PLAYERS OF
COOPERSTOWN

BASEBALL'S
HALL OF FAME

PUBLICATIONS INTERNATIONAL, LTD.

COPYRIGHT © 1992 PUBLICATIONS
INTERNATIONAL, LTD. ALL RIGHTS RESERVED.
THIS BOOK MAY NOT BE REPRODUCED OR
QUOTED IN WHOLE OR IN PART BY
MIMEOGRAPH OR ANY OTHER PRINTED OR
ELECTRONIC MEANS, OR FOR PRESENTATION
ON RADIO, TELEVISION, VIDEOTAPE, OR FILM
WITHOUT WRITTEN PERMISSION FROM:

LOUIS WEBER, C.E.O.
PUBLICATIONS INTERNATIONAL, LTD.
7373 NORTH CICERO AVENUE
LINCOLNWOOD, ILLINOIS 60646

PERMISSION IS NEVER GRANTED FOR
COMMERCIAL PURPOSES.

MANUFACTURED IN CROATIA, ZRINSKI.

8 7 6 5 4 3 2 1

ISBN: 1-56173-074-2

LIBRARY OF CONGRESS CATALOG CARD
NUMBER: 92-80274

Contributing Writers:
David Nemec
Matthew D. Greenberger
Dan Schlossberg
Dick Johnson

David Nemec is a baseball historian,
author of *Great Baseball Feats, Facts &
Firsts* and a co-author of *20th Century
Baseball Chronicle*, *1992 Baseball
Almanac*, and the *Ultimate Baseball
Book*. He has written numerous baseball history, quiz, and memorabilia
books as well as franchise histories for
major league team yearbooks.

Matthew D. Greenberger is a free-lance
sports writer and was a contributing
editor for *The Scouting Report: 1990*,
the commissioner for the Bill James
Fantasy Baseball game and a senior
sports statistician for STATS, Inc. He
was a contributing writer for the *1991
Baseball Almanac* and has worked on
the *Major League Handbook* series.

Dan Schlossberg is a free-lance sports
writer whose work has appeared in *Grand
Slam Baseball Magazine*, *Petersen's Pro
Baseball Yearbook* and *Street & Smith's
Baseball Yearbook*. He is the author of
12 books, including *The Baseball I.Q.
Challenge* and *1991 Baseball's
Hottest Players*.

Dick Johnson serves as associate director
and curator of The Sports Museum in
Boston, where he has mounted exhibits
on the history of Fenway Park, the Boston
Braves, and the Boston Bruins, among
others. He is book review editor of
Diehard, the Red Sox monthly, and serves
as an active member of the Society for
American Baseball Research (SABR).
He is the co-author of *20th Century
Baseball Chronicle* and *Ted Williams,
A Portrait in Words and Pictures*.

Contributing photo researcher: Mark
Rucker

Special thanks to Pat Kelly from the
National Baseball Hall of Fame in
Cooperstown, N.Y.

CONTENTS

Honus Wagner

Joe DiMaggio (left)

CHAPTER FOUR
Home Front
America's Pastime at War . . . 156

CHAPTER FIVE
Equal Opportunity
Robinson Erases the Line . . . 184

Willie Mays

Tom Seaver

Enshrinement is the Highest Honor

THE NATIONAL BASEBALL HALL of Fame and Museum is the oldest and most revered of all the sports Halls of Fame. Enshrinement is the highest honor a major league player can receive.

Though *Baseball Magazine* used the term "Hall of Fame" as early as 1908 to describe a list of pitchers who had thrown no-hit games, its meaning changed when baseball decided to honor its premier performers. Today, the term embraces all three branches of the sport's shrine: the gallery where the plaques of the Hall of Fame players hang, as well as the adjacent museum and library.

Wandering the halls of the Hall triggers constant questions as wide-eyed youngsters ogle the artifacts and engage their elders in lively debate. Who was the best player of all time? What baseball records will never be broken?

In the last 30 years alone, players reached new plateaus in career hits, home runs, and stolen bases, plus homers and steals in a single season. Experts once considered all of those records unobtainable. Is Lou Gehrig's streak of 2,130 consecutive games played in the same category? Or Joe DiMaggio's 56-game hitting streak? How about Cy Young's 511 victories or Connie

Mack's 53 years as a major league manager? Ty Cobb's .367 career average may be safe, but his stolen base records have been superseded so many times that nothing seems certain.

Odds against election are overwhelming: about 1,500-to-1 for the typical major leaguer. That's approximately one player out of every 167 starting lineups. Entering in the first year of eligibility is even tougher: Only one out of about nine Hall of Famers entered on their first try. To qualify for the ballot, a player must have played at least 10 years in the major leagues and be retired for five—requirements that are sometimes waived for special cases, such as the untimely death of Roberto Clemente in 1972.

Addie Joss had 160 victories and a career earned run average of 1.88 but was one game short of 10-year status when tubercular meningitis killed him just before the opening of the 1911 season. He was finally admitted by the Veterans Committee in 1978. The history of Hall of Fame elections is filled with policy changes. After holding annual elections from 1936 to '39, the Baseball Writers Association of America (BBWAA) opted to vote only at three-year intervals. They returned to annual elections in

Right: The Hall of Fame in Cooperstown, New York. Opposite page, top: Several of the all-time greats, such as Ty Cobb and Cy Young, receive their own display case inside the Hall. Opposite page, bottom: This is the awards display case.

Tyrus Raymond Cobb

Ty Cobb won more batting championships (12) and compiled a higher lifetime average (.367) than any player in the game's history.

Denton True Young

Cy Young won 511 games—more than any other pitcher—during his 22-year career in the major leagues.

the game's over-achievers. Silver bats have long been associated with batting prowess. The Most Valuable Player Award was initially given in 1911 and was originally called the Chalmers Award. Rookie of the Year Awards date back to 1946 and the first Cy Young Award to the year's outstanding pitcher(s) was first presented in 1956. Gold Glove for fielding excellence originated the following year and the Rolaids Award for relief pitchers debuted...

Most Valuable Player

Gold Glove

Cy Young Award

Silver Bat

Above: *This baseball board-game card features Buck Ewing as a third baseman, one of the many positions that he played, though he made his reputation as a catcher.* Right: *Ty Cobb (left) greets Tris Speaker.*

1946, then decided on every-other-year intervals 10 years later. Annual elections returned again in 1966. The five-year wait rule began in 1954, superseding the one-year wait that had been in effect from 1946 to 1953.

A six-member screening committee prepares the annual ballot and selected players remain eligible for 15 years—unless they receive less than 5 percent of the vote. That system keeps the ballot from becoming unwieldy and makes it easier for voters to choose up to 10 candidates per year. Many writers, however, select only a few top choices and leave the remainder of their ballots blank. Electors must have covered major league baseball for at least 10 years.

Various special committees have also been given the power to enshrine baseball personalities. They were the Centennial Commission of 1937 and '38, Old Timers Committee of 1939 to 1949, Negro Leagues Committee of 1971 to 1977, and current Veterans Committee, created in 1953. The Veterans Committee considers players retired at least 23 years who received at least 100 votes from the BBWAA, and can enshrine managers, umpires, or executives but is permitted to name only one nonplayer per year. It usually chooses no more than two candidates annually but has named as many as seven in a single voting session (1971). To be elected by the committee, a manager, umpire, or executive must be retired five years or be six months past his 65th birthday (a rule passed for Casey Stengel in 1966).

Hitting 500 homers, collecting 3,000 hits, or winning 300 games does not produce an automatic ticket to Cooperstown. In fact, there is no statistical guideline. Voting baseball writers are instructed to judge each candidate on ability, integrity, sportsmanship, character, and contribution to the team or teams on which he played—as well as to baseball in general.

The Hall of Fame, though, is living proof that baseball is more wedded to statistics than any other sport. Fans speak in alphabetized codes about ERA and RBI and devour boxscores with the intensity of archaeologists deciphering hieroglyphics.

The seeds of the game's statistical foundation were planted by pioneer baseball writer Henry Chadwick long before the National League began play in 1876. Chadwick, who spent most of his 45-year journalism career with the *Brooklyn Eagle*, devised a system of scorekeeping, created the first boxscore, and refined the game through changes he instituted as chairman of an early rules committee.

Chadwick, the only writer among the more than 200 baseball immortals whose plaques hang in the Hall of Fame gallery, was indirectly responsible for the placement of the baseball shrine in the tiny lakeside hamlet of Cooperstown, New York. As editor of *Spalding's Baseball*

Opposite page: *This piece features some of the top stars of the 1800s. Keefe, Anson, and Kelly have been inducted into the Hall of Fame. Charlie Bennett was a popular Detroit star whose career came to an end when he lost both legs in a train accident.*

TIMOTHY KEEFE.

ADRIAN C. ANSON.

CHAS. W. BENNETT.

MIKE KELLY.

The Vanity Fair *impression of Babe Ruth was not far removed from the one harbored by most American League pitchers of his day (above).*

Guide, Chadwick wrote in 1903 that baseball was a direct descendant of the British game of rounders, which he had played as a youth in England. Albert G. Spalding, the former pitcher and manager who owned the publication, printed a rebuttal that said baseball had actually developed from the colonial American game of One Old Cat.

Spalding not only called for the appointment of a special commission to settle the dispute but also hand-picked its seven members. His choices were hardly impartial: commission chairman A.G. Mills had told a New York banquet audience six years earlier that "patriotism and research" had established baseball as uniquely American and not descended from the English rounders.

Honored guests at that banquet were players who had participated in baseball's first world tour—organized and led by Al Spalding. During tour stops in England, Australia, and New Zealand, American players had been subjected to razzing from spectators who charged them with stealing the idea for the game.

Spalding, still seething from the teasing and also searching for ways to publicize his growing sporting-goods business, viewed the Commission as a way to kill two birds with one stone. The panel based its findings almost entirely on a letter Spalding obtained from former Cooperstown resident Abner Graves, then a Denver mining engineer. In his letter, Graves said he witnessed Doubleday interrupt a game of marbles behind a tailor shop to draw a diamond diagram in the dirt and explain and name the game.

That was all the Commission needed. Its final report, published on December 30, 1907, after three years of gathering evidence, stated, "The first scheme for playing baseball, according to the best evidence obtainable to date, was devised by Abner Doubleday at Cooperstown, New York in 1839. Baseball is of American origin and has no connection with rounders or any other foreign game."

Chadwick, among others, disagreed vehemently. In a note to Mills published in the 1908 *Spalding Baseball Guide*, he wrote, "Your decision in the case of Chadwick vs. Spalding is a masterly piece of special pleading that lets my dear old friend Albert escape a bad defeat. The whole matter was a joke between Albert and myself." That joke has evolved into a multi-million dollar enterprise.

Before the century's turn, historians agreed that baseball became separate from rounders only when its rules were amended by Alexander Cartwright's New York Knickerbockers in 1845.

Cartwright, a New York bank teller whose rules were introduced seven years after Doubleday's alleged "invention" of baseball, was the first man to suggest teams of nine players, regular batting orders, equidistant bases, and three outs per inning. Because the nine-inning concept was developed later, the first game under Cartwright's rules ended when the New York Nine scored their 21st run (called an *ace*) in the fourth inning (called a *hand*), then added two more tallies to pin a 23-1 defeat on the Knickerbockers.

That game was played on June 19, 1846, at the Elysian Fields of Hoboken, New Jersey—a town many feel is the true birthplace of baseball. Even Hall of Fame officials view Cooperstown more as a symbol of the game's birth rather than its actual cradle.

Twelve years after publication of the Mills report, a group of Cooperstown residents bought the Phinney lot that Graves had identified as the birthplace of baseball. After receiving a Chamber of Commerce delegation seeking his support for a national baseball shrine, National League president John A. Heydler came to Cooperstown for the 1923 dedication of Doubleday Field. It was not until 1934, however, that the Doubleday legend received national recognition.

That was the year a tattered old baseball was discovered in a dusty trunk tucked away in a farmhouse attic in Fly Creek, a village three miles from Cooperstown. Since the trunk had belonged to Abner Graves, local historians leapt to the conclusion that the ball had been used by Abner Doubleday in the first baseball game.

Stephen C. Clark, a local resident and heir to the Singer Sewing Machine fortune, bought the ball for $5, enclosed it in a glass case, and placed it on the fireplace mantle of the Village Club, a combination library and boys club. After the addition of other baseball memorabilia, the exhibit became so popular that sentiment for a national museum soared. Clark took the idea to new National League president Ford Frick, who not only embraced the concept but suggested the inclusion of a Hall of Fame for the game's heroes.

The Depression-weary baseball establishment —desperate for a gimmick that might start the turnstiles spinning again—began making elaborate plans for the game's 100th birthday. Those plans, announced in March 1936, would tie the Centennial with the museum, Hall of Fame, and Doubleday Field in a nationwide party, sponsored in part by a $100,000 grant from the major leagues. Cooperstown announced 27 "days," including the first official Induction Day, a Minor League Day, and even an Alexander Cartwright Day for those who refused to accept the Doubleday legend.

Clark spent $44,000 of his own money—about half the original construction cost—to help convert the village gym into the National Baseball Hall of Fame and Museum and served 21 years as its first president. Filling the hall was left to baseball.

There were two elections in 1936: one by 226 members of the Baseball Writers Association of America and another by a special 78-member veterans committee. Because no guidelines were set regarding eligibility, several active players received strong support. The only five able to muster the required 75 percent of the vote, however, were all retired: Ty Cobb (222), Babe Ruth and Honus Wagner (215 each), Christy Mathewson (205), and Walter Johnson (189).

The first election, plus three subsequent annual tallies, gave the Hall 26 members by the time it was ready to open on June 12, 1939. All 11 living members appeared for the induction ceremonies, along with a number of future Hall of Famers.

As Carl Hubbell stepped off the train, the great lefthander—his arm permanently twisted from years of throwing the screwball—took one look at the elm-lined streets and said, "So this is where all the grief started!" Maybe so or maybe not. But the immortals gathered for the first induction agreed that baseball could not have found a better spot for its shrine.

Some of the treasures the shrine holds include the shoes of Shoeless Joe (he picked up the nickname as a youngster who couldn't afford proper foot attire). The baseball museum also has Christy Mathewson's piano (with baseball bats as supporting legs), Babe Ruth's bowling ball, Moe Berg's medal for wartime spy service, a

17-foot bat carved as a gift for Ted Williams, a whisk broom used by umpire Jocko Conlan, and a crown given "King Carl" Hubbell.

The library has long been regarded as baseball heaven by writers, researchers, and historians. Even before the latest expansion work started, it housed five million newspaper documents, 200,000 player data cards, 125,000 photographs, 100,000 autographs, 15,000 baseball books, 2,000 pamphlets, and 400 videotapes, plus radio tapes, movie reels, sheet music, team files, team publications (including yearbooks and media guides), baseball magazines, and various documents of the game dating back to 1840. Its archives also included boxscores of every game in baseball history, complete collections of *The Sporting News, Sporting Life,* and *Sports Illustrated.*

The collection honors not only the relative handful of Hall of Fame players but also the game itself. They trace the game's history from pre-Civil War sandlot days through the development of domed ballparks, divisional play, and free agency. Many baseball historians consider only the "modern era" of the game, beginning with the 1901 advent of the American League. But not the national baseball museum.

Although much of 19th century baseball was played under rules and conditions that seem completely foreign to followers of today's game, Cooperstown remembers its heritage.

This is one of the uniforms Ted Williams wore when he earned six American League batting championships and four home run crowns. Williams won his first hitting title in 1941 when he was age 23 and his last 17 years later after he turned 40 (above). Casey Stengel said that Mickey Mantle (opposite page) had more raw talent than any other player in history.

When Stan Musial retired, he owned every Cardinals career batting record except for highest batting average, which belongs to Rogers Hornsby.

Birth of the Game
Cartwright's Cornerstone

BASEBALL WAS NOT ORIGINATED BY ABNER Doubleday, Alexander Cartwright, or any individual. Instead, it evolved gradually as various American regions adapted elements of British base-and-ball games, such as rounders, to their styles of play.

The New York and Massachusetts games competed with many other versions for popularity. The New York version of "Base Ball" took precedence; the first organized team, Cartwright's Knickerbocker Base Ball Club, formed in 1845 and played the first game under his rules a year later. The Civil War put development of the game between the lines on hold but spread its popularity. An 1857 convention in New York City attended by 16 clubs formulated a single set of rules. The National Association of Base Ball Players, created by the convention, soon had more than 200 members and countless fans.

Baseball's Wright Brothers—Harry and George—became the highest-paid members of the first all-professional team, the Cincinnati Red Stockings, in 1869. This team's prosperity emboldened professionals to form the National Association in 1871, making it the first modern professional league. Riddled by disorganization and financial hardship, the NA collapsed after five years. William Hulbert formed the National League in the NA's place in 1876.

The National League was a success, and it survives to this day, despite challenges from several rival leagues, including the American Association and the Players' League. By the turn of the century, however, the National League had to face its most successful challenger.

This pin was given to one of the greatest sluggers of baseball's early era, Dan Brouthers. He led his league in slugging percentage seven different seasons, including six in a row from 1881 to 1886. He also finished in the top three in ten seasons.

Opposite page: *Harry Wright managed baseball's first all-professional team, the undefeated 1869 Cincinnati Red Stockings, and later won four championships in the National Association and two in the National League.* Below: *This plate, from 1887, features four Hall of Famers: (clockwise from upper left) Mickey Welch, Monte Ward, Roger Connor, and Tim Keefe.*

13

ALEXANDER JOY CARTWRIGHT, Jr.
"FATHER OF MODERN BASE BALL."
SET BASES 90 FEET APART.
ESTABLISHED 9 INNINGS AS GAME
AND 9 PLAYERS AS TEAM. ORGANIZED
THE KNICKERBOCKER BASEBALL CLUB
OF N.Y. IN 1845. CARRIED BASEBALL
TO PACIFIC COAST AND HAWAII
IN PIONEER DAYS.

Right: Cartwright was responsible for the baseball's development. Below: The Knickerbockers Club was the first baseball team. Cartwright is at top center.

THE PRECISE ORIGINS OF BASE-ball are probably forever impossible to determine. The likelihood is that it evolved gradually from several different games that had only one common element: They all utilized a ball and an object with which to strike it. Thus, we cannot fairly credit the invention of baseball to any one individual. What can be unequivocally stated, however, is that Alexander Cartwright—Alick, to his friends—had a large hand in the development of the game as we now know it.

Curiously, Cartwright's contribution for years remained buried and might still be unrecognized were it not for the creation of the Hall of Fame. In 1907, Al Spalding established a commission to unearth the origins of baseball. The man named to head it was former National League President A. G. Mills. After undergoing a perfunctory investigation, Mills attributed the game's invention to his old friend General Abner Doubleday, who purportedly staged the first contest one afternoon in 1839 in Cooperstown, New York, while still a West Point cadet.

Mills's findings were accepted as gospel despite an alarming absence of supporting evidence, and the Baseball Hall of Fame was accordingly placed in Cooperstown, with a centennial celebration of the game's birth planned for 1939. About a year before the gala event, however, Bruce Cartwright, grandson of Alexander, wrote a letter when the hoopla reached all the way to Hawaii, where Bruce resided. With his letter, Cartwright produced his grandfather's diaries. The diaries, which charted Alexander Cartwright's early baseball

experiences, touched off an investigation that seemed to establish that the Mills Commission's findings were fallacious and Cartwright was the true originator of baseball. The Hall of Fame officials, after due deliberation, decided to revise their position. As a result, Abner Doubleday, the man responsible for the shrine being placed in Cooperstown, has himself never been enshrined. Cartwright was inducted in 1938.

Alexander Joy Cartwright (1820-1892) helped form the Knickerbocker Base Ball Club on September 23, 1845, and drafted a set of 20 rules that were intended to set baseball apart from other bat-and-ball games. The following spring, on June 19 at Elysian Field in Hoboken, New Jersey, the Knickerbocker Club played a game for the first time against another team. With Cartwright umpiring, the Knickerbockers were drubbed by the New York Nine, 23-1.

Cartwright remained in New York until March 1, 1849, and then, lured by the Gold Rush, went to the West Coast. After a short, disillusioning time there, he set sail for Hawaii and made the islands his home until his death on July 12, 1892.

This 1888 Old Judge card featured manager Harry Wright of the Philadelphia Quakers.

HARRY WRIGHT WAS A GOOD player in his heyday but certainly never in the class of his younger brother George. When Harry was selected for the Hall of Fame in 1953, it was largely for his contributions as a baseball pioneer and innovator. A case can be made, though, that he is worthy of inclusion for his managerial record as well. Wright managed baseball's first all-professional team, the undefeated 1869 Cincinnati Red Stockings, and later won four championships in the National Association and two in the National League while serving at the helm of the Boston Red Caps.

Born in Sheffield, England, William Henry Wright (1835-1895) was the son of a professional cricket player; hence his sport of choice was cricket after the family emigrated to New York. When baseball became the new rage in the 1850s, he joined the amateur Knickerbockers club as an outfielder while continuing to make his living in the jewelry trade.

In 1865, Harry took a position as an instructor at the Union Cricket Club in Cincinnati. The following year he organized the Cincinnati Red Stockings Base Ball team and soon found himself devoting all his energy to the diamond sport. In his desire to put his newly formed team on the map, Wright recruited the finest baseball players in the country, beginning with his brother George. The result was that from 1869 to 1870, the Red Stockings won a record 130 consecutive games before losing a violently disputed extra-inning contest to the Brooklyn Atlantics. Soon thereafter the Red Stockings disbanded and Harry moved on to help form the National Association, the first professional league. Taking the reins of the Boston entry, he lost the 1871 flag to Philadelphia but then proceeded to sweep four straight pennants before the loop folded following the 1875 season owing to competitive imbalance, player drunkenness, and rampant rumors of fixed games.

Harry was nearly through as a player in 1876 when the National League began in the stead of the National Association, but he managed for 18 more seasons, first with Boston and later with Providence and Philadelphia. Although in his last five years as a helmsman he never won a pennant, he introduced many elements that have become an integral part of baseball, such as having his teams take pregame batting practice and fungoing fly balls to outfielders before a game.

Following the 1893 season, his vision failing, Harry retired as manager of the Philadelphia Phillies and became chief of umpires. After serving for two years in the newly created post, Wright died in Atlantic City, New Jersey, on October 3, 1895.

Outfielder
Boston Red Stockings
1871–1875
Boston Red Caps
1876–1877

Manager
Boston Red Stockings
1871–1875
225–60
Boston Red Caps
1876–1881
Providence Grays
1882–1883
Philadelphia Quakers
1884–1893
1,000–825

This is a team photo of the 1868 Cincinnati Red Stockings, now recognized to be the first all-salaried baseball team. Manager and organizer Harry Wright is seated at far left.

Major League Totals				
BA	G	AB	R	H
.261	181	858	182	224

GEORGE WRIGHT

GEORGE WRIGHT
STAR OF BASEBALL'S FIRST
PROFESSIONAL TEAM, THE
CINCINNATI RED STOCKINGS OF 1869.
GREAT SHORTSTOP AND CAPTAIN OF
CHAMPION BOSTONS IN NATIONAL
LEAGUE'S PIONEER YEARS.

Shortstop
Cincinnati Red Stockings
  1869–1870
Boston Red Stockings
  1871–1875
Boston Red Caps
  1876–1878;
  1880–1881
Providence Grays
  1879; 1882

Manager
Providence Grays 1879
85–59

George Wright, the leading player of his day, is depicted in 1870.

THE STAR SHORTSTOP OF THE legendary Cincinnati Red Stockings team that went undefeated for the entire 1869 season, George Wright was elected to the Hall of Fame in 1937 for his contributions as both a player and a baseball pioneer. When his brother Harry, a lesser athlete but a more influential trailblazer, joined him in Cooperstown 16 years later, the Wrights became the first pair of siblings to be enshrined.

Known as the first "King of Shortstops"— considered to be the key position on the diamond even in the 1860s—George Wright (1847-1937) was without an equal in the game's infant days as both a hitter and a fielder. Thus, he was also the highest paid performer. So talented was George that wherever he went, championships almost always followed. After the Cincinnati Red Stockings disbanded following the 1870 season, the Wright brothers signed with Boston in the fledgling National Association. After Philadelphia captured the initial National Association flag by dint of several forfeit wins, the Wrights took charge and led Boston to four straight pennants.

In his five seasons in the National Association, George consistently ranked among the loop's top hitters and had no peer as a playmaker. When the league folded after the 1875 season, Wright remained in Boston along with his brother to play for the Red Caps in the newly formed National League. On April 22, 1876, George became the first batter in NL history when he led off the inaugural game at Philadelphia by grounding out to short.

Boston finished fourth in the first National League season but then copped two straight pennants. Wright jumped the club following the Red Caps' second triumph to become player-manager of the Providence Grays. In his one and only season as a major league skipper, George brought the Grays home first ahead of brother Harry's Red Caps.

Although only age 32, Wright never again played regularly after the 1879 season. Unlike most shortstops, his fielding skills were not what deserted him with encroaching age. Beginning in 1876, with more and more pitchers learning how to throw curveballs, Wright's batting deteriorated alarmingly. In 1878, his final full year with Boston, he hit .225. Four years later, when he attempted to make a comeback with Providence, he was forced to abandon the notion after hitting just .162 in 46 games.

In 1884, George was one of the backers of the Union Association (a short-lived third major league), buying the Boston Reds franchise. The league collapsed after just one season, but Wright continued his affiliation with the game until his death at age 90 in Boston in 1937.

Major League Totals				
BA	G	AB	R	H
.303	591	2,894	663	877

Chadwick was so prolific that his byline appeared in most major newspapers.

THE ONLY SPORTSWRITER TO be honored with a plaque in the Hall of Fame, the British-born Henry Chadwick was called by none other than Teddy Roosevelt (himself an avid sportsman) the "Father of Baseball."

After emigrating to the United States from England in 1837 at age 13, Henry Chadwick (1824-1908) settled in Brooklyn with his family. He remained a Brooklynite for the rest of his life. At first a devotee of cricket, the national game of his native country, he gradually found himself drawn to baseball. Upon joining the New York *Clipper* as a sportswriter in 1857, he decided to use his post to remedy a problem with the game that had long disturbed him. Chadwick thereupon set about designing his own system for scoring a baseball contest. After some thinking, he came up with an instrument that is remarkably like the modern box score.

Chadwick himself was anything but a modernist. During his long career as a writer he never owned a typewriter, always penning his newspaper columns and books in longhand. He also continued to expect players to behave like gentlemen, railing against rowdyism and the evils of drink long after most other baseball writers had accepted the two as part and parcel of the game.

Yet at the same time that he was an anachronism, Chadwick was an astonishingly prolific innovator. He was the first to compile reference books on baseball, and instructional guides on how to play the game. In 1872, he assembled the first listing of all professional baseball players, containing their heights, weights, and dates and places of birth. Chadwick's work provided the main source for future historians seeking the vital statistics of participants in the first major league, the National Association. In addition, his writing was peppered with many descriptive words and phrases about baseball that are still in vogue.

Beginning in 1881, Chadwick edited the *Spalding Official Baseball Guide* until his death. Included in the guide were not only yearly standings and individual batting, pitching, and fielding statistics, but Chadwick's trenchant commentary on the game. So expert and revered was he that when he happened to be in attendance umpires frequently stopped play to confer with him about a rule interpretation.

Chadwick contracted pneumonia after attending the Giants' opening game at the Polo Grounds in 1908 despite a fever and died shortly thereafter on April 20. The following day flags in every major league park were lowered to half-mast. In 1938, Chadwick was selected for the Hall of Fame.

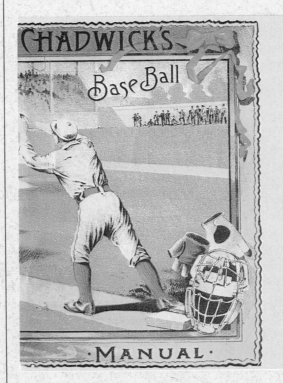

This is the cover from one of the multitude of baseball manuals Chadwick produced. He also wrote instructional books on cricket, handball, and chess, all sports and games in which he was recognized as an authority.

ALBERT GOODWILL SPALDING
ORGANIZATIONAL GENIUS OF BASEBALL'S
PIONEER DAYS. STAR PITCHER OF FOREST
CITY CLUB IN LATE 1860's, 4-YEAR
CHAMPION BOSTONS 1871-1875 AND
MANAGER - PITCHER OF CHAMPION
CHICAGOS IN NATIONAL LEAGUE'S FIRST
YEAR. CHICAGO PRESIDENT FOR 10
YEARS. ORGANIZER OF BASEBALL'S FIRST
ROUND-THE-WORLD TOUR IN 1888.

Pitcher; infielder; executive
Boston Red Stockings
1871–1875
Chicago White Stockings
1876–1878

In 1877, Spalding produced his first official Baseball Guide. *It proved so successful that the Spalding guide was an annual until 1942.*

Major League Totals		
W	L	PCT
255	69	.787

BORN IN BYRON, ILLINOIS, INTO a prosperous farming family, Albert Goodwill Spalding (1850-1915) was forced to go to work as a grocery boy at age nine because his father died. By the time Spalding was age 16, he was already pitching for the Rockford Forest Citys, one of the top teams in the Midwest. After beating the George Wright-led Washington Nationals the following year, he was offered $40 per week to pitch for the Chicago Excelsiors.

Back with the Forest Citys in 1869, Al played on a team that lost only four games that season, all to the undefeated Cincinnati Red Stockings. Two years later, Spalding accepted a $1,500-a-year offer from Harry Wright to join the Boston team in what was to be baseball's first all professional league, the National Association. In his five years with the Red Stockings, Spalding posted a 207-56 record and played on four pennant winners. The Hub team was so good that the NA collapsed after 1875 because of a lack of competitive balance.

Spalding became instrumental in the demise of the National Association when he deserted the circuit to join the Chicago club in the newly formed National League as a player-manager. Pitcher Spalding proved to be manager Spalding's greatest asset, winning 47 games in

Spalding won 255 games then retired to own a club and a sporting goods business.

60 decisions and sparking the White Stockings to an easy pennant. After his remarkable showing, nevertheless, Spalding pitched just one more victory in the National League and then switched to playing the infield. Soon thereafter, though only at age 27, he quit as a player altogether. The reason for his early retirement was that the curveball had become an integral part of the game by the mid-1870s, and Spalding could neither learn to throw one nor to hit one.

Al and his younger brother, J. Walter Spalding, opened their first sporting goods store in 1876. The following year, the brothers produced their first official *Spalding Baseball Guide*. When William Hulbert died in 1882, Spalding assumed the presidency of the Chicago White Stockings, a role he held until 1890.

Spalding was affiliated with baseball only peripherally after the 1891 season. Politics and his sporting goods business consumed most of his attention. He was instrumental, however, in negotiating the peace settlement between the American and National Leagues in 1903. Two years later, he started a committee to investigate the origins of baseball; the committee concluded that Abner Doubleday invented the game. Spalding died in California in 1915 and was elected to the Hall of Fame in 1939 as both a player and a pioneer.

WILLIAM ARTHUR CUMMINGS (1848-1924) came by his nickname of Candy in the late 1860s. During that period, when Cummings was first gaining prominence as a pitcher, "candy" was a popular term for anything that was one of the best of its kind. Cummings was clearly that. Pitching for the Excelsior Club of Brooklyn, Candy regularly beat the best amateur teams of his day despite his unimposing physical dimensions. He stood but 5'9" and never weighed more than 120 pounds during his baseball career.

Cummings's forte was a baffling curveball. Some historians believe he invented the pitch. Others think that at most he had a part in its evolution. Cummings was inducted into the Hall of Fame among the first batch of immortals in 1939. Since there is little to cite in his major league career—he played just six seasons—one must assume that the historians who deemed him the creator of the curveball held sway when the first Hall of Fame ballots were cast.

From the Excelsiors, Cummings moved to a team called the Stars of Brooklyn. He remained with them for four years and then joined the New York Mutuals of the National Association. "Revolving," or changing teams at will, was a common practice in the 1870s, and Cummings took full advantage of the privilege. In his six professional seasons he played in five different cities, allowing only Hartford the benefit of his curves for more than one campaign.

A stalwart hurler in the National Association, Cummings was nearly finished by the time the National League was formed in 1876. Although only age 28, he was forced to cede his title as

Hartford's ace pitcher to 20-year-old Tommy Bond. The following year the Hartford Blues put up little fuss when Candy declared his intention to sign with Cincinnati.

His experience in the Queen City was one that Cummings could have done without. When he won just five games in 19 decisions, one paper described his record as "sickening" and his presence on the team as "demoralizing." Upon learning at the end of the season that he was leaving the team, the same paper said, "No one who has pride in the game will mourn his loss to the club."

After leaving baseball, Cummings ran a paint and wallpaper business for many years. He moved to Toledo, Ohio, in 1920 and died there on May 17, 1924.

W. A. "CANDY" CUMMINGS
PITCHED FIRST CURVE BALL IN BASEBALL HISTORY. INVENTED CURVE AS AMATEUR ACE OF BROOKLYN STARS IN 1867. ENDED LONG CAREER AS HARTFORD PITCHER IN NATIONAL LEAGUE'S FIRST YEAR 1876.

Pitcher
Brooklyn Excelsiors
   1866–1867
Stars of Brooklyn
   1868–1872
New York Mutuals 1872
Lord Baltimores 1873
Philadelphia Athletics
   1874
Hartford Dark Blues
   1875–1876
Cincinnati Reds 1877

Top: Cummings (left) and a teammate with the Brooklyn Stars. Cummings joined the Stars in 1868 and pitched for them for four years. Right: Cummings (top row, center) won 35 games for Hartford in 1875, sparking the club to third place in the NA.

Major League Totals		
W	L	G
146	92	245

MORGAN BULKELEY

HON. MORGAN G. BULKELEY
FIRST PRESIDENT OF THE NATIONAL
LEAGUE AND A LEADER IN ITS
ORGANIZATION IN 1876 WHICH
LAID THE FOUNDATION OF THE
NATIONAL GAME FOR POSTERITY.

IF MORGAN GARDNER BULKELEY had been told in 1876 that he would one day have a plaque in the pantheon honoring the greatest contributors to the game of baseball, he probably would have shaken his head incredulously. He is without question the most obscure baseball personage in the Hall of Fame. Yet he may also be its most estimable figure.

Bulkeley's lone significant connection with baseball is that in 1876, as a 39-year-old executive, he represented the Hartford Blues at the National League's first club owners' meeting. Previously, he had been a principal backer of the Hartford entry in the old National Association but had long since declared that baseball to him was a mere pastime; his true devotion was to the Aetna Life Insurance Company, which had been founded by his father Eliphalet.

It was Bulkeley's business background and sterling reputation that intrigued William Hulbert of Chicago, the National League's creator. Hulbert saw in Bulkeley the perfect man to serve as the loop's first president. For one, Bulkeley's impeccable credentials would give Hulbert's enterprise instant respectability. Equally impor-

tant, Bulkeley (1837-1922) was an Easterner and as such would act to counter the view that the National League was strictly the brainchild of maverick Westerners. Hulbert nominated Bulkeley for president and a drawing was conducted. Bulkeley's name was the first one chosen by lot, and by that stroke of luck he became the first president of the National League.

Bulkeley served just one year. At the post-season meeting in December he was not even present when Hulbert was named his successor. After the Hartford club moved to Brooklyn in 1877, Bulkeley's connection with baseball was severed. Named president of Aetna in 1879, he remained at that post for the rest of his life. He died on November 6, 1922.

In 1937, when all agreed that Ban Johnson as the first president of the American League should be among the original Hall of Fame enshrinees, it seemed only appropriate that the first National League president should be likewise commemorated. Hence Bulkeley has a place in the Hall of Fame while William Hulbert, the true founder of the National League, is nowhere to be found.

Bulkeley held the NL presidency for only one year and was not even present at the final league meeting in 1876 when the vote was taken to expel New York and Philadelphia.

ADRIAN CONSTANTINE ANSON
"CAP"
GREATEST HITTER AND GREATEST
NATIONAL LEAGUE PLAYER-MANAGER
OF 19TH CENTURY. STARTED WITH
CHICAGOS IN NATIONAL LEAGUE'S
FIRST YEAR 1876. CHICAGO MANAGER
FROM 1879 TO 1897, WINNING 5 PENNANTS.
WAS .300 CLASS HITTER 20 YEARS,
BATTING CHAMPION 4 TIMES.

BORN IN MARSHALLTOWN, Iowa, Adrian Constantine Anson (1852-1922) was one of the very few early stars whose father encouraged him to pursue a career in professional baseball. The elder Anson even wrote a letter to the Chicago team in 1869 recommending his son. The letter was ignored, and Anson instead entered Notre Dame in 1870. A year later he left school to join the Rockford team in the newly formed National Association.

The following year, Anson signed with the Philadelphia Athletics and remained with them through 1875. When the National League was formed in 1876, he deserted Philadelphia along with several other Athletics stars. Anson cast his lot with the Chicago White Stockings seven years after his father had tried to interest a Chicago team in him. For the next 22 seasons he was a fixture there, setting a 19th century loyalty record for the longest stint by a player with one team.

Still primarily a third baseman when he first came to the White Stockings, Anson moved to first base when he became the club's manager in 1879. Fielding was never Anson's strong point. It was at the plate that he excelled. Only three times in his 27-year career did he bat below .300, and he was the first player to accumulate 3,000

career hits. Although a line-drive hitter, Cap also could hit with power, and he was particularly dangerous with men on base. Anson led the National League in RBI no less than nine times in the 12-year period between 1880 and 1891. Furthermore, he headed the loop twice in batting average and on three occasions in slugging average. As a player-manager, Anson led Chicago to five pennants.

Anson was not without flaws, however. His language on the field was often so vile that it evoked fines from umpires, and rival fans called him "Crybaby" Anson because of the way he whined and moaned when events did not go his way. Moreover, Anson was a racist, believing the major league game should be the province only of white players. Because of his threat to organize a strike, several black performers were clandestinely barred from the major leagues before the 1885 season, a ban that lingered, albeit unofficially, until 1947.

After the 1897 campaign, White Stockings president James Hart demanded that Cap resign his manager's seat. When Anson refused he was summarily fired. The White Stockings, minus Anson for the first time in their 23-year history, became known as the Orphans. In 1939, Anson was elected to the Hall of Fame.

**First baseman;
third baseman**
Rockford Forest Citys 1871
Philadelphia Athletics
1872–1875

First baseman
Chicago White Stockings
1876–1897

Manager
Philadelphia Athletics
1875
4–2
Chicago White Stockings
1879–1897
New York Giants 1898
1,292–945

*Top: White Stockings
manager-first baseman
Anson by 1888 was
being called "Pop" by
many of his players.
Left: A plate featuring
Anson's visage.*

National League Totals

BA	G	AB	R	H	2B	3B	HR	RBI	SB
.329	2,276	9,108	1,719	3,000	528	124	96	1,715	247

JIM O'ROURKE

JAMES H. O'ROURKE

"ORATOR JIM" PLAYED BALL UNTIL HE WAS PAST FIFTY, INCLUDING TWENTY-ONE MAJOR LEAGUE SEASONS. AN OUTFIELDER AND CATCHER FOR THE BOSTON RED STOCKINGS OF 1873, HE LATER WORE THE UNIFORMS OF THE CHAMPIONSHIP PROVIDENCE TEAM OF 1879, BUFFALO, NEW YORK AND WASHINGTON.

Outfielder; catcher
Boston Red Caps
  (Beaneaters)
  1876–1878; 1880
Providence Grays 1879
Buffalo Bisons 1881–1884
New York Giants
  1885–1889; 1891–1892
New York Giants (PL) 1890
Washington Senators 1893

Manager
Buffalo Bisons 1881–1884
Washington Senators 1893
246-258

Top Right: In the early days players on championship teams received medals rather than rings. This one was given to O'Rourke in 1879. Right: In 1880, O'Rourke and his brother, John, became the first pair of siblings to play in the same outfield.

THE MOST ELOQUENT PLAYER of the 19th century, Jim O'Rourke was called "Orator" and another O'Rourke (no relation) was dubbed "Voiceless Tim" because he lacked Jim's eloquence.

A native of Bridgeport, Connecticut, James Henry O'Rourke (1852-1919) joined the Mansfields, an outstanding amateur team in the nearby community of Middletown, in 1867 although he had not yet turned age 15. When the Mansfields went professional in 1872 and entered the National Association, O'Rourke accompanied them after a club official found a replacement for him on the family farm. The Mansfields folded after only one year, allowing O'Rourke to sign with the champion Boston Red Caps. He stayed with the club for six seasons, during which time they became more commonly known as the Red Stockings.

An attempt by Boston to deduct $20 from his pay to cover the cost of his uniform prompted O'Rourke to move to Providence in 1879. After hitting .351 to help spur the Grays to the National League pennant, O'Rourke returned to Boston for one last season in 1880 and then signed as player-manager of the Buffalo Bisons. Three years in the dual role convinced him to return to the playing ranks only.

O'Rourke signed with the New York Giants in 1885 and remained with them through the 1892 season with a year out to participate in the Players League experiment. After a single season as player-manager of the Washington Nationals, O'Rourke became part owner, player, and manager of the Bridgeport team in the Victor League. Later renamed the Connecticut League, the circuit had the benefit of O'Rourke's services through the 1908 season. Except for the final campaign, when he only managed the club, he remained an active player during all that time — and a catcher, no less. Because of his remarkable fitness for a man his age, O'Rourke was enlisted by Giants manager John McGraw to catch the entire game that clinched the 1904 pennant for New York. Although age 52 at the time, O'Rourke went 1-for-4 and scored a run.

The 1904 appearance enabled O'Rourke to become the first player in major league history to be active in four different decades. Oddly, although he played every position on the diamond during his career, he never excelled at any of them. The Orator was somewhat of a liability in the field but made up for it by being a reliable and productive hitter. He was elected to the Hall of Fame in 1945.

Major League Totals

BA	G	AB	R	H	2B	3B	HR	RBI	SB
.310	1,774	7,435	1,446	2,304	414	132	51	830	177

MIKE KELLY

BECAUSE HIS CAREER WAS shortened by alcoholism and a general disinclination to take care of himself, Mike Kelly is viewed by many historians as a colorful but vastly overrated performer whose press clippings far exceeded his deeds on the diamond. The truth, though, is that for at least a few years he may have been the best player in the game. Certainly Kelly was one of the most versatile. He could play every position on the field and even took a turn on occasion as a pitcher, although it was the only job he never performed with distinction.

This lithograph shows Kelly in 1887, his first season in Boston. He occupied every spot that year but first base.

Born in Lansingburgh, New York, Michael Joseph Kelly (1857-1894) gravitated to Ohio to play semipro ball in his late teens. In 1878, he joined the Cincinnati Reds and was put in right field but also served infrequently at third base and behind the plate. The following season, playing mostly as a third baseman, Kelly hit .348 and drew the interest of Chicago White Stockings player-manager Cap Anson. When Cincinnati neglected to put Kelly on its reserve list of protected players, Anson promptly snatched him up.

Kelly was an instant sensation in Chicago. Windy City fans nicknamed him "King" and were so enamored of his daring base-running

techniques, particularly the hook slide that he reportedly originated, that they chanted "Slide, Kelly, slide," whenever he got on base. They were seldom without an opportunity at least once during a game, for Kelly twice led the National League in batting while in Chicago and three times in runs. Although never really the regular catcher for the White Stockings, Kelly was usually behind the bat in big games. Part of the reason was his remarkable ingenuity. Kelly is credited with being the first backstopper to use signals that alerted his infielders to the type of pitch being thrown; the infielders, in turn, positioned themselves accordingly.

Kelly's high living and penchant for gambling, however, caused Anson, something of a Puritan, to grow disenchanted with him despite the five pennants the White Stockings won in Kelly's seven seasons with the club. Chicago sold him to Boston for a then record sum of $10,000 before the 1887 season.

Called "The $10,000 Beauty," Kelly served on two National League pennant winners in the Hub. He also piloted the Boston Reds to the Players League title in 1890. By 1892, however, Kelly's lifestyle had robbed him of his skills, and he could hit only .189 in 78 games. Kelly was named to the Hall of Fame in 1945.

MIKE J. (KING) KELLY
COLORFUL PLAYER AND AUDACIOUS BASE-RUNNER. IN 1887 FOR BOSTON HE HIT .394 AND STOLE 84 BASES. HIS SALE FOR $10,000 WAS ONE OF THE BIGGEST DEALS OF BASEBALL'S EARLY HISTORY.

Catcher; outfielder; infielder
Cincinnati Reds
   1878–1879
Chicago White Stockings
   1880–1886
Boston Beaneaters
   1887–1889; 1891–1892
Boston Reds 1890
Cincinnati Kellys, 1891
Boston Reds 1891
New York Giants 1893
Manager
Boston Beaneaters 1887
Boston Reds 1890
Cincinnati Kellys 1891
173-148

Kelly was the most popular player in each city that he played. He played on pennant-winning teams in three different major leagues.

Major League Totals										
BA	G	AB	R	H	2B	3B	HR	RBI	SB
.308	1,455	5,894	1,357	1,813	359	102	69	793	315

JOHN MONTGOMERY WARD
1873-1894
PITCHING PIONEER WHO WON 158,
LOST 102 GAMES IN SEVEN YEARS.
PITCHED PERFECT GAME FOR PROVIDENCE
OF N.L. IN 1880.
TURNED TO SHORTSTOP AND MADE 2,151 HITS.
MANAGED NEW YORK AND BROOKLYN IN N.L.
PRESIDENT OF BOSTON, N.L. 1911-1912.
PLAYED IMPORTANT PART IN ESTABLISHING
MODERN ORGANIZED BASEBALL.

Pitcher; infielder; executive
Providence Grays
1878-1882
New York Giants
1883-1889; 1893-1894
Brooklyn Wonders 1890
Brooklyn Bridegrooms
1891-1892

Manager
Providence Grays 1880
New York Giants 1884;
1893-1894
Brooklyn Wonders 1890
Brooklyn Bridegrooms
1891-1892
412-320

Monte Ward was featured in this postcard (top) and a picture plate (right). He is the only member of the Hall of Fame who compiled more than 150 wins as a hurler and more than 2,000 hits.

JOHN MONTGOMERY WARD (1860-1925) compiled 108 major league wins before his 21st birthday. When his arm went sour, he became one of the better fielding shortstops of his time and a more than competent offensive performer, good enough to collect 2,105 hits and twice pace the National League in stolen bases. Besides his playing credentials, Ward organized the Brotherhood of Professional Base Ball Players (an early attempt at player unionization) and was later a manager, owner, and chair of the rules committee. Few, if any, players or executives in the last century made a greater contribution to the game than Ward. Yet he was not selected for the Hall of Fame until 1964.

Ward's professional debut was on July 15, 1878. A mere 18 years old at the time, he was hired by the Providence Grays of the National League. Although the campaign was well under way by the time Ward hurled his first game, he finished among the leaders in every major pitching department. The following year, he topped the NL with 47 wins and led in strikeouts and winning percentage as the Grays copped the pennant.

On the morning of June 17, 1880, Ward tossed a perfect game, 5-0 victory over Buffalo, missing by only five days the distinction of

becoming the first pitcher to hurl a full nine-inning game without allowing a single enemy baserunner. Two years later, he notched the longest complete-game shutout win ever, an 18-inning 1-0 triumph over Detroit. By the end of that season, however, Ward's arm had already begun to fail, and he began the conversion to shortstop after he was sold to New York before the 1883 campaign.

Ward was appointed the field captain of the New York club soon after his arrival. During the off-season, he attended law school, graduating from Columbia in 1885. His legal training served him in good stead after he became president of the Brotherhood of Professional Base Ball Players. In 1887, he wrote an article denouncing the reserve clause. Two years later, upon returning from a postseason world tour to find that owners had imposed a cap on players' salaries, he organized the Players League rebellion. Many say this kept Ward out of the Hall of Fame for so long.

In 1891, Monte was appointed player-manager of the Brooklyn Bridegrooms. After two years with Brooklyn, he returned to the New York Giants in an identical role. Ward left the game following the 1894 season to practice law. In 1911, he bought a part interest in the Boston Braves, selling his share less than a year later.

Major League Totals

BA	G	AB	R	H	2B	3B	HR	RBI	SB
.275	1,825	7,647	1,408	2,105	231	97	26	686	504

PUD GALVIN

ONE OF THE MOST COLORFUL performers in the last century, Pud Galvin is the only pitcher in history to win 20 or more games on 10 different occasions without ever playing on a pennant winner. Owing partly to this piece of bad luck and partly to never being a league leader in any of the three triple-crown pitching departments—wins, strikeouts, or ERA—Galvin was not elected to the Hall of Fame until 1965 despite collecting 361 career victories, more than any other hurler who played exclusively in the 19th century.

James Francis "Pud" Galvin (1856-1902) reportedly got his odd nickname because he made a hitter look like a pudding, a 19th century slang term for a dud. In addition, he was called "Gentle Jeems" because he was a mild, unassuming individual who rarely drank or questioned umpires.

Born in St. Louis on Christmas Day in 1856, Galvin broke in with the first professional team in the Mound City, the St. Louis Reds, a member of the National Association in 1875. Pud then pitched for teams in Pittsburgh and Buffalo for the next three years before returning to the major leagues in 1879 when Buffalo, his 1878 club, became a member of the National League.

During his six full seasons with Buffalo, Galvin won 206 games and threw two no-hitters. The first gem came in 1881 when the pitcher's box was only 45 feet from the plate. His second masterpiece came in 1884 after the box had been moved to a 50-foot distance.

But the Bisons, while a respectable team, never quite became a contender. Part of the problem was that Buffalo in the 1880s was a small city in a poor climate and thus faced the dual handicap of skimpy attendance and frequent postponements. Late in the 1885 season, with the franchise on the rocks, he was sold to the Pittsburgh Alleghenys in the American Association for $2,500.

A weak team before the acquisition of Galvin, Pittsburgh almost immediately became competitive. Teaming with southpaw sensation Cannonball Morris, Galvin led the Alleghenys to a second-place finish in the Association in 1886. The team then opted to cast its lot in the National League the following season. The move proved a mistake. Although Galvin continued to be a workhorse for several more seasons, Pittsburgh never again finished in the first division until he was no longer with the club. A finger injury and soaring weight finished Pud in 1892. He tried umpiring in the NL and then pitched a while for a minor league team in Buffalo.

JAMES F. (PUD) GALVIN
ST. LOUIS N.A. 1875
BUFFALO N.L. 1879-1885
PITTSBURGH A.A. 1885-1886
PITTSBURGH N.L. 1887-1889 1891-1892
PITTSBURGH P.L. 1890
ST. LOUIS N.L. 1892
WON 365 GAMES, LOST 311.
WHEN ELECTED ONLY FOUR PITCHERS
HAD WON MORE GAMES.
PITCHED NO-HIT GAMES IN 1880 AND 1884.
PITCHED 649 COMPLETE GAMES.

Pitcher
Buffalo Bisons 1879-1885
Pittsburgh Alleghenys
    1885-1892
St. Louis Browns 1892

Manager
Buffalo Bisons 1885
7-17

Top: *This ad shows the 1878 International Association champion Bisons, with Galvin at top right. The IA title helped Buffalo gain access to the NL in '79. Left: Galvin has the most wins of any hurler who didn't play on a big league pennant winner.*

		Major League Totals							
W	**L**	**ERA**	**G**	**CG**	**IP**	**H**	**ER**	**BB**	**SO**
361	308	2.87	697	639	5,941.1	6,352	1,894	744	1,799

DAN BROUTHERS

HARD-HITTING FIRST BASEMAN OF EIGHT MAJOR LEAGUE CLUBS, HE WAS PART OF ORIGINAL "BIG FOUR" OF BUFFALO. TRADED WITH OTHER MEMBERS OF THAT COMBINATION TO DETROIT, HE HIT .419 AS CITY WON ITS ONLY NATIONAL LEAGUE CHAMPIONSHIP IN 1887.

First baseman
Troy Trojans 1879-1880
Buffalo Bisons 1881-1885
Detroit Wolverines
    1886-1888
Boston Beaneaters 1889
Boston Reds 1890-1891
Brooklyn Bridegrooms
    1892-1893
Baltimore Orioles
    1894-1895
Louisville Colonels 1895
Philadelphia Phillies 1896
New York Giants 1904

BY ANY STANDARD, DAN Brouthers was the greatest hitter in the game's first period from 1871 (the founding of the National Association) to 1893, when the pitcher's mound was established at its present 60'6" distance from home plate. Brouthers captured five hitting titles and was at one time or another a league leader in every major batting department.

Dennis Joseph Brouthers (1858-1932) was initially a pitcher. He reached the National League in 1879 with the Troy Trojans. After three undistinguished twirling efforts, he was converted to a full-time first baseman.

Unlike most great hitters, Brouthers struggled at the plate in the majors at the outset, returning to semipro ball in 1880 for further seasoning. Back in the NL the following year with Buffalo Big Dan teamed with Deacon White, Hardy Richardson, and Jack Rowe to give the Bisons an attack so devastating that the quartet came to be labeled "The Big Four." Brouthers soon emerged as the acknowledged club leader and one of the game's first great stars by topping the circuit in batting in 1882 and 1883.

When Buffalo encountered severe financial problems in 1885, the entire Big Four was sold to Detroit in mid-September for $7,500.

National League president Nick Young attempted to void the deal, believing it would swing the pennant unfairly to Detroit. When the quartet refused to return to Buffalo, however, Young allowed them to remain in Detroit provided they not play in any games against pennant contenders. So, the Big Four had to sit out the last three weeks of the season as all Detroit's remaining games were with teams in the race for the flag.

Allowed to play for Detroit in 1886, Brouthers led the league in homers. The following season, he sparked the Wolverines to their only pennant. Poor attendance forced Detroit to fold after a fifth-place finish in 1888. The Big Four broke up as a result, with Brouthers being awarded to the Boston Beaneaters. In his first year in the Hub, Big Dan promptly won his third batting title. In 1890 Brouthers won a flag with the Boston Reds in the Players League, and the following season he was on the pennant-winning Boston Reds in the American Association. He played on one last pennant winner in 1894 with the fabled Baltimore Orioles.

Altogether, Brouthers played on a record nine different National League teams during his career. The ninth and last was the New York Giants, for whom he got into two games toward the end of the 1904 campaign at age 46. He was elected to the Hall of Fame in 1945.

Top right: Brouthers sports the colors of the 1887 Wolverines. Above: A lithograph of the game's most prolific batting champion before 1900.

Major League Totals

BA	G	AB	R	H	2B	3B	HR	RBI	SB
.342	1,673	6,711	1,523	2,296	460	205	106	1,057	235

WHETHER INTENTIONALLY OR accidentally, Charley Radbourn ended up giving himself his nickname. During his extraordinary 1884 season, while in the midst of winning a record 60 games for the Providence Grays, Radbourn would warm up in the outfield before a game until he finally proclaimed, "Old Hoss is ready." By the end of the season, Old Hoss had logged so many innings that he could scarcely lift his arm to comb his hair. Never again was he much more than an average hurler, but his Hall of Fame plaque nonetheless says that he was the "greatest of all 19th-century pitchers."

There is no disputing that Charles Gardner Radbourn (1854-1897) was the game's supreme pitcher—for one year anyway—although no one would have predicted it as late as July 1884. On July 16, in fact, he was suspended without pay by Providence Grays manager Frank Bancroft for a combination of drunkenness and lack of effort. When the club's other pitcher, Charlie Sweeney, jumped to the Union Association, Bancroft was forced to reinstate Radbourn. Hoss deigned to return on two conditions: that he receive his

Pitcher
Buffalo Bisons 1880
Providence Grays
**   1881-1885**
Boston Beaneaters
**   1886-1889**
Boston Reds 1890
Cincinnati Reds 1891

release from Providence at the end of the season and that, in the meantime, he be allowed to pitch every remaining game in return for a hefty bonus.

Providence was in a tight pennant race at the time. With Radbourn back in the box on a daily basis, the Grays soon pulled away, romping home 10½ games ahead of the pack in the National League. It was therefore not necessary for Radbourn to hurl every game, and toward the end of the season he did take a day off now and then. The damage to his arm was already done, however. After winning 167 games in his first four years in the National League, Radbourn collected just 144 more victories before his wing finally gave out altogether during the 1891 campaign.

Radbourn returned to his hometown of Bloomington, Illinois, and opened a billiard parlor. A hunting accident in April 1894 rendered his face partially paralyzed. Self-conscious, he retired to a back room, where he sat most of the time in dim light to conceal his disfigurement. On February 5, 1897, he died, just a few weeks after his birthday.

Old Hoss Radbourn was elected to the Hall of Fame in 1939. The Old Timers voters who selected him remembered him not just for his fabled 60-win season and his 311 career victories, but also for his all-around ability.

Top: Radbourn often played other positions when he wasn't pitching. In 1882, Radbourn collected 326 at bats, about as many as the average NL regular that year. Left: This advertising clipping is from his first year in Boston, 1886, when he was 27-31.

			Major League Totals						
W	**L**	**ERA**	**G**	**CG**	**IP**	**H**	**ER**	**BB**	**SO**
311	194	2.67	528	489	4,535.1	4,335	1,345	875	1,830

MICHAEL FRANCIS WELCH
"SMILING MICKEY"
TROY N.L. 1880-1882
NEW YORK N.L. 1883-1892
CREDITED WITH MORE THAN 300 VICTORIES
DURING 13 SEASONS IN MAJORS. WON 17
GAMES IN A ROW IN 1885 WHILE COMPILING
44-11 RECORD FOR LEAGUE-LEADING .800
WINNING PERCENTAGE. TOPPED 30-VICTORY
TOTAL IN FOUR YEARS.

Pitcher
Troy Trojans 1880-1882
New York Giants
    1883-1892

"SMILING MICKEY" WELCH, SO tagged because of his nonchalant smile that never dimmed no matter how many errors his teammates made behind him, attributed his remarkable pitching success to drinking beer. He even coined a short ditty that embodied his philosophy: "Pure elixir of malt and hops/Beats all the drugs and all the drops." Whatever the secret Welch knew that most other pitchers did not, he had the second shortest career of any 300-game winner in history. Only Old Hoss Radbourn toiled fewer than Welch's 13 seasons in top company.

Born in Brooklyn, New York, Michael Francis Welch (1859-1941) made his professional debut in 1878 with Auburn in the minor league National Association. The following year, he was with Holyoke in the same circuit. Hired by the Troy Trojans of the National League for the 1880 season, Mickey was installed as the team's ace pitcher. Welch came through with 34 wins in 64 starts and 574 innings as a rookie. Despite his extraordinary yearling season, Mickey was replaced as Troy's ace the following year by Tim Keefe.

MICHAEL WELCH

After again playing second fiddle to Keefe in 1882, Welch regained his status as the club's No. 1 pitcher when Troy moved to New York for the 1883 season and Keefe was shifted from the Gothams National League franchise to the New York Metropolitans of the American Association. To Welch fell the honor of pitching the first game for the home team in the original Polo Grounds. The forerunner of the New York Giants got full value from Mickey, a 25-game winner in 1883 and a 39-game winner the next season. In 1885, when Keefe returned to the club from the Metropolitans, the pair won 76 games between them, with Welch contributing 44 victories.

Despite having what was probably the strongest pitching tandem in the game, the New Yorkers were unable to garner their first flag until 1888. Welch netted 26 wins for the pennant winners, then another 27 victories a year later, when the Giants repeated as champions by capturing the title on the last day of the season in the closest pennant race in history to that point.

With most of the leading stars gone to the Players League in 1890, Welch toppled to just 17 wins. Used sparingly the following season, he started only 15 games, winning six and losing nine. After being knocked out of the box in an early season start in 1892, Mickey was shipped to Troy in the Eastern League. Despite his 308 career wins, he was neglected by Hall of Fame voters until the Veterans Committee named him for enshrinement in 1973.

Top: Welch adorns the cover of this 1887 Giants scorecard. By the mid-1880s the baseball concession business was already thriving. Right: An early baseball card of Mickey. Welch played his entire career for the same franchise.

			Major League Totals							
W	**L**	**ERA**	**G**	**CG**	**IP**	**H**	**ER**	**BB**	**SO**
308	209	2.71	564	525	4,802.0	4,587	1,446	1,297	1,850

TIM KEEFE

As VIRTUALLY ALL THE 19TH century's 300-game winners, Tim Keefe had the luxury of playing for good teams for the better part of his career. In an era when most quality pitchers started upward of 50 games a season, winning 30 or 35 games with a contender was a routine matter, provided a hurler was durable—and Keefe was certainly that. In his first nine full seasons in the major leagues, he labored 4,103 innings and racked up 285 victories. Although he posted only a 57-51 record for the remaining five seasons of his 14-year career, he totaled 342 wins, the eighth most in history.

During his 14-year career, Keefe led the National League in every major pitching department at least once.

Born in Cambridge, Massachusetts, Timothy John Keefe (1857-1933) played for local amateur teams until he was 22 years old. He joined the Utica team of the National Association in 1879. By the middle of the following season, he was in the majors with the Troy Trojans of the National League. In 1880, Troy already had an outstanding rookie pitcher in Mickey Welch, and Keefe seemed destined to become no more than the club's second-line hurler. Early in the 1881 season, however, Keefe slowly but steadily began to prove himself the more tireless worker.

When the Troy franchise moved to New York in 1883, the pitching duo of Keefe and Welch was split up, with Keefe going to the Metropolitans, the New York representative in the rival American Association. After the Metropolitans won the Association pennant in 1884, Keefe and several other of the team's stars were quickly transferred to the National League entry in New York, soon to be renamed the Giants. What made the shift an easy matter, albeit somewhat unethical, was that both Gotham clubs were under the same ownership.

Reunited in 1885, Keefe and Mickey Welch helped carry the Giants to National League pennants in 1888 and 1889. On both occasions, New York beat the American Association champion in the World Series with comparative ease, giving Gotham fans cause to believe a dynasty was in the making. After the 1889 season, though, the Brotherhood revolted and formed the Players League. Along with most of the other Giants stars, Keefe jumped to the New York franchise in the Brotherhood circuit, which was managed by Buck Ewing, his former catcher on the Giants.

Although the best team on paper, Ewing's club could finish no better than third when Keefe was held to 17 victories by arm trouble. Returning to the National League after the Brotherhood League failed, he pitched three more seasons without much distinction, then became an umpire. Keefe was named to the Hall of Fame in 1964.

Pitcher
Troy Trojans 1880-1882
New York Metropolitans
1883-1884
New York Giants
1885-1889; 1891
New York Giants (PL) 1890
Philadelphia Phillies
1891-1893

This 1887 Tobin litho depicts Keefe in his third season with the New York Giants. In 1886, his second year there, he led the NL with 42 wins.

Major League Totals

W	L	ERA	G	CG	IP	H	ER	BB	SO
342	225	2.62	600	557	5,061.1	4,452	1,473	1,224	2,527

BUCK EWING

WM. B. "BUCK" EWING
GREATEST 19TH CENTURY CATCHER. GIANT
IN STATURE AND GIANT CAPTAIN OF
NEW YORK'S FIRST NATIONAL LEAGUE
CHAMPIONS 1888 AND 1889. WAS GENIUS
AS FIELD LEADER, UNSURPASSED IN
THROWING TO BASES. GREAT LONG-RANGE
HITTER. NATIONAL LEAGUE CAREER
1881 TO 1899 TROY, N.Y. GIANTS AND
CLEVELAND; CINCINNATI MANAGER.

Catcher; infielder; outfielder
Troy Trojans 1880-1882
New York Giants
1883-1889; 1891-1892
New York Giants (PL) 1890
Cleveland Spiders
1893-1894
Cincinnati Reds
1895-1897
Manager
New York Giants
1890; 1900
Cincinnati Reds
1895-1899
489-395

In 1895, this medal (the equivalent of a Gold Glove) was given to first baseman Buck Ewing.

AT A GLANCE, BUCK EWING'S career seems noteworthy but in no way extraordinary. He led the National League in home runs in 1883 and in triples in 1884, but his accomplishments otherwise appear to have been on the modest side. In Ewing's case, however, statistics are deceiving. In 1919, Francis Richter, one of the leading sportswriters of his day, deemed Ewing, Ty Cobb, and Honus Wagner the three greatest players in baseball to that time. Richter went on to say that Ewing might have been the best of them all according to "supreme excellence in all departments—batting, catching, fielding, baserunning, throwing, and baseball brains—a player without a weakness of any kind, physical, mental, or temperamental."

Ewing is shown leaving the batter's box on this cover of Leslie's weekly.

William Ewing (1859-1906) was one of the first players from the Cincinnati area to become a major league star. A weak hitter early in his career, Ewing batted only .178 in a brief trial with Troy in 1880 and finished at an even .250 the following year in his first full big league season. Any hitting Buck did was a bonus, however. From the very outset of his career, he was viewed as an outstanding defensive catcher, the most demanding position on the diamond.

Ewing's chest protector and mask are surprisingly similar to today's devices.

Ewing was one of the first catchers to catalogue each opposing batter's weakness and then share the knowledge in pregame clubhouse meetings. John Foster wrote that "as a thrower to bases, Ewing never had a superior. Ewing was the man of whom it was said, 'he handed the ball to the second baseman from the batter's box.'"

Great as Ewing was behind the plate, he could not play there every day. The position was so physically taxing that catchers in the last century seldom worked more than half their team's games. While most backstops simply took that day off, Ewing customarily played another position. So versatile was Buck that he could fill in anywhere on the diamond. In 1889, with the Giants in a drive for the pennant, Ewing even pitched and won two complete games. He jumped to the Players League the following year and was named manager of the New York Giants. The 1890 season was Ewing's last as a regular catcher.

Ewing finished his playing career in Cincy in 1897. A player-manager at the time, he remained with the Reds for two more years as a manager. A diabetic, he succumbed to the disease on October 20, 1906, at age 47. In 1936, he tied for first place in the initial vote of the old-timers for the Hall of Fame. Buck was inducted in 1939.

			Major League Totals							
BA	G	AB	R	H	2B	3B	HR	RBI	SB	
.303	1,315	5,363	1,129	1,625	250	178	70	738	336	

ROGER CONNOR

ORN OF IRISH PARENTAGE IN Waterbury, Connecticut, Roger Connor (1857-1931) started his baseball career as a lefthanded third baseman with the local team in 1876. Three years later, while playing for Holyoke, Massachusetts, Connor caught the eye of Bob Ferguson, the manager of a rival team in Springfield. When named manager of the Troy Trojans in the National League the following year, Ferguson made it a priority to sign both Connor and Mickey Welch, a pitcher on the Holyoke team.

Still a third baseman, Connor might have been the earliest to play that position for his entire career and subsequently make the Hall of Fame were it not for an injury. A dislocated shoulder necessitated his move to first base and there he stayed for most of his 17 remaining seasons in the majors.

Connor was one of the game's first noteworthy sluggers. Early in his career, though, the mark of a long ball hitter was not the number of home runs he tallied but rather his other extra base hit totals (triples in particular). Connor's 233 career triples are fifth on the all-time list and first among players active solely in the last century. He was also the only player before 1900 to collect more than 1,000 walks. In addition, his 136 home runs stood as the career record until Babe Ruth surpassed the mark in 1921.

The neglect into which Connor's reputation fell after his retirement in 1897 is puzzling. Not only are his career totals in almost every major batting department among the highest of any player in the last century, but he played during his prime years for the New York Giants, a team that was always in the limelight. Moreover, the Giants won two pennants during his tenure and were contenders on several other occasions.

Traded to the lowly St. Louis Browns early in the 1894 season, Connor played parts of four seasons there before departing the majors to extend his career in the minors. Flashing a new pair of glasses, he served as owner, manager, and first baseman in 1898 of the Waterbury team in the Connecticut League. The loop's batting leader, he remained its most renowned player until his retirement in 1903.

A school inspector in Waterbury, he withdrew more from the public eye with each passing year until his death in 1931. Until Hank Aaron's pursuit of Babe Ruth's career home run record made historians wonder whose record Ruth had broken, Connor was largely forgotten. In 1976, Connor was at long last selected for the Hall of Fame.

First baseman
Troy Trojans 1880-1882
New York Giants
  1883-1889; 1891;
  1893-1994
New York Giants (PL) 1890
Philadelphia Phillies 1892
St. Louis Browns
  1894-1897
Manager
St. Louis Browns 1896
8-37

This 1886 New York Giants scorecard features Connor. He led the NL with 20 triples that year.

In 1882, Troy had four Hall of Famers: Buck Ewing (middle row, far left), Roger Connor (middle row, second from right), Mickey Welch (top, fourth from right), and Tim Keefe (top, far right).

		Major League Totals							
BA	**G**	**AB**	**R**	**H**	**2B**	**3B**	**HR**	**RBI**	**SB**
.317	1,998	7,794	1,620	2,467	441	233	136	1,125	227

JOHN GIBSON CLARKSON
WORCESTER, N.L. 1882
CHICAGO, N.L. 1884-87
BOSTON, N.L. 1888-92
CLEVELAND, N.L. 1892-94
PITCHED 4 TO 0 NO-HIT GAME AGAINST
PROVIDENCE IN 1885. WON 328 LOST 179
PCT. 652 LED LEAGUE WITH 55 VICTORIES
IN 1885 (INCLUDING 10 SHUTOUTS) 38 IN
1887, 49 IN 1888 AND 49 IN 1889. HAD
2013 STRIKEOUTS IN 4514 INNINGS.

Pitcher
Worcester Ruby Legs 1882
Chicago White Stockings
   1884-1887
Boston Beaneaters
   1888-1892
Cleveland Spiders
   1892-1894

Below: *The 1886 NL Champion White Stockings contained three Hall of Famers: Cap Anson (top row, center), King Kelly (top row, far right), and John Clarkson (bottom row, second from right). Top: Clarkson won 33 games in 1888, his first season in Boston.*

I N ALMOST EVERY RESPECT, John Gibson Clarkson (1861-1909) was an anomaly. He was born in Cambridge, Massachusetts, the son of a wealthy jewelry manufacturer. He was badly out of step with the rough-and-tumble era in which he played. The miracle is not so much that he won 326 games but that he played 12 seasons in the majors before his mental makeup overcame him.

Clarkson's introduction to the professional game was even atypical. He debuted at the major league level, with Worcester of the National League in 1882. When the club disbanded at the close of the season, the meek Clarkson didn't join his teammates in scrambling for a place on another major league team but instead headed for the minors. In 1884, while in the midst of winning 31 games for Saginaw in the Northwestern League, he was scouted by Cap Anson of the Chicago White Stockings, who desperately needed another pitcher to spell Larry Corcoran, the staff workhorse.

Signed by Chicago, Clarkson won 10 games for Anson's men before the season was out. The following year, when the overworked Corcoran fell prey to arm trouble, Clarkson inherited his job. Only age 23 when the season began, he fashioned a 53-16 record (the second-highest number of victories in history) to vault the White Stockings to the pennant by a two-game margin over the New York Giants. Proving that he was not just a one-year wonder, Clarkson followed up on his mammoth season by logging 35 victories in 1886 and 38 in 1887.

His league-leading record in 1887 notwithstanding, Clarkson was sold to Boston for $10,000 before the 1888 season. Chicago fans were up in arms over the deal that followed on the heels of the sale of Clarkson's battery mate, King Kelly, to Boston. Manager Anson defended the transactions by claiming that both men were detrimental to his team: Kelly because of his undisciplined nature, and Clarkson because of his overly sensitive one.

In any case, Clarkson was hardly shattered by the move. He won 82 games during his first two seasons in Boston, giving him a record 209 wins over a five-year period. Failing to beat Pittsburgh on the final day of the 1889 season, however, he helped cost Boston the pennant.

Although Clarkson remained loyal to the Beaneaters during the Players League insurrection in 1890, he was nevertheless shipped to Cleveland two years later. He retired after the 1894 season, in part because he was unable to adapt to the increased 60'6" pitching distance put into effect the previous year. Clarkson was elected to the Hall of Fame in 1963.

Major League Totals										
W	L	ERA	G	CG	IP	H	ER	BB	SO
326	177	2.81	531	485	4,536.1	4,295	1,416	1,191	1,978

AS A PITCHER, TOMMY McCarthy had an 0-7 career record. He played just nine full seasons in the majors and was never a league leader in a single batting or fielding department. His only ostensible distinction was that he topped the American Association in stolen bases in 1890, a year when most of the loop's better performers were participating in the Players League rebellion. Yet Thomas Francis Michael McCarthy (1863-1922) was named to the Hall of Fame in 1946, long before many players who produced career statistical totals that were nearly double those that he had tallied.

Perhaps McCarthy's most obvious attribute was that he was the other half of the Boston Beaneaters' famous "Heavenly Twins" of the early 1890s. Splitting his time between playing right and left field, McCarthy was stationed beside center gardener Hugh Duffy. The Irish duo swiftly became the darlings of Boston fans. Duffy was by far the better player, but McCarthy had his moments as well, though trickery rather than talent seems to have been his long suit. McCarthy has been credited for developing the fake bunt, a device used to draw in opposing

T. McCARTHY, C. F.,
St. Louis Browns
Copyrighted by GOODWIN & CO. 1887.
OLD JUDGE
CIGARETTES.
GOODWIN & CO., New York.

infielders and then slap the ball past them, and the outfield trap play. Reputedly, McCarthy's penchant for snaring pop flies on the short bounce and then forcing runners trying to advance was instrumental in the creation of the modern infield fly rule.

McCarthy is the only participant in the ill-fated Union Association experiment in 1884 who is now enshrined in Cooperstown. A rookie at the time with the Boston Reds, he hit just .215 and was tagged with seven quick losses when tried as a hurler.

After his retirement as an active player, McCarthy worked as a scout, a college coach, and, for one season, a minor league manager. For many years, he operated a combination bowling alley and saloon in his hometown of Boston. Called "Duffy and McCarthy" to appeal to a clientele who remembered the "Heavenly Twins," it closed its doors long before McCarthy's death on August 5, 1922.

THOMAS F. McCARTHY
ONE OF BOSTON'S "HEAVENLY TWINS" UNDER MANAGER FRANK SELEE. OUTSTANDING BASE RUNNER WHO STOLE 109 BASES FOR THE BROWNS IN 1888. PIONEER IN TRAPPING FLY BALLS IN THE OUTFIELD. HOLDS N.L. RECORD FOR ASSISTS IN OUTFIELD-53 WITH BOSTON IN 1893. PLAYED 1268 GAMES IN MAJOR LEAGUES.

Outfielder
Boston Reds 1884
Boston Beaneaters 1885;
  1892-1895
Philadelphia Quakers
  1886-1887
St. Louis Browns
  1888-1891
Brooklyn Bridegrooms
  1896
Manager
St. Louis Browns 1890
11-11

McCarthy appeared in two Old Judge cigarette cards. **Left:** *Note that home plate at that time was in the shape of a diamond.* **Top:** *Although this picture was copyrighted late in 1887, McCarthy actually did not first appear with the St. Louis Browns until the 1888 season.*

McCARTHY, 2d B. St. Louis
COPYRIGHTED BY GOODWIN & CO. 1887.
OLD JUDGE
CIGARETTES.
GOODWIN & CO., New York.

Major League Totals

BA	G	AB	R	H	2B	3B	HR	RBI	SB
.292	1,275	5,128	1,069	1,496	193	55	44	666	467

SAMUEL LUTHER THOMPSON
DETROIT N.L., PHILADELPHIA N.L.
1885-1898; DETROIT A.L. 1906
ONE OF THE FOREMOST SLUGGERS OF
HIS DAY. LIFETIME BATTING AVERAGE
.336, BATTED BETTER THAN .400 TWICE.
GREAT CLUTCH HITTER. COLLECTED
200 OR MORE HITS IN A SEASON THREE
TIMES. TOPPED N.L. IN HOME RUNS AND
RUNS BATTED IN TWICE.

Outfielder
Detroit Wolverines
    1885-1888
Philadelphia Quakers
    (Phillies) 1889-1898
Detroit Tigers 1906

Top: This die cut of Thompson was manufactured in 1887, when he led the National League in batting and slugging averages, RBI, total bases, triples, and hits. Right: Thompson was the most prolific batter ever at knocking in runs—.921 per game.

S AMUEL LUTHER THOMPSON (1860-1922) was already 24 years old and seemingly destined to spend his life as a carpenter in his hometown of Danville, Indiana, when a scout for the Evansville club in the Northwest League bade him to give professional baseball a try. The scout was more interested in Thompson's older brother Cy, then demurred when he discovered that Cy was past age 26.

After playing only five games with Evansville, Sam ended up out of a job when the club folded. Thompson signed with Indianapolis of the Western League in 1885. When Thompson got off to a fast start in 1885, manager Hustling Dan O'Leary, an off-season resident of Detroit, convinced Detroit owner Fredrick Stearns to purchase Big Sam.

Joining the Wolverines in early July, Thompson tallied 11 hits in his first 26 at bats and claimed the club's right field job. He led Detroit in batting in 1886, his first full campaign in the majors. In 1887, he paced the entire National League as he hit .372 and bagged a 19th century record 166 RBI. Still, Thompson's

talents as a hitter went largely unrecognized in his time (RBI totals were kept on an informal basis). As a result, it was not until long after Thompson retired that historians revealed him to be the most prolific of any player ever at driving in runs—.921 per game. The home run, another Thompson specialty, was regarded as a trivial accomplishment by many of the game's authorities in the late 1800s.

Thompson, however, was not merely a slugger. He also led the National League on three occasions in hits, twice in doubles, and once in triples. A good outfielder, he had one of the strongest arms in the game. The Detroit franchise collapsed after the 1888 season, and Sam was sold to the Philadelphia Phillies.

In the early 1890s, Big Sam was joined by Ed Delahanty and Billy Hamilton, giving Philadelphia a trio of future Hall of Fame outfielders. While Hamilton batted .399, the other two topped the .400 mark in 1894. The following year, Thompson hit .392 and led the National League with 18 homers and 165 RBI, coming within one marker of tying his own 19th century record. A bad back shelved him early in the 1897 season. He made several unsuccessful comeback attempts, the final one with the Detroit Tigers in 1906. Then 46 years old, Thompson found himself playing beside 19-year-old Ty Cobb for a few days in Cobb's first full season. Thompson was named to the Hall of Fame by the Veterans Committee in 1974.

				Major League Totals					
BA	**G**	**AB**	**R**	**H**	**2B**	**3B**	**HR**	**RBI**	**SB**
.331	1,410	6,005	1,263	1,986	340	160	128	1,299	221

INORDINATELY SMALL AS A BOY, chunky, and equipped with heavy legs, Billy Hamilton seemed to have little future in baseball. If he had any hope at all, it would appear to have been as a catcher. As it turned out, Hamilton became the speediest center fielder and most prolific base thief of his time. Moreover, he scored 1,692 runs in 1,593 games to become one of only two players in major league history to average more than a run per game (Harry Stovey, the old American Association slugging and basestealing star, is the other.).

Born in Newark, New Jersey, William Robert Hamilton (1866-1940) broke into baseball with Worcester in the New England League in 1888—and was in the majors with Kansas City of the American Association by the end of the season. When the Cowboys folded after the 1889 campaign, Hamilton joined the Philadelphia Phillies in the National League.

During the six seasons he spent with the Phils, Sliding Billy twice topped the circuit in batting and set a post-1893 club record for stolen bases, swiping 98 sacks in 1894—a season in which he tallied an all-time record 192 runs. Hamilton was part of the Phillies' all-.400-hitting outfield that year (Hamilton in center, Ed Delahanty in left, and Sam Thompson in right).

After the 1895 season, Hamilton was traded to the Boston Beaneaters for third baseman

Billy Nash—a deal that amounted to highway robbery, as Nash was through as a regular player while Hamilton was just reaching his peak. With Boston, Hamilton played on pennant winners in 1897 and again in 1898, but was limited to 110 games in the latter campaign by a knee injury.

An outstanding leadoff man, Hamilton continued to compile large walk totals and on-base percentages—he topped the National League in on-base percentage six times—but suffered defensively and as a basestealer when he sustained another leg injury in 1899. After rebounding in 1900 to lead the senior circuit in on-base percentage one last time, Sliding Billy played just one more season in the majors. He then began a long career as a player-manager in the New England and Tri-State Leagues. He led the former loop in batting on three occasions, the last in 1909 at age 43.

Because of judicious real estate investments, Hamilton lived comfortably after he left baseball. He died in Worcester, Massachusetts, on December 16, 1940. Despite his exceptional run and stolen base totals and his .344 career batting average, Hamilton was not selected for the Hall of Fame until 1961.

Outfielder
Kansas City Cowboys
1888-1889
Philadelphia Phillies
1890-1895
Boston Beaneaters
1896-1901

Left: *Hamilton, with the 1900 Boston Beaneaters, was in his final season as a full-time regular.* Top: *This baseball card shows Billy in 1889, his first full major league season. His Kansas City team finished next to last in the American Association that year.*

Major League Totals

BA	G	AB	R	H	2B	3B	HR	RBI	SB
.344	1,593	6,284	1,692	2,163	242	94	40	736	915

ED DELAHANTY

ED DELAHANTY
ONE OF THE GAME'S GREATEST SLUGGERS. LED NATIONAL LEAGUE HITTERS IN 1899 WITH AN AVERAGE OF .408 FOR PHILADELPHIA; AMERICAN LEAGUE BATTERS IN 1902 WITH A MARK OF .376 FOR WASHINGTON. MADE 6 HITS IN 6 TIMES AT BAT TWICE DURING CAREER AND ONCE HIT 4 HOME RUNS IN A GAME.

Outfielder
Philadelphia Quakers
(Phillies) 1888-1889;
1891-1901
Cleveland Infants 1890
Washington Nationals
1902-1903

SOME ANALYSTS CONSIDER ED Delahanty to be the greatest righthanded hitter of all-time. The most famous and the eldest of the only family to produce five brothers who became major league players, Ed batted over .400 three times and took batting titles in both the National League and American League (the only player to accomplish the feat). Yet with the sole exception of Lou Gehrig, Delahanty is baseball's most tragic figure.

Born in Cleveland, Edward James Delahanty (1867-1903) broke in with the Philadelphia Phillies as a second baseman in 1888. He put in four seasons before he first topped the .300 mark. After batting .306 in 1892, however, he never again hit below .323.

Called "Big Ed" more for his strength than his size, Delahanty played for the Phillies all but one of his first 14 seasons. He joined the Players League in 1890 with the Cleveland Infants. Returning to the National League in 1891, Delahanty found the Phillies considerably improved. With Big Ed in left field, the club had the strongest hitting attack in the game for the next four years. Despite a team batting average that soared to an all-time record high .349 in

1894, however, the Phils could never rise above third place.

During the 19th century's last decade, Delahanty led the NL in almost every major hitting department at least once. In 1899, while rapping .410 and also pacing the loop in hits and RBI, Delahanty ripped 55 doubles, a major league record that stood until 1923.

In 1901, Delahanty and Nap Lajoie, the Phillies' two biggest stars, both jumped to the new circuit; Delahanty went to Washington. The following year, he became the second former Phillie to capture the American League hitting crown when he stroked .376 (Lajoie led the circuit in batting in 1901).

Washington was a poor team, however, and Delahanty longed to play on a pennant winner. Before the 1903 season he struck a bargain with John McGraw to join the New York Giants, but a peace settlement between the two leagues froze all players with their old teams. Stuck in Washington, owing McGraw money he had been advanced, and experiencing marital trouble, Delahanty grew despondent and began drinking heavily. On the night of July 2, 1903, he was ejected from a train that was about to cross the International Bridge over Niagara Falls. Drunk and frustrated, he set off in pursuit of the locomotive but had difficulty negotiating the railway ties. He tumbled through the ties and plunged to his death into the Niagara River. His body was not found for days. In 1945, Delahanty was named to the Hall of Fame.

EDWARD J. DELAHANTY, Captain and Left Fielder.
PHILADELPHIA CLUB, 1899

Top: This portrait of Delahanty was produced in 1894, the season he hit .400 as part of Philadelphia's .400-batting average outfield. Right: In 1899, Delahanty paced the National League in batting with a .410 mark and replaced Hugh Duffy as the game's premier left fielder.

			Major League Totals							
BA	G	AB	R	H	2B	3B	HR	RBI	SB	
.346	1,835	7,509	1,601	2,597	520	183	100	1,464	455	

36

FOR YEARS, HUGH DUFFY WAS listed in the record books as the player with the highest single-season batting average in major league history (a .438 mark in 1894). A re-examination of that season's box scores recently divulged that the record books may have been wrong all this time. Duffy may have actually hit .440 in 1894.

On the other hand, a similar reassessment altered Duffy's career batting average from .330 to .324, and most of his other career totals have also suffered a reduction. Even after the modification of his achievements, however, Duffy remains one of the outstanding hitters of the last century.

Hugh Duffy (1866-1954) began his major league career with the Chicago White Stockings in 1888. Standing 5'9" and slim, Duffy was mistaken at first by Chicago manager Cap Anson for a batboy. Unwilling to believe any outfielder so small could cut it with his heavy-hitting team, Anson kept Duffy on the bench for several weeks until regular right fielder Billy Sunday, later a famous evangelist, was traded to Pittsburgh. Given his chance, Duffy quickly showed he belonged in top company. By the end of the season, Duffy was stationed at the more demanding center field spot.

After a solid season in 1889, Duffy jumped to the Players League the following year and led the rebel loop in both hits and runs. Rather than return to the White Stockings when the circuit folded, Duffy signed on with the Boston Reds of the American Association. In his first year in the Hub, Duffy played on his premier pennant winner.

The following year, the American Association combined with the National League to form a twelve-team circuit, and Duffy, a free agent, signed with the defending National League champion Beaneaters. Also joining the Beaneaters in 1892 was right fielder Tommy McCarthy. The two Irish fly chasers were quickly embraced by Boston fans for their heady play and became known as the "Heavenly Twins." Boston won pennants in each of the first two seasons the pair played together, then gave way to a newly emerging dynasty in Baltimore. When the Orioles grabbed the 1894 flag and repeated the next year, the Heavenly Twins were split up; McCarthy was sent to Brooklyn to make room for Billy Hamilton, who had been acquired from Philadelphia.

Duffy remained with the Beaneaters throughout the 1900 season. He then became player-manager with the Milwaukee Brewers of the reorganized American League. He stayed on in Milwaukee after the franchise joined the minor Western League. Duffy was inducted into the Hall of Fame in 1945.

Outfielder
Chicago White Stockings
  1888-1889
Chicago Pirates 1890
Boston Reds 1891
Boston Beaneaters
  1892-1900
Milwaukee Brewers 1901
Philadelphia Phillies
  1904-1906

Manager
Milwaukee Brewers 1901
Philadelphia Phillies
  1904-1906
Chicago White Sox
  1910-1911
Boston Red Sox
  1921-1922
535-671

Duffy's 1910 White Sox club set an AL record for the lowest slugging average (.261). Hugh used this bat in 1894 (top).

HUGH DUFFY, Captain.
BOSTON, 1910.

In 1898, Duffy batted .298 with 108 RBI.

Major League Totals

BA	G	AB	R	H	2B	3B	HR	RBI	SB
.324	1,736	7,043	1,551	2,283	324	116	105	1,299	583

JAKE BECKLEY

JACOB PETER BECKLEY
"OLD EAGLE EYE"
1888-1907
FAMED NATIONAL LEAGUE SLUGGER
MADE 2,930 HITS FOR LIFETIME .309 BATTING
AVERAGE. HOLDS RECORD IN MAJORS FOR
FIRST BASE: FOR CHANCES ACCEPTED 25,000,
MOST PUTOUTS 23,696, MOST GAMES 2,368.
PLAYED 20 SEASONS WITH PITTSBURGH,
NEW YORK, CINCINNATI AND ST. LOUIS.

First baseman
Pittsburgh Alleghenys
    (Pirates) 1888-1889;
    1891-1896
Pittsburgh Burghers 1890
New York Giants
    1896-1897
Cincinnati Reds
    1897-1903
St. Louis Cardinals
    1904-1907

Right: *In 1894, Beckley had his best season, batting .343, with 121 runs and 120 RBI. Top: He played with five different teams over the course of his career but only once, in 1893, found himself on a club that was in a pennant race.*

WHEN JAKE BECKLEY WAS named to the Hall of Fame, not a single member of the Veterans Committee that selected him had ever seen him play. Moreover, few knew him as anything more than the owner of the record for having played the most career games at first base. The first man to play 20 years in the majors without ever being on a pennant winner, Beckley had the misfortune to leave the game with 2,931 hits (just 69 short of the coveted 3,000 benchmark), and to die at age 50 on June 25, 1918. All three facts combined to keep him out of the Hall of Fame until 1971.

Born in Hannibal, Missouri, Jacob Peter Beckley (1867-1918) grew up on the Mississippi River. At age 19, he left his job in a machine shop and his place as a lefthanded second baseman on the local semipro team to try his luck with the Leavenworth club of the Western League. Although an instant success at the plate—he debuted with three hits, including a home run—his work at the keystone sack left much to be desired. Moved to first base where

his notoriously weak arm could do less harm, Beckley hit .401 the next year, attracting the attention of several major league scouts.

Purchased midway through the 1888 season by Pittsburgh for $4,000—an eye-popping sum at the time—Beckley quickly proved his worth, stroking a neat .343 in his rookie outing. With a year out to participate in the Players League rebellion in 1890, he remained in the Smoke City until the summer of 1896, when he was sent to New York for Harry Davis (a future four-time home run leader in the American League).

A disappointment with the Giants, Beckley was released early in the 1897 season. Signing with Cincinnati, he pumped up his average to .345, and on September 26 became the last player until 1922 to hit three home runs in a game.

Beckley remained with Cincinnati in the early 1900s despite several attractive offers from teams in the upstart American League. It was not so much loyalty as the Reds' willingness to match rival bids that bound him. During the Players League war in 1890, Beckley said, "I'm only in this game for the money anyway." It was a statement he often reiterated, although his longevity as a player suggests there was a strong love for the game as well. Nicknamed "Eagle Eye" for his hitting skill, he was a memorable figure with his lean features and dashing handlebar mustache. Beckley spent the final four years of his career in St. Louis.

				Major League Totals						
BA	**G**	**AB**	**R**	**H**	**2B**	**3B**	**HR**	**RBI**	**SB**
.308	2,386	9,527	1,600	2,931	476	243	88	1,575	315

AMOS RUSIE

Copyright 1889 Goodwin & Co

AMOS WILSON RUSIE
"THE HOOSIER THUNDERBOLT"
INDIANAPOLIS N.L., NEW YORK N.L.,
CINCINNATI N.L., 1889-1895,
1897-1898 AND 1901
GENERALLY CONSIDERED FIREBALL KING OF
NINETEENTH-CENTURY MOUNDSMEN. NOTCHED
BETTER THAN 240 VICTORIES IN TEN-YEAR
CAREER. ACHIEVED 30-VICTORY MARK FOUR
YEARS IN A ROW AND WON 20 OR MORE GAMES
EIGHT SUCCESSIVE TIMES. LED LEAGUE IN
STRIKEOUTS FIVE YEARS AND LED OR TIED
FOR MOST SHUTOUTS FIVE TIMES.

Pitcher
Indianapolis Hoosiers
    1889
New York Giants
    1890-1895, 1897-1898
Cincinnati Reds 1901

AMOS RUSIE IS ONE OF THE few players in the Hall of Fame who spent fewer than 10 seasons in the major leagues. Rusie's career was abbreviated by two bitter holdouts he staged against New York Giants owner Andrew Freedman.

Born in Mooresville, Indiana, Amos Wilson Rusie (1871-1942) was still a child when his family moved to Indianapolis. At age 16, he quit school to work in a factory and pitch for a local amateur team. Less than two years later, Rusie was pitching for the Indianapolis Hoosiers (then in the National League), who signed the local boy for both his drawing card appeal and blinding speed.

In 1890, the 19-year-old Rusie led all National League hurlers with 341 strikeouts. Indianapolis had folded by then, and most of the team's better players (Rusie included) had become the property of the New York Giants. The Gotham City was not an ideal milieu for the young fireballer. By the time he was in his early 20s, he had a drinking problem. Worse, he could not escape Freedman, who was both vindictive and a cheapskate, a lethal combination in an owner during the 1890s (the most repressive era in major league history).

In the pitcher's box, though, "The Hoosier Thunderbolt" was in his element. More than any other hurler, Rusie prompted the last significant change in the geometric design of the playing field. During the 1892 season, batting averages plummeted to a record low. The game's rulemakers then decided to move the pitching distance from 50' from home plate to 60'6".

Although Rusie's strikeouts dipped sharply in 1893, the first year the mound was situated at its present location, he still led the league by a total nearly double that of runner-up Brickyard Kennedy. After topping the loop in whiffs again the next two seasons, Rusie sat out all 1896 when Freedman first attempted to fine him $200 and then cut his pay. Returning in 1897, when the other clubs kicked in $5,000 to reimburse him for the salary he had lost in 1896, Rusie had two more strong years with the Giants. Wounded by Freedman's skinflint methods again, Amos skipped the 1899 season, then was prevented by personal problems from playing in 1900.

Reds' owner John Brush was about to purchase part of the Giants in 1901. So before the 1901 campaign, Rusie was traded to Cincinnati for Christy Mathewson in a one-sided deal. While Mathewson went on to win 372 games in the majors, Rusie proved to be all washed up. Rusie was, however, named to the Hall of Fame in 1977.

Newsboy

175.
Amos Rusie

NEW YORK.

Left: In 1894, Hall of Famer Amos Rusie and 33-game winner Jouett Meekin were 1-2 in the National League in wins and ERA. Top: Just age 17, Rusie won 12 decisions in his 1889 rookie season. He won his 246th and last game nine years later when he was still only 27.

				Major League Totals						
W	L	ERA	G	CG	IP	H	ER	BB	SO
246	174	3.07	462	392	3,769.2	3,384	1,286	1,704	1,934

JESSE C. BURKETT
BATTING STAR WHO PLAYED OUTFIELD FOR
THE NEW YORK, CLEVELAND AND ST. LOUIS
N.L. TEAMS AND THE ST. LOUIS AND BOSTON
A.L. TEAMS. SHARES WITH ROGERS HORNSBY
AND TY COBB THE RECORD OF HITTING .400
OR BETTER THE MOST TIMES. ACCOMPLISHED
THIS ON THREE OCCASIONS. TOPPED THE
N.L. IN HITTING THREE TIMES, BATTING
OVER .400 TO GAIN THE CHAMPIONSHIP
IN 1895 AND 1896.

Outfielder
New York Giants 1890
Cleveland Spiders
　　1891-1898
St. Louis Perfectos
　　(Cardinals) 1899-1901
St. Louis Browns
　　1902-1904
Boston Pilgrims 1905

JESSE BURKETT MADE THE river his second home in his youth. In his early teens, he plunged into its swirling waters in a valiant but unsuccessful effort to save a drowning girl. The incident proved to be the most memorable moment in his life, even more than his baseball exploits.

Jesse Cail Burkett (1868-1953), born and raised in Wheeling, West Virginia, began his pro career as a pitcher, winning 39 games for Worcester of the Atlantic Association in 1889. Hammered regularly the following season in his rookie big league campaign with the New York Giants, however, he was transferred to the outfield. Exhibiting only flashes of the exceptional bat control that would make him one of the game's premier hitters in the 1890s, Burkett was returned to the minors after being purchased by Cleveland in 1891.

The following year, his first as a regular with the feisty Spiders, he hit just .275 — nevertheless ranking among the club's top batters as averages all over the National League were down in 1892, the last season in which the pitchers' box was only 50' from home plate. When 10'6" were added the next year, Burkett's average jumped to .348; he didn't bat below .340 again until 1902. In the nine intervening seasons, Burkett twice topped the .400 mark and on three occasions led the National League in batting.

Popular with sportswriters because of his readiness to discuss hitting, Burkett was less of a hit with fans. Thus while his surly manner and frequent battles with umpires early in his career earned him the nickname "The Crab," he was always available to instruct young admirers about batting and could usually be found after a game nursing a vanilla ice cream cone.

In 1899, Burkett was switched to St. Louis along with most of Cleveland's better players in an effort by the Robison brothers, who owned both the Cleveland and St. Louis franchises, to punish Clevelanders for poor attendance of the Spiders' games. After three years with the Cardinals, he was persuaded to jump to the American League in 1902 by St. Louis Browns manager Jimmy McAleer, a former Spiders teammate. Burkett hit .306 in his initial campaign

Between 1893 and 1901, Burkett never hit below .341 and twice topped the hallowed .400 mark.

with the Browns, then declined rapidly. Traded to the Boston Pilgrims for rookie outfielder George Stone before the 1905 season, the transaction proved to be one of the most one-sided deals ever. While Stone was winning the 1906 American League batting title, Burkett was in the minors serving as player-owner-manager of Worcester in the New England League. Burkett was elected to the Hall of Fame in 1946.

Major League Totals

BA	G	AB	R	H	2B	3B	HR	RBI	SB
.339	2,070	8,413	1,718	2,853	322	183	75	952	389

KID NICHOLS

WHEN HE FIRST JOINED THE Boston Beaneaters in 1890, Charlie Nichols looked so youthful and so physically unprepossessing that he was called "Kid." The nickname stuck with him for the remainder of his life. Nichols is the only 300-game winner in major league history who got by with just one pitch. He had a fastball, period. And at that, it was by no means an overpowering fastball. What Nichols did possess in spades, however, was control. When he walked a batter, it was usually only because he was afraid to let him hit. Later in his career, Nichols developed a changeup but infrequently used it. Until the end of his career, his fastball remained his "out" pitch.

Charles Augustus Nichols (1869-1953) began his career in 1887 with his hometown Kansas City club in the Western League. After two years, Nichols landed with Omaha in the Western Association, managed by 29-year-old Frank Selee (already a keen judge of talent). Selee was hired as the Beaneaters manager the following year and proceeded to sign Nichols.

Nichols won 27 games as a rookie in 1890 and 273 games in his first 10 seasons, more than any other pitcher during the decade of the 1890s. On eight occasions he collected 30 or more victories, reaching a high of 35 in 1892. Never a strikeout or an ERA leader, Kid nevertheless topped the National League three times in shutouts and always ranked among the leaders in both complete games and saves (staff leaders were also often used as stoppers then).

The Boston Beaneaters were in the 1890s the most formidable team in the game, and no one had more to do with Boston's success than Nichols, who had 10 straight winning seasons. In 1898, Ted Lewis, Vic Willis, and Nichols (who won 31 games) teamed up to win 82 games among them, bringing the Beaneaters their fifth flag in the decade. The club began to falter after that, however. When team owner Arthur Soden lost several stars to the American League by refusing to match the offers made them by junior loop clubs, Nichols quit the Beaneaters and bought a part interest in the Kansas City team in the Western League.

After two years as a player-manager with Kansas City, Kid was lured back to the majors by the St. Louis Cardinals, who offered him the same dual role. He won 21 games for St. Louis in 1904. When the club got off to a poor start the next year, Nichols was released, finishing his career with the Phillies. Despite winning 361 games, Nichols was not named to the Hall of Fame until 1949.

Pitcher
Boston Beaneaters
   1890-1901
St. Louis Cardinals
   1904-1905
Philadelphia Phillies
   1905-1906
Manager
St. Louis Cardinals
   1904-1905
80-88

CHARLES A. NICHOLS, Pitcher,
BOSTON, 1898.

Top: In 1904, Nichols unretired and proceeded to lead St. Louis in wins with 21. Besides 1946, no other pitcher has come back to the majors and won 20 games after a two-year hiatus. Left: He was the game's top pitcher during the 1890s.

Major League Totals

W	L	ERA	G	CG	IP	H	ER	BB	SO
361	208	2.94	620	532	5,084	4,912	1,661	1,272	1,877

JOE KELLEY

JOSEPH JAMES KELLEY
1891-1908
STANDOUT HITTER AND LEFT FIELDER OF
CHAMPION 1894-95-96 BALTIMORE ORIOLES
AND 1899-1900 BROOKLYN SUPERBAS. BATTED
OVER .300 FOR 11 CONSECUTIVE YEARS, WITH
HIGH OF .391 IN 1894. EQUALLED RECORD
WITH 9 HITS IN 9 AT-BATS IN DOUBLEHEADER.
ALSO PLAYED FOR BOSTON, PITTSBURGH AND
CINCINNATI OF N.L. AND BALTIMORE OF A.L.
MANAGED CINCINNATI 1902 TO 1905 AND
BOSTON N.L. IN 1908.

Outfielder
Boston Beaneaters
1891; 1908
Pittsburgh Pirates
1891-1892
Baltimore Orioles
1892-1898
Brooklyn Superbas
1899-1901
Baltimore Orioles (AL)
1902
Cincinnati Reds
1902-1906
Manager
Cincinnati Reds
1902-1905
Boston Doves 1908
337-321

JOE KELLEY WAS A GOOD OUTfielder and a productive hitter who might not be remembered at all today had he not been traded late in the 1892 season from Pittsburgh to Baltimore. In 1893, Kelley's first full campaign in Baltimore, Orioles manager Ned Hanlon (a fine outfielder in his own day) made Joe his pet project. Hanlon dragged Kelley out to the park early every morning to work on improving his fielding and hitting fundamentals. With Hanlon hounding him, Kelley in short order became the most complete player on the National League's best team during the mid-1890s.

Beginning in 1893, Cambridge, Massachusetts, native Joseph James Kelley (1871-1943) topped the .300 mark in 11 consecutive seasons, reaching a high of .393 in 1894. Although never a league leader in a major batting department, he would usually score well over 100 runs each season and knock home nearly the same amount. A deft basestealer, he paced the loop with 87 thefts in 1896. It was for his imagination and crowd-pleasing antics, however, that Kelley was best known. He is credited with originating the trick of concealing baseballs in the high outfield grass at the Baltimore park, allowing Orioles gardeners to make seemingly impossible stops on balls hit into the gap and then throw out startled baserunners.

Right: This mid-1890s shot portrays Joe Kelley in Union Park, the home of the fabled Baltimore Orioles. Kelley was Baltimore's most popular player. Top: Like several other members of the mid-1890s Orioles, Joe later played for the AL entry in Baltimore.

Along with Hanlon, Hughie Jennings, Willie Keeler, and several other Baltimore stars, Kelley was shifted to Brooklyn before the 1899 season when the Orioles encountered financial difficulties. Kelley, the team captain in Baltimore, was named to the same position in Brooklyn by Hanlon after Hanlon became the Superbas manager. Between Kelley's leadership on the field and Hanlon's on the bench, Brooklyn took the National League flag in 1899 and 1900.

The upstart American League prevented a third straight pennant by luring several Brooklyn stars into its camp. Kelley joined them in 1902, jumping to Baltimore's entry (also called the Orioles), where he was reunited with John McGraw and Wilbert Robinson, two other important cogs from the great Orioles teams of a few years earlier. McGraw soon deserted Baltimore, though, to return to the National League. A few weeks later, with the Orioles deep in last place, Kelley defected as well, signing with Cincinnati. Named manager of the Reds after only two weeks with the club, he remained at the helm through the 1905 season and then lingered one more year in Cincinnati as a player only. After hitting just .228 in 1906, he drifted down to the minors. Kelley was named to the Hall of Fame in 1971.

			Major League Totals							
BA	G	AB	R	H	2B	3B	HR	RBI	SB
.319	1,845	7,018	1,426	2,242	356	194	65	1,193	443

A CATCHER IN YOUTH, HUGH Ambrose Jennings (1869-1928) was held back at the backstop position by arm trouble, a problem that haunted him throughout his career. Converted to shortstop when he turned pro, Hughie played just 13 games in the minors before joining the Louisville Colonels of the American Association in 1891. The loop was in its last year of existence and in disarray, enabling Jennings to hit .292 as a rookie. The following season, when the Louisville franchise was absorbed by the National League, Jennings batted just .222.

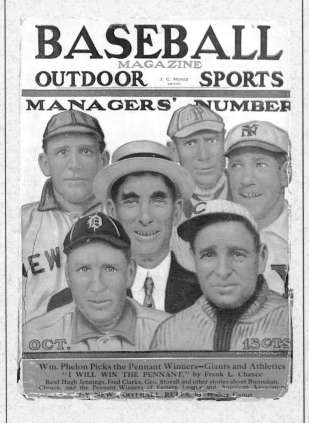

Traded to the Baltimore Orioles in June 1893, Jennings was held to a mere 39 games that year because of injuries and continued weak hitting, making the deal seem insignificant at first. But in 1894, Jennings suddenly emerged as one of the premier shortstops in the game and a clubhouse leader. Appointed team captain by Orioles manager Ned Hanlon, Hughie helped spark Baltimore to three straight pennants. His personal-best season came in 1896 when he belted .401, a record for shortstops, and collected 121 RBI despite not hitting a single home run. In addition, he was hit by 49 pitches, a record that Ron Hunt of the Expos broke in 1971.

A lame arm forced Jennings to move to first base after the 1898 season. The injury shortened his playing career but had an unexpected benefit. It made him turn to managing, where he was destined to make his greatest mark on the game. In 1907, after spending several years in the minors learning his new trade, Jennings was hired to manage the Tigers. After swiftly capturing three straight pennants for Detroit, he piloted the Motor City entry for 11 more years without ever winning another.

Replaced by Ty Cobb at the Tigers helm in 1921, Jennings was hired as a third base coach by New York Giants manager John McGraw, a former Orioles teammate. With Jennings in the coaching box exhorting the club with his patented "Ee-yah" cry and McGraw in the dugout, the Giants swept a National League record four straight pennants.

The job was not without stress. Below the surface of the Giants' success ran an undercurrent of duplicity and scandal. When McGraw took ill in 1925, leaving Jennings in charge of the team, the burden proved too much. Hughie suffered a nervous breakdown and had to be put in a sanatorium. He never returned to baseball. After contracting spinal meningitis early in 1928, Jennings died in Scranton, Pennsylvania, on February 1. He was elected to the Hall of Fame in 1945.

HUGHIE JENNINGS
OF BALTIMORE'S FAMOUS OLD ORIOLES,
HE WAS ONE OF THE GAME'S MIGHTY
MITES. A STAR SHORTSTOP HE WAS A
CONSTANT THREAT AT THE PLATE.
ONCE HIT .397. PILOTED DETROIT
TO THREE CHAMPIONSHIPS.

Shortstop; first baseman; second baseman
Louisville Colonels
 1891-1893
Baltimore Orioles
 1893-1899
Brooklyn Superbas
 1899-1900; 1903
Philadelphia Phillies
 1901-1902
Detroit Tigers 1907, 1909, 1912, 1918
Manager
Detroit Tigers 1907-1920
New York Giants 1925
1,163-984

Left: *The October 1910* Baseball Magazine *featured skippers, with Jennings at lower left.* Above: *Hugh teaches sliding.*

		Major League Totals							
BA	G	AB	R	H	2B	3B	HR	RBI	SB
.312	1,285	4,903	993	1,532	235	87	18	840	359

CHAPTER TWO

Dead-Ball Era
Emergence of the AL

THE NATIONAL LEAGUE'S DECISION TO REDUCE to eight clubs in 1900 created a reservoir of surplus talent and unoccupied ballparks—and a climate conducive to the launch of a rival major league.

In the late 1890s, Ban Johnson had built the Western League into a minor league power. In 1901, he renamed his circuit the American League and declared it a major league. The American League filled former NL territories, and planted rival clubs in both Philadelphia and Chicago. Using high salaries as bait, the upstart AL convinced many established stars to switch leagues. In its first year, some 110 of the 185 players who appeared in the American League had NL experience. In January 1903, the NL came to terms with the AL, and the two leagues concluded a new National Agreement. There were to be no changes in the baseball map for 50 years.

At the start of the century, teams manufactured runs through bunts, hit-and-run plays, and stolen bases. Pitchers used trick deliveries and applied foreign substances to the ball. The balls themselves were so dead that swinging for the fences was futile. Pitchers were expected to work long and often; relief pitching was as rare as a home run.

At the end of the 1920 season eight members of the Chicago White Sox were accused of fixing the 1919 World Series against the underdog Cincinnati Reds. The eight Black Sox were banned for life by Kenesaw Mountain Landis—baseball's first commissioner.

Christy Mathewson was baseball's original role model, and he was the game's best pitcher in the first decade of this century.

Opposite page: Kenesaw Mountain Landis was baseball's first commissioner. He was called in to save baseball's reputation after the 1919 Black Sox scandal. Below: This pin celebrates Pittsburgh's World Championship of 1909, and pictures Honus Wagner. Hans was the greatest shortstop in the game's history. Wagner led the NL in batting eight times, RBI five times, and every other major batting department except homers at least once.

CY YOUNG

DENTON T. (CY) YOUNG
CLEVELAND (N) 1890-98
ST. LOUIS (N) 1899-1900
BOSTON (A) 1901-08
CLEVELAND (A) 1909-11
BOSTON (N) 1911
ONLY PITCHER IN FIRST HUNDRED
YEARS OF BASEBALL TO WIN 500 GAMES.
AMONG HIS 511 VICTORIES WERE 3
NO-HIT SHUTOUTS. PITCHED PERFECT
GAME MAY 5, 1904, NO OPPOSING
BATSMAN REACHING FIRST BASE.

Pitcher
Cleveland Spiders
 1890-1898
St. Louis Perfectos
 (Cardinals) 1899-1900
Boston Somersets
 (Pilgrims, Red Sox)
 1901-1908
Cleveland Naps 1909-1911
Boston Braves 1911
Manager
Boston Red Sox 1907
3-3

SHORTLY AFTER BEING SIGNED by Canton of the Tri-State League in 1890, the 23-year-old Cy Young was spotted warming up against a wooden fence on a farm near Gilmore, Ohio. The ensuing damage to the barrier, as legend has it, was likened to that of a cyclone hitting a wall. An enterprising sportswriter shortened "cyclone" to "Cy," and Young would never again be known by any other name during his professional career.

Denton True Young (1867-1955) made his big league debut with the Cleveland Spiders on August 6, 1890. Most of the game's stars were playing in the Players League that season; one of those who were not was Cap Anson, player-manager of the Chicago White Stockings, Young's foes in his inaugural outing. Anson had scouted Young while he was at Canton and rejected him as being "just another big farmer." When Cy beat the White Stockings 8-1 and allowed only three hits, Anson strove to purchase him from Cleveland.

Throughout the 1890s, Young, Kid Nichols, and Amos Rusie vied for recognition as the top pitcher in the game. Although Nichols pitched for the best team and collected the most wins,

and Rusie regularly logged the most strikeouts and lowest ERAs, it was Young who reached the top of the league in all three departments. He blended stamina, guile, and excellent control in almost equal measures to make him a pitcher who rarely had a bad game. A pennant for the Spiders never materialized, however, and when attendance sagged in Cleveland, Young and most of the team's other stars were shipped to St. Louis in 1899.

Above: A Young autographed baseball. Left: Young in 1907, at age 40, had 21 wins and a 1.99 ERA. He won 21 in '08.

Turning 33 years old in 1900, Young slipped to just 19 wins, his lowest output since his rookie season. Speculation that he was nearly through gave St. Louis some consolation when Young deserted the club to sign with Boston in the newly reorganized American League. The rumors of Young's imminent departure from the game soon were dispelled after he led the yearling major league in wins in 1901, then repeated his feat the next two years.

Cy went on to win 20 or more games six times for the Boston Americans, pitch on two pennant winners, and participate in the first modern World Series in 1903. Perhaps the finest effort of his career came on May 5, 1904, when he pitched a perfect game to beat Rube Waddell of the Philadelphia Athletics 3-0.

Sold to Cleveland at age 42 in 1909, Young again defied time by leading the Naps mound staff with 19 wins. It was his last good season. Two years later, after winning seven games in a campaign split between Cleveland and the Boston Braves, Young retired with 511 career victories.

Major League Totals

W	L	ERA	G	CG	IP	H	ER	BB	SO
511	315	2.63	906	750	7,356.0	7,092	2,147	1,217	2,796

Young's secrets were exceptional upper body strength and amazing control.

Statistical Juggernaut

Was Cy Young the greatest pitcher of all time? Unfortunately no films exist of this legendary pitcher in his prime for historians to investigate in split-screen analysis with the likes of Lefty Grove, Walter Johnson, Dizzy Dean, and Sandy Koufax. Our only research sources are newspaper accounts, interviews with colleagues, and a bevy of statistics.

Consider what it would take a modern performer to match Young's record of 511 career victories. Try 25 seasons with 20 or more wins. Yet, even if one averaged 20 wins for a quarter century there would still be the matter of winning those extra 11 games. On five occasions, the big righthander won 30 games or more. He won 20 or more games for 15 years. Interestingly, he only led the league in victories on four occasions and games pitched twice.

Many of his records are based on sheer endurance and grit, witness his 7,356 innings pitched, which is nearly 1,500 innings more than his nearest rival, Pud Galvin. He also pitched 750 complete games, considering the combined complete games of Warren Spahn (382) and Robin Roberts (305) still don't come close to Young's astounding record.

To the day he last took off his uniform, he boasted that he had never had a sore arm or spent a single minute on the trainer's table.

Continuing to follow the game closely after retiring to his farm near Peoli, Ohio, Young felt wounded when he was passed over in the initial Hall of Fame election in 1936. The oversight was rectified the following year, however, allowing him to be among the original group of inductees in 1939.

Shortly after Young's death on November 4, 1955, Commissioner Ford Frick originated the Cy Young Award, an annual honor bestowed upon the pitcher deemed most valuable.

WILLIE KEELER
"HIT 'EM WHERE THEY AINT;"
BASEBALL'S GREATEST PLACE-HITTER;
BEST BUNTER. BIG LEAGUE CAREER
1892 TO 1910 WITH N.Y. GIANTS,
BALTIMORE ORIOLES, BROOKLYN SUPERBAS,
N.Y. HIGHLANDERS. NATIONAL LEAGUE
BATTING CHAMPION '97-'98.

Outfielder
New York Giants
 1892-1893; 1910
Brooklyn Bridegrooms
 (Superbas) 1893;
 1899-1902
Baltimore Orioles
 1894-1898
New York Highlanders
 1903-1909

WILLIE KEELER IS PERHAPS the major league's most difficult player to evaluate. Nicknamed "Wee Willie" because of his 5'4", 120-pound stature, Keeler nevertheless compiled 2,947 hits and 1,727 runs, twice led the National League in batting, and posted a .343 career batting average. His forte, as he himself put it, was to "hit 'em where they ain't," and there has probably never been a batter more skillful at poking a ball through a vacated hole in the infield or executing a hit-and-run play.

The difficulty in analyzing him is that William Henry Keeler (1872-1923) played in an era that gave him advantages that comparable players who came along later didn't have. During most of his career, for example, Keeler was able to foul off pitches at will without having them count against him as strikes. For a while, he was even able to bunt balls foul deliberately without being charged with a strike. Every hitter in Keeler's time had the same options, however, and none used them better than he did.

In all likelihood, none of Keeler's achievements would be suspect if his performance had not slipped dramatically almost as soon as foul balls became considered strikes. Part of the drop-off can be explained by age—once he turned 29 years old, his career batting average declined every year thereafter—but in several seasons his output was so minuscule, it seemed he was being retained for his name alone.

Keeler finished his career in the dead-ball era, however, a time when few players were able to hit .300. He was an integral member of one of baseball's most famous teams—the Baltimore Orioles of 1894 to 1898. While his teammates—such as John McGraw, Wilbert Robinson, and Hughie Jennings—played the reckless, exciting, and at times deceitful brand of baseball for which the team became renowned, Keeler was shy and retiring almost to the point of invisibility. Were it not for his small size, he might, curiously, have gone without notice. Because he was barely bigger than a bat boy, he became instead a fan favorite.

When the great Baltimore team was broken up after the 1898 season, Keeler moved with most of its other stars to Brooklyn. He played four years with the Superbas before jumping to the fledgling New York entry in the American League. Keeler played seven years for the Highlanders. Upon finishing his big league career, Keeler played a year in the minors and was later a coach. When the Hall of Fame opened in 1939, Keeler was among its first inductees.

Top: *Keeler in 1898, his last year with the O's.*
Above: *Willie lays one down.*

		Major League Totals							
BA	G	AB	R	H	2B	3B	HR	RBI	SB
.343	2,124	8,585	1,727	2,947	237	150	34	810	495

CHARLIE COMISKEY WAS ONE of a small group of players in his generation who saw the future of pro baseball and parlayed his vision into team ownership. He was part of the baseball wars of 1890, when the upstart Players League tried and failed to establish a rival to the National League. Ten years later, he joined Ban Johnson in launching the American League, and "Commy" was one of its prime movers for three decades as owner of the Chicago White Sox.

CHARLES A. COMISKEY
"THE OLD ROMAN"
STARTED 50 YEARS OF BASEBALL AS ST. LOUIS BROWNS FIRST-BASEMAN IN 1882 AND WAS FIRST MAN AT THIS POSITION TO PLAY AWAY FROM THE BAG FOR BATTERS. AS BROWNS' MANAGER-CAPTAIN-PLAYER WON 4 STRAIGHT AMERICAN ASSOCIATION PENNANTS STARTING 1885, WORLD CHAMPIONS FIRST 2 YEARS. OWNER AND PRESIDENT CHICAGO WHITE SOX 1900 TO 1931.

Comiskey was featured on the cover of the December 1917 Baseball Magazine.

Charles Albert Comiskey (1859-1931) was a fine first baseman, though his later fame may have magnified his playing ability. As player-manager, he led the St. Louis Browns to four straight American Association pennants, from 1885 to 1888. After purchasing a franchise in the minor Western League in 1895, Comiskey transferred the team to Chicago in 1899 in preparation to make the Western League a major league. He induced Clark Griffith to jump from the Cubs in 1901, signaling the beginning of hostilities between the two circuits, and the White Sox won the first AL pennant that year. The

White Sox won the World Series in 1906, and were terrifically successful at the gate. In 1910 Comiskey built "The Baseball Palace of the World," the biggest, most modern park in baseball. Comiskey Park set the standard for more than a generation of parks. In 1917, after he purchased stars like Eddie Collins, the Sox won their second World Series. (Collins had his Philadelphia salary written into his new contract before the deal to protect himself from Comiskey.)

In 1919, the White Sox powerhouse, with left fielder Shoeless Joe Jackson, Collins, pitcher Eddie Cicotte, and a terrific supporting cast, returned to the World Series. Though heavily favored, the team bowed to Cincinnati amid rumors of fixes and bribes. Cicotte, Jackson, and at least six other players had participated in or known about efforts to throw the Series. Judge Kenesaw Mountain Landis, the new commissioner of baseball, in 1920 banned the eight from baseball.

Comiskey was the worst-paying owner, despite owning the best-drawing franchise. His miserly approach did not extend to purchasing players; he paid top dollar for Collins. It did not extend to other owners; Comiskey gave Clark Griffith $10,000 so that Griffith could keep Walter Johnson from jumping to the Federal League. When it came to his own players, however, he was inflexible, and even irrational. Comiskey nourished, with his vision and industry, the creation of the American League. However, he was the carrier of a greed that nearly destroyed it. Comiskey entered the Hall of Fame in 1939.

Manager
St. Louis Browns
 1883-1889; 1891
Chicago Pirates 1890
Cincinnati Reds
 1892-1894
First baseman
St. Louis Browns
 1882-1889; 1891
Chicago Pirates 1890
Cincinnati Reds
 1892-1894

Top: *On the cover of this wooden box are the rules for the McLaughlin Baseball Game and illustrations of Bob Ferguson (left) and Charlie Comiskey. The game was a popular one in 1888, the season in which Comiskey's St. Louis Browns became the first major league team ever to collect four consecutive pennants.*

Major League Managing Totals				
W	L	T	PCT	G
840	541	23	.608	1,407

Major League Totals									
BA	G	AB	R	H	2B	3B	HR	RBI	SB
.264	1,390	5,796	994	1,531	206	68	29	467	378

FRED CLARKE

THE FIRST OF THE SUCCESSFUL "BOY MANAGERS," AT TWENTY-FOUR HE PILOTED LOUISVILLE'S COLONELS IN THE NATIONAL LEAGUE. WON 4 PENNANTS FOR PITTSBURGH AND A WORLD CHAMPIONSHIP IN 1909. STARRED AS AN OUTFIELDER FOR 22 SEASONS.

Outfielder
Louisville Colonels
  1894-1899
Pittsburgh Pirates
  1900-1915
Manager
Louisville Colonels
  1897-1899
Pittsburgh Pirates
  1900-1915

Top: *Clarke was a member of the worst team of his era—the Louisville Colonels—before landing on Pittsburgh, one of the era's best.* Below: *Members of the Pirates receive tutelage from Clarke.*

FRED CLARKE IS AMONG THE few members of the Hall of Fame who could justifiably have been selected as either a player or a manager. When he let go of the Pittsburgh reins at the conclusion of the 1915 season, he had racked up a then-record 1,602 managerial wins. A few days earlier, on September 23, Pittsburgh fans organized a "Fred Clarke Day" at Forbes Field in recognition of his long service. Clarke came out of retirement to play a few innings, collecting his 2,675th hit to conclude his career with a .312 batting average (a mark that would almost certainly have been higher had he not been burdened with the dual job of playing and managing for much of his career).

The Iowa-born Fred Clifford Clarke (1872-1960) made his entry into baseball when he took a delivery job with a Des Moines newspaper that was managed by Ed Barrow, the organizer of the "Newsboy's League." A minor leaguer by 1892, Clarke was shipped north by Savannah in the Southern League in 1894 when Barney Dreyfuss, owner of the Louisville club in the National League, offered to get the Georgia team out of the red in return for the contract of their star left fielder.

Clarke had the most auspicious debut of any major leaguer. Facing Philadelphia's Gus Weyhing on June 30, 1894, he was a perfect 5-for-5 with four singles and a triple. Reality set in, however, and Clarke wound up hitting just .268 in his inaugural season.

Louisville was a poor team, but Clarke played well for them. In 1897, when the Colonels finished 11th, he hit a personal-high .390. Named the team's manager midway through that season, he immediately clashed with a brash recruit pitcher named Rube Waddell, who quit the team in response. Another rookie, Honus Wagner, won Clarke's instant admiration.

In 1900, after Louisville was dropped from the National League, Dreyfuss was given the Pittsburgh franchise and allowed to keep any of the Colonels' players he wanted. The owner retained Clarke and Wagner as well as pitcher Jack Chesbro and a somewhat chastened Waddell, who had returned to the fold in 1899.

It took Clarke a year to blend the new Louisville blood with the incumbent Pittsburgh talent. Beginning in 1901, he skippered the Pirates to three consecutive pennants then won again in 1909, after narrowly missing the flag the previous year. He retired to his ranch in Kansas following the 1915 season.

Elected to the Hall of Fame in 1945, Clarke died 15 years later in Winfield, Kansas, just a few days before what would have been his 88th birthday.

Major League Totals									
BA	G	AB	R	H	2B	3B	HR	RBI	SB
.312	2,244	8,570	1,621	2,675	361	220	67	1,015	506

Major League Managing Totals				
W	L	T	PCT	G
1,602	1,181	40	.576	2,829

WHEN RHODERICK JOHN WALlace (1873-1960) was inducted into the Hall of Fame in 1953, he was the first former American League shortstop to be enshrined. Since Wallace never played on a pennant winner, was a failure as a manager, and had a career batting average of only .266, the presumed reason for his selection is that he was a great fielder.

No doubt that Wallace was a great fielder, but even here the ground is somewhat shaky. He played in an era when the best fielders were not necessarily record setters or fielding-average leaders and so long ago that only anecdotal material can be offered in support of his glove prowess. Rather amazingly, there is almost nothing on this score either to be said in his behalf, save that he supposedly was one of the first shortstops to scoop up slow-hit grounders barehanded so that he could get rid of the ball more quickly in order to nail speedy runners.

What can be stated is that Wallace began his career as a pitcher and leaped straight from the amateur ranks in western Pennsylvania to the Cleveland Spiders in 1894. Thrashed in his first start, he went on to win two games before the season ended. Relegated to spot starting assignments by 1896, Wallace was informed the following spring him that he would be replacing the recently departed Chippy McGarr at third base.

Despite never having played the hot corner before on a regular basis, Bobby had in some

Pitcher; third baseman
Cleveland Spiders
    1894-1898
Shortstop
St. Louis Cardinals
    1899-1901; 1917-1918
 St. Louis Browns
    1902-1916

ways his finest season in 1897. He hit .335 and also registered career highs in hits, runs, slugging average, triples, and RBI. After a less successful season statistically in 1898, Wallace moved the next year to St. Louis along with most of Cleveland's better players and was switched to shortstop to replace a fading Ed McKean. By 1901, Bobby was generally recognized as the best shortstop in the majors.

Wallace's salary was frozen at $2,400, however, the maximum that National League owners would pay a player, so he jumped to the crosstown St. Louis Browns in the American League for a reported five-year $32,500 contract that included a no-trade clause. In retrospect, Wallace might have regretted that contingency, for he labored 15 seasons with the Browns, most of them spent on teams that finished deep in the second division. Too, Honus Wagner usurped Bobby's title as the game's best shortstop.

Left: *Player-manager Wallace is shown on a 1911 Helmar stamp.* Top: *A 1911 Turkey Red tobacco card of Bobby Wallace shows him with a bat in hand even though he was noted by then almost strictly for his ability with his glove.*

Major League Totals										
BA	G	AB	R	H	2B	3B	HR	RBI	SB
.266	2,383	8,642	1,059	2,303	391	153	35	1,121	201

JIMMY COLLINS

JAMES COLLINS
CONSIDERED BY MANY THE GAME'S GREATEST THIRD BASEMAN, HE REVOLUTIONIZED STYLE OF PLAY AT THAT BAG. LED BOSTON RED SOX TO FIRST WORLD CHAMPIONSHIP IN 1903. A CONSISTENT BATTER, HIS DEFENSIVE PLAY THRILLED FANS OF BOTH MAJOR LEAGUES.

Third baseman
Boston Beaneaters 1895;
   1896-1900
Louisville Colonels 1895
Boston Somersets
   (Pilgrims, Red Sox)
   1901-1907
Philadelphia Athletics
   1907-1908
Manager
Boston Somersets
   (Pilgrims, Red Sox)
   1901-1906
455-376

B Y 1908, THE YEAR THAT HOME Run Baker made his debut with the Philadelphia Athletics, major league baseball had existed for 36 seasons; only one third baseman who played before Baker's appearance, however, is in the Hall of Fame. Simply put, Jimmy Collins was the most outstanding third sacker in the last century.

Those who witnessed James Joseph Collins (1870-1943) play claimed he was without even a close rival. The first to charge bunts and play them barehanded, he also could range equally well toward the line or into the shortstop's territory to his left. Playing for the Boston Beaneaters in 1899, he accepted a record 593 chances. The following year, he set a 20th century mark when he accumulated 251 putouts.

Adding more weight to his heavy credentials, Collins was also a productive hitter (pacing the National League in home runs in 1898) and a fine manager. He piloted the Boston Pilgrims to the championship in the first modern World Series in 1903, then garnered a second pennant the following year. He was denied a chance for another world title, though, when the 1904 NL champion New York Giants refused a postseason match.

Collins was anything but an immediate success in baseball. Already past age 25 when he reached

JAMES J. COLLINS, Third Baseman.
BOSTON CLUB, 1899.

the majors with the Beaneaters in 1895, Jimmy was judged by manager Frank Selee to be in need of polishing. Boston thereupon loaned Collins to the last-place Louisville Colonels, a maneuver that was done occasionally at the time when a player on a contending team needed further seasoning. Recalled to Boston in 1896, he held down the hot corner for the Beaneaters for five seasons. To the dismay of owner Arthur Soden, Collins then grabbed an offer from Charlie Somers, the magnate of the Boston team in the newly revamped American League. The theft of Collins caused Somers's club to be called the Invaders initially.

Installed as the manager and third baseman of the new Hub entry, Collins surrendered the former post late in the 1906 season when it became obvious that his charges were doomed to last place. The following year, Collins began spring training to play under new manager Chick Stahl, a former teammate. Collins's roommate, Stahl committed suicide on March 28, 1907.

Two months later, the BoSox traded Collins to the Athletics. Hitting just .217 in 1908, his second and last season with Philadelphia, he was released. His replacement was Baker, the only time in history that one future Hall of Fame third baseman was succeeded by another. Collins was selected for the Hall of Fame in 1945.

Top: *Collins on an 1899 magazine premium.*
Above: *He is at center of this photo.*

Major League Totals

BA	G	AB	R	H	2B	3B	HR	RBI	SB
.294	1,728	6,796	1,055	1,997	352	116	65	983	194

NAP LAJOIE

IN 1896, NAPOLEON LAJOIE (1874-1959) was purchased by the Phillies from Fall River of the New England League. By Nap's fifth year with the Phillies, the club seemed ready to mount a serious pennant bid. A salary hassle with Phillies owner Colonel Rogers, however, induced Lajoie to jump to the Philadelphia Athletics of the fledgling American League when A's manager Connie Mack offered him a four-year, $6,000-per-season pact. It seemed as if this would be sufficient enticement for Lajoie, who set a 20th century record by batting .422 and winning the Triple Crown in 1901, the AL's first campaign as a major league.

The Phillies, however, were not about to surrender their great second sacker. After considerable litigation, a state court injunction prohibited Lajoie and another former Phillies star, Elmer Flick, from playing with any other team in Philadelphia. Since the injunction applied only in the state of Pennsylvania, Mack sent Lajoie and Flick to Cleveland, for which they could play in every other AL city but Philadelphia. Owing to all the legal wrangling, Lajoie got into only 87 games in 1902. Nap swiftly made up for the setback by winning the hitting titles in 1903 and 1904.

In all, Lajoie won three American League bat crowns, with one, in 1910, that is still in dispute.

That year, Nap edged Ty Cobb by a single point after making eight hits in a season-ending doubleheader, six of them bunts that Lajoie was able to beat out because St. Louis Browns third baseman Red Corriden was playing deep on orders from his manager Jack O'Connor, to deny the hated Cobb the hit title.

None of Lajoie's many other accomplishments are tainted or diminished, however. For the first 13 years of the 20th century, he was the American League's equivalent of Honus Wagner—the greatest fielder of his time at his position who was also one of the game's greatest hitters.

Unlike Wagner, who played on four pennant winners in Pittsburgh, Lajoie was never on a championship team. The closest he came was in 1908, when Cleveland lost the pennant to Detroit by a half-game. Lajoie was then in his fourth season as Cleveland's player-manager. He was so popular in the Forest City that the team was renamed the "Naps" in his honor.

Although Lajoie stepped down as manager following the 1909 season, he remained with Cleveland for five more seasons as a second baseman. He concluded his major league career with a two-year stint with the A's. Lajoie was elected to the Hall of Fame in 1936.

Second baseman
Philadelphia Phillies
  1896-1900
Philadelphia Athletics
  1901-1902; 1915-1916
Cleveland Blues (Naps)
  1902-1914
Manager
Cleveland Naps 1905-1909
377-309

Top: *Lajoie outhit the average American Leaguer by 149 points in 1901 when he batted .422, the highest batting average in this century.* Left: *This is a 1913 baseball board game card of him. In 1913, he hit .335, the sixth best average in the AL.* Above: *A 1909 Helmar stamp of Lajoie.*

Major League Totals

BA	G	AB	R	H	2B	3B	HR	RBI	SB
.338	2,479	9,592	1,503	3,244	658	161	83	1,599	382

Infielder; outfielder
Louisville Colonels
1897-1899
Shortstop
Pittsburgh Pirates
1900-1917

J OHN PETER WAGNER (1874-1955) was a rarity, the son of an immigrant father who thought baseball was an acceptable profession. One reason the elder Wagner held such a sanguine opinion was that Honus's older brother Albert had previously tried his hand at the game with fair success.

By 1898, Honus was an established star with the Louisville Colonels of the National League. Good as he was as a hitter, though, Honus had something of a problem: He could not find a regular position. The Colonels used him at first base, second base, third base, and the outfield during his three seasons with them. When the franchise folded after the 1899 season, owner Barney Dreyfuss, who also owned the Pittsburgh Pirates, was permitted to take his best players to the Steel City with him. Dreyfuss naturally retained Wagner, a .336 hitter in 1899.

Player-manager Fred Clarke used Wagner mainly in the outfield in 1900 and was rewarded when Honus won the first of his record eight National League batting titles and also led the loop in doubles, triples, and slugging average. When Bones Ely slumped to .208 in 1901, Wagner spelled him for nearly half the season at shortstop. In 1902, he was returned to the outfield as Wid Conroy handled the shortstop post for most of a season that saw the Pirates win the pennant by a record 27½ games. The team was so strong that it could survive several defections to the American League and still triumph for a third successive season in 1903. When Conroy was one of the players to jump ship, Clarke decided to give Honus the shortstop job on a permanent basis. Finally, for the first time in his career, Wagner had a position he could call his own, and the rest is history.

Wagner was so great a shortstop that contemporary players must have considered it a cruel act of providence that he was also blessed with such incredible talent as a hitter. During his 21-year career Wagner was a league leader at least twice in every major offensive department except home runs and walks. When he retired he had compiled more hits, runs, total bases, RBI, and stolen bases than any player in history to that point. All these career records have since been broken, but no other shortstop in the game's long history has even approached Wagner's overall achievements. Honus was among the elite group of five players named to the Hall of Fame in 1936 when the first vote for enshrinement was conducted.

Above: An ancient but well-preserved ball autographed by Wagner. Right: Since this example of one of Wagner's uniforms is white, it is likely a home uniform. Until 1911, late in Wagner's career, it was not mandatory for a home team to wear white garb and a visiting club dark.

WAGNER, PITTSBURG

The $451,000 Baseball Card

Pittsburgh Pirate Hall of Fame shortstop Honus Wagner is remembered by youngsters today principally for the staggering value of his 1910 American Tobacco Company "T-206" baseball card.

In May 1991, Los Angeles Kings NHL hockey team owner Bruce McNall and hockey star Wayne Gretzky purchased one of the 20 or so known Wagner cards at auction for $451,000. Over the years the value of the card has remained high because so few of the cards are known to exist. Baseball cards, like stamps and coins, are priced according to scarcity not beauty.

Today, only a handful of the Wagner T-206s survive in the excellent condition of the card auctioned to McNall and Gretzky. While they are not the rarest cards, they are the most treasured.

Wagner was still Pittsburgh's top shortstop in 1916 when he was 42. His legs were shot, but still, his .287 average was 40 points above the league norm.

Major League Totals

BA	G	AB	R	H	2B	3B	HR	RBI	SB
.327	2,789	10,441	1,735	3,418	643	252	101	1,732	722

ROGER BRESNAHAN
BATTERY MATE OF CHRISTY MATHEWSON
WITH THE NEW YORK GIANTS, HE WAS
ONE OF THE GAME'S MOST NATURAL
PLAYERS AND MIGHT HAVE STARRED
AT ANY POSITION. THE "DUKE OF TRALEE"
WAS ONE OF THE FEW MAJOR LEAGUE
CATCHERS FAST ENOUGH TO BE USED
AS A LEADOFF MAN.

Catcher; outfielder; infielder
Washington Senators
    1897
Chicago Cubs 1900;
    1913-1915
Baltimore Orioles
    1901-1902
New York Giants
    1902-1908
St. Louis Cardinals
    1909-1912

Manager
St. Louis Cardinals
    1909-1912
Chicago Cubs 1915
328-432

Right: Bresnahan—on the cover of this instructional guide—was generally credited with introducing shin-guards for catchers. Top: This photo shows him in 1905, the year that he was given the Giants' catcher job that year by John McGraw, after the starting catcher in 1904 hit .199.

IF HALL OF FAME MEMBERSHIP was based upon ongoing contributions to the game and involvement in some of the most memorable incidents in baseball history, then Roger Bresnahan is among the Hall's most qualified members.

Claiming to hail from Tralee, Ireland, Roger Philip Bresnahan (1879-1944) earned the nickname "The Duke of Tralee" (although he was born in Toledo, Ohio). Roger first made his mark on major league baseball as an 18-year-old pitcher for Washington in 1897. He was 4-0 in six late-season games. The Senators, however, penurious and mistake-prone even then, could not meet his terms. He later surfaced in Baltimore, where he pitched and played nearly every other position. He was part of John McGraw's bold power play to enter the National League in 1902. McGraw persuaded Cincinnati owner John T. Brush to buy an interest in the American League Baltimore club, and then release McGraw, Bresnahan, Joe McGinnity, and others. They quickly caught on with the Giants, Brush sold the Cincinnati club and bought the Giants, and a powerhouse was born.

Bresnahan became a catcher and outfielder and a disciple of the fiery, win-at-all-costs McGraw. Roger was a favorite of McGraw's and would manage the new players in spring training

until McGraw and the veterans would report. In an effort to stay in the lineup more, Bresnahan developed shin guards and a chest protector for catchers. Although only a .280 lifetime batter, he was a solid hitter, attaining the lofty mark of .350 in 1903. He had exceptional speed for a catcher and was a terrific baserunner, allowing McGraw to use him in the leadoff spot. He stole 212 bases during his career, an unheard-of number for catchers.

He is forever linked with Christy Mathewson, whom Bresnahan caught from 1902 to 1908, including the 1905 fall classic. In the only World Series in which he played, Roger hit .313 and had the distinction of catching four shutouts, including three by Mathewson, as the Giants beat Connie Mack's Philadelphia A's four games to one.

Bresnahan became player-manager of the Cardinals in 1909, and though he matched McGraw in determination and became notorious as an umpire-baiter and a fighter, he could not match McGraw's success. After four years in St. Louis, he moved on to coach the Chicago Cubs in 1913 and retired after managing the 1915 season. He later managed in the minors and coached in the majors.

Elected to the Hall of Fame in 1945, one year after his death, Bresnahan became the first catcher honored in Cooperstown.

Major League Totals										
BA	G	AB	R	H	2B	3B	HR	RBI	SB	
.280	1,430	4,480	683	1,253	223	71	26	530	212	

RUBE WADDELL

THE BASEBALL PUBLIC KNEW George Edward Waddell (1876-1914) only as Rube. Although Waddell detested the nickname, he was so uneducated and so ill-equipped to deal with even the simple exigencies of life that he seemed born to be called Rube.

At the art of pitching a baseball, however, there have been few more worldly. Waddell was so talented that he pitched for the Louisville Colonels in 1897 without any previous professional experience. However, even the lowly Colonels were unable to tolerate his utter lack of self-discipline. After only two games with the club, Waddell was fined $50 for excessive drinking by manager Fred Clarke.

Thus began a love-hate relationship between Waddell and Clarke that lasted until 1901. Waddell by then was in his third tour of duty under Fred, who in 1901 was the player-manger of Pittsburgh. After Waddell once again displayed his appetite for an unstructured lifestyle, Clarke despaired and traded Waddell to Chicago. Chicago had no better luck in restraining Waddell and jettisoned him even though he led the team in wins.

Waddell began the 1902 season in the Pacific Coast League but by midsummer found himself in Philadelphia pitching for the Athletics of Connie Mack, perhaps the only manager at the

Pleasant Moments in sports

time who could cope with the carefree southpaw. Mack treated Waddell as a father would an unruly child. He doled out Waddell's pay in small amounts as if he were giving him an allowance, assigned catcher Ossee Schreckengost (who had a high threshold for eccentrics) to room with him on the road, and tried his best to ignore Waddell's frequent disappearances to chase fire engines or go fishing. Mack's reward was having on his team the best lefthanded pitcher in baseball. In each of his first four seasons with the Athletics, Waddell was a 20-game winner and led the AL in strikeouts. His top overall campaign was 1904 when he collected 25 victories and fanned 349 hitters, a modern single-season record that endured until 1965.

In 1905, after leading the league with 27 wins and a 1.46 ERA, he put himself in Mack's doghouse when Waddell injured his shoulder during horseplay on the eve of the 1905 World Series and was unable to pitch. Mack never completely forgave Waddell and sold him to the St. Louis Browns two years later. Waddell remained with the Browns until early in the 1910 season.

Early in 1912, Waddell developed tuberculosis after working shoulder-deep in icy river water to help save a Kentucky town during a flood. He died on April 1, 1914. In 1946, Waddell was elected to the Hall of Fame.

GEORGE EDWARD WADDELL
"RUBE"
COLORFUL LEFTHANDED PITCHER WHO WAS IN BOTH LEAGUES, BUT WHO GAINED FAME AS A MEMBER OF THE PHILADELPHIA A.L. TEAM. WON MORE THAN 20 GAMES IN FIRST FOUR SEASONS WITH THAT CLUB AND COMPILED MORE THAN 200 VICTORIES DURING MAJOR LEAGUE CAREER. WAS NOTED FOR HIS STRIKEOUT ACHIEVEMENTS.

Pitcher
Louisville Colonels
    1897; 1899
Pittsburgh Pirates
    1900-1901
Chicago Orphans 1901
Philadelphia Athletics
    1902-1907
St. Louis Browns
    1908-1910

Far left: In 1900, before foul balls were counted as strikes, Waddell led the NL in Ks with just 130. Four years later, with foul balls now strikes, Waddell fanned 349 AL hitters, a post-1893 record that stood until Sandy Koufax appeared. Top: Waddell is the centerpiece in this PM Whiskey ad.

Major League Totals

W	L	ERA	G	CG	IP	H	ER	BB	SO
191	145	2.16	407	261	2,961.1	2,460	711	803	2,316

ELMER FLICK

ELMER HARRISON FLICK
PHILADELPHIA, N.L. 1898-1902
CLEVELAND, A.L. 1902-1910
OUTFIELDER WHO BATTED .378 FOR
1900 PHILLIES. LEFT LIFETIME MARK
OF .315 FOR 13 SEASONS. A.L. BATTING
CHAMPION IN 1905. LED A.L. IN TRIPLES,
1905-06-07, AND IN STEALS, 1904, TYING
FOR LEADERSHIP AGAIN IN 1906.

Outfielder
Philadelphia Phillies
    1898-1901
Philadelphia Athletics
    1901
Cleveland Blues (Naps)
    1901-1910

Above right: During his heyday with Cleveland, Elmer Flick was viewed as the team's top slugger even though his high marks were five home runs and 64 RBIs. Right: These are two early baseball cards, a T-206 card (left) and a Sporting Life *premium.*

DURING SPRING TRAINING IN 1907, Cleveland owner Charley Somers was talking to sporstwriters in his hotel room in Macon, Georgia, one evening when the phone rang. Excusing himself to answer it, Somers found Hughie Jennings, the new Detroit manager, on the other end of the line. "We'll give you Ty Cobb for Elmer Flick," Jennings said, "even up." Somers took a while to think. He knew Cobb had hit .316 in his first full season and had shown himself to be a daring baserunner and fierce competitor. He also knew that Cobb was unpopular with his teammates and had been limited by injuries, most of them caused by his ferocious play, to only 98 games. Would Cobb, though just age 20, be able to play long enough at his feverish pitch to prove more valuable than Flick who, at age 31, was seemingly in his prime? Somers believed not. "I think we'll just keep Flick," he told Jennings. Had Somers guessed right Cleveland, and not Detroit, might have reeled off three straight pennants beginning in 1907.

Born in Bedford, Ohio, Elmer Harrison Flick (1876-1971) started his career with the Phillies in 1898. He seemed slated to sit on the bench for most of the season, however a bad back idled Sam Thompson, forcing the Phils to throw the rookie Flick into the fray.

Elmer hit .302 as a frosh, followed up by stroking .342 in 1899, and then began the new century by slapping .367 and topping the NL in RBI. When another good year in 1901 failed to

get him the raise he felt he merited, Flick signed for the 1902 season with Connie Mack's Philadelphia Athletics. The Phillies, still rocked by the loss of stars Nap Lajoie and Ed Delahanty the previous year, pursued the matter in state court. The judicial decision enjoined Flick and other ex-Phillies from playing for any other team but the Phils while in the state of Pennsylvania. Unwilling to retain players who could play only road games, Mack sent both Lajoie and Flick to Cleveland.

Elmer produced several fine seasons in Cleveland. Three times he paced the AL in triples, once he led it in runs, and in 1905 he topped all AL hitters with a .308 average, the lowest figure to win a batting crown before 1968. Flick became disabled by a mysterious stomach ailment and other nagging injuries, and he never played regularly after the 1907 season. He remained with Cleveland through 1910.

When he was selected for the Hall of Fame in 1963, Flick was 88 years old. His induction ceremony was one of the most moving in the shrine's history.

Major League Totals

BA	G	AB	R	H	2B	3B	HR	RBI	SB
.313	1,484	5,601	950	1,755	267	166	48	756	334

TOM CONNOLLY WAS A RARITY in his day, a great umpire who had never served a stint as a ballplayer.

Born in Manchester, England, Thomas Henry Connolly (1870-1961) came to America at age 13. Upon settling with his family in Nattick, Massachusetts, he observed that the most popular game in town was one that he hadn't seen played before. Learning it was called baseball, he discovered that while he had no overwhelming desire to play it, he nevertheless found it fascinating. Acquiring a book of rules, he studied them until he knew enough about the game that he began to be called on to umpire.

National League umpire Tim Hurst spotted Connolly officiating amateur games and recommended Tommy to Tim Murnane, a former major leaguer who was then the president of the New England League. After four seasons in the minor league circuit, Connolly graduated to the National League in 1898.

On the small and quiet side, Connolly quit the senior circuit during the 1900 season because he felt that umpires didn't get sufficient support from league moguls in disputes with unruly players. He came out of his brief retirement to join the newly formed American League the following year, after Connie Mack recommended him to loop president Ban Johnson, who had pledged that umpires in the young circuit would receive his full backing.

Connolly had the honor of umpiring the first American League game on April 24, 1901, between Chicago and Cleveland. In 1903, he was selected to umpire in the first modern World Series between Boston and Pittsburgh. Unobtrusive but stern when he had to be, Connolly umpired a total of eight World Series and 34 seasons in the majors. He took great pride in his ability to placate even the most hotheaded players and seldom resorted to ejection. The last player he benched was Babe Ruth in 1922 (it was Ruth's last ejection as well).

After retiring as an umpire, Connolly took on a newly created position as the chief of staff of American League umpires. Attending games to watch his umpiring crews at work, Connolly remained in the post of overseer until 1954 (he was 83 years old at the time). The previous year, he and Bill Klem were the first umpires selected for enshrinement in the Hall of Fame. Connolly died at his home in Nattick on April 25, 1961.

Above: *Connolly flourishes the typical umpire's garb of his time.* **Below:** *Connolly is the home-plate umpire at the bottom of this 1910 all-star cartoon fan.*

JOHN DWIGHT CHESBRO
"HAPPY JACK"
FAMED PITCHER WHO LED BOTH LEAGUES
IN PERCENTAGE–NATIONAL LEAGUE IN
1902; AMERICAN LEAGUE IN 1904; SERVED
WITH PITTSBURGH N.L. AND THE NEW YORK
AND BOSTON A.L. WON 41 GAMES, TOPS
IN MAJORS, IN 1904 AND DURING BIG
LEAGUE CAREER COMPILED 192 VICTORIES
WHILE LOSING ONLY 128.

Pitcher
Pittsburgh Pirates
1899-1902
New York Highlanders
1903-1909
Boston Red Sox 1909

Center column: *This 1909 card pictures Chesbro at the end of his career. From 1900 to 1908, he collected 193 triumphs, an average of better than 21 per season.* Top right: *In 1904, Chesbro loomed as large on the baseball diamond as he did in this picture.*

O N OCTOBER 10, 1904, THE LAST day of the season, Jack Chesbro pitched the first game of a doubleheader for the New York Highlanders against the Boston Pilgrims. Had Chesbro won the game it would have been his 42nd victory; more important, the Highlanders would have been mere percentage points behind the Pilgrims and positioned to cop the American League pennant if they took the second game as well. At the top of the ninth inning, with the score two-all and Boston catcher Lou Criger on third base with two out, Chesbro unleashed a spitball on an 0-2 count to Boston shortstop Freddy Parent. Reports conflict whether the pitch sailed over the head of New York catcher Red Kleinow or whether Kleinow was slow in getting his glove up to spear it. The ball rolled to the backstop, enabling Criger to tally the run that gave Boston the game and the pennant.

Chesbro, New York, A.L.

The stigma attached to that loss and what was officially labeled a wild pitch marred the remainder of Chesbro's life. More than his modern-record 41 wins, that game came to be his most vivid memory for John Dwight Chesbro (1874-1931). Long after his death, his widow continued her unavailing efforts to have the scorer's decision on the pitch officially changed to a passed ball.

"Happy Jack," Chesbro's nickname, won only six games in his 1899 rookie year with the Pittsburgh Pirates. Showing only intermittent brilliance during his first two seasons, in 1901 he emerged as the ace of the Pittsburgh staff by

snaring 21 victories and pacing the National League in winning percentage.

Repeating as the winning percentage champ in 1902 and leading the loop with 28 triumphs, Chesbro was pitching for perhaps the most dominant team of all time. Playing only a 140-game schedule, the 1902 Pirates won the pennant by 27½ games, the widest margin in major league history.

The New York Highlanders in 1903 made Chesbro an offer so enticing that he jumped to the junior loop. After falling to only 21 wins that year, he exceeded all expectations the following year—at least until the last weekend of the season. For Happy Jack not only lost the game that decided the pennant; he was also defeated two days earlier by Boston. Incredibly, Chesbro had a 41-10 record before suffering those setbacks.

After the 1904 campaign, Chesbro reached the 20-game plateau only one more time, in 1906, when he bagged 24 wins. He began the 1909 season just one victory short of 200 but was released after collecting five defeats in five starts. He was named to the Hall of Fame in 1946.

Major League Totals

W	L	ERA	G	CG	IP	H	ER	BB	SO
199	131	2.68	392	261	2,897	2,642	864	690	1,265

ALTHOUGH HIS "IRON MAN" nickname arose from his previous employment as an ironworker, Joseph Jerome McGinnity (1871-1929) could easily have earned the alias for his pitching exploits. In 1901, McGinnity became the first pitcher in the 20th century to work both ends of a twin bill, accomplishing the feat twice while with Baltimore of the American League and splitting the decisions on each occasion. In 1903, he won a record three doubleheaders in a single month for the New York Giants. Moreover, in his first eight seasons in the major leagues, McGinnity averaged over 40 starts per year and won 218 games.

He had, curiously, seemed too fragile only a few years earlier to make a mark in baseball. In 1894, after two forgettable seasons in the minor leagues and with his health questionable, he had even quit the game altogether and opened a saloon in his home state of Illinois. During his layoff, however, McGinnity not only regained his strength, he developed a new pitch—a tantalizingly slow sidearm curveball that he called "Old Sal." Returning to the professional ranks in 1898, he won 10 games for Peoria of the Western Association.

The Baltimore club, then in its last year in the National League, had seen enough promise to offer McGinnity a contract for 1899. The 28-year-old rookie won a loop-leading 28 games

JOSEPH McGINNITY, Pitcher.
BROOKLYN, 1900.

that year. In 1900, with the Baltimore franchise dropped and the senior circuit pared to eight teams, he moved to Brooklyn, where he paced the National League again with 29 victories.

McGinnity joined the mass exodus of NL stars to the upstart American League in 1901, reuniting with John McGraw, his manager in his rookie season in Baltimore. Midway through the 1902 campaign, both men jumped back to the senior circuit, signing with the New York Giants. McGinnity remained with the Giants for the rest of his 10-year major league career, topping the NL in wins three times. In 1903, McGinnity set a 20th century National League record with 44 complete games. Reaching his pinnacle in 1904, he bagged 35 victories and combined with Christy Mathewson to post 68 wins, a 20th century record for two pitchers on the same team.

Gauged by McGraw to be slipping when he logged only 11 wins in 1908, Joe was released at age 37. Although he never again pitched in the major leagues, he was still taking his regular turn on the mound in the minors as late as 1925, at the age of 54. The game's most durable pitcher, Iron Man retired in 1926 to take a coaching job with Brooklyn. McGinnity was elected to the Hall of Fame in 1945.

JOSEPH JEROME McGINNITY
"IRONMAN"
DISTINGUISHED AS THE PITCHER WHO HURLED
TWO GAMES ON ONE DAY THE MOST TIMES. DID
THIS ON FIVE OCCASIONS. WON BOTH GAMES
THREE TIMES. PLAYED WITH BALTIMORE,
BROOKLYN AND NEW YORK TEAMS IN N.L.
AND BALTIMORE IN A.L. GAINED MORE THAN
200 VICTORIES DURING CAREER. RECORDED
20 OR MORE VICTORIES SEVEN TIMES. IN TWO
SUCCESSIVE SEASONS WON AT LEAST 30 GAMES

Pitcher
Baltimore Orioles (NL)
   1899
Brooklyn Superbas 1900
Baltimore Orioles (AL)
   1901-1902
New York Giants
   1902-1908

Top: *This is a 1900 copper-plate print of McGinnity, when he was with Brooklyn.* Left: *In 1903, even though both leagues still played only a 140-game schedule, he set the 20th century NL record for innings pitched with 434.*

		Major League Totals							
W	**L**	**ERA**	**G**	**CG**	**IP**	**H**	**ER**	**BB**	**SO**
247	144	2.64	465	314	3,458.2	3,276	1,011	812	1,068

SAMUEL EARL CRAWFORD
"WAHOO SAM"
CINCINNATI N.L. 1899-1902
DETROIT A.L. 1903-1917
HAD LIFETIME RECORD OF 2964 HITS,
BATTING AVERAGE OF .309. PLAYED 2905
GAMES. HOLDS MAJOR LEAGUE RECORD
FOR MOST TRIPLES, 312. LEAGUE LEADER
ONE OR MORE SEASONS IN DOUBLES, TRIPLES,
RUNS BATTED IN, RUNS SCORED, CHANCES
ACCEPTED, HOME RUNS (N.L. 1901-A.L. 1908)
AND TOTAL BASES (N.L. 1902-A.L. 1913).

Outfielder
Cincinnati Reds 1899-1902
Detroit Tigers 1903-1917

IN SAM CRAWFORD'S TIME THE mark of a great slugger was still not how many home runs he hit but how many triples. By that standard Crawford was the dead-ball era's most prolific long-ball hitter. He left the majors in 1917 with 312 triples. Crawford still holds the distinction of being the only player in this century to lead both major leagues in home runs.

Born in Wahoo, Nebraska, Samuel Earl Crawford (1880-1968) was tagged "Wahoo Sam" early in his professional career and grew so fond of the nickname that he asked that it be inscribed on his Hall of Fame plaque. Crawford first played pro baseball in 1899 and did so well that Cincinnati purchased him near the end of the season. Still just 19 years old when he made his debut with the Reds on September 10, 1899, Crawford hit .307 in the 31 games that remained and collected eight triples in just 127 at bats.

After the 1902 season, Crawford seized what might be his last chance to escape the lowly Reds, a cellar finisher in 1901 despite his loop-leading 16 homers. He jumped to Detroit in the American League. Wahoo Sam promptly hit

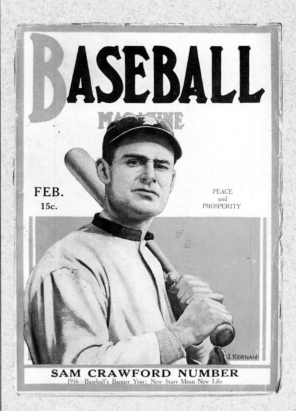

FEB.
15c.

PEACE
and
PROSPERITY

SAM CRAWFORD NUMBER
1916—Baseball's Banner Year; New Stars Mean New Life

.335 in his first year with the Bengals and cracked 25 triples, an AL record that stood until 1913 when Joe Jackson notched 26 three-baggers, a total that Crawford himself matched a year later. Even with Crawford's slugging, nonetheless, Detroit remained a second-division team until it added Ty Cobb to its cast in 1905. While not the hitter for average that Cobb was, Crawford was his superior as an extra-base-hit producer. Playing side by side in the same outfield, the pair spearheaded the 1907 to '09 Tigers, the first team in American League history to garner three consecutive pennants.

Crawford fashioned a .309 career batting average in 2,517 games and logged at least 10 triples in every full season he played. He was a loop leader in three-baggers six times and also topped the AL on three occasions in RBI.

During his long tour of duty with Detroit, Crawford became very popular with Motor City fans, to the envy of Cobb. The relationship between the two grew so strained that purportedly the only time they spoke to each other was when a ball was hit between them. Their animosity lasted even after both retired, but ironically it was Cobb who campaigned the hardest for Crawford when Wahoo Sam continued to be passed over for selection to the Hall of Fame. In 1957, Crawford received the long-overdue honor.

Top: *After pacing the AL in both triples and RBI in 1915, Crawford was featured on a preseason cover of* Baseball Magazine. Right: *In 1901, he clubbed 16 dingers for the Reds to set a 20th century club mark. It was broken in 1930 by Harry Heilmann—the man who took Crawford's job on the Tigers in 1917.*

					Major League Totals					
BA	G	AB	R	H	2B	3B	HR	RBI	SB
.309	2,517	9,580	1,393	2,964	457	312	97	1,525	366

CHRISTY MATHEWSON

CHRISTY MATHEWSON LEFT Bucknell University in 1899 to sign his first baseball contract. Seventeen years later he retired with 373 victories and an almost universal recognition as the greatest pitcher in National League history to that time.

Christopher Mathewson (1880-1925) probably did more than any other performer of his day to enhance the image of a professional baseball player. Educated, intelligent, and a consummate gentleman, he seemed almost too good to be true.

Mathewson was originally the property of the New York Giants but was drafted by Cincinnati for $100 when he won 20 games for Norfolk of the Virginia League in 1900, after doing poorly in an early season trial with the New York club. John Brush, who owned a piece of the Reds and knew he would soon be serving the Giants in a similar capacity, clandestinely arranged to return Matty to New York for a badly worn Amos Rusie.

After winning 20 games for the Giants in 1901, Matty tumbled to just 14 victories the next year. After that, however, he reeled off 12 straight seasons in which he won 20 or more games. "Big Six" won over 30 games on four occasions with a high of 37 in 1908. The net result of his extraordinary run of success was that he had 300 career victories by the time he was 32 years old.

Sometimes, though, Mathewson seemed to have trouble winning the big games. In his last three World Series appearances—1911, 1912, and 1913—Matty won just two games while losing five. In his defense, the Giants consistently displayed defensive lapses at crucial moments when he was on the mound and scored only seven runs in the last 39 innings he hurled in Series play.

However, Mathewson's work in championship contests did not always end in disappointment. In 1905, his first World Series appearance, he twirled a record three complete-game shutouts and 27 scoreless innings against the Philadelphia Athletics to lead the Giants to victory in their first 20th century postseason affair. Matty's feat is generally considered to be the most outstanding performance in World Series history.

In 1916, with his famed screwball or "fadeaway" no longer effective, Mathewson was traded to Cincinnati so that he could become the Reds player-manager. After only one mound appearance in the Queen City, he became a bench pilot only. In 1918, Matty entered the Army in August. While serving overseas in World War I, he accidentally inhaled poison gas, permanently damaging his lungs. He died on October 7, 1925. In 1936, Christy was among the first group of five players elected to the Hall of Fame.

Pitcher
New York Giants
   1900-1916
Cincinnati Reds 1916
Manager
Cincinnati Reds
   1916-1918
164-176

Matty's last win, ironically, came as a member of the Reds in 1916.

"Big Six" was one of Matty's nicknames; its origin still remains a puzzle.

Major League Totals

W	L	ERA	G	CG	IP	H	ER	BB	SO
373	188	2.13	634	435	4,782.0	2,502	1,132	838	2,502

EDWARD S. PLANK
"GETTYSBURG EDDIE"
ONE OF GREATEST LEFTHANDED PITCHERS OF
MAJOR LEAGUES.NEVER PITCHED FOR A MINOR
LEAGUE TEAM, GOING FROM GETTYSBURG
COLLEGE TO THE PHILADELPHIA A.L. TEAM
WITH WHICH HE SERVED FROM 1901 THROUGH
1914. MEMBER OF ST. LOUIS F.L. IN 1915 AND
ST. LOUIS A.L. IN 1916-17. ONE OF FEW
PITCHERS TO WIN MORE THAN 300 GAMES
IN BIG LEAGUES. IN EIGHT OF 17 SEASONS,
WON 20 OR MORE GAMES.

Pitcher
Philadelphia Athletics
1901-1914
St. Louis Terriers 1915
St. Louis Browns
1916-1917

Above: *In 1911, the season that
he was the subject of this
caramel card, Plank won 23
games and led the AL in both
shutouts and saves. Right:
Consistency was his main
strength. Between 1901 and
1916 he never won more than
26 games in a season or fewer
than 14.*

BEFORE ENROLLING AT GET-tysburg College, Eddie Plank had no organized baseball experience. Moreover, he was age 21 at the time and had spent his entire life on a farm in Gettysburg. However, the Gettysburg coach was Frank Foreman, a former major league pitcher whose roots in the game reached back to the old Union Association in 1884. Foreman cajoled Plank into trying out for the Gettysburg varsity and soon realized that he had a prize pitcher.

Although nearly age 26 when he was graduated from Gettysburg in 1901, Edward Stewart Plank (1875-1926) was signed by Connie Mack of the Philadelphia A's, who were about to embark on their first season in the fledgling American League. Proceeding straight to the A's without a day in the minors, Plank won 17 games as a rookie and quickly became a bane not only of enemy hitters but also of American League umpires. Although his pitches were quite straightforward—he had only a fastball and a curve—he worked so deliberately that he seemed to take forever between deliveries. Plank claimed that he slowed the pace of the game to rattle

*Plank models in this Royal Tailor ad in 1914,
his last season with the A's.*

hitters. Additionally, he kept them off balance by talking to himself on the mound. Sportswriters found him poor copy; he was so colorless he was almost dull.

Plank's achievements, though, were anything but lackluster. He won 20 or more games in a season seven times for the A's, a club record that he shares with Lefty Grove. Plank nevertheless failed to lead the American League in wins, ERA, or strikeouts, nor was he ever considered the A's staff ace. He became one of the few Hall of Famers to ride the bench for an entire World Series when Mack preferred to go with Jack Coombs and Chief Bender against the Cubs in the 1910 classic.

After slipping to 15 wins in 1914 and losing the second game of the World Series that fall, a heartbreaking 1-0 verdict to Bill James of the Miracle Braves, Plank deserted the A's that winter to play in the renegade Federal League. Thus it was that his 300th win came in the uniform of the 1915 St. Louis Terriers.

The following year, the St. Louis Browns signed Plank, and he finished out his career with them in 1917, the first southpaw in major league history to win 300 games. Plank still holds the record for the most wins and the most shutouts by an American League portsider.

Eddie pitched semipro ball for several years after leaving the majors and was elected to the Hall of Fame in 1946.

			Major League Totals						
W	L	ERA	G	CG	IP	H	ER	BB	SO
327	193	2.34	622	412	4,505.1	3,956	1,173	1,072	2,246

CLARK GRIFFITH

ALTHOUGH HE LIVED TO BE age 85, Clark Griffith was given the nickname "The Old Fox" while in his 20s. Pitching for Cap Anson's Chicago White Stockings at the time, Griffith was known for having more guile than ability. He was one of the first hurlers to scuff up baseballs and doctor them with foreign substances to make his pitches more difficult to hit. After building his career around trick deliveries, Griffith, while serving as owner of the Washington Senators, ironically became a staunch advocate for the abolition of the spitball in 1920.

One of the last players to be born in a log cabin, Clark Calvin Griffith (1869-1955) joined his hometown Bloomington, Illinois, team in the Central Interstate League in 1887. Four years later, he reached the majors with St. Louis of the American Association. Sold to the Boston Association team late in the 1891 season, he came down with a sore arm and was released.

Griffith then returned to the minors for one and one-half years. By 1894, he had become a mainstay of the Chicago White Stockings mound staff. He won 20 or more games six years in a row and led the NL with a 1.88 ERA in 1898. When the American League declared itself a major circuit in 1901, Griffith was one of the first stars to jump to the new loop, joining the Chicago entry as a pitcher-manager and signaling the start of hostilities between the two leagues. In his very first season with the Chicago Americans, he not only bagged 24 victories but became the only pitcher in this century to win a pennant while functioning as a player-manager.

Griffith left Chicago in 1903 to manage the new AL New York entry. Still a pitcher and a manager, he became predominantly a pilot after the 1906 season. Although in later years he occasionally hurled a few innings, he never added to his 240 career wins.

Griffith quit the Highlanders during the 1908 season, managed the Cincinnati Reds for three years, and then became the manager and part owner of the Washington Nationals in 1912. After nine years in the dual role, Griffith devoted himself entirely to front office duties. A crafty and, at times, daring owner for many years, the Old Fox helped bring the nation's capital three pennant winners. During the last two decades he ran the club, however, he grew increasingly nepotistic and unimaginative. By the time he died on October 27, 1955, the Senators had become the most moribund franchise in the majors. Griffith was elected to the Hall of Fame in 1946.

Manager
Chicago White Stockings
    1901-1902
New York Highlanders
    1903-1908
Cincinnati Reds
    1909-1911
Washington Nationals
    1912-1920
Pitcher
St. Louis Browns 1891
Boston Reds 1891
Chicago Colts (Orphans)
    1893-1900
Chicago White Sox
    1901-1902
New York Highlanders
    1903-1907
Cincinnati Reds
    1909-1910
Washington Nationals
    1912-1914

Far left: *"The Old Fox" managed four ballclubs for 20 years.* Left: *Never generous with players, Griffith grew all the more tightfisted during the war years. In 1945, though, with the most ill-paid lineup in the majors, the Senators contended until the season's final day.*

Major League Managing Totals				
W	L	T	PCT	G
1,491	1,367	58	.522	2,918

Major League Totals									
W	L	ERA	G	CG	IP	H	ER	BB	SO
240	144	3.31	453	337	3,386.1	3,670	1,245	774	955

BAN JOHNSON

BYRON BANCROFT JOHNSON
ORGANIZER OF THE AMERICAN
LEAGUE AND ITS PRESIDENT FROM
ITS ORGANIZATION IN 1900 UNTIL
HIS RESIGNATION BECAUSE OF
ILL HEALTH IN 1927.
A GREAT EXECUTIVE.

IN 1893, CHARLES COMISKEY returned from a scouting trip through the Western League full of plans. He shared his ideas with his drinking buddy, Cincinnati sportswriter Ban Johnson. Johnson should assume control of the Western League, which was weak but had teams in valuable cities. Johnson's leadership proved so strong and successful, that after Comiskey, Connie Mack bought into the league. When the National League contracted from 12 to eight teams in 1900, the circuit made its move. Renamed the American League, it moved into eastern territories abandoned by the NL, declared itself a major league, and began a series of player raids. When the new league opened in 1901, 111 of the league's 185 players had NL experience.

Byron Bancroft Johnson (1864-1931) was a catcher at Marietta College in Ohio, and took a job as a sportswriter at the Cincinnati *Commercial-Gazette*. It was in the Queen City that he developed his friendship with then-Cincinnati Reds manager Comiskey. Though 300 pounds, Ban was an active man with great vision.

"My determination was to pattern baseball in this new league along the lines of scholastic contests, to make ability and brains and clean, honorable play, not the swinging of clenched fists, coarse oaths, riots, or assaults on the umpires, decide the issue," Johnson said. He was determined to keep his league free of the "rowdyism" that pervaded the NL in the late 1800s.

John McGraw was attracted to run the Baltimore franchise in 1901, and he used every tactic of rowdy ball. Despite McGraw being a favorite in Baltimore, Johnson drove him back to the NL. The new league flourished under Johnson, and the National Agreement, signed in 1903, ended the raiding wars between the circuits and established a World Series.

Johnson felt that his founding of the league granted him dictatorial power over its operations. In the beginning it did, but as the league gained its own momentum, it took more power than one man could muster to swing the circuit to his will. Johnson almost immediately alienated his old friend Comiskey; Ban through the years got on the wrong side of most of the league's strong-willed owners.

When the first rumor of a fix in the 1919 World Series broke, Johnson took the opportunity to insult Comiskey and became deeply involved in the investigation. The election of Judge Kenesaw Mountain Landis put an end to Johnson's power. After a long struggle, Ban retired in 1927. McGraw, though they never reconciled, called Johnson "a great fighter and organizer" and said the American League was "a monument to his genius."

Ban Johnson stands in the doorway of the office he occupied for some 26 years as the czar and first president of the American League.

Shortstop
Chicago Cubs
    1902-1912; 1916
Cincinnati Reds 1913
Chicago Chi-Feds (Whales)
    1914-1915
Manager
Cincinnati Reds 1913
Chicago Chi-Feds (Whales)
    1914-1915
Chicago Cubs 1916
304-308

JOE TINKER IS THE LEAST known member of the Chicago Cubs' immortal infield trio in the first decade of the 20th century. Thus, there is a strong temptation to believe that he was a lesser player than his two comrades, Johnny Evers and Frank Chance, and probably made the Hall of Fame on their coattails. The actual truth may be that Tinker was the best of the three. He was a superior fielder to Evers and Chance, an important consideration since it was for their alleged skill at executing double plays that the trio gained renown.

Joseph Bert Tinker (1880-1948) was signed to his first professional contract by Denver of the Western League while he was performing with a semipro team in Coffeyville, a town near his Muscotah, Kansas, home. In Denver's thin air he got off to so poor a start in 1900 that he was shipped north to the Montana State League. A good season with Portland of the Pacific Northwest League in 1901 earned Tinker a berth with the Chicago Cubs the following spring. The Windy City was the farthest east he had ever been in his life to that time, but he seemed at home almost from the first day he arrived.

Initially Tinker played shortstop beside the veteran Bobby Lowe, but when Lowe broke his leg late in the season, a young second baseman named Johnny Evers was summoned to replace him. On September 13, 1902, Tinker, Evers, and Chance appeared in their first game together for the Cubs. Two days later the trio recorded their first double play.

Ironically, Tinker was never overly fond of Chance and actually disliked Evers. The keystone pair culminated their brewing feud in a fistfight on the field during an exhibition game in 1905 and subsequently went without speaking to each other for nearly three years. Nevertheless, the Cubs won four pennants with them anchoring the two key infield positions.

Tinker remained a regular with the Cubs for 11 seasons, longer than either Evers or Chance. In 1913, he became player-manager of the Reds after an off-season trade. Although he hit .317, Cincinnati finished seventh. The following season Joe joined the Chicago Whales of the Federal League as player-manager and piloted them to a pennant in 1915. His success caused the Cubs to name him their manager in 1916. The job lasted only one year, after which Joe spent several years managing in the minors. In 1946, while scouting for the Cubs, he, Chance, and Evers were named to the Hall of Fame as a unit.

Top: *When the Chicago Federal League entry signed Tinker as their player-manager prior to the 1914 season, they immediately flaunted him on their club pennant.* Left: *In 1908, when the Cubs won their last Championship, he led the team with 68 RBI.*

Major League Totals

BA	G	AB	R	H	2B	3B	HR	RBI	SB
.263	1,805	6,441	773	1,695	264	114	31	782	336

JOHNNY EVERS

JOHN JOSEPH EVERS
"THE TROJAN"
MIDDLE MAN OF THE FAMOUS DOUBLE
PLAY COMBINATION OF TINKER TO EVERS
TO CHANCE WITH THE PENNANT WINNING
CHICAGO CUBS OF 1906, 7, 8, 9 & 10, AND WITH
THE BOSTON BRAVES' MIRACLE TEAM OF
1914. VOTED MOST VALUABLE PLAYER IN N.L.
IN 1914. SERVED AS PLAYER, COACH AND
MANAGER IN BIG LEAGUES AND AS A SCOUT
FROM 1902 THROUGH 1934. SHARES RECORD
FOR MAKING MOST SINGLES IN FOUR
GAME WORLD SERIES.

Second baseman
Chicago Cubs 1902-1913
Boston Braves
    1914-1917; 1929
Philadelphia Phillies 1917
Chicago White Sox 1922
Manager
Chicago Cubs 1913; 1921
Chicago White Sox 1924

Below: *Evers (left) and Tris Speaker appear on this Darby Chocolate box cover in 1909.*

JOHN JOSEPH EVERS (1881-1947) was a devout student of the game. Even in a time when players were much more concerned with its history and its intricacies than they are today, Evers stood alone in his almost fanatical obsession with the nuances of his chosen profession.

His diligence was attributed to his having to gain every extra advantage he could, owing to his size. At 5'9" Evers was about average height for his time, but he weighed barely 100 pounds when he turned professional in 1902. Whatever the reason, though, for Johnny's ruthless devotion to learning everything there was to know about baseball, it paid off for him. Not only did he enjoy an extraordinarily successful major league career after initially being judged too fragile to last even in a single game in top company, but in 1908 he played a key role in perhaps the most important incident in a major league game that turned on a rule interpretation.

It happened in a late-September contest at the Polo Grounds between the Giants and Evers's Cubs. The Cubs, shooting for their third straight pennant, seemingly were about to be dethroned when Al Bridwell of the Giants singled in the bottom of the ninth inning to bring home Moose

Evers used a very heavy bat and choked up a good six to ten inches on the handle.

McCormick with the apparent winning run. Evers, always on the alert, noticed that Fred Merkle, the Giants runner at first base, headed for the clubhouse in center field as soon as Bridwell delivered his hit. Calling for the ball, Evers began screaming to umpire Hank O'Day that Merkle was out on a force play at second base since he had neglected to touch the bag before leaving. O'Day had been through this same scenario before with Evers earlier in the season and was disposed to make the only decision that complied with the rule book. He declared Merkle out at second, provoking a near riot that prevented the game, now tied again, from continuing.

When the Giants and the Cubs finished the season deadlocked, the teams replayed the tie game with the Cubs winning. Thanks largely to Evers, the Cubs thus captured their third straight flag.

Johnny played on four pennant winners altogether in Chicago. In 1914 he played on a fifth flag team, the Miracle Braves of Boston. Evers's role in Boston's triumph was deemed to have been so critical that he was voted the NL's MVP. Although he was only age 31, it was his final season as a full-time player. Evers was inducted into the Hall of Fame in 1946.

			Major League Totals						
BA	G	AB	R	H	2B	3B	HR	RBI	SB
.270	1,783	6,134	919	1,658	216	70	12	538	324

FRANK LEROY CHANCE
FAMOUS LEADER OF CHICAGO CUBS. WON
PENNANT WITH CUBS IN FIRST FULL SEASON
AS MANAGER IN 1906-THAT TEAM COMPILED
116 VICTORIES UNEQUALED IN MAJOR
LEAGUE HISTORY-ALSO WON PENNANTS
IN 1907, 08 AND 1910 AND WORLD SERIES
WINNER IN 07 AND 08. STARTED WITH
CHICAGO IN 1895. ALSO MANAGER
NEW YORK A.L. AND BOSTON A.L.

First baseman; catcher
Chicago Orphans (Cubs)
1898-1912
New York Yankees
1913-1914
Manager
Chicago Cubs 1905-1912
New York Yankees
1913-1914
Boston Red Sox 1923
946-648

forced Selee to step down as manager. His last act was to appoint Chance his successor.

Under Chance's guidance, the Cubs won four pennants in the next five years and their only two World Championships. When the club won a record 116 games in 1906, Chance's nickname of Husk gave way to the name "The Peerless Leader."

Although only age 31 at the finish of the 1908 season, Chance was never again a full-time player. He began to be plagued by headaches, a result of many beanings. Reduced to a bench role, Chance was fired after the Cubs finished third in 1912. The Yankees immediately hired him in the hope that he could instill some spark in what to that point had been a listless team, but Chance quit after less than two seasons. In 1946, Tinker, Evers, and Chance were all inducted into the Hall of Fame.

BORN IN FRESNO, FRANK LEROY Chance (1877-1924) was one of the first native Californians to achieve stardom in "The Eastern Game," as it was then known.

Cal McVey, a member of the legendary 1859 Cincinnati Red Stockings, observed him catching for a semipro team. On McVey's recommendation, Chance was signed by the Chicago Orphans in 1898 and made the club as a backup receiver. Nicknamed "Husk," his size worked against him, as he lacked the necessary agility in back of the plate.

It took the canny Frank Selee to recognize that Chance was playing the wrong position. Selee switched Frank to first base in 1902. At the outset Chance opposed the move, even threatening to quit. When he hit .327 in 1903, his first full season as a regular, and then swiped 67 bases the following year to lead the National League and set a modern season record for first basemen, however, his catching ambitions were forgotten.

By 1905, the Orphans had long since come to be called the Cubs and were about to take their place among the premier teams in baseball history. Along with stationing Chance at first base, Selee had nurtured two young keystoners, second baseman Johnny Evers and shortstop Joe Tinker, who were soon to join Chance in becoming the most celebrated infield trio in the game's history. In July of 1905, tuberculosis

Top: *Chance, bat in hand, is pictured on this 1907 sheet music cover. Left: Chance began his career as a catcher and then converted to first base when he lacked the defensive skills to play regularly behind the plate.*

			Major League Totals							
BA	**G**	**AB**	**R**	**H**	**2B**	**3B**	**HR**	**RBI**	**SB**
.296	1,286	4,293	798	1,272	200	79	20	596	405

MORDECAI PETER BROWN
(THREE-FINGERED AND MINER)
MEMBER OF CHICAGO N.L. CHAMPIONSHIP
TEAM OF 1906,'07,'08,'10. A RIGHT HANDED
PITCHER, WON 239 GAMES DURING MAJOR
LEAGUE CAREER THAT ALSO INCLUDED
ST. LOUIS AND CINCINNATI N.L. AND CLUBS
IN F.L. FIRST MAJOR LEAGUER TO PITCH
FOUR CONSECUTIVE SHUTOUTS, ACHIEVING
THIS FEAT ON JUNE 13, JUNE 25, JULY 2
AND JULY 4 IN 1908.

Pitcher
St. Louis Cardinals 1903
Chicago Cubs
   1904-1912; 1916
Cincinnati Reds 1913
St. Louis Terriers 1914
Brooklyn Tip-Tops 1914
Chicago Whales 1915

THREE FINGER BROWN WAS ONE of a kind. He became a great pitcher because of rather than in spite of a crippling injury.

At the age of seven, while visiting his uncle's farm in Indiana, Mordecai Peter Centennial Brown (1876-1948) accidentally stuck his right hand under a corn chopper. Before he could retrieve the hand, half of his index finger was torn off and the thumb and middle finger were also permanently impaired.

The damaged hand hampered Brown whenever he tried to play his preferred position of third base but strangely seemed to work to his advantage when he turned to pitching in his early 20s. Brown found that the unnatural grip he had to employ on the ball caused many of his straight pitches to behave like knuckleballs and imparted an extra dip to his curves. The irony is that Brown lacked a major league fastball and might never have risen above semipro competition were it not for his uncle's corn chopper.

Brown joined the Cardinals in 1903; thinking that his crippled hand would handicap him in the long term, the Cardinals dealt him to the Cubs before the 1904 season. With Chicago,

Top: *Brown—pictured on a 1909 tobacco baseball card— led the NL in wins, appearances, complete games, innings, and saves that year.* Right: *Only Christy Mathewson prevented Brown from being recognized as the NL's best pitcher during his prime.*

BROWN
Pitcher, Chicago N. L.

Brown achieved almost instant stardom and became the linchpin of the mound staff.

On June 13, 1905, Brown and Christy Mathewson of the Giants hooked up in one of the greatest pitching duels ever. Brown surrendered just one hit but came out a loser, 1-0, when Mathewson held the Cubs hitless. To Mathewson's dismay, it turned out to be the last time he bested Brown until the 1909 season. In between, Brown topped the great Matty on nine consecutive occasions.

With Brown's right arm leading the way, the Cubs won four pennants between 1906 and 1910 and two World Series. The second and last championship came in 1908 against Detroit and saw Brown win two games and post a perfect 0.00 ERA. Two years earlier Brown came through the regular season with a 1.04 ERA to set a 20th century National League record.

Used not only as a starting pitcher but also as the Cubs main stopper, Brown topped the NL in 1911 with 53 mound appearances while compiling a 21-11 record. It was the last of his six consecutive 20-win seasons. Brown returned to the Cubs in 1916 after two years in the Federal League. Fittingly, his final big league appearance came on Labor Day that season against Mathewson, who was also making his final bow. Matty, for once, took Brown's measure, winning 10-8. Brown died in 1948, one year before he was elected to the Hall of Fame.

Major League Totals

W	L	ERA	G	CG	IP	H	ER	BB	SO
239	129	2.06	481	271	3,172.1	2,708	726	673	1,375

ADDIE JOSS'S CAREER WINNING percentage of .623 is the highest of any pitcher involved in 200 or more decisions who was never on a pennant winner. He also had the shortest career of any player in the Hall of Fame. Joss played only nine seasons, all with Cleveland. Since a minimum of 10 years as an active player is required for enshrinement in Cooperstown, Addie was denied entry until 1978 when the Veterans Committee made a special exception in his case.

Adrian Joss (1880-1911) grew up in Juneau, Wisconsin. In 1900, while playing semipro ball and attending the University of Wisconsin, he was signed by former National League outfielder Bob Gilks, then a player-manager for Toledo in the Inter-State League. Joss won 19 games in 1900, and after notching 25 victories for Toledo in 1901, Addie was purchased by Cleveland.

In his rookie year with Cleveland, Joss led the American League in shutouts with five. Two years later his 1.59 ERA paced the loop. In 1908, Joss was again the hardest pitcher in the AL to score against as he posted a 1.16 ERA. Indeed, except for his first seasons, Joss always contrived to keep his ERA remarkably low even for the dead-ball era. As a result, his career ERA

of 1.88 is second on the all-time list. Joss was, moreover, the most difficult pitcher in history to reach base against. Parsimonious with walks and nearly unhittable when he was on his game, he allowed a record-low 8.73 baserunners per nine innings, excluding errors.

Joss began to peak in 1905. In each of the next four seasons he won 20 or more games. His high mark came in 1907 when he collected 27 victories to pace the AL, but his greatest day in baseball occurred the following year. On October 2, 1908, with a possible pennant hanging in the balance, Joss dueled Big Ed Walsh of the White Sox. When Walsh allowed a run on a wild pitch, that was all Addie needed. He shut the White Sox down cold without a single baserunner and thus registered only the fourth perfect game in major league history.

Arm and elbow trouble plagued Joss in 1909 and 1910. Seemingly on the comeback trail during spring training in 1911, Joss fainted on the field in an exhibition contest in April. He shrugged the incident off initially. Within a week, however, Joss was hospitalized with tubercular meningitis, and on April 14, 1911, he died. His funeral was held on what would have been Opening Day, but his Cleveland teammates refused en masse to play the game in order to attend.

Pitcher
Cleveland Blues (Naps)
1902-1910

Top: *Only 14-13 in 1909, Joss posted a 1.71 ERA, the fourth-best in the AL, and completed 24 of 28 starts.* Above: *This tobacco card of Joss was issued as he lay near death in 1911 at his home in Toledo, Ohio. He succumbed to meningitis two days before his Cleveland team before the 1911 season in St. Louis.*

Joss warms up before a game in 1908. He led the majors that year with a 1.16 ERA.

					Major League Totals					
W	L	ERA	G	CG	IP	H	ER	BB	SO
160	97	1.88	286	234	2,336.0	1,895	489	370	926

CHARLES ALBERT BENDER
"CHIEF"
PHILADELPHIA A.L. 1903-1914
PHILADELPHIA N.L. 1916-1917
CHICAGO A.L. 1925
FAMOUS CHIPPEWA INDIAN. WON OVER 200
GAMES. PITCHED FOR ATHLETICS IN 1905-
1910-1911-1913-1914 WORLD SERIES.
DEFEATED N.Y. GIANTS 3-0 FOR A'S ONLY
VICTORY IN 1905 FIRST PITCHER IN
WORLD SERIES OF 6 GAMES (1911) TO PITCH
3 COMPLETE GAMES PITCHED NO-HIT GAME
AGAINST CLEVELAND IN 1910.
HIGHEST A.L. PERCENTAGES IN
1910-1911-1914.

Pitcher
Philadelphia Athletics
    1903-1914
Baltimore Terrapins 1915
Philadelphia Phillies
    1916-1917
Chicago White Sox 1925

AS A MEMBER OF CONNIE Mack's Philadelphia A's from 1903 to 1914, Charles Albert Bender (1884-1954) was surrounded by fellow All-Star pitchers Eddie Plank and Rube Waddell and backed up by the famous "$100,000 Infield." Pitching for five pennant winning teams, Bender won six World Series games in ten starts, including two apiece in the 1911 and 1913 fall classics.

Bender won 20 or more games only twice in an era when 40 wins were not uncommon, but he led the league in winning percentage twice with 23-5 and 17-3 seasons in 1910 and '11. The Chief also figured in a host of the biggest games of the era. In only the second World Series (1905), Bender led the A's to their only victory of the Series, beating Iron Man Joe McGinnity with a four-hit shutout in game two, but lost the final game to Christy Mathewson, in Matty's third victory in the five-game series. Despite this, Mack called Bender the best clutch pitcher on the Athletics.

Bender, half Chippewa Indian, left the White Earth Indian reservation in Minnesota at age eight to attend school in Philadelphia. After attending the Carlisle Indian School, Bender skipped the minor leagues and jumped straight

from semipro ball to the bigs. He was one of the bigger pitchers of his day at 6'2", and although he didn't rack up many total strikeouts, he was often near the top of the AL in strikeouts per game during his stint with the A's. A good fastball pitcher, he also threw a "talcum" pitch. The Chief would rub one side of a baseball with talcum powder until the ball would drop; the pitch was legal in his time.

In 1906, Bender replaced outfielder Topsy Hartsel in a contest and slugged two home runs in one game, a rare feat in the dead-ball era. After winning three World Series with Connie Mack's A's, Bender was lured to the Federal League in 1915. He returned to Philadelphia for the 1916 and 1917 seasons as a member of the National League's Phillies, before contributing to the war effort during the entire 1918 campaign. He came back at age 36 to post a 29-2 record in the minor leagues. He tossed one inning for the White Sox in 1925 at age 41 before retiring for good. In his 16-year major league career, Bender posted a 210-127 won-lost record and a stellar 2.46 earned run average.

He went on to coaching chores, serving stints with Connie Mack, John McGraw, and the U.S. Naval Academy. Elected to the Hall of Fame in 1953, Bender worked in baseball until his death in 1954.

REMEMBER ME TO MY OLD GAL

SUCCESSFULLY INTRODUCED BY
THOSE THREE GREAT BALL PLAYERS
CHIEF BENDER, COOMBS
AND MORGAN
THE HEROES OF THE
WORLD'S SERIES

WORDS BY
GEORGE MORIARITY
CAPTAIN OF THE DETROIT BASE-BALL TEAM
MUSIC BY
AL. W. BROWN AND J. BRANDON WALSH

HAROLD ROSSITER MUSIC COMPANY

Top: Bender topped the AL in winning percentage three times during the 1910s. Right: Like other ballplayers of the era, Bender was involved in entertainment in the off-season.

Major League Totals

W	L	ERA	G	CG	IP	H	ER	BB	SO
210	127	2.46	459	256	3,017.0	2,645	825	712	1,711

EDWARD ARTHUR WALSH
"BIG ED"
OUTSTANDING RIGHTHANDED PITCHER OF CHICAGO A.L. FROM 1904 THROUGH 1916. WON 40 GAMES IN 1908 AND WON TWO GAMES IN THE 1906 WORLD SERIES. TWICE PITCHED AND WON TWO GAMES IN ONE DAY, ALLOWING ONLY ONE RUN IN DOUBLEHEADER AGAINST BOSTON ON SEPT. 29, 1908. FINISHED BIG LEAGUE PITCHING CAREER WITH BOSTON N.L. IN 1917.

Pitcher
Chicago White Sox
1904-1916
Boston Braves 1917

ORIGINALLY, EDWARD AUGUStine Walsh (1881-1959) had an overpowering fastball and little else. In 1904, however, while in spring training with the Chicago White Sox, he learned how to throw a spitball from teammate Elmer Stricklett, reputedly the first hurler to master the pitch. Walsh's spitter became so effective that Sam Crawford once said of it, "I think the ball disintegrated on the way to the plate and the catcher put it back together again."

Besides acquiring the best spitter in the game, Walsh also worked overtime to improve his fielding. A liability to himself early in his career, Walsh by 1907 had become his own biggest asset. That year he collected 227 assists, an all-time record for pitchers. Walsh also won 24 games in 1907 and worked 422 innings, but both figures were dwarfed by what he accomplished the following year.

In 1908, Walsh labored an American League record 464 innings, hurled 42 complete games, and became the last pitcher in major league history to notch 40 victories in a season. Notwithstanding his superhuman achievement, the White Sox finished third. The team's problem, a weak attack, was most glaringly in evidence on October 2 when Walsh ceded Cleveland just one run and fanned 15 batters but lost 1-0 because his mates were unable to get a single man on base against Addie Joss.

The Joss perfect-game defeat was typical of Walsh's fate all during his career with the White Sox. Two years later, when he led the AL with a magnificent 1.27 ERA, he nonetheless had a losing record (18-20) as the Sox hit just .211 and scored a meager 457 runs in 156 games.

Despite a woeful dearth of offensive support, Walsh never lacked for confidence in his own ability. Charles Dryden called him the only man who "could strut while standing still." Another Chicago writer, Ring Lardner, made Big Ed his model for Jack Keefe, the cocky bumpkin hero of *You Know Me Al*, the classic baseball novel.

Playing for the notoriously penurious Charlie Comiskey, Walsh never earned more than $7,000 in a season and usually had to pitch well over 400 innings just to avoid having his salary cut. By 1913, overwork had taken its toll, and he was never again a front-line hurler. Although Ed hung on until 1917, he won only 13 games in his last five seasons and thus ended his career five short of 200 victories. What he lacked in wins, however, he more than compensated for in other departments. His 1.82 career ERA is the lowest of all-time. Walsh was elected to the Hall of Fame in 1946.

Top: *Walsh's 1.82 career ERA is the best in history.* Left: *He adorned the White Sox club pennant in 1910. Owing to a lack of support, he lost 20 games and won but 18 despite pacing the majors with a 1.27 ERA.*

Major League Totals									
W	L	ERA	G	CG	IP	H	ER	BB	SO
195	126	1.82	430	250	2,964.1	2,346	598	617	1,736

TYRUS RAYMOND COBB
DETROIT·PHILADELPHIA, A.L.·1905-1928
LED AMERICAN LEAGUE IN BATTING
TWELVE TIMES AND CREATED OR
EQUALLED MORE MAJOR LEAGUE
RECORDS THAN ANY OTHER PLAYER.
RETIRED WITH 4191 MAJOR LEAGUE HITS.

Outfielder
Detroit Tigers 1906-1926
Philadelphia Athletics
    1927-1928
Manager
Detroit Tigers 1921-1926
479-444

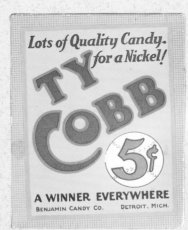

Above: *Cobb's name was used to promote virtually every product during the 1910s. Top: In 1927, though he was past 40, he was third in the AL in steals with 22. Below: Cobb's bat. At the end of his career, he set a single-game AL record for total bases (16) that still stands.*

WHEN THE FIRST HALL OF Fame vote was taken in 1936, Ty Cobb was named on 222 of the 226 ballots cast, to lead all candidates for enshrinement. The shock was not that "The Georgia Peach" outpolled every other player in major league history to that time, including Babe Ruth and Honus Wagner, but that four voters could ignore Cobb's towering credentials. This slight was understandable only when it was taken into consideration that he was not just the greatest player who ever lived—he was also the most despised.

Tyrus Raymond Cobb (1886-1961) himself saw no paradox in that. Throughout his life he contended that he was far from being a great athlete. What made him such a superb player was his unparalleled desire to achieve, to excel, and, above all, to win. No story better illustrates both his fiery determination and the reason for his unpopularity with opponents and teammates alike than the one told about a 1905 fracas between Cobb and Nap Rucker, his roommate while both were playing in the minors for Augusta. Rucker returned to their hotel room ahead of Cobb after a game and drew a bath for himself. When Cobb found him in the tub and began upbraiding him, Rucker only looked bewildered. "Don't you understand yet?" Cobb roared. "I've got to be first all the time—in everything."

About any other player but Cobb such a tale might seem apocryphal. In any case, there is no common explanation to account for zealous desire he brought to a baseball diamond. As a result of his unquenchable thirst to win and his reckless slides with spikes high whenever he tried to take a base, he was shunned by other players. Yet, if wanting to be first was what ignited Cobb, no one can deny that he got his wish. When he retired in 1928 after 24 seasons in the majors, he held almost every major career and single season batting and base-running record. Most have since been broken, owing largely to the longer schedule now played, but one that almost certainly never will be is his mark for the highest career batting average. Precious few players in the past half century have managed to hit .367 for one season, let alone a 24-year period.

Cobb's deepest regret was that he never played on a World Series winner. The closest he came to it was in 1909, when the Tigers took the Pirates to seven games before succumbing. Only age 22 at the time and playing on his third consecutive American League champion, Cobb seemed destined to play in many more World Series before he was done. Sadly, the 1909 classic proved to be his last taste of postseason competition.

Not just a slap hitter, Cobb could always go deep when the occasion warranted.

The First Millionaire Ballplayer

Not only was Ty Cobb one of the most competitive athletes of all time, he was also one of the shrewdest. Although he never made more than $80,000 in a season, he became the first millionaire athlete in America.

Cobb invested in a number of extremely successful ventures. In 1908, he began a lifelong friendship with Coca Cola chief executive Robert Woodruff. Cobb made endorsements for the fledgling Atlanta company and wisely took remuneration in stock. By the time he was named manager of the Tigers in 1921, he owned more than 20,000 shares of Coca Cola stock.

Early in his career Cobb would make it a point to hobnob with Detroit's business elite, picking up the information he wisely parlayed into major investments. His contract with Louisville Slugger allowed him free bats for his endorsement, the standard arrangement given to most major leaguers to this day.

Whether playing for an also-ran or a contender, though, Cobb gave the same relentless effort. It was thus difficult to credit a story that surfaced after he was fired as the Tigers player-manager following the 1926 season. Reportedly both he and Tris Speaker had helped rig a 1919 game between Detroit and Cleveland. The only part of the story that was consistent with the Cobb everyone knew was that it had been foreordained that Detroit would win the contest. Cobb, not even for all the money in the world, would ever have agreed to finish less than first in something.

Despite the 1926 scandal, Cobb was allowed to sign with the Philadelphia Athletics. He retired after two seasons in Philadelphia, never again to have a full-time job in baseball. For the next 33 years he continued to live on the terms under which he had played, comfortably fixed but essentially alone. Cobb died in Atlanta, Georgia, on July 17, 1961.

Major League Totals

BA	G	AB	R	H	2B	3B	HR	RBI	SB
.367	3,034	11,429	2,245	4,191	724	297	118	1,961	892

EDDIE COLLINS

EDWARD TROWBRIDGE COLLINS
PHILADELPHIA · CHICAGO
PHILADELPHIA, A.L.·1906-1930
FAMED AS BATSMAN, BASE RUNNER
AND SECOND BASEMAN AND ALSO AS
FIELD CAPTAIN. BATTED .333 DURING
MAJOR LEAGUE CAREER, SECOND ONLY
TO TY COBB IN MODERN BASE STEALING.
MADE 3313 HITS IN 2826 GAMES.

Second baseman
Philadelphia Athletics
    1906-1914; 1927-1930
Chicago White Sox
    1915-1926
Manager
Chicago White Sox
    1924-1926
174-160

Above: Baseball Magazine
*dressed Collins in a Sox uniform
for its March 1915 cover
though he had yet to wear one.*
Right: *Collins just once made
200 hits in a season. Consistency
and longevity were his
trademarks.*

JOHN McGRAW ONCE SAID THAT Eddie Collins was the best ballplayer he'd ever seen. Connie Mack (who managed both Collins and Nap Lajoie) called Collins the best second baseman he ever saw. Those are strong endorsements coming from two men who saw a lot of baseball. Collins played in 25 seasons, and turned in one outstanding season after another for nearly 20 years, and is arguably the greatest second baseman in history.

Edward Trowbridge Collins Sr. (1887-1951) was a college star for Columbia, but evidence that he appeared as a professional under an assumed name in six games in 1906 ended his amateur status. He joined Connie Mack's Philadelphia Athletics after graduation. Eddie teamed with Jack Barry at shortstop, Stuffy

In 1914, Collins received a Chalmers automobile as the AL's MVP.

McInnis at first, and Frank Baker at third to form the famous "$100,000 Infield." In Collins's first World Series, in 1910, he hit .429 and set four hitting records, after a regular season that included a then-record 81 stolen bases. In all, he won three championships with the A's.

When the Athletics were broken up and sold off after the devastating salary raids of the upstart Federal League, Collins fetched the highest price paid for a player until Babe Ruth went to the Yankees. The White Sox gave $50,000 for "Cocky" after his MVP 1914 season. He led the Sox to a World Series triumph in 1917. One of the clean players on the 1919 Black Sox, Eddie never forgave the eight players who sold out. The 1919 World Series was Eddie's last, but he left behind a stack of World Series records.

Collins hit for average and not power, but played in an era when power was not as much a part of the game as now. He finished with a .333 lifetime batting average and a .406 career on-base average. He hit over .340 ten times, and almost never struck out. Collins owns many fielding records for second basemen, including most putouts, assists, and total chances. Few have been able to match Eddie's abilities and longevity. His skill at adapting his aggressive style of play to the changing style of baseball may have been his greatest asset.

Collins was named player-manager of the White Sox in 1924 but never finished higher than fifth in his two years at the helm. He returned to Philadelphia in 1927 but played less and less until he retired from playing in 1930.

After retiring, Collins persuaded long-time friend Tom Yawkey to buy the BoSox. As the Red Sox general manager, Collins signed Ted Williams and Bobby Doerr during one trip. Eddie was enshrined in Cooperstown in 1939.

Major League Totals

BA	G	AB	R	H	2B	3B	HR	RBI	SB
.333	2,826	9,949	1,818	3,311	437	187	47	1,299	743

BILLY EVANS

WILLIAM GEORGE EVANS
UMPIRE AND EXECUTIVE
EMPLOYED BY AMERICAN LEAGUE IN
1906 AT AGE 22, MAKING HIM YOUNGEST
UMPIRE EVER IN MAJORS. SERVED ON A.L.
STAFF THROUGH 1927. OFFICIATED IN
SIX WORLD SERIES. GENERAL MANAGER
OF CLEVELAND INDIANS, 1927-1935. FARM
DIRECTOR OF BOSTON RED SOX 1936-1940
PRESIDENT OF SOUTHERN ASSOCIATION,
1942-1946. GENERAL MANAGER OF
DETROIT TIGERS, 1947-1951.

ALTHOUGH BORN IN CHICAGO, William George Evans (1884-1956) grew up in the Youngstown, Ohio, area. Evans matriculated at Cornell University. At Cornell he played four sports but only as a sideline. His future was charted clearly: He was going to be a lawyer.

After two years of college, however, Evans had to leave Cornell abruptly when his father died. He got a job as a reporter on the Youngstown *Vindicator*. Soon he moved up to the sports editor's position, where one of his assignments was to cover local semipro baseball games. At one of them he was drafted out of the stands to officiate when the regular umpire failed to show up. Although not smitten by the work, Evans continued doing it as a way of supplementing his income.

In 1905, while still working as a sportswriter, Billy joined the umpiring staff of the Ohio-Pennsylvania League. His work in that circuit was so impressive that he was hired by the American League for the 1906 season. Barely age 22 at the time, Evans became the youngest full-time umpire in major league history.

In his second season as an umpire, Billy nearly died when he was struck in the head by a bottle thrown by an irate fan at a Detroit-St. Louis game. The incident contributed to the banning of bottles at big league games. In 1910, Evans became the first active baseball figure to write a regular newspaper column. It proved so successful that it was syndicated to more than 100 newspapers.

On the field, Evans was instrumental in the number of umpires in a World Series game being increased in 1909 from two to four—at the time it was still common for umpires to work regular season games alone. Not above being pugnacious despite his "college-boy" image, Billy took Ty Cobb up on a challenge to a postgame fight in 1921 and emerged the loser but with Cobb's everlasting respect.

In 1927, Evans resigned his umpire's post to take a newly created job as general manager of the Cleveland Indians. Eight years later, refusing to accept a pay cut during the Depression, Billy left the Tribe to become farm director of the Red Sox. During World War II, Evans served as president of the Southern Association. In 1946 he returned to the major leagues as vice president and general manager of the Tigers, retiring in 1951. In 1973, Evans became the third umpire to be elected to the Hall of Fame.

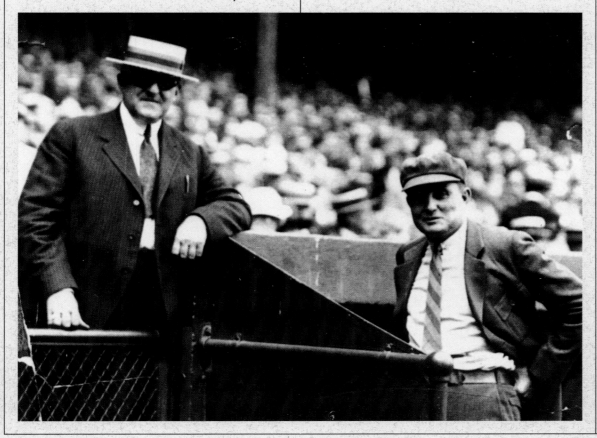

Evans poses at right in the dugout prior to umpiring a game at Yankee Stadium. In his early 40s, at an age when most arbiters are reaching their peak, Evans left to become general manager of the Indians.

WALTER PERRY JOHNSON
WASHINGTON–1907-1927
CONCEDED TO BE FASTEST BALL PITCHER
IN HISTORY OF GAME. WON 414 GAMES
WITH LOSING TEAM BEHIND HIM MANY YEARS
HOLDER OF STRIKE OUT AND SHUTOUT RECORDS

Pitcher
Washington Senators
 1907-1927
Manager
Washington Senators
 1929-1932
Cleveland Indians
 1933-1935
529-432

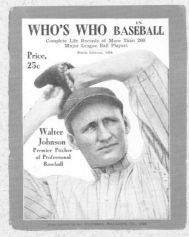

Above: *Johnson was an apt choice for the cover of the 1924 edition of* Who's Who in Baseball. *He rejuvenated his 37-year-old arm in 1924 to lead the AL in wins, Ks, and ERA.* Right: *He displays perfect hitting form. In 1925, he set a modern record for pitchers when he hit .433 and slugged .577.*

WHEN WALTER JOHNSON joined the Washington Senators in August 1907, they were the worst team in the American League. Then in their seventh year of existence, the Senators had yet to finish higher than sixth place or have a pitcher who won 20 games in a season.

Walter Perry Johnson (1887-1946) soon remedied the latter shortcoming, but not even his mammoth talents could immediately lift the team out of the nether regions. The Senators finished last or next to last in each of Walter's first five seasons with them even though he twice won 25 games. Then in 1912, Washington vaulted all the way to second place as Johnson seemingly had a career season with 32 wins, 303 strikeouts, and a 1.39 ERA. When Walter surpassed belief the following year, winning 36 games and posting a 1.09 ERA, the lowest in American League history by a pitcher with more than 300 innings, the Senators repeated their second-place finish. Eleven years would pass, however, before Washington again returned to contention, and by then Johnson seemed nearly done. He was age 36 and had not won more than 17 games in a season for four years.

Those who had written Walter off, though, were in for a surprise. In 1924, with Washington locked in a season-long battle with the Yankees for the pennant, Johnson paced the junior loop in winning percentage, strikeouts, and ERA. More important, his league-leading 23 wins played an essential role in bringing the Senators their first flag. In the World Series that fall, Johnson was beaten twice by the New York Giants but recovered to win the deciding seventh game in relief. The following season he spurred Washington to a second consecutive pennant when he again was a 20-game winner. The Pirates, however, proved him mortal in the World Series, topping him in the seventh game after he had twice bested them in earlier rounds.

Nicknamed "The Big Train" by sportswriter Grantland Rice, who was reminded of an express train by Walter's size and the velocity of his pitches, Johnson was also called "Barney" by intimates. Although race car driver Barney Oldfield was the source for the name, it was not inspired by Johnson's blazing fastball but rather by the reckless and erratic manner in which he operated an automobile. In any case, it was bestowed on Walter by his teammates with an affection that was wholly understandable. In his 21 years with the Senators, Johnson won 416

Universally well-liked, Johnson compiled a record 110 shutouts in his career.

The Lure of the Federal League

In 1913, Walter Johnson became the first pitcher to win the Chalmers Award. He was 36-7 with a league-leading 11 shutouts and 243 strikeouts. Historians have argued that this may have been the best season by any pitcher. Walter followed this season with 28 victories in 1914.

It was on the heels of such greatness that Johnson was lured from the Washington Senators by an offer to join the upstart Federal League for a guaranteed contract of $25,000 per season for three years. At the time Senators owner Clark Griffith was only paying his ace $12,000 per year.

When it appeared that Johnson was going to join the new league Griffith pleaded with American League President Ban Johnson to help him stop the move. When the AL President refused to contribute league funds to his effort, Griffith convinced White Sox owner Charles Comiskey that if he didn't want Walter Johnson pitching for the Chicago Federals, he had better advance $10,000.

games. No other pitcher in this century has won so many. More to the point, no other pitcher could have won nearly as many games with the teams for which Johnson played. Except for 1926, when he had little left, Johnson's winning percentage exceeded his team's winning percentage in every season that he worked 200 or more innings. Most of the time the difference was well over 100 points.

The Big Train retired as a player after the 1927 season when he was unable to rebound from a broken leg he sustained in a spring training inter-squad game. In 1929, Johnson was appointed manager of the Senators. Replaced in his fourth season at the Washington helm, Walter signed in 1933 to pilot Cleveland. As with most great players, nevertheless, Johnson did not make a good manager.

Johnson was elected to the Hall of Fame in 1936 along with Ty Cobb, Babe Ruth, Honus Wagner, and Christy Mathewson. It was only fitting that the greatest righthanded pitcher in history should be among the elite first group selected for enshrinement.

Major League Totals

W	L	ERA	G	CG	IP	H	ER	BB	SO
416	279	2.17	801	531	5,923.0	4,921	1,427	1,355	3,508

TRIS SPEAKER

TRISTRAM E. (TRIS) SPEAKER
BOSTON (A) 1909-15
CLEVELAND (A) 1916-26
WASHINGTON (A) 1927
PHILADELPHIA (A) 1928
GREATEST CENTREFIELDER OF HIS
DAY. LIFETIME MAJOR LEAGUE BATTING
AVERAGE OF .344. MANAGER IN 1920
WHEN CLEVELAND WON ITS FIRST
PENNANT AND WORLD CHAMPIONSHIP.

Outfielder
Boston Red Sox 1907-1915
Cleveland Indians
 1916-1926
Washington Senators 1927
Philadelphia Athletics
 1928
Manager
Cleveland Indians
 1919-1926
617-520

WHETHER TRIS SPEAKER WAS the greatest fielding center fielder of all time is an argument that can never finally be settled. All the statistical evidence shows that he was the best outfielder of his era, if not ever, and there is no dispute that he revolutionized outfield play more than any other performer in history. His achievements as a defensive player, however, are so prodigious that they can mask the fact that he was also an outstanding hitter.

Born in Hubbard, Texas, Tristram E Speaker (1888-1958) broke his right arm so badly as a child that he had to relearn how to bat and throw lefthanded. Originally a pitcher, Speaker moved into the outfield and from the beginning played such a shallow center field that he was in effect a fifth infielder at times. In the dead-ball era, when long drives were rare, other outfielders copied Speaker in order to cut down on bloop hits. With the coming of the lively ball era in the early 1920s, however, many observers believed that Speaker's style of play would be rendered outdated. In a sense, they were right. The sudden explosion of long hits made playing shallow impossible—for virtually every outfielder but Speaker.

WHO'S WHO in BASEBALL

Tris joined the Boston Red Sox for good near the end of the 1908 season. A lackluster team at the time, Boston quickly vaulted back into contention because of Speaker's presence. In 1912, he played on his first of two World Championship teams in the Hub while pacing the American League in doubles, home runs, and on-base percentage. During his career, "The Grey Eagle" topped the junior circuit in two-base hits a record eight times, amassing 792 doubles, more than any other player in history.

A salary dispute resulted in his being traded to Cleveland after the 1915 season. In his first year with the Indians, he wrested the batting crown from Ty Cobb. In July 1919, the Indians named Speaker player-manager. Under his guidance Cleveland shot up to second place. In 1920, Cleveland gained its first pennant with Tris batting .388.

In December 1926, he suddenly quit the Indians without explanation. A few weeks later it emerged that he feared being implicated in an alleged plot to fix a game in 1919 between Detroit and Cleveland with Ty Cobb. The two stars were exonerated, though, when Dutch Leonard, a former pitcher who bore a grudge against both Cobb and Speaker, refused to confront the pair in person with his accusations of their crime.

In 1937, Speaker was named to the Hall of Fame.

Top: *Speaker earned the 1917 cover of* Who's Who in Baseball *by breaking Ty Cobb's stranglehold on the AL hitting crown in 1916. Tris rapped .386 in his first season with Cleveland.* Right: *While his reputation was built with his glove, Tris was one of the best hitters in history.*

Major League Totals

BA	G	AB	R	H	2B	3B	HR	RBI	SB
.344	2,789	10,208	1,881	3,515	792	223	117	1,559	433

HOME RUN BAKER

JOHN FRANKLIN BAKER (1886-1963) was born on a farm in Trappe, Maryland, the only home he ever knew. After flunking a brief trial with the Baltimore Orioles of the Eastern League in 1907, Frank in '08 joined Reading of the Tri-State League on the recommendation of Buck Herzog, a fellow Marylander who saw promise in the young third sacker. Herzog was virtually alone, though, in his estimation of Baker's talents. It came as a surprise to most observers when Connie Mack purchased Baker for the Philadelphia Athletics on August 28, 1908.

Baker comprised part of what for three years, starting in 1912, was known as the "$100,000 Infield." The other three members were first baseman Stuffy McInnis, second baseman Eddie Collins, and shortstop Jack Barry. The 1912 season was also Baker's best; he led the AL in both homers and RBI and hit .347, a record for junior circuit third basemen that stood until 1980, when George Brett batted .390.

Baker's tenure with the A's remained pleasurable and productive until the finish of the 1914 season. After the A's were swept embarrassingly in the World Series by the "Miracle" Braves, Mack opted to break up his team by either trading high-salaried stars or refusing to pay them what they were worth. Baker was in the latter category. He sat out the entire 1915 campaign when Mack stubbornly refused to give him a raise. The following year, the Yankees purchased Baker from the A's for $35,000. A year away from the game apparently affected Baker. In 1916, he had his poorest season, hitting just .269, and was never again an important offensive force in the majors.

When his first wife died in 1920, Baker again chose to retire temporarily. He returned to the Yankees the following spring, just in time to play on the club's first pennant winner. He retired, this time for good, in 1922. He was elected to the Hall of Fame in 1955.

Third baseman
Philadelphia Athletics
1908-1914
New York Yankees
1916-1919; 1921-1922

Above: *Baker led the AL in homers four years in a row.* Right: *He led the AL 16 times in fielding categories.*

By the conclusion of the 1909 season, Mack's judgment was more than vindicated. In his rookie season Baker hit .305 and 19 triples, still an American League yearling record.

Two years later Baker received his nickname of "Home Run" when he topped the AL in four-baggers and clubbed two more homers in the World Series that fall against the New York Giants. The first came off Rube Marquard, who was chastised the next day in a newspaper column by Christy Mathewson for pitching "carelessly" to Baker. By that evening Mathewson himself had been victimized by the new slugging star, surrendering a game-tying home run in the ninth inning.

			Major League Totals						
BA	G	AB	R	H	2B	3B	HR	RBI	SB
.307	1,575	5,985	887	1,838	313	103	96	1,103	235

RICHARD WILLIAM MARQUARD
"RUBE"
NEW YORK N.L., BROOKLYN N.L.,
CINCINNATI N.L., BOSTON N.L.
1908-1925
THREE-TIME 20-GAME WINNER WITH
GIANT CHAMPIONS OF 1911-12-13. TIED ALL-TIME
RECORD WITH 19 VICTORIES IN A ROW WHILE
WINNING 26 AND LOSING 11 IN 1912. LED
N.L. IN WINNING PERCENTAGE AND
STRIKEOUTS IN 1911. TIED FOR MOST
VICTORIES, 1912. HURLED NO-HIT GAME
AGAINST DODGERS IN 1915.

Pitcher
New York Giants
    1908-1915
Brooklyn Dodgers
    1915-1920
Cincinnati Reds 1921
Boston Braves 1922-1925

A SANDLOT STAR IN HIS HOME-town of Cleveland, Ohio, Richard William Marquard (1889-1980) signed his first contract with Indianapolis in 1907. After two strong years on the farm, the Giants purchased the tall lefty's contract for a then-record $11,000. He joined the Giants as an 18-year-old rookie in 1908, just in time to watch Fred Merkle make his infamous boner. Marquard became a footnote to the exhilarating 1908 pennant race when he was pushed around in his greatly anticipated debut.

An Indianapolis newspaper tagged him with the name "Rube," not because of his physical resemblance to the great Rube Waddell, but rather because his pitching abilities were reminiscent of Waddell. The thin Marquard (6'3", 180 pounds) had two mediocre seasons in 1909 and 1910 before he exploded in 1911. Rube went 25-7 that year, leading the league in winning percentage and strikeouts. Teamed with ace Christy Mathewson, Marquard led the Giants to the first of three consecutive pennants. In the World Series that fall, it was a Marquard fastball that Frank Baker of the Athletics turned on, knocking it out of the park, thus earning the nickname "Home Run."

Rube turned in his best seasons for McGraw's Giants in those three pennant years, 1911 to '13. He won 73 games and lost just 28 in that span, including 19 straight in 1912, tying the mark set by Tim Keefe. Marquard was good in the 1911 Series, terrific in 1912, and bad in 1913, but to little effect; the Giants lost all three championships. He compiled a 201-177 lifetime record by relying on pinpoint control and a forkball and changeup rather than a fastball, insisting he never once had a sore arm.

When Rube bombed to 12-22 in 1914, McGraw lost patience with him. McGraw was spoiled, because during the flag-winning years the New Yorkers also had front-line hurlers Jeff Tesreau, Doc Crandall, Red Ames, Al Demaree, and Hooks Wiltse, besides Matty. In 1915, Marquard arranged his own trade to Brooklyn, with the Giants receiving the minimum waiver fee. In his first two full seasons with the Dodgers, Rube was 13-6 and 19-12, his last outstanding seasons. He appeared in two more World Series with the Dodgers but came up short both years. He pitched with Cincinnati and Boston before retiring after the 1925 season.

A popular personality with show-business aspirations, Marquard appeared in vaudeville sketches, and in several movies and skits with his wife, Broadway actress Blossom Seeley, during his baseball career. He managed and scouted for several minor league teams before working for many years at horse racetracks in Florida and Maryland. The Veterans Committee recognized Rube Marquard in 1971.

Top: *Etched on this leather premium is an image of Marquard, the National League's best southpaw for three consecutive seasons in the early 1910s.* Right: *In World Series action, Rube, unfortunately, fared poorly, suffering five defeats in seven decisions.*

			Major League Totals						
W	**L**	**ERA**	**G**	**CG**	**IP**	**H**	**ER**	**BB**	**SO**
201	177	3.08	536	197	3,306.2	3,233	1,130	858	1,593

ANDREW FOSTER (1878-1930) RAN away from home, like many teenage boys, to become a baseball player. Only this was the 1890s, and Foster was an African-American. The few cracks in organized ball that the occasional black player had slipped through were closed by then, and it was a hard life for black ballplayers. Foster did his best to make it better, earning the title, "Father of Black Baseball."

An outstanding pitcher in the first decade of the 20th century, Foster was a big man with a big fastball. He joined the Cuban-X Giants in 1902, and after an initial defeat, won 44 games in a row. He pitched and prevailed in four of the five black World Series games against the Philadelphia Giants. That year he also beat Rube Waddell, of the pennant-winning Athletics, appropriating his nickname in the contest. Foster drew raves from black and white players alike. The Chicago *Inter-Ocean* wrote: "Rube Foster is a pitcher with the tricks of a Radbourne, with the speed of a Rusie, and with the coolness and deliberation of a Cy Young."

In 1909, Foster was pitching for the Leland Giants in Chicago when he wrested control of the team from owner Frank Leland. Rube led the renamed American Giants to prominence as the top black team in the country. As a manager he was John McGraw's counterpart, using every one-run strategy of the bunt and the hit-and-run, and even his own unique bunt-and-run, to give every edge to his speedy team. His team packed the old White Sox park, giving the AL Sox in Comiskey Park and the crosstown Cubs a run for their attendance money.

In 1919, Foster put together the Negro National League, an eight-team league with seven black owners. It took a substantial, sustained effort, and much of his own money. Rube often worked 15-hour days with no pay. He even had to send his own players to bolster the other teams in the league at times. Foster had a dream, and he drummed it into the heads of the players of his times. He wanted them to play at a high level of excellence, so that when integration finally came about, black players would be ready. The effort finally got to Foster. In 1926, he was taken to an asylum after a spate of erratic behavior. He died in 1930 in Chicago and his funeral drew an immense crowd. The dream came true, however, and the players were ready. Foster was inducted in the Hall of Fame in 1981.

Foster's place in baseball history is similar to that of both Alexander Cartwright and Henry Chadwick as a pioneer and an organizer.

ANDREW (RUBE) FOSTER

RATED FOREMOST MANAGER AND EXECUTIVE IN HISTORY OF NEGRO LEAGUES. ACCLAIMED TOP PITCHER IN BLACK BASEBALL FOR NEARLY A DECADE IN EARLY 1900'S. FORMED CHICAGO AMERICAN GIANTS IN 1911 AND BUILT THEM INTO MIDWEST'S DOMINANT BLACK TEAM. IN 1920 HE ORGANIZED NEGRO NATIONAL LEAGUE. HEADED LEAGUE AND MANAGED CHICAGO TEAM UNTIL RETIREMENT FOLLOWING 1926 SEASON.

Pitcher; executive teams include:
Chicago Union Giants, Cuban Giants, Cuban X-Giants, Philadelphia Giants, Chicago Leland Giants, Chicago American Giants 1902-1926

Foster's statistics are unavailable.

Among the many teams Foster pitched for in the first decade of the century was the Royal Pongiana club.

Outfielder
Boston Red Sox 1909-1920
Chicago White Sox
        1921-1925

Top: *Hooper is the only outfielder in the Hall of Fame who hit .235 in mid-career— and for a pennant winner—and never had more tha 80 RBI in a season.* Right: *It's probable that few Red Sox fans ever learned all the words to this ditty, but all quickly mastered the refrain: "Hoop, hoop, Hooper" was chanted at Sox games from 1909 to 1920.*

Harry Hooper is the only outfielder who was elected to the Hall of Fame primarily because of his defensive skills. Although he made 2,466 hits and was an excellent leadoff batter with good speed, Hooper was never a league leader in a single major offensive department.

A native of Santa Clara County in California, Harry Bartholomew Hooper's (1887-1974) driving ambition was to become an engineer. While at St. Mary's College, however, he joined the Oakland team in the outlaw California State League to help pay his tuition. During the 1907 season, Charlie Graham, manager of the Sacramento club, purchased Harry and cajoled him to play in Sacramento on the agreement that he was free to quit the game anytime and pursue an engineering career. When Harry did well for Sacramento, however, he opted to play a second year there.

During the 1908 campaign, Boston Red Sox owner John Taylor saw Hooper play while visiting his wife's relatives in California. Urged by Graham to give major league baseball a whirl, Harry agreed to go east when Taylor offered Hooper a contract for $2,800. As a further inducement, Taylor told Hooper that the Red

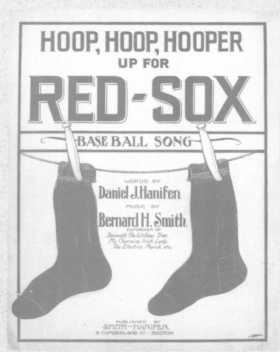

Sox might utilize his engineering knowledge in building Fenway Park, then still in the planning steps.

Hooper never again worked as an engineer and had no role in the construction of Fenway Park, but he was an important cog on four Red Sox World Championship teams during the 1910s. Stationed in right field, he played beside Tris Speaker, arguably the greatest center fielder in history. Speaker played so shallow that Hooper was left to cover not only his position but also balls hit to deep right-center field. The left fielder on the club, Duffy Lewis, also was a very good, fast fielder. Until the threesome was broken up after the 1915 season, they were the most famous outfield trio of their time.

In 1915, after hitting a personal-low .235, Hooper emerged as the hero of the World Series against the Philadelphia Phillies. In the fifth and final game, played at Philadelphia, Hooper hit two ground-rule home runs into the temporary seats built around the outfield. The second blow gave the Red Sox a 5-4 win and their second World Championship during Hooper's tenure with the club.

Harry remained in Boston until 1921 when the Red Sox traded him to the Chicago White Sox, where he played five seasons. After a stint in the minors, Hooper served two years as the head baseball coach at Princeton University. He was named to the Hall of Fame in 1971.

Major League Totals

BA	G	AB	R	H	2B	3B	HR	RBI	SB
.281	2,308	8,785	1,429	2,466	389	160	75	817	375

Outfielder
Brooklyn Superbas
(Dodgers, Robins)
1909-1926
Philadelphia Athletics
1927

AFTER WINNING THE NATIONAL League pennant in 1900, the Brooklyn Dodgers fell upon hard times. Throughout most of the 20th century's first decade they were one of the most uninspired teams in the majors. That began to change in 1909 when Zachariah Davis Wheat (1888-1972) joined them in September after being purchased from Mobile of the Southern Association. For the next 17 years Wheat occupied left field for the Dodgers. By the time he left the team at the finish of the 1927 season, he held almost every existing Brooklyn Dodgers career offensive record. Only three of his marks—for runs, home runs, and stolen bases—were subsequently broken.

A quiet, almost colorless performer, Wheat was never ejected from a game by an umpire. Later in his career, when the team acquired a reputation for zaniness under manager Wilbert Robinson, Wheat was something of an anachronism. Not only did he never argue with umpires, he got along well with Brooklyn owner Charlie Ebbets, the bane of several other Dodgers players, and on two occasions even lent Ebbets money to help him out of financial straits. So popular was Wheat with Brooklyn fans that local advertisers outdid their imaginations to link him to their products. One year there was a billboard on the outfield wall in Ebbets Field

that read: "Zach Wheat caught 400 flies last season—Tanglewood Fly Paper Caught 10 million."

Wheat played on his first pennant winner in 1916 and had his finest season to date that same year when he topped the National League in slugging average and total bases. Two years later, in 1918, Zach led the senior loop in batting but notched the fewest total bases ever by a hit crown winner with over 400 at bats, as he became the last batting leader in NL history to go homerless for an entire season. In 1918 the dead-ball era was still in full sway, but beginning two years later, when the advent of Babe Ruth abruptly changed the nature of the game, Wheat joined in the increased offensive output. Although never a slugger, Zach regularly began posting home run totals in double figures.

After hitting well above .350 three straight seasons, Wheat sagged to .290 in 1926 and was accused of not hustling. The actual culprit, however, was age. Nearing age 40, Zach was released by the Dodgers and caught on with the Philadelphia A's for one last season. After batting .324 in 88 games for Connie Mack's 1927 crew, Wheat played a few months for Minneapolis in the American Association and then retired. Wheat was named to the Hall of Fame in 1959.

Top: *Baseball Magazine of August 1925 identified Wheat (left) as the new Brooklyn manager. In truth, however, Wheat never really managed the Dodgers. Although Wheat was appointed manager by president Wilbert Robinson, Robinson was still the manager.* Left: *Wheat compiled 2,884 hits, all but 80 of them in a Brooklyn uniform.*

Major League Totals

BA	G	AB	R	H	2B	3B	HR	RBI	SB
.317	2,410	9,106	1,289	2,884	476	172	132	1,261	205

RAYMOND WILLIAM SCHALK
CHICAGO A.L. 1912 TO 1928
NEW YORK N.L. 1929
HOLDER OF MAJOR LEAGUE RECORD FOR
MOST YEARS LEADING CATCHER IN FIELDING,
EIGHT YEARS; MOST PUTOUTS, NINE YEARS;
MOST ASSISTS IN ONE MAJOR LEAGUE (1810)
MOST CHANCES ACCEPTED (8965). CAUGHT
FOUR NO-HIT GAMES INCLUDING PERFECT
GAME IN 1922.

Catcher
Chicago White Sox
    1912-1928
New York Giants 1929

Manager
Chicago White Sox
    1927-1928
102-125

Wilson used Schalk's name to sell catcher's mitts. He holds the record for catching the most no-hitters.

RAY SCHALK'S CAREER BATTING average of .253 is the lowest of any position player in the Hall of Fame. That he was selected for enshrinement in 1955 is largely a tribute to his outstanding defensive skills. Schalk's one claim to fame from an offensive standpoint is that in 1915 he stole 30 bases, a record for an American League receiver until it was broken in 1982 by John Wathan.

Born in Harvel, Illinois, Raymond William Schalk (1892-1970) played semipro ball in 1911 after leaving high school until a minor league team offered him $65 a month to sign. He hit well in the low minors, but he was not a superb batsman thereafter in the high minor leagues. After a two and one-half year training period in the minors, Schalk joined the Chicago White Sox in August 1912. He was promoted solely on his catching skills, but many in the ChiSox organization (including Charles Comiskey himself) were skeptical that Ray would stick around the Windy City for long. Except for a five-game stint with the New York Giants in 1929, his last major league season, Ray never played for any other team.

The White Sox regular backstopper from nearly the day he arrived in Chicago until 1927, he caught 100 or more games for 11 straight seasons at one point in his career, at the time a

When Schalk retired in 1929, he held the major league records for most games caught (1,726) and putouts (7,171).

major league record. When Schalk retired, he held the mark for most games played behind the plate with 1,726. Though all his longevity records have since been broken, his 176 career stolen bases are still the most by a catcher.

Ray was on pennant winning teams in 1917 and again in 1919. The latter club, considered to be the best in White Sox history, is infamous for having had eight players who conspired to throw the World Series to the Cincinnati Reds. Schalk, second baseman Eddie Collins, and right fielder Nemo Leibold were the only regulars who were not part of the Black Sox cabal. Ray not only had a fine World Series in 1919, hitting .304 while catching in all eight games, but tried valiantly to the thwart the fixers. He knew something was amiss because Eddie Cicotte and Lefty Williams, the club's two mound aces who were both part of the conspiracy, continually crossed him up on pitches.

In 1927, with Schalk's playing career nearing its end, the White Sox named him player-manager. He lasted on the job only a season and a half. Ray remained one of the White Sox' most loyal supporters until his death in Chicago from cancer on May 19, 1970.

				Major League Totals					
BA	G	AB	R	H	2B	3B	HR	RBI	SB
.253	1,760	5,306	579	1,345	199	48	12	594	176

JOHN HENRY LLOYD
"POP"
NEGRO LEAGUES 1906-1932
REGARDED AS FINEST SHORTSTOP TO PLAY
IN NEGRO BASEBALL. SCIENTIFIC HITTER
BATTED OVER .400 SEVERAL TIMES DURING
HIS 27-YEAR CAREER. PERSONIFIED BEST
QUALITIES OF ATHLETE BOTH ON AND OFF
FIELD. INSTRUMENTAL IN HELPING OPEN
YANKEE STADIUM TO NEGRO BASEBALL IN
1930. MANAGED MORE THAN TEN SEASONS.

Shortstop; first baseman; catcher; manager teams include:
Macon Acmes, Cuban X-Giants, Brooklyn Royal Giants, Philadelphia Giants, Leland Giants, New York Lincoln Giants, Chicago American Giants, Columbus Buckeyes, Atlantic City Bacharach Giants, Philadelphia Hilldales, New York Harlem Stars 1905-1932

POP LLOYD FIRST JUMPED FROM semipro baseball to the black professional leagues in 1905 at age 21, and was a good enough player to play semipro until he was age 58. He was a very good defensive shortstop for most of the early days in his career, and he showcased a line-drive stroke that drove his average to dizzying heights.

Born in northeast Florida, John Henry Lloyd (1884-1964) started playing semipro ball in his midteens. Moving to the Cuban X-Giants in 1905, Pop, like other gifted players of his generation, began his career as a catcher. By 1907, he was a shortstop and a cleanup hitter. Lloyd played for whatever team could pay him. He spent time on various Philadelphia teams, New York and New Jersey teams, and with the Chicago American Giants, among others. As a star player, Lloyd was in demand for All-Star games and tours to Cuba and the West Coast, but the uncertain financial situation of the black leagues forced him to miss spring training at times in order to work a conventional job.

In a 1910 12-game exhibition series in Cuba against the Detroit Tigers, Lloyd went 11-for-22. While the Bengals won seven games, Ty Cobb (who batted .370) was sufficiently embarrassed to vow never to play against blacks again. In 1914, Rube Foster enticed Pop to play for the Chicago American Giants. In the Windy City he teamed with "Home Run" Johnson in a legendary double-play combination. He helped lead the American Giants to championships in 1914 and 1917.

Lloyd was often likened to Honus Wagner, a comparison Wagner was proud to acknowledge. It was an apt analogy, because like Honus, Lloyd was highly regarded, was a terrific hitter, and was known to scoop up dirt and pebbles along with ground balls. From his playing days in Cuba, Pop's other nickname was *"El Cuchara,"* Spanish for "The Shovel."

At age 44 in 1928, still in the pros, Pop hit .564 in 37 games, with 11 homers and 10 steals. The next year, he hit .388. Pitcher Sam Streeter said "Everything he hit was just like you were hanging out clothes on a line." Not only was Pop a great hitter, but he had an intimate knowledge of the game. In 1915, Lloyd had the first of many stints as a player-manager, and in 1921 he took charge of the short-lived Columbus, Ohio, franchise in Rube Foster's new Negro National League. It was there that he finally acquired his nickname, and he was mentor to a new generation. He was named to the Hall of Fame in 1977.

Left: The umpire autographing a ball for some lucky fan is Pop Lloyd. He added arbitrating to his numerous baseball roles after his days as an active major Negro League player.
Top: He continued to perform, however, for semipro teams until he was deep into his 50s.

		Negro League Totals*					
BA	**G**	**AB**	**H**	**2B**	**3B**	**HR**	**SB**
.368	477	1,769	651	90	18	26	56

*Note: Lloyd's stats are games that were recorded from 1914 to 1932 only.

EDGAR CHARLES (SAM) RICE
WASHINGTON, A.L. 1915 TO 1933
CLEVELAND, A.L. 1934
AT BAT 600 OR MORE TIMES EIGHT
DIFFERENT SEASONS, HAD 200 OR MORE HITS
IN EACH OF SIX SEASONS. BATTED .322
FOR 20-YEAR CAREER AND HAD 2,987 HITS.
SET A.L. RECORD WITH 182 SINGLES IN
1925. LED A.L. IN NUMBER OF HITS 216
IN 1924 AND 1926. LED A.L. IN PUTOUTS
FOR OUTFIELDERS WITH 454 IN 1920 AND
385 IN 1922.

Outfielder
Washington Senators
1915-1933
Cleveland Indians 1934

Top: After being released by Washington, Rice signed with Cleveland and held down right field for the Indians in 1934 at age 44.

BY THE TIME THAT SENATORS skipper Clark Griffith gave Sam Rice a job in the Washington outfield late in the 1916 season, Rice was already past 26 years old. Sam seemed unlikely to wind up playing 20 years in the major leagues, let alone to compile more hits than any other player in Washington history, particularly since he missed most of the 1918 season while serving in the Army. Upon returning to the Senators in 1919 at age 29, with only one full season as a regular under his belt, Rice embarked on a tear that would leave him only 13 hits short of the hallowed 3,000 total when he retired 15 years later.

Edgar Charles Rice (1890-1974) enlisted in the Navy in 1913. While aboard the U.S.S. *Hampshire*, Rice pitched for the ship's baseball team and drew the attention of the Petersburg club in the Virginia League. Signing with Petersburg when his Navy hitch was up, he closed the 1914 season with nine wins and also hit .310 while playing the outfield occasionally. In August 1915, Rice was sold to Washington. Still pitching, his mound work failed to impress Griffith during the 1915 season. Griffith switched Sam to the outfield full-time at the end of 1916.

Rice's prime years were in the middle 1920s. During a four-year span he led the American League twice in hits and once in triples. Additionally, he played on Washington's first two pennant-winning teams in 1924 and 1925. After hitting just .214 in the 1924 World Series, Sam covered himself with glory in fall play the next year as he batted .364 with 12 hits, a Series

record that endured until 1964. The greatest moment of Rice's career, however, came in the eighth inning of the third game when he snared a long drive off the bat of Pittsburgh's Earl Smith while tumbling into the temporary right field bleachers in Griffith Stadium. Pirates players vehemently insisted that Rice dropped the ball when he landed in the seats, but umpire Cy Rigler ruled it a fair catch. Asked whether he had held the ball, Rice was evasive but later sent a sealed letter to the Hall of Fame that was not to be opened until after his death. After he died, in 1974, the letter revealed that Rice asserted, "At no time did I lose possession of the ball."

Rice's inclusion in the Hall of Fame was delayed for many years because he was 13 hits shy of 3,000 base hits. In 1934, when Sam retired, making 3,000 hits was not considered particularly important. As it was, he had to wait until 1963 to be named to Cooperstown.

Rice was age 43 when this card appeared. He is one of a very few players to make more hits after age 40 than before age 30.

Major League Totals

BA	G	AB	R	H	2B	3B	HR	RBI	SB
.322	2,404	9,269	1,515	2,987	497	184	34	1,078	351

MAX CAREY

AX CAREY WAS BORN MAXI-
millian Carnarius (1890-1976) in Terre
Haute, Indiana, to deeply religious German
parents. He entered Concordia College in Fort
Wayne, intending to become a Lutheran minister.
Before his senior year, though, his career plans
changed after he saw a minor league game and
felt he could do better than most of the players in
it. Signed after a tryout, he changed his name to
Max Carey to protect his college eligibility.

A weak-hitting shortstop in his first season,
Carey was converted to the outfield in 1910.
When his hitting improved and his extraordinary
speed on the bases became apparent, he was
purchased by the Pirates.

Almost from the day Carey arrived in
Pittsburgh, Pirates star Honus Wagner took
him under his wing. Wagner counseled Carey to
take extra care to keep his legs in shape, believing
that speed was the tool with which Carey would
make his mark. A righthanded hitter like Wagner,
but without Wagner's power or ability to handle
breaking balls, Carey also saw the wisdom of
learning to switch-hit.

Brooklyn was in contention for the NL flag when
this edition of Baseball Magazine hit the stands
in June 1932.

Beginning in 1911, Max became a fixture in
the Pittsburgh outfield for 16 years. A left field
fill-in at first for injured player-manager Fred
Clarke, Max was switched to center when Clarke
returned to the lineup and given the assignment
of batting leadoff. Carey swiftly demonstrated
his skills were tailor-made for the job. He twice
topped the National League in walks, regularly
led the Pirates in runs, and ten times copped the
senior loop stolen base crown. In the process, he
swiped 738 cushions, a modern National League
record that lasted until Lou Brock broke it
in 1974.

During the late 1910s, with Clarke gone and
Wagner on the wane, the Pirates were a lackluster
team, but Carey gave Pittsburgh fans hope of
better days to come and daily excitement in the
meantime. A scientific base-stealer who mastered
his craft by diligently studying pitchers and
learning their pickoff moves, Carey was the rare
thief who grew better as he grew older. In 1921,
with base-stealing nearly a forgotten part of the
game, Pirates fans were treated to the sight of
Carey pilfering 51 sacks in 53 attempts, a record
for proficiency that has never been surpassed.

Waived to Brooklyn in 1926, Max managed
that team for two seasons. Carey was inducted
into the Hall of Fame in 1961.

MAX GEORGE CAREY
PITTSBURGH N.L. 1910-1926, 1930
BROOKLYN N.L. 1926-1929, 1932-1933
HOLDS NATIONAL LEAGUE RECORDS FOR OUT-
FIELDERS: GAMES PLAYED, 2421; PUT OUTS,
6363; ASSISTS, 339; TOTAL CHANGES,
6702. MODERN LEAGUE RECORD FOR MOST
STOLEN BASES, 738. MAJOR LEAGUE RECORD
MOST YEARS LEADING LEAGUE IN STOLEN
BASES, 10. BATTING AVERAGE .285 FOR
20 SEASONS. IN 1922 51 STOLEN BASES
IN 53 ATTEMPTS.

Outfielder
Pittsburgh Pirates
1910-1926
Brooklyn Dodgers
1926-1929

Manager
Brooklyn Dodgers
1932-1933
146-161

Left: *At the plate, Carey was an
line-drive hitter. His base
thievery gave him an extra
dimension. Even though he
began his professional career as
a shortstop, Max never played
a single inning in the majors
anywhere but in the outfield.*

			Major League Totals						
BA	G	AB	R	H	2B	3B	HR	RBI	SB
.285	2,476	9,363	1,545	2,665	419	159	69	800	738

GROVER CLEVELAND ALEXANDER
GREAT NATIONAL LEAGUE PITCHER
FOR TWO DECADES WITH PHILLIES,
CUBS AND CARDINALS STARTING
IN 1911. WON 1926 WORLD CHAMPIONSHIP
FOR CARDINALS BY STRIKING OUT
LAZZERI WITH BASES FULL IN
FINAL CRISIS AT YANKEE STADIUM.

Pitcher
Philadelphia Phillies
1911-1917; 1930
Chicago Cubs 1918-1926
St. Louis Cardinals
1926-1929

Right: World War I vet Alexander was featured on the cover of Who's Who in Baseball. *After returning, he paced the 1919 NL with a 1.72 ERA and nine shutouts. Top: After he won 30 games for the 1917 Phillies, he was traded, in part because the Phils didn't want to meet his salary demands. The Phils had to wait 33 years before they again had a 20-game winner (Robin Roberts in 1950).*

GROVER CLEVELAND ALEXANDER (1887-1950) paced the New York State League at age 23 with 29 wins in 1910, and Syracuse sold him to the Philadelphia Phillies for $750.

With the acquisition of Alexander, the Phillies almost instantly became a contender. In 1911, "Pete" won 28 games, a modern rookie record, and also set National League rookie marks for strikeouts and shutouts that have since been broken.

Pete's seven years in Philadelphia were the most successful and probably the happiest of his life. In 1915, his 31 wins spearheaded the Phillies to their only pennant before 1950. The following season Alexander scored a personal-high 33 victories and notched an all-time record 16 shutouts. When he won 30 again in 1917, he became the last pitcher to be a 30-game winner in two consecutive seasons, let alone three.

With the United States involved in World War I, the Phillies traded Pete to the Cubs, thinking he would soon be drafted. After pitching just three games for the Cubs in 1918, Pete was sent to France with the 89th Infantry Division. Serving on the front lines, he lost the hearing in

WHO'S WHO in BASEBALL

FACTS FOR FANS

PRICE 15c.

GROVER CLEVELAND ALEXANDER

Published by the BASEBALL MAGAZINE CO. 70 FIFTH AVE. NEW YORK

Copyrighted, 1919, by the Baseball Magazine Co., N. Y.

one ear as a result of a shelling and also began experiencing the first symptoms of epilepsy. Between the illness and the shell shock he had suffered, Alexander came to rely more and more on alcohol for solace.

Upon his return from overseas, Pete rejoined the Cubs and had several outstanding years with Chicago. Waived to the Cardinals in early 1926, now known as "Old Pete," he came to St. Louis with a chronic sore arm and a reputation for no longer being able to keep his drinking under control. In the Mound City his arm revived, however, enabling him to win nine games for the Cardinals down the stretch and the stage to be set for the most dramatic moment of his career.

In the 1926 World Series against the Yankees, Pete won both the second and sixth games in a starting role and then went out on the town, believing his work to be done. But in game seven, when New York loaded the bases in the seventh inning with two out, Alexander was called out of the bullpen to protect a 3-2 St. Louis lead. Despite nursing a monumental hangover, he proceeded to fan rookie slugging sensation Tony Lazzeri on four pitches. Pete then set down the vaunted New Yorkers in the final two innings without surrendering a hit.

Pete won 21 games in 1927, the ninth and last time he reached the magic circle. His professional career ended in 1930, and he was named to the Hall of Fame in 1938.

Major League Totals

W	L	ERA	G	CG	IP	H	ER	BB	SO
373	208	2.56	696	438	5,189.1	4,868	1,474	953	2,199

CONNIE MACK

A STAR CATCHER BUT FAMED MORE AS MANAGER OF THE PHILADELPHIA ATHLETICS SINCE 1901. WINNER OF 9 PENNANTS AND 5 WORLD CHAMPIONSHIPS. RECEIVED THE BOK AWARD IN PHILADELPHIA FOR 1929.

Manager
Pittsburgh Pirates
1894-1896
Philadelphia Athletics
1901-1950

CONNIE MACK HAD THE LONG-est career on a baseball field that any man has ever had—66 years as a player and manager, starting in the 19th century and lasting through the first half of the 20th.

Like many managers, Cornelius Alexander Mack (born McGillicuddy, 1862-1956) was a catcher in his playing days, a soft hitter who lasted 11 years starting in 1886. Mack became player-manager in 1894 with the Pittsburgh Pirates, taking over a talented but disappointing team. The club remained in relatively the same position the next two years that he was the manager, and he was fired after the 1896 season.

At that point one of Mack's friends, Western League commissioner Ban Johnson, invited Connie to pilot the Milwaukee franchise, which he did for four years. In 1901, when Johnson elevated the status of the minor circuit to the major American League, he gave the Philadelphia franchise to Connie. Mack remained the A's manager through the 1950 season.

Mack first gained attention for his "White Elephants" in 1901 by buying star Napoleon Lajoie away from the crosstown NL Phillies. Lajoie was gone in 1902, but Mack built a championship club around pitchers Eddie Plank, Rube Waddell, and Chief Bender, to win pennants in 1902 and 1905. Behind hurlers Bender and Jack Coombs, and the "$100,000 Infield" (featuring second baseman Eddie Collins), the A's won three World Championships in 1910, '11, and '13.

The upstart Federal League had begun to raid the two established leagues, and Mack could see his team unraveling as Boston swept them in the 1914 Series. "If the players were going to cash in and leave me to hold the bag,

there was nothing for me to do but to cash in too," Mack said. Selling off his best players, he doomed the club to a record seven straight last-place finishes.

Mack's methods were to buy hot prospects from the flourishing minor league teams of the times, trusting his ability to discover stars. In the mid-1920s, Mack's charges were usually in pennant races. By 1929, the A's exploded. Young stars like Al Simmons, Jimmie Foxx, Mickey Cochrane, and Lefty Grove won three straight pennants and the World Series in 1929 and 1930.

Unfortunately for Mack, the Depression forced him to sell many of his best players to better-heeled teams. He wallowed in the second division for the rest of his career. "The Tall Tactician," who dressed in his severe dark suits, was age 87 when he managed his last team. Always the gentleman, Mack was beloved by his players and was among the first people inducted into the Hall of Fame, in 1937.

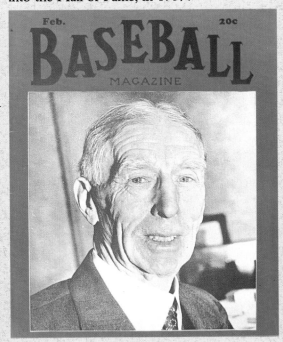

Feb. 20c
BASEBALL MAGAZINE

Major League Managing Totals

W	L	T	PCT	G
3,731	3,948	75	.486	7,755

Top: *This cigar cutter, bearing Connie Mack's signature, was presented to him in the 1890s. In 1890, backstopping for Buffalo in the Players League, he had become the first major league catcher to accumulate 500 at bats in a season.* Left: *When he appeared on the cover of* Baseball Magazine *in February 1941, his A's had just come off a season in which they lost 100 games.*

CHAPTER THREE

Brawny Baseball
Ruth Rescues the Game

EVEN AFTER 24 WINS IN 1917, PITCHER BABE Ruth's batting proved too tempting for the Red Sox. In 95 games in 1918, the occasional outfielder led the league with 11 home runs. Still a part-time pitcher, he startled the baseball world by hitting a record 29 home runs in 1919.

When Red Sox owner Harry Frazee needed funds to underwrite his theater productions, he sold Ruth to the Yankees. Nine months later — thanks to the cozy dimensions of the Polo Grounds, the new cork-centered ball, and the banning of the spitball — Ruth swatted 54 home runs. His .378 average, 59 homers, and 171 runs batted in of 1921 emphasized that baseball's nature had changed. The slugger's popularity had boomed in direct proportion to his bat, and the fans flocked to the ballpark to see Ruth play, in New York and on the road. After the Black Sox fiasco, the Babe lifted the game back to its spot as the nation's pastime.

When they saw how well Ruth and the Yankees were drawing, the baseball owners decided to gear the game toward offense. By the end of the 1920s, such sluggers as Lou Gehrig, Mel Ott, and Jimmie Foxx were featured. In 1930, a souped-up ball in the NL inflated batting figures so wildly that it had to be deadened a year later. Eleven players on the pennant-winning Cardinals hit .300, and even the last-place Phillies hit .315, not enough to compensate for a record 6.71 team ERA. While pitchers eventually lessened the gap, baseball had survived the Depression.

Opposite page: From 1920 through 1929, Babe Ruth hit 467 home runs in regular season play, 13 in World Series action, and countless more in exhibition games. Left: Carl Hubbell, one of the era's greatest hurlers, won two MVP awards, in 1933 and '36. Below: The makeshift knots in the webbing of Frankie Frisch's favorite glove are a testimony both to Frisch's fondness for the fielding tool and the longevity gloves enjoyed in his day.

93

STANLEY ANTHONY COVELESKI
PHILADELPHIA A.L. 1912
CLEVELAND A.L. 1916-1924
WASHINGTON A.L. 1925-1927
NEW YORK A.L. 1928
STAR PITCHER WITH A RECORD OF 214 WINS,
141 LOSSES, AVERAGE .603, E.R.A. 2.88,
WON 20 OR MORE GAMES IN 5 SEASONS, WON
13 STRAIGHT GAMES IN 1925. PITCHED AND
WON 3 GAMES FOR CLEVELAND IN 1920
WORLD SERIES WITH E.R.A. 0.67.

Pitcher
Philadelphia Athletics
1912
Cleveland Indians
1916-1924
Washington Senators
1925-1927
New York Yankees 1928

(57) STANLEY COVELESKIE

Top: In 1924, Covaleskie had a 4.04 ERA. Thought to be through, he was traded to Washington in 1925. That year he went 20-5 with a loop-best 2.84 ERA. He won 14 games in '26. Above: This 1916 baseball card shows Stan in his rookie year, when he won 15 games for the Indians.

BORN STANISLAUS KOWALEW-skie in Shamokin, Pennsylvania, a coal-mining town near Scranton, Stanley Covaleskie (1889-1984) was one of five sons produced by Polish immigrant parents. All five boys entertained dreams of a professional baseball career as a way of escaping life in the mines, but only two made it to the top—Stan and Harry. Harry was a southpaw who received the nickname "The Giant Killer" after beating the New York Giants three times late in the heated 1908 National League pennant race.

Harry later became a 20-game winner for Detroit, by which time Stan had joined Cleveland. Despite pleas from the owners of both clubs, who envisioned the crowds the two might draw if they pitched against one another, the brothers declined, claiming neither wanted to be responsible for the other's defeat.

Although only three years younger than Harry, Stan took nearly a decade longer to reach the majors. He was nearly age 27 and had been in the minors eight seasons before he joined Cleveland in 1916. A fast worker who showcased exceptional control and a puzzling spitball, Covy

was a manager's dream. Almost always ahead in the count, he once worked a contest in which he did not have a ball called against him until the eighth inning. Too, his games were usually over, win or lose, in little more than an hour.

Covy won 20 or more games for four straight years between 1918 and 1921. Overshadowed by 31-game winner Jim Bagby in 1920 when Cleveland won its first pennant, Stan emerged as the team's hero that autumn when he registered three World Series triumphs against the Brooklyn Dodgers.

Covaleskie was so reserved and unassuming that he would not even correct sportswriters who spelled his name without an "E" on the end rather than as he and his brother Harry did after legally changing their surname. As a result, Covy's Hall of Fame plaque has his name spelled incorrectly, as that was the name under which he played.

After nine years with Cleveland, Stan was traded to Washington in December of 1924. Thought to be through, he rebounded the following season to collect an even 20 victories and lead the American League in winning percentage while assisting the Senators to their second consecutive pennant. In two World Series starts against the Pirates, however, he was beaten in both. Covy was elected to the Hall of Fame in 1969.

Major League Pitching Totals									
W	L	ERA	G	CG	IP	H	ER	BB	SO
215	142	2.88	450	225	3,092	3,055	990	802	981

JOHN McGRAW

JOHN McGRAW WAS THE MOST controversial, notorious, hateful, inspiring manager in baseball history, and he is the winningest manager in National League history.

John Joseph McGraw (1873-1934) played in an era when "rowdyism" was rampant, and he was among the worst offenders as he battled with opponents, umpires, and fans for any edge he could grasp. He played mostly third base from 1891 to 1906; a spike wound cut short his playing career. His infamous Baltimore Oriole club twice won the Temple Cup. He had his first taste of managing in 1899, when he steered the club along with teammate Wilbert Robinson.

McGraw and Robinson were sold to St. Louis in 1900, but elected to leave in 1901 to join the nascent American League, taking over the new Orioles. McGraw did not get along with AL founder Ban Johnson and began to listen to the siren of the firmly established National League. He persuaded John Brush to buy an interest in the Orioles, and then release McGraw and some

of the team's bright young stars. They went to New York, and Brush sold his Cincinnati club and bought the restocked Giants. McGraw was then age 29, and he managed the team for the next 30 years.

Fans anticipated fireworks when McGraw and young, gentlemanly pitching sensation Christy Mathewson met, but the two became fast friends. The Giants won pennants in 1904 and 1905. There was no World Series in 1904, as owner Brush scoffed at the AL. In 1905, the Giants beat Philadelphia for the first of three World Championships for the McGraw-led Giants, though McGraw was doomed to lose six World Series in his long career.

In 1908, "Merkle's Boner" cost the Giants a pennant, though many historians thought that the accountability lay with McGraw. "Little Napoleon" put together three pennants from 1911 to '13, and another in 1917. McGraw was a fine field general who knew all the tricks for manufacturing runs in that low-scoring era. He was the "absolute czar" of the team, relying on discipline and fear. John once said "Nine mediocre players pulling together under one competent head will do better work than nine individuals of greater ability without unified control." His record is dotted with problems with umpires, and his violent nature often got him into trouble off the field and on.

McGraw built a powerhouse in the early 1920s, winning a record four straight pennants from 1921 to '24, with World Series victories in 1921 and 1922. With the advent of lively ball strategies, baseball changed and the '24 pennant was to be his last. McGraw was elected to the Hall of Fame in 1937.

Manager
Baltimore Orioles 1899
Baltimore Orioles (AL)
    1901-1902
New York Giants
    1902-1932

Top: *McGraw was a top third baseman for the Orioles. He twice led the NL in both bases on balls and runs scored in 1898 and 1899.* Below: *When this trolley poster was in circulation, in the early 1910s, McGraw was busy leading the New Yorkers to three straight pennants, from 1911 to 1913.*

Major League Managing Totals				
W	L	T	PCT	G
2,784	1,959	57	.587	4,801

95

BILL KLEM

WILLIAM J. KLEM
UMPIRE
NATIONAL LEAGUE · 1905-1951
KNOWN AS "THE OLD ARBITRATOR" UMPIRED
IN 18 WORLD SERIES. CREDITED WITH
INTRODUCING ARM SIGNALS INDICATING
STRIKES AND FAIR OR FOUL BALLS. FAMOUS
QUOTE "BASEBALL IS MORE THAN A GAME
TO ME-IT'S A RELIGION" RETIRED AS ACTIVE
UMPIRE IN 1940, NAMED CHIEF OF N.L.
STAFF IN 1941.

Klem was one of baseball's most quotable umpires. He was fond of telling players who inquired whether a ball was fair or foul, "It ain't nothing until I call it." He also retired with the knowledge that, "I never missed one in my heart."

WILLIAM JOSEPH KLEM (1874-1951), born in Rochester, New York, wanted desperately to be a professional baseball player as a boy. His small size and his failure to stand out in trials with professional teams, however, relegated him to sandlot ball. Then in the early 1900s, while working in a Pennsylvania steel mill, Klem began umpiring semipro games. Silk O'Loughlin, an American League umpire at the time, urged him not to make a profession of officiating, calling it a rotten business. It was too late, however, for Klem had found his calling.

After serving a three-year apprenticeship in the minors, Klem was hired by National League president Harry Pulliam for $1,500 before the 1905 season. The job lasted a record 37 years. Klem was recognized early on as the best arbiter in baseball. When he first joined the National League, umpires often worked games alone. Even after more officials began to be used, Klem continued always to serve as the home plate umpire, owing both to his ability to take control of a game and his impeccable judgment at calling balls and strikes. Only in 1921, after 16 consecutive years behind the plate, did Klem begin

to rotate with the other umpires in his crew and take a turn working the bases.

From the outset of his career, he strove to establish his authority. In an era when umpires often got into fistfights with players and fans and were universally loathed, Klem was never less than a gentleman. During arguments with players or managers, he would draw a line on the field with the toe of his shoe. Protestors were then warned that if they crossed that mark, they were gone. Klem would then calmly walk away. He nonetheless could lose his cool on occasion. One challenge that was almost guaranteed to provoke him was to call him "Catfish." Since he truly did resemble the piscine creature, the sensitive umpire would often vehemently eject his offender.

Klem retired from officiating after the 1941 season to become chief of National League umpires, a position he held until his death in Miami, Florida, on September 16, 1951. During his long career, he officiated in a record 18 World Series, the last of which was played out in 1940. Klem was elected to the Hall of Fame in 1953.

HERB PENNOCK

Herb was age 29 and barely a .500 pitcher when he arrived in the Bronx, but in his first season there he led the league in winning percentage at .760 (19-6). He went on to two 20-win seasons for the Yankees and a 162-90 record in 11 seasons.

"The Squire of Kennett Square" was known for his smooth, effortless delivery, his finesse, and his guile. Ruth believed Pennock was the smartest of all lefthanders. He amassed a 240-162 career record, with a 3.61 ERA. Pennock was a perfect 5-0 in World Series competition. He appeared briefly for the 1914 Athletics, and in 1923 he won two games and saved a third as the Yankees finally overcame two previous disappointments against John McGraw's Giants. In the 1927 Series, Pennock retired the first 22 batters he faced and pitched a three-hitter in the Yankee sweep. In 1932, 18 years after his first World Series, he saved two games.

Pennock made a final stop with Boston in 1934 before retiring that year. He coached with the Red Sox for five years before becoming the supervisor of their farm system. He became the Phillies general manager in 1944 and held the position until his death in 1948, the year of his induction into the Hall of Fame. He will always be associated with the Babe and with New York, where he notched many big-game victories.

Pitcher
Philadelphia Athletics
  1912-1915
Boston Red Sox
  1915-1922
New York Yankees
  1923-1933
Boston Red Sox 1934

HERB PENNOCK WAS ANOTHER of Connie Mack's discoveries, a terrific lefthander who would eventually become the best-remembered pitcher of Babe Ruth's Yankees.

Hailing from affluent Kennett Square, Pennsylvania (near Philadelphia), Herbert Jefferis Pennock (1894-1948) went directly from prep school to Connie Mack's Philadelphia Athletics in 1912 when he was just 18 years old. Mack did arrange for Herb to pitch on the semipro level during his summer vacation from school.

Pennock was involved in two of baseball's historical fire sales. In 1915, Mack, trying to fend off the assault of the Federal League, sold Pennock to Boston, where the gentlemanly Pennock first met Ruth. The two became friends despite their different temperaments. In 1923, Boston owner Harry Frazee continued his piecemeal sale of the Red Sox and sent Pennock to join Ruth on the Yankees.

While with the A's, Herb didn't receive the opportunity to pitch much until 1914, when at age 20 he was 11-4 with a 2.79 ERA. With Boston in 1915 and '16, he again was not a front-line pitcher, and the Red Sox farmed him out both seasons. After a mediocre 1917 season, Herb was in the Navy during World War I and missed the 1918 campaign. Back in the Hub in 1919, Pennock finally became a starter, posting ordinary numbers from 1919 to 1922.

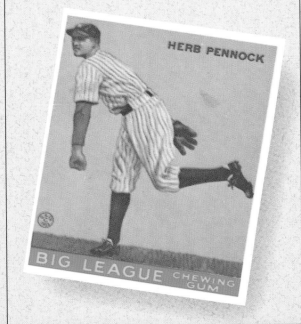

Top: *Pennock, like other good control pitchers, had trouble overcoming the weaknesses of bad teams but was able to fully take advantage of good teams.* Left: *When this 1933 Goudey card was released, Herb was at the end of his successful 11-year run with the Yankees.*

Major League Totals									
W	L	ERA	G	CG	IP	H	ER	BB	SO
240	162	3.61	617	248	3,558.1	3,900	1,427	916	1,227

WALTER J.V. MARANVILLE
"RABBIT"
BOSTON, PITTSBURGH, CHICAGO,
BROOKLYN AND ST. LOUIS,
NATIONAL LEAGUE, 1912-1935
PLAYED MORE GAMES, 2153, AT SHORTSTOP
THAN ANY OTHER NATIONAL LEAGUE PLAYER
AT BAT TOTAL 10075. SURPASSED BY ONLY
ONE NATIONAL LEAGUER. HONUS WAGNER
MADE 2605 HITS IN 23 SEASONS. MEMBER
OF 1914 BOSTON BRAVES "MIRACLE TEAM"
THAT WON PENNANT, THEN WORLD SERIES
FROM ATHLETICS IN 4 GAMES.

Shortstop
Boston Braves 1912-1920;
    1929-1933; 1935
Pittsburgh Pirates
    1921-1924
Chicago Cubs 1925
Brooklyn Dodgers 1926
St. Louis Cardinals
    1927-1928

Manager
Chicago Cubs 1925
23-30

Right: Baseball Magazine *selected Maranville for its cover in August 1931 when he celebrated his 20th season in the major leagues. In 1932, he was moved to second base by the Braves and proceeded to lead all NL second sackers in fielding average.*

WALTER JAMES VINCENT Maranville (1891-1954) was nicknamed "Rabbit" by fans who were captivated by the way the diminutive shortstop scurried and hopped about the infield. At 5'5½" and 155 pounds, Maranville is the smallest 20th century player in the Hall of Fame. He is also the only enshrinee who was demoted to the minors in midcareer because he no longer seemed able to cut it on a major league level. Maranville posted only a .258 career batting average and a .318 on-base percentage. It was for his glove and his leadership that Maranville earned his reputation, and in that respect he had few peers.

Maranville was purchased from the minors in 1912 by the Boston Braves. During spring training in 1913, Maranville beat out Art Bues (the nephew of Braves manager George Stallings) with a combination of hustle and self-confidence that could only earn the admiration of Stallings, himself a marginal player who had gotten by more on brains than muscle. A poor team for over a decade, the Braves showed signs of revival in 1913 and then took the National League pennant a year later after being in last place as late as July 4. Stallings was nicknamed "The Miracle Worker" for the team's stunning triumph and second baseman Johnny Evers received the

BASEBALL MAGAZINE
Aug.   20c
MARANVILLE, the MIDGET MARVEL
OVER 500,000 FANS READ THE BASEBALL MAGAZINE

"Rabbit" Maranville

Maranville survived during the dead-ball era almost exclusively on his fielding prowess and leadership.

Most Valuable Player Award, but most analysts felt that the real catalyst of the Braves' unexpected surge to the top was Maranville.

Renowned for his impulsive and zany off-the-field antics, Rabbit once dove fully clothed into a hotel fountain on a dare and reportedly surfaced with a goldfish clenched between his teeth. Traded to Pittsburgh following the 1920 season, he continued to carouse but nevertheless produced his finest year as a hitter in 1922 when he batted .295 and scored 115 runs. Maranville began slipping in the field, though, and was sent to the Cubs in 1925. Appointed player-manager in July, he wore out his welcome in the Chicago dugout after only eight weeks and was fired and subsequently released to Brooklyn on waivers. Idled most of the 1926 season by an injury, he was banished to the minors in 1927. The pink slip so shocked Rabbit that he stopped drinking. By the end of the season he had been recalled by the Cardinals, who needed a shortstop after Tommy Thevenow was hurt.

Maranville remained a major league regular until 1934 when he sustained a broken leg in an exhibition game. On January 5, 1954, Rabbit died in New York after suffering a heart attack. Several weeks later he was named to the Hall of Fame.

			Major League Totals							
BA	G	AB	R	H	2B	3B	HR	RBI	SB
.258	2,670	10,078	1,255	2,605	380	177	28	884	291

EPPA RIXEY

Pitcher
Philadelphia Phillies
1912-1920
Cincinnati Reds
1921-1933

PRIOR TO WARREN SPAHN, EPPA Rixey held the National League record for the most career wins by a lefthanded pitcher with 266. He still holds the major league record for the most career losses (251) by a southpaw.

The son of a wealthy Virginia family, Eppa Rixey (1891-1963) was a chemistry major at the University of Virginia when his pitching skill on the college team was noted by National League umpire Cy Rigler. Recommended to the Phillies by Rigler, Rixey joined the National League team in 1912 without any previous professional experience. Although he stood 6'5" and weighed 210 pounds, Eppa was anything but a fireballer. From the outset of his career his strong point was control and keeping hitters off balance with an assortment of breaking pitches and changeups.

Rixey's first four seasons with the Phillies were undistinguished. Even when the club won the National League pennant in 1915, he could fashion no better than an 11-12 record. In 1916, however, Eppa broke through in a big way, winning 22 games and giving the Phils, who featured Pete Alexander, the best lefty-righty

mound tandem in the game. When Alexander was traded to the Cubs after the 1917 season, the Phils immediately fell out of contention. After missing the 1918 campaign while serving in an Army chemical warfare unit, Rixey returned to the Phillies early in 1919 but could do nothing to prevent the club's tumble into the cellar. The Phils sank even deeper into the basement the following year as Eppa lost a loop-high 22 games. To his relief, Philadelphia owner William Baker traded him to Cincinnati just before the 1921 season began.

Rixey toiled for 13 years with the Reds, three times winning 20 or more games in a season. His pinnacle came in 1922 when his 25 victories paced the National League. Nicknamed "Jeptha" by Cincinnati sportswriter William Phelon, Rixey remained one of the mainstays of the Reds mound staff through the 1920s. He retired from baseball in 1933. When Spahn broke his National League mark for the most career victories by a southpaw, Rixey said, "I'm glad somebody finally did it. If Warren hadn't broken my record, no one would have ever known who set it."

Named to the Hall of Fame in 1963, Rixey died in Cincinnati little more than a month later, on February 28. In 1969 he was voted the greatest lefthanded pitcher in Reds history.

Top: This Rixey card was issued while he toiled for the 1933 Reds. That team finished in the NL cellar despite setting a 20th century NL record for the fewest walks allowed (257).
Left: Rixey featured exceptional control and a surplus of guile.

Major League Totals									
W	L	ERA	G	CG	IP	H	ER	BB	SO
266	251	3.15	692	290	4,494.2	4633	1,572	1,082	1,350

MILLER JAMES HUGGINS
1904—1929
MANAGER OF ST. LOUIS CARDINALS
AND NEW YORK YANKEES.
LED YANKEES TO 6 PENNANTS
IN 1921, 1922, 1923, 1926, 1927 AND 1928 AND
3 WORLD SERIES VICTORIES 1923, 1927 AND 1928.
SECOND BASEMAN IN PLAYING DAYS
WITH REDS AND CARDINALS, 1904-1916.

Manager
St. Louis Cardinals
1913-1917
New York Yankees
1918-1929

Top: *A smiling Huggins tops a composite scoreboard of the 1928 World Series on the cover of* Baseball Magazine. *His Yankees needed only four games to dispose of the Cardinals.* Right: *A master at getting on base any way he could, Huggins led the NL four times in free passes and scored nearly 1,000 runs in his career, but he amassed only 318 RBI in 13 seasons.*

LIKE PETE ROSE, MILLER HUG-gins was a native of Cincinnati who broke in as a switch-hitting second baseman with the hometown Reds. Unlike Rose, Huggins was barely 5'6", earned his keep chiefly with his glove, and entered the Hall of Fame as a manager.

Miller James Huggins (1879-1929) gained his first pro experience with Mansfield, Ohio, of the Inter-State League, in 1899. "Hug" needed five years of minor league apprenticeship before he was judged ready for the majors. When he reported to the Reds in the spring of 1904, most observers were dubious at first of Miller's small size, but he was soon proving that he had enough ability. One of the best of his time at working pitchers for walks, he played 13 years for Cincinnati and St. Louis.

In 1913, he was named manager of the Cards after Roger Bresnahan was fired. Under Hug's leadership the Cardinals rose to third place in 1914, the highest ever by a St. Louis team in the NL to that point.

Following the 1917 season, Hug was fired when he was still unable to lift the Cardinals to a pennant. Within days, however, he was hired by Jake Ruppert to manage the Yankees. In Miller's first two seasons at the New York helm, the club

finished fourth then third. After the 1919 campaign, the Yankees purchased Babe Ruth from the Red Sox at Huggins's behest. The move made the team an instant contender. In the hunt all the way in 1920, only to fall short at the end, the Yankees then reeled off three straight pennants. When the club lost a close race in 1924 to Washington and followed by plummeting to seventh place in 1925, however, Hug locked horns with his superstar, Babe Ruth, whose undisciplined approach to life Huggins felt was costing the team. Ruth was fined $5,000 and suspended indefinitely, an action that solidified Hug's position as team leader when the decision was upheld by Ruppert. Beginning in 1926, Hug's crew put together a second string of three consecutive pennants. The 1927 Yankees, known as "The Murders' Row," were one of the greatest teams ever, and the 1928 club was only a cut below them. Heavily favored to win a fourth straight pennant in 1929, the Yankees staggered instead and were out of the race by mid-September. Huggins, a natural worrywart, appeared even more overwrought than usual. His weight began dropping. In late September, he entered a New York hospital suffering from erysipelas. He died on September 25, 1929. In 1964, Huggins was elected to the Hall of Fame.

Major League Managing Totals

W	L	T	PCT	G
1,413	1,134	23	.555	2,570

EDD J ROUSH (1893-1988) WAS born in Oakland City, Indiana, to a father who had been a noted local semipro player. He never revealed the reason for the unorthodox spelling of his first name but did admit that he was given only a middle initial so as not to offend either of his uncles, who were named Joseph and James. It was one of the few personal tidbits that the close-mouthed and iconoclastic Roush shared with the world.

Although lefthanded exclusively during his major league career, Edd was ambidextrous by nature and could throw well enough with his right arm to create the myth that he had to develop it after incurring an injury to his left. His first professional baseball job was with Henderson of the Kitty League in 1911. In 1912, he moved to Evansville in the same league and stayed for a year and one-half. Late in the 1913 season, the Chicago White Sox bought his contract, and he appeared in nine games there before being shipped to the Western League. The next season, Roush elected to sign with the Indianapolis Hoosiers of the outlaw Federal League, then endeavoring to become a third major circuit.

When the Federal League collapsed after the 1915 season, the New York Giants garnered Roush for $7,500. Roush disliked the notion of playing for John McGraw, though, who he viewed as a taskmaster. When Edd hit only .188 in 39

In 1919, Roush's .321 mark topped Rogers Hornsby's .318. Not until 1926 would another NL hitter beat out Hornsby.

EDD J. ROUSH
CHICAGO A.L. 1913
NEW YORK N.L. 1916, 1927 TO 1930
CINCINNATI N.L. 1916 TO 1926, 1931
LEADING N.L. BATTER IN 1917 AND 1919
BATTED .352 IN 1921, .352 IN 1922, .351
IN 1923, .348 IN 1924. BATTED OVER
.300 - 13 SEASONS. LIFETIME BATTING
AVERAGE OF .323. MOST OUTFIELD
PUTOUTS, 410 IN 1920. F.L. 1914-1915.

Outfielder
Chicago White Sox 1913
Indianapolis Hoosiers 1914
Newark Peppers 1915
New York Giants 1916; 1927-1929
Cincinnati Reds 1916-1926; 1931

games with the Giants, he was thrown into the deal that resulted in Christy Mathewson joining Cincinnati as the Reds player-manager.

Holdouts became an almost annual event for Roush, as he loathed spring training. Edd contended that he needed 10 days maximum to get into playing shape and could do his conditioning on his own. The evidence supports him. In 1917, despite holding out that spring, he won his first National League batting crown. In 1919, Roush hit .321 not only to cop hitting honors but spark the Reds to their first pennant. That fall, in the only World Series of his career, Edd hit just .214, but was a member of the winning team as eight players on the Chicago White Sox conspired to throw the Series.

After 11 seasons with Cincinnati, Roush was traded to the Giants in 1927 where he played for three years. He then held out the entire 1930 season before returning to Cincinnati for his final big league bow.

In 1962 Roush was elected to the Hall of Fame. At the time of his death on March 21, 1988, in Bradenton, Florida, he was the last surviving Federal League participant.

EDDIE ROUSCH.
C. FIELD   CINN.   22

Roush's name is misspelled on this strip card, but that was typical for him. Usually, though, it was his first name that suffered. Not even Roush had an explanation for why it had two "Ds".

Bunting was only one of the many talents that aided Edd Roush in winning two National League batting crowns.

			Major League Totals							
BA	G	AB	R	H	2B	3B	HR	RBI	SB
.323	1,967	7,363	1,099	2,376	339	182	68	981	268

HARRY HEILMANN

HARRY EDWIN HEILMANN
DETROIT, A.L.–CINCINNATI, N.L.
1916–1932
RIGHT HANDED HITTING OUTFIELDER AND
FIRST BASEMAN, WON AMERICAN LEAGUE
BATTING CHAMPIONSHIP FOUR TIMES
1921,'23,'25 AND '27. IN 1923, BATTED .403.
COLLECTED 2660 HITS AND 183 HOME RUNS
IN 2,146 MAJOR LEAGUE GAMES. HAD
LIFETIME BATTING AVERAGE OF .342 AND
FIELDING MARK OF .975.

Outfielder; infielder
Detroit Tigers 1914-1929
Cincinnati Reds
1930; 1932

Below: *As this advertisement suggests, Heilmann was "the world's leading batter" in 1923 and again in 1927.*

HARRY HEILMANN WAS THE last righthanded batter in the American League to hit over .400. Had he made just one more hit in 1927 and four more hits in both 1921 and 1925, he would have been the only player in major league history to top the .400 mark four times. As it was, he won four AL batting titles and became the first player to hit at least one home run in every major league park in use during his career. Yet, for all his accomplishments, Heilmann was not elected to the Hall of Fame until 1952, the winter after his death. Critics claimed that his .342 career batting average was inflated because he played during the 1920s when astronomical averages were the norm.

Born in San Francisco and raised in Oakland, Harry Edwin Heilmann (1894-1951) signed his first professional contract with Portland of the Pacific Coast League. Optioned to the Northwest League, he hit .305 in 122 games and tagged 11 home runs, prompting the Tigers to draft him. Heilmann was a bust in 1914, however, his initial season in the majors. Moved from the outfield to first base in 1919, he topped the .300 barrier for the first time when he posted a .320 average with 95 RBI for Detroit.

When Ty Cobb became the Detroit manager in 1921, he returned Heilmann to the outfield. Cobb also spent considerable time tutoring Harry at the plate. The extra instruction paid immediate dividends when he won the AL batting title in Cobb's first season at the Detroit helm, a feat Heilmann would repeat every other season for

Heilmann seemed headed back to the minors before Ty Cobb's lessons were absorbed. Harry finished with four hitting crowns.

the next six years (1921, 1923, '25, and '27). He also had more than 200 base hits in each of the four years that he won the hit crown. One consequence of the successful teacher-pupil relationship between Cobb and Heilmann was that the pair became lifelong friends. Heilmann was also close to Babe Ruth and may have been the only contemporary of the two temperamental superstars who was on excellent terms with both.

Following the 1929 season, Harry was waived out of the American League despite hitting .344 for the Tigers and netting 120 RBI. Picked up by Cincinnati, he batted .333 and set a new Reds' record when he hammered 19 home runs. Unfortunately, arthritis caused him to miss the entire 1931 season. After playing just 15 games in 1932, he stepped down as an active player and became a coach for the Reds.

In 1933 the Tigers hired Heilmann to announce their games on the radio. He remained at the Detroit microphone until his death from lung cancer on July 9, 1951.

Major League Totals										
BA	G	AB	R	H	2B	3B	HR	RBI	SB	
.342	2,146	7,787	1,291	2,660	542	151	183	1,551	112	

WILBERT ROBINSON

Manager
Baltimore Orioles 1902
Brooklyn Robins
1914-1931

CATCHING FOR THE LAST-PLACE Baltimore Orioles in a game against the St. Louis Browns on June 10, 1892, Wilbert Robinson enjoyed probably the greatest batting day in history. In seven plate appearances, he collected seven hits and 11 RBI. Only once since then has a player totaled more than 11 RBI in a game, and no one has ever improved on Robinson's perfect 7-for-7 showing.

Born in Hudson, Massachusetts, Wilbert Robinson (1863-1934) was a latecomer to professional baseball, not making his entry until nearly age 22 in 1885. The following season, the Philadelphia Athletics of the American Association hired him to do the bulk of their mask work. Sent to Baltimore late in the 1890 season, Robinson had become the regular backstopper of the famous Orioles by the time the club was absorbed by the National League at the end of the following year. He remained the Orioles regular catcher throughout the decade.

During his golden years in Baltimore, Robinson formed a close friendship with third baseman John McGraw. The relationship grew into a business partnership when the two opened a local saloon called The Diamond. When McGraw was named the American League Baltimore Orioles' first manager, Robinson became his coach. McGraw defected to the National League in July 1902 to manage the New York Giants; Robinson replaced him as the Orioles skipper and then retired from the game after the club was moved to New York

before the 1903 season. He stayed out of baseball until McGraw hired him to be the Giants pitching coach in 1911.

During the 1913 season, the two old friends began to quarrel over strategy and what pitches to call. The arguments swiftly flared into a feud that made them enemies; in addition, the already intense rivalry between the Giants and the Dodgers was heightened when Robinson was hired the following spring to pilot the Brooklyn club.

Before his first year in Brooklyn was out, Robinson had been nicknamed "Uncle Robbie" and sportswriters had begun calling his team the "Robins." Hailed by Brooklyn fans as a genius after he brought home pennant winners in 1916 and 1920, Robinson later was beloved for his absentmindedness and casual approach to life that in turn became the trademarks of his team. By the late 1920s, the Dodgers were known as the Daffiness Boys, and Robinson seemed almost to revel in the team's reputation for zaniness and boneheaded plays. Following the 1931 season, he ended his 18-year association with the club when he resigned under pressure from the front office. Robinson was elected to the Hall of Fame in 1945.

Major League Managing Totals				
W	L	T	PCT	G
1,399	1,398	21	.500	2,819

Top: *The cover of the 1916 World Series program sold at Ebbets Field. Brooklyn won the third contest, the first postseason clash to be played at Ebbets. Robinson's popularity was already such that his team was dubbed the Robins by Brooklyn beat writers. Left: He was a reliable hitter until the end of his career. In 1902, his final season, he hit .293.*

URBAN CLARENCE FABER
CHICAGO A.L. 1914-1933
DURABLE RIGHTHANDER WHO WON 253,
LOST 211. E.R.A. 3.13 GAMES IN TWO DECADES
WITH WHITE SOX. VICTOR IN 3 GAMES
OF 1917 WORLD'S SERIES AGAINST GIANTS.
WON 20 OR MORE GAMES IN SEASON
FOUR TIMES, THREE IN SUCCESSION.

Pitcher
Chicago White Sox
1914-1933

Faber is one of the few pitchers in big league history to win back-to-back ERA crowns, in 1921 and 1922. Faber won 254 games for the White Sox over a 20-year span. In his first season Buck Weaver was the club's shortstop, and Luke Appling held down the post in Red's finale.

WHEN RED FABER POSTED HIS 254th and last victory in 1933, it was the next to last game won by an American League pitcher legally permitted to throw a spitball. Then 45 years old, Faber felt that he would still have been good for a few more years had it not been for a bum knee.

Urban Charles Faber (1888-1976) did all his pitching for the Chicago White Sox. Red joined the Pale Hose in 1914, still early enough in their history that he was on two pennant-winning teams. Faber won three games for the Sox in the 1917 World Series and was the main reason they garnered their second World Championship that fall.

In 1919, when the Sox again claimed the American League title, they were so heavily favored over the Reds in the World Series that fall that little concern was felt in Chicago when it was announced that an ankle injury would force Faber to miss the occasion. In retrospect, though, Faber's disablement may have changed the course of baseball history. Had Red been healthy enough

The July 1933 Baseball Magazine *feted Faber during his 20th major league season.*

to take his regular turn on the mound, there might well have never been a Black Sox scandal. Faber in 1919 was just reaching his peak and would win 20 or more games in each of the next three seasons.

Unfortunately for Red, though, after the scandal broke in 1920 he never again pitched in a game of much importance. A steady first-division team and a frequent contender during the first 20 American League seasons, the White Sox never finished higher than fifth in Faber's remaining 13 years with them.

Nicknamed Red because of the flaming color of his hair in his youth, Faber was a mature 26 years old when he reached the majors in 1914. However, he had already left an impression on certain big league hitters. The previous fall, after being purchased from Des Moines of the Western League, Faber had been loaned by the White Sox to the New York Giants when Christy Mathewson backed out a few days before the two teams were slated to set off on a world tour. Faber thus began his major league career by doing battle against the only team for which he would ever pitch in official competition. By the end of the tour Giants manager John McGraw was so enamored of Red that he offered White Sox owner Charlie Comiskey $50,000 for him, but Comiskey too had seen enough by then to know he had a gem. Faber was elected to the Hall of Fame in 1964.

					Major League Totals				
W	L	ERA	G	CG	IP	H	ER	BB	SO
254	213	3.15	669	274	4,087.2	4,106	1,430	1,213	1,471

GEORGE HAROLD SISLER
ST. LOUIS-WASHINGTON A.L.
BOSTON, N.L.-1915-1930
HOLDS TWO AMERICAN LEAGUE RECORDS,
MAKING 257 HITS IN 1920 AND BATTING
.41979 IN 1922. RETIRED WITH MAJOR
LEAGUE AVERAGE OF .341. CREDITED WITH
BEING ONE OF BEST TWO FIELDING FIRST
BASEMEN IN HISTORY OF GAME.

First baseman
St. Louis Browns
1915-1927
Washington Senators
1928
Boston Braves 1928-1930

GEORGE SISLER WAS ONE OF the best first basemen who ever played the game, despite performing at peak capacity for only about half of his career. He had amply demonstrated, though, that he might well have been the greatest hitter of them all.

George Harold Sisler (1893-1973) grew up in Akron, Ohio, and signed a contract with the Akron entry in the Ohio-Penn League while still in high school, though he received no money. He later enrolled at Michigan to play under Branch Rickey, and Sisler was considered one of the best college players. His Akron contract became the property of the Pittsburgh Pirates, but after college George signed with Rickey's St. Louis Browns. After much controversy, the National Commission ruled in favor of the Browns, because George was a minor when he signed the Akron contract.

Like Babe Ruth, George began his career as a pitcher. Shortly after joining St. Louis, Sisler beat Walter Johnson in a classic pitcher's duel. Stationed at first base in 1916, Sisler hit .305 in his first full season. After three successive seasons in which he batted around .350, George went wild in 1920. Not only did he top the American League with a .407 average, but he collected an all-time record 257 hits and set a new 20th century mark for first basemen with 19 home runs.

Two years later Sisler again cracked the .400 barrier when he soared to .420. Since he also paced the AL in runs, hits, and triples, he became the natural choice for the league's MVP Award. With all Sisler's heroics, the Browns still could not land their first pennant, losing to the Yankees by a single game. Sisler finished his career without ever appearing in a World Series.

After the 1922 season, George began to develop double vision, stemming from his infected sinuses. An operation only partially remedied the problem. When Sisler returned to the Browns in 1924 as a player-manager, he slumped to .305. He rebounded somewhat in 1925 when he batted .345 and knocked home 105 runs. However, he quickly regressed, falling to .290 in 1926, his lowest average ever for a full season's work.

Sold to Washington in 1928, Sisler played just 20 games for the Senators before finishing his career with the Boston Braves. His son Dick hit a dramatic three-run homer on the final day of the 1950 season to give the Phillies the NL pennant. Sisler's other two sons, David and George Jr., also became professional players. Dad Sisler was elected to the Hall of Fame in 1939.

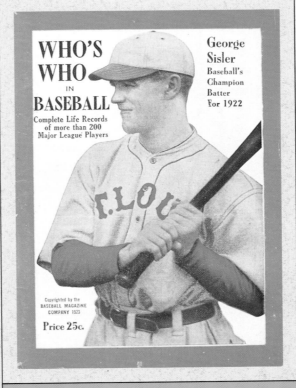

WHO'S WHO IN BASEBALL

Complete Life Records of more than 200 Major League Players

George Sisler Baseball's Champion Batter For 1922

Copyrighted by the BASEBALL MAGAZINE COMPANY 1923

Price 25c.

Top: *Sisler set an all-time major league record in 1920 when he garnered 257 hits.*
Left: *After making the cover of the 1923* Who's Who in Baseball, *Sisler was shelved for the entire year. The only other defending batting titlist who failed to play so much as a single game owing to injury or illness the year after he won the crown was Rico Carty in 1971.*

Major League Totals									
BA	G	AB	R	H	2B	3B	HR	RBI	SB
.340	2,055	8,267	1,284	2,812	425	165	100	1,175	375

BABE RUTH

GEORGE HERMAN (BABE) RUTH
BOSTON-NEW YORK, A.L.; BOSTON, N.L.
1915-1935
GREATEST DRAWING CARD IN HISTORY OF
BASEBALL, HOLDER OF MANY HOME RUN
AND OTHER BATTING RECORDS. GATHERED
714 HOME RUNS IN ADDITION TO FIFTEEN
IN WORLD SERIES.

Pitcher; outfielder
Boston Red Sox
1914-1919
Outfielder
New York Yankees
 1920-1934
Boston Braves 1935

IN 1917, WHEN BABE RUTH WAS age 22, he was 6'2" and a slim 180 pounds of muscle, and a superb lefthanded pitcher who had a lifetime record of 67-34. His prowess with the bat, however, prompted his manager to cut in half the number of starts of this young ace in 1918, and give him 317 at bats playing as a regular outfielder. He went 13-7 on the mound and led the league with 11 home runs. The kid became the talk of both leagues. The finest player in the history of the game was just beginning to flex his muscles, but everyone already knew about Ruth.

In 1919, George Herman Ruth (1895-1948) set a single-season record with 29 home runs and led the league in RBI and runs for the Boston Red Sox. Red Sox owner Harry Frazee's financial needs prompted Ruth's sale to the New York Yankees. "The Sultan of Swat" brought $100,000, more than twice the price of any previous player, and a $300,000 loan. The Red Sox, winners of the 1916 and 1918 World Series (Ruth was 3-0 as a pitcher in the fall classic), have not won a World Series since, but the Yankees went on to become the most successful franchise in history.

In 1920 Ruth took baseball, New York, and America by storm. His 54 home runs were more than any other American League team. His .847 slugging average still stands as the single-season

This patch is from the Babe's barnstorming, for which he was suspended for the first 40 games of the '22 season.

record, and he hit .376 with a league-leading 158 runs and 137 RBI. He dominated the AL almost up to his 1935 retirement. He had a batting title in 1924, twelve home run titles, eight times a league leader in runs, six in RBI, and 13 times in slugging. He might have won more honors, but in 1922 he was suspended by the commissioner for barnstorming, and he played in only 110 games. He was limited to only 98 games in 1925, when he was sidelined with an intestinal abscess; "Babe's Bellyache" was front page news across the country. Despite his big swing, the Bambino never struck out 100 times in a season, and he led the league in walks 11 times, including a record 170 in 1923. He still holds lifetime marks in walks and slugging. He led the way for a new, offense-oriented game of baseball that packed in fans in record numbers, and helped heal the wounds left by the 1919 Black Sox scandal.

The Babe led the Yankees to seven World Series appearances and four championships. He teamed with Lou Gehrig to form the most feared one-two punch in baseball history, and in 1927 the fabled "Murderers Row" of the Yankees won 110 games and lost just 44. Ruth set a record that year that was to capture the imagination like no other, hitting 60 home runs in a single season. He further added to baseball lore in the 1932 World Series, when, as legend has it, he made his famous "Called Shot." He reportedly pointed to the center field bleachers before homering against the Cubs.

Besides his on-field heroics, Ruth—one of the first five players inducted into the Hall of Fame in 1936—was a legend for his off-the-field

Ruth's worldly satchel. Yankee roommate Ping Brodie once said, "I don't room with Babe. I room with his suitcase."

"He never let [fans] down, not once. He was the greatest crowd pleaser of them all," said Waite Hoyt.

The Marketing of the Babe

Ruth was not only the greatest baseball player in history but also the first athlete in any sport to become a mini-conglomerate. There never was a product that Ruth wouldn't have considered endorsing.

In his prime, the Bambino made $80,000 per season with the Yankees and at least as much in outside income from various business enterprises. At various points in his career he endorsed the following products: Babe Ruth underwear, Bambino Tobacco, Ruth's Home Run Candy, Puffed Wheat, Wheaties, Babe Ruth Gum, Barbasol Shave Cream, Lee Union Suits, Remington Shot Guns, Louisville Slugger bats, Spalding baseball gloves, and much more. Also included in his business interests were the licensing of items such as the clock pictured.

Even though Ruth has been dead for 40-plus years, his heirs continue to derive significant income from the licensing of his name and image to countless advertisements and products. No other athlete has had such a grip on the American imagination and wallet.

adventures as well. He was genial and absent-minded, with an appetite for life that led him to every excess. He made friends everywhere—while he ate everything, drank everything, tried everything. Rube Bressler said that Ruth was "one of the greatest pitchers of all time, and then he became a great judge of a fly ball, never threw to the wrong base when he was playing the outfield, terrific arm, good base runner, could hit the ball twice a far as any other human being. He was like an animal. He had that instinct. They know when it's going to rain. Nature, that was Ruth!" He was the most beloved player ever to play the game. The Hall of Fame was created for players like Babe Ruth. He died in 1948 of throat cancer.

Major League Totals

BA	G	AB	R	H	2B	3B	HR	RBI	SB
.342	2,503	8,399	2,174	2,873	506	136	714	2,211	123

DAVE BANCROFT

DAVID JAMES BANCROFT
"BEAUTY"
PHILADELPHIA N.L., NEW YORK N.L.,
BOSTON N.L., BROOKLYN N.L.
1915-1930
SET MAJOR LEAGUE RECORD FOR CHANCES
HANDLED BY A SHORTSTOP IN A SEASON—984
IN 1922, LED LEAGUE IN PUTOUTS FOR SHORT-
STOPS IN 1918-1920-1921-1922. HIT .319 IN 1921,
.321 IN 1922 AND .304 IN 1923 WITH
NEW YORK GIANTS. HIT .319 IN 1925 AND
.311 IN 1926 WITH BOSTON.
PLAYER-MANAGER OF BRAVES, 1924-1927.

Shortstop
Philadelphia Phillies
  1915-1920
New York Giants
  1920-1923; 1930
Boston Braves 1924-1927
Brooklyn Robins
  1928-1929

Manager
Boston Braves 1924-1927
238-336

Top: *Bancroft was one of the Braves' few bright spots in that era. As the club's manager, his chief asset was himself. In 1925, he hit .319 and led the NL in fielding to help spur the Braves into fifth place, their highest finish under his tenure. Right: Exhibit cards like this one of Bancroft could be found in penny arcade machines during the 1920s.*

WHEN DAVE BANCROFT WAS traded by the Phillies to the Giants in June 1920, he was taken aside by John McGraw on his first day in New York livery for instruction in the team's signs. Bancroft quietly confided to the famous skipper that the lesson was unnecessary. He knew all the Giants' signs while he was with Philadelphia. McGraw was so impressed by this new shortstop's wherewithal that he named Bancroft the team captain in his first year with the Giants.

Recognition had not always come so quickly, though, for David James "Beauty" Bancroft (1891-1972). He languished in the minors for six years before his first big league opportunity with the 1915 Phillies. Even then he was still so unpolished a hitter that he batted crosshanded. The Phils, a sixth-place team in 1914, reluctantly threw him into the breach and were rewarded at the season's end with the first pennant in team history. Manager Pat Moran publicly acclaimed Bancroft the key to the club's success.

Although the Phils did not win again during Bancroft's sojourn with them, he improved both at bat and in the field so that by the late 1910s he was rated the top all-around shortstop in the National League. Perhaps his two greatest assets

were his outstanding range and his skill at working the hit-and-run play.

Upon coming to the Giants, Bancroft was installed in the No. 2 slot in the batting order, behind George Burns, one of the best leadoff men in the game. With such outstanding hitters as Frankie Frisch, Ross Youngs, Irish Meusel, and George Kelly following him, Bancroft began to see better pitches and blossomed accordingly at the plate.

It was with his glove, however, that Dave made his reputation. In 1922, he topped the senior circuit in both putouts and assists and set a major league record that still stands by accepting 984 fielding chances. At the close of the following season, after playing in his third straight World Series with the Giants, Bancroft was traded to the Boston Braves. Before making the swap, McGraw privately arranged for his shortstop to become the Boston player-manager in 1924.

A natural leader, Bancroft seemed the ideal choice to lead the Braves out of the doldrums. The Braves, though, finished dead last in 1924 and fared little better in the next three seasons under Bancroft's guidance. At the end of 1927, Dave was sold to Brooklyn. He closed his career in 1930 by serving as a player-coach with the Giants. Bancroft was inducted into the Hall of Fame in 1971.

DAVID BANCROFT
BOSTON, N. L.

Major League Totals

BA	G	AB	R	H	2B	3B	HR	RBI	SB
.279	1,913	7,182	1,048	2,004	320	77	32	591	145

GEORGE KELLY

GEORGE KELLY WAS A KEY player in the last glory years of John McGraw's Giants, helping win four straight pennants from 1921 to 1924 and two World Championships.

George Lange Kelly (1895-1984) was born in San Francisco one of nine children. His uncle was Bill Lange, an outfielder in the late 1890s for the Chicago White Stockings. By age 16, George was playing semipro ball at Golden Gate Park. Three years later, uncle Bill recommended George to Mike Lynch, another former Chicago player, to play in the Northwestern League. After he signed, George hit .250 that first year, in 1914. He improved his average almost 50 points the next year when he was signed by the New York Giants.

At 6'4" and 190 pounds, George was tagged with the nickname "Highpockets" upon arriving in the Gotham City in 1915. When Giants manager John McGraw threw Kelly into the fray, however, he was overmatched. He hit .158 in 1916, and McGraw sent George to Pittsburgh in '17 on the condition that he would return if he didn't make the Pirates. Luckily for New York, George hit .067 that year and was returned. McGraw optioned Kelly to the International League, where he hit .300.

After a year in the military, Kelly returned to the IL to bat .356 in 1919. He then hit .290 in the NL during the last 32 games of the campaign.

GEORGE KELLY
Oaks Coach

George surpassed all judgments when he led the NL with 94 RBI in 1920, and he then led the league in home runs in 1921. Kelly was a good first baseman, and a good enough fielder to play more than 100 games at second base in 1925 when Bill Terry was stationed at first base. Kelly led the league in fielding categories 12 times.

Although Kelly hit just .248 in Series play, he had some big hits, including a three-hit game in 1921, and the game-winning hit in game four of the Giants sweep of the Yankees in 1922. His best Series, a .290 average and seven runs in 1924, was his last, and the last pennant for McGraw.

Kelly hit .300 in six seasons and drove in 100 runs four seasons for the Giants, but when Terry was finally ready to play full-time, George in 1927 was sent to the Cincinnati Reds for one of the best center fielders of that time, Edd Roush. George had one good season for the Reds in 1929, notching 103 RBI. Cincy released Kelly in 1930. He played for the Cubs that year, and he played half a season for the Dodgers in 1932 before retiring for good. George was inducted into the Hall of Fame in 1973.

First baseman
New York Giants
    1915-1917; 1919-1926
Pittsburgh Pirates 1917
Cincinnati Reds
    1927-1930
Chicago Cubs 1930
Brooklyn Dodgers 1932

Left: *Kelly played in a Brooklyn uniform, the one he wears here, for just one season, in 1932. He hit .243 after spending all of the previous season in the minors.* Top: *A Pacific Coast League baseball card of Kelly in 1950 when he was a coach for the Oakland Oaks. A native of San Francisco, he was active in West Coast baseball circles up until his death in 1984.*

		Major League Totals							
BA	G	AB	R	H	2B	3B	HR	RBI	SB
.297	1,622	5,993	819	1,778	337	76	148	1,020	65

ROGERS HORNSBY
NATIONAL LEAGUE BATTING CHAMPION
7 YEARS - 1920 TO 1925; 1928. LIFETIME
BATTING AVERAGE .358 HIGHEST IN
NATIONAL LEAGUE HISTORY. HIT .424 IN
1924, 20TH CENTURY MAJOR LEAGUE RECORD.
MANAGER 1926 WORLD CHAMPION ST. LOUIS
CARDINALS. MOST-VALUABLE-PLAYER
1925 AND 1929.

**Second baseman;
shortstop; third baseman**
St. Louis Cardinals
    1915-1926; 1933
New York Giants 1927
Boston Braves 1928
Chicago Cubs 1929-1932
St. Louis Browns
    1933-1937

Manager
St. Louis Cardinals
    1925-1926
Boston Braves 1928
Chicago Cubs 1930-1932
St. Louis Browns
    1933-1937; 1952
Cincinnati Reds
    1952-1953
680-798

Right: *The Rogers Hornsby
fielders glove was one of Wilson's
big sellers in the 1930s.
Hornsby's critics disparaged his
fielding, but he is among the
select few players in history to
perform regularly at three
infield positions—second base,
shortstop, and third base.* Top:
*Pitchers first learned to fear the
Rajah in 1917 when he led the
NL in slugging average as a
scrawny 21-year-old shortstop.*

WITH THE LONE EXCEPTION of Ty Cobb, no superstar was more disliked than Rogers Hornsby. Hornsby was aloof, independent, and brutally honest. As a consequence, he was probably the least understood great player. Modern authorities cite his defensive lapses as a drawback, but Hornsby was the greatest righthanded hitter in history.

Rogers Hornsby (1896-1963) was given his unusual first name by his mother, whose maiden name was Rogers. Hornsby began as a shortstop in the Texas-Oklahoma League in 1914. Weighing just 140 pounds at age 18, he hit only .232. In 1915, Rogers was still a light-hitting and erratic-fielding shortstop, but the Cardinals saw enough talent in him to fork over $500 for his contract.

After putting on weight in the off-season, Hornsby hit .313 for St. Louis as a rookie and played a surprisingly adequate shortstop. In 1917, his second full season, he topped the National League in slugging and was second in batting. Moreover, he led all league shortstops in double plays.

Hornsby slipped below the .300 mark for the only time in his major league career in 1918, but continued to rank high in all slugging departments. Moved to third base in 1919, "The Rajah" again finished second in the National League batting race. The following spring, Hornsby earned the batting and RBI crowns in his first season as a second baseman. His .370 average was the highest in the 20th century by an NL second baseman.

No one expected Rogers to duplicate that figure in 1921, and he did not. Instead he hit .397 and then followed up by hitting .401 in 1922, .384 in 1923, .424 in 1924, and .403 in 1925 to make him the only player in history to average over .400 for a five-year span. During the 1920s, Hornsby hit below .361 on just one occasion. That came in 1926 after he was made player-manager of the Cardinals. The dual responsibility held Rogers to a .317 mark, but the Cardinals nevertheless brought the first pennant in National League history to St. Louis under his leadership.

A fierce dispute with St. Louis owner Sam Breadon resulted in Hornsby being traded to the Giants before the 1927 season. In his lone season in New York, Hornsby set a new Giants season batting average record (since broken). Before the decade was out Rogers had also established season batting average franchise records for both the Braves and the Cubs. His .424 mark with the Cardinals in 1924 is also a 20th century NL record. Hampered by injuries, Hornsby quit as a full-time player after the 1931 season. Rogers was elected to the Hall of Fame in 1942.

Major League Totals

BA	G	AB	R	H	2B	3B	HR	RBI	SB
.358	2,259	8,173	1,579	2,930	541	169	301	1,584	135

Charleston embraces baseball clown "King Tut" (left) and "Peanuts" Morgan.

OSCAR CHARLESTON PUT punch in the lineups of no less than a dozen teams in his 35 year career. He was a barrel-chested man of great strength, a long-hitter who could hit for average and run like the wind. Only Josh Gibson, whose memory is fresher, challenges Oscar's reputation as a slugger, and only Cool Papa Bell is mentioned with him when the best center fielders of the Negro Leagues are named.

Born in Indianapolis, Oscar McKinley Charleston (1896-1954) began his career in organized baseball in 1912 at age 15 in the Philippines as a member of the Army. He also ran track proficiently. Two years later, he was the only African-American in the Manila League. Discharged in 1915, Charleston signed on with the Indianapolis ABCs.

John B. Holway wrote "there were three things Oscar Charleston excelled at on the field: hitting, fielding, and fighting. He loved all three, and it's a toss-up which he was best at." Each of the three is documented. Charleston's lifetime average is .357. Newt Allen said "He hit so hard, he'd knock gloves off you." Charleston's 11 homers against major league pitchers in exhibition games ties for the highest total recorded, and he hit them for distance, too. In the field, Oscar was just as impressive, with an arm more accurate than strong, and the speed to run down drives in any part of the park easily. Right fielder Dave Malarcher, who played alongside Charleston, said: "He could play all the outfield. I just caught foul balls. I stayed on the lines." His spectacular catches are legendary.

Infielders got out of Oscar's way as he sped around the bases. They knew he would use all his considerable strength and speed against them, and that he had a mean streak. Off the field he was just as formidable. Cool Papa Bell said that Charleston ripped the hood off a "mouthy" Klansman in Florida in 1935; the Klansman elected to drop the matter. Charleston also resembled white baseball's biggest star, Babe Ruth, in his attraction to and for women and the good life. Like the Babe, Oscar is remembered as a genial, good-natured fellow, though few were blind to his faults.

Charleston stayed on past his prime as a player-manager, mainly with the great Pittsburgh Crawfords. He switched to first base after a chronic weight problem got the best of him. During World War II, Oscar played for the Philadelphia quartermaster's team, where he worked. Charleston was elected to the Hall of Fame in 1976.

OSCAR McKINLEY CHARLESTON
NEGRO LEAGUES 1915-1944
RATED AMONG ALL-TIME GREATS OF NEGRO LEAGUES. VERSATILE STAR BATTED WELL OVER .300 MOST YEARS. SPEED, STRONG ARM AND FIELDING INSTINCTS MADE HIM STANDOUT CENTER FIELDER. LATER MOVED TO FIRST BASE. ALSO MANAGED SEVERAL TEAMS DURING 40 YEARS IN NEGRO BASEBALL.

Outfielder; first baseman; manager
teams include:
Indianapolis ABCs,
Harrisburg Giants,
Detroit Stars, Chicago
American Giants,
St. Louis Giants,
Harrisburg Giants,
Homestead Grays,
Pittsburgh Crawfords,
Toledo Crawfords,
Philadelphia Stars,
Brooklyn Brown
Dodgers 1915-1954

Charleston in 1942 as a first baseman and manager of the Philadelphia Stars. He began as a center fielder.

Negro League Batting Stats*

BA	G	AB	H	2B	3B	HR	SB
.357	821	2,992	1,069	184	63	151	153

*Note: Charleston's career stats are incomplete.

BURLEIGH GRIMES

BURLEIGH ARLAND GRIMES
1916–1934
ONE OF THE GREAT SPITBALL PITCHERS.
WON 270 GAMES, LOST 212 FOR 7 MAJOR
LEAGUE CLUBS. FIVE 20 VICTORY SEASONS.
WON 13 IN ROW FOR GIANTS IN 1927.
MANAGED DODGERS IN 1937 AND 1938.
LIFETIME E.R.A. 3.52.

Pitcher
Pittsburgh Pirates
    1916-1917; 1928-1929;
    1934
Brooklyn Robins
    1918-1926
New York Giants 1927
Boston Braves 1930
St. Louis Cardinals
    1930-1931; 1933-1934
Chicago Cubs 1932-1933
New York Yankees 1934

Manager
Brooklyn Dodgers
    1937-1938
131-171

Top: *Grimes was the last pitcher to be legally allowed to throw a spitball in a major league game. He won 269 games in the NL before his 270th win with the Yankees, in a relief role. It was the final win by a spitballer—the final legal win anyway.* Right: *This pin was one of the prizes a purchaser of Orbit gum could obtain in 1932.*

WHEN BURLEIGH ARLAND Grimes (1893-1985), pitching in relief for the Yankees, won his 270th game in 1934, it was not only his final victory, it was also the last game in major league history won by a pitcher legally permitted to throw a spitball.

Oddly, Grimes's landmark victory was both his only win with the Yankees and his only win in the American League. His previous 269 triumphs had been divided among six National League teams over a 19-year period.

The Pirates were the beneficiaries of both Burleigh's first and last NL victories and also of his biggest season, in 1928, when he won 25 games. Even though Grimes served three stints with Pittsburgh, the brunt of his work was done with Brooklyn. Burleigh was traded to the Dodgers by Pittsburgh before the 1918 season after suffering through a 3-16 campaign the previous year, including 13 straight losses. With almost his first outing in Brooklyn, he suddenly became a different pitcher.

Grimes won 19 games for the Dodgers in 1918 and led the league in winning percentage two years later while netting 23 victories. On his first pennant winner in 1920, Burleigh shut out Cleveland, 3-0, in his first World Series appearance but then was beaten twice by the Tribe as the Dodgers lost five games to two.

Ten years later, when Grimes next played on a pennant winner, the 1930 Cardinals, he was a loser in both his World Series starts against the

GRIMES
CHICAGO "CUBS"

Philadelphia A's. The following year, however, Burleigh turned the tables on the A's, topping them twice. His second victory came in the crucial seventh game of the 1931 Series and was his last decision in fall play. Traded to the Cubs the following year, he closed out his postseason career with two relief appearances in the 1932 World Series.

Nicknamed "Ol' Stubblebeard" because of his habit of never shaving on days he was slated to pitch, Burleigh's rugged visage was only one of the weapons he used to intimidate batters. His spitball was among the most effective ever, often breaking some seven or eight inches, but the threat of it was equally valuable. Grimes would fake a spitter on almost every pitch so that a batter could never rid his mind of the possibility of it. In actuality, Burleigh employed his pet delivery rather sparingly and was proudest when he could win a game without using it at all.

After his playing career ended, he was hired by the Dodgers to replace Casey Stengel as their skipper in 1937 and lasted two seasons. Grimes was elected to the Hall of Fame in 1964.

				Major League	Totals				
W	**L**	**ERA**	**G**	**CG**	**IP**	**H**	**ER**	**BB**	**SO**
270	212	3.53	617	314	4,179	4,412	1,636	1,295	1,512

ROSS YOUNGS

Outfielder
New York Giants
1917-1926

WHEN THE GREAT WALTER Johnson finally pitched a World Series game after 18 years in the majors, he lost in the 12th inning on a bases loaded single by Ross Youngs. Johnson and the Senators won the final game of the Series, but during that game he intentionally walked a man twice to get to Hall of Famer George Kelly. The man he walked was Ross Youngs.

Royce Middlebrook Youngs (1897-1927) grew up in West Texas as a football star in high school, but he was more interested in playing baseball. In 1914, Ross signed with the Austin club of the Texas League at age 17, but he was released after hitting only .097. The next season, he played for two circuits that folded during the season, the Mid-Texas League and the Central Texas League. He blossomed in the Western Association in 1916, batting .362. John McGraw signed Ross that year and sent him to Rochester of the International League in 1917. Youngs hit .356, proving that the stocky 5'8" outfielder was ready for the bigs.

In the old box scores and articles, "Youngs" is nearly always spelled with no "s." McGraw called Youngs "the greatest outfielder I ever saw," and "Pep" was a fixture on McGraw's four-straight pennant-winning teams of 1921 to 1924. He was a prototypical McGraw star: a fast, high-average hitter who had little power but played great defense. He had a fearsome arm, three times leading loop right fielders in assists.

At the plate, Ross batted over .300 in nine of his ten seasons. He had a good eye, posting a lifetime on-base average of .399, and scored at least 90 runs in each of the Giants' four pennant-winning seasons, leading the league with 121 in 1923. He was a fine World Series performer, batting .280, .375, and .348 in the first three; he

hit just .185 in the fourth, but he scared Walter Johnson witless.

Youngs struggled during the 1925 season, finishing at .264, the only season he fell below .300. In the spring of 1926, he was diagnosed as suffering from Bright's disease, a terminal kidney illness. The Giants hired a full-time nurse to travel with the team, and Pep spent the season teaching young Mel Ott everything he knew about baseball. Though the disease was taking its toll, Ross still hit .306.

Youngs died in 1927 in San Antonio at age 30. He was such a soft-hearted man that when he died he was owed over $15,000 by his debtors. The Veterans Committee selected Ross to the Hall of Fame in 1972.

Top: *Youngs was John McGraw's idea of the perfect Giant.* Above: *Youngs had a career .322 batting average.*

Major League Totals									
BA	G	AB	R	H	2B	3B	HR	RBI	SB
.322	1,211	4,627	812	1,491	236	93	42	592	153

WAITE HOYT

WAITE CHARLES HOYT
"SCHOOLBOY"
NEW YORK YANKEE PITCHER 1921-1930.
LIFETIME RECORD: 237 GAMES WON, 182
GAMES LOST, .566 AVERAGE. EARNED RUN
AVERAGE 3.59. PITCHED 3 GAMES IN 1921
WORLD SERIES AND GAVE NO EARNED RUNS.
ALSO PITCHED FOR BOSTON, DETROIT AND
PHILADELPHIA A.L. AND BROOKLYN,
NEW YORK AND PITTSBURGH N.L.

Pitcher
New York Giants 1918;
   1932
Boston Red Sox
   1919-1920
New York Yankees
   1921-1930
Detroit Tigers 1930-1931
Philadelphia Athletics
   1931
Brooklyn Dodgers 1932;
   1937-1938
Pittsburgh Pirates
   1933-1937

After his playing career was concluded, Hoyt became the radio voice of the Cincinnati Reds.

In the 1921 World Series, Hoyt pitched three complete games for the Yankees without allowing an earned run.

ONE OF MANY PITCHERS THAT rode the Babe Ruth and Lou Gehrig led Yankees to the Hall of Fame, Waite Hoyt labored in the major leagues for 21 years, pitching in six World Series and winning five Championships with the Yankees. His career in baseball spanned many eras, and he played a part in many of the richest moments in baseball history.

Born in Brooklyn at the turn of the century, Waite Charles Hoyt (1899-1984) pitched three no-hitters in high school and had ambitions to pitch for the Dodgers as early as 1916. The Brooklyn club was not interested in the boy. John McGraw found Waite intriguing however, signed the 17-year-old righthander, and sent him to the minors, where he went 4-5 in his first year. In 1917, his second pro year, "Schoolboy" won ten games but lost 28. He wasn't promoted to the bigs until mid-1918, after a 5-10 record in the Southern Association.

Waite pitched in one inning for the Giants (striking out two batters) before he was shipped back to the minors. Waite became disillusioned with the Giants organization but was lucky when the Red Sox bought his contract in 1919. Following a 6-6 record in the 1920 season, Waite was traded to the Yankees. In his first season with the Bombers, Hoyt won 19 games,

helping New York to its first AL pennant. In that year's nine-game World Series, he won twice in three games while not allowing a single run in his 27 innings of work. It was the first of three straight championships for the Yanks.

In 1924, the Yankees began to slip, falling to seventh by 1926. In 1927, Hoyt enjoyed the finest year of his 21-year career. He led the league with a 22-7 record while posting a 2.63 ERA for the '27 Yanks, perhaps the most awesome team ever to take the field. He bounced back in 1928 to post a 23-7 record. It was his last effective year as a starter.

After appearing in six World Series and winning 157 games for the Yankees, Hoyt began his travels, and would eventually see action with seven teams without much success. He had mild success as a reliever for the Pirates in the early 1930s, however. Hoyt retired from pitching after the 1938 season.

In 1941, Waite jumped into broadcasting and became the voice of the Reds, a position he held for 24 years. He was a prime agitator when Reds fans stuffed the ballot boxes with preprinted ballots and had their fourth-place team elected practically *en masse* to the 1957 All-Star Game. Waite was inducted into the Hall of Fame in 1969.

Major League Totals									
W	L	ERA	G	CG	IP	H	ER	BB	SO
237	182	3.59	674	224	3,762.2	4,037	1,501	1,003	1,206

JESSE HAINES SERVED A ST. Louis Cardinals-record 18-year stint on the mound, surprising since he was age 27 before he became a regular pitcher in the major leagues. A three-time 20-game winner, he did some of his best work in World Series competition.

An overpowering pitcher as a schoolboy in Clayton, a small town in western Ohio, Jesse Joseph Haines (1893-1978) compiled a 17-14 record in the South Michigan League in 1914 and 10-5 in 1915. The Tigers were impressed enough to sign him in mid-1915, though he never saw action in Detroit. With Springfield of the Central League, he was 23-12 in 1916 and 19-10 in 1917. Cincinnati finally purchased his contract in 1918.

The Reds used Haines in only one game before shipping him back to the minors. He didn't make it back to the bigs until the Cardinals gave him a chance in 1920. St. Louis manager Branch Rickey spent $10,000 to obtain Haines's contract, the last purchase the Cardinals would make for 25 years.

Haines relied on a blistering fastball and a baffling knuckleball that he learned from Athletics ace Eddie Rommell. Haines compiled 20 losses in his rookie year in 1920, but he won 13 games in 1926 and lost just four, helping the Cardinals to the pennant. In the World Series that year he won two games without a loss and posted a 1.08 ERA. In game seven, Haines was leading the Yankees 3-2 with the bases loaded

Pitcher
Cincinnati Reds 1918
St. Louis Cardinals
1920-1937

and two outs when 39-year-old Grover Cleveland Alexander (to whom Haines gave the nickname "Old Low and Away") came in from the bullpen to face Tony Lazzeri. Alexander's striking out of Tony Lazzeri is one of the most famous events in baseball history.

Jesse's best year came in 1927, when he compiled a 24-10 record, while leading the league with 25 complete games and six shutouts. His knuckler proved too tough a puzzle for the league to solve the following year as well, as "Pop" notched a 20-8 record in leading the Red Birds to another pennant. Haines was roughed up when the Cardinals returned to the fall classic that year, though. He appeared in the 1934 Series at age 41, and allowed no runs while fanning two in two-thirds of an inning as the Cards beat Detroit.

Pop hung up his spikes after the 1937 season, and he not only pitched more years in a Cardinal uniform than any other pitcher, but his 210 wins stand behind only Bob Gibson's 251 for Cardinal wins. Pop remained in baseball for the 1938 season as the pitching coach for Brooklyn. The Veterans Committee selected him into the Hall of Fame in 1970.

Top: *Haines won 210 games and once led the National League in both complete games and shutouts. He is among a handful of 200 winners who notched fewer than 1,000 career strikeouts. Left: A 1933 Goudey card of Haines.*

Major League Totals

W	L	ERA	G	CG	IP	H	ER	BB	SO
210	158	3.64	555	209	3,208.2	3,460	1,298	871	981

WILLIAM JULIUS JOHNSON
"JUDY"
NEGRO LEAGUES 1923-1937

CONSIDERED BEST THIRD BASEMAN OF HIS DAY IN NEGRO LEAGUES. OUTSTANDING AS FIELDER AND EXCELLENT CLUTCH HITTER WHO BATTED OVER .300 MOST OF CAREER. HELPED HILLDALE TEAM WIN THREE FLAGS IN ROW, 1923-24-25. ALSO PLAYED FOR 1935 CHAMPION PITTSBURGH CRAWFORDS.

**Third baseman;
  infielder; manager**
teams include:
    Madison Stars,
    Philadelphia Hilldales,
    Homestead Grays,
    Darby Daisies,
    Pittsburgh Crawfords
    1919-1938

O F THE FEW NEGRO LEAGUE players recognized by the Hall of Fame, Judy Johnson (inducted in 1975) has perhaps the weakest batting stats. His fielding at third base is usually described as steady or intelligent rather than spectacular. Yet everyone who played with him or saw him play agreed that he was a great ballplayer.

William Julius Johnson (1900-1989) was born in Snow Hill, Maryland. He started his career in 1918 as a semipro, getting his break when World War I called many black players away from baseball. He was a worthy fill-in during the war, but he still needed seasoning, and by 1918 was playing for the Madison Stars, a farm team.

He returned to one of the powerhouse teams in the east, the Philadelphia Hilldales, in 1921, taking over the third base job. He was a line-drive hitter who drove in a high number of runs, despite not hitting a great amount of homers.

Johnson played for Philadelphia 11 years (from 1921 to '29, and 1931 and 1932), and played winter ball in Cuba. He hit a career-high

Johnson was the best third baseman in Negro League history.

.406 in 1929, a year in black baseball that matched white baseball for unprecedented offensive totals. He was chosen MVP by sportswriter Rollo Wilson for the season. Judy moved to the Homestead Grays as a player-manager for the 1930 season.

Johnson was a member of perhaps the best Negro Leagues team in history when he joined Gus Greenlee's Pittsburgh Crawfords in 1932. Greenlee built the first stadium completely owned by an African-American. To fill his new ballpark, Greenlee was determined to have the best talent that he could find, raiding the Pittsburgh-based Homestead Grays and other teams for the best black players money could buy. The Crawfords were managed by Oscar Charleston and included Josh Gibson, Satchel Paige, and Cool Papa Bell. Johnson finished his playing career with the Crawfords in 1938.

Later, Johnson became one of the most astute scouts for the majors, when organized baseball began to accept black players. "I could have gotten Hank Aaron [for the Athletics] for $3,500," said Judy. "I got my boss out of bed and told him I had a good prospect and he wouldn't cost too much, and he cussed me out for waking him up at one o' clock in the morning." Johnson would also go to spring training with the Phils until he retired in 1974.

The 1932 Pittsburgh Crawfords "Big Five" included, left to right, player-manager Oscar Charleston, Ted Page, Josh Gibson, Judy Johnson, and Jud Wilson.

Negro League Stats*

BA	G	AB	H	2B	3B	HR	SB
.303	728	2,692	816	125	44	19	51

*Note: Johnson's career stats are incomplete.

FRANKIE FRISCH

FRANKIE FRISCH WAS A FOOT-ball and baseball star at Fordham University, with a degree in chemistry and a competitive drive that made him a natural leader on the field. There could be only one leader on a team managed by John McGraw, but McGraw realized that the talents of "The Fordham Flash" could help the New York Giants. In 1919 Frisch joined the club, and by 1921 the Giants won the first of four straight pennants.

This carving shows Frisch awaiting a throw at second base.

Frank Francis Frisch (1898-1973) was born in the Bronx and attended Fordham Prep before going to the university. He briefly left college during World War I to join the Student Army Training Corps. Back at school, Frankie learned how to play baseball under former New York Giant third baseman Art Devlin, Fordham's baseball coach. Devlin tipped McGraw about Frankie, and when all reports were positive, Frisch was signed to a professional contract.

McGraw's Giants won the World Series in 1921 and 1922, with Frisch hitting .300 and .471 in the two tournaments, and he captured the imagination of baseball fans with his slick fielding (he played third in 1921 and second in 1922) and his timely hitting. In 1923 he led the league with 223 hits, establishing himself as one of the great stars of the day.

The lively ball era began to produce terrific power numbers, but Frisch was not a slugger. He never hit more than a dozen home runs in a season, but hit over .300 13 times, including 11 in a row, from 1921 to 1931.

Frisch was an exceptional fielder. The *New York Times* called him "possibly the flashiest second baseman of any day" after one of the most talked-about trades of the time. Frank had a serious clash with McGraw and walked off the club in 1926. After suspending Frisch, McGraw traded him in 1927 to St. Louis for Rogers Hornsby, equally at odds with the St. Louis club. The fiery Frisch had finally worn out his welcome with McGraw, though the Flash later said, "I could have flopped as a ballplayer under any other teacher."

Frisch had learned to win, and as a second baseman of the famous "Gas House Gang," he appeared in four World Series, winning one in 1931, and leading the team to another in 1934, a year after becoming player-manager. Well-respected by his contemporaries, Frisch in 1931 won the first MVP Award in the National League, after a year that was not his best (a .311 average, 96 runs, 82 RBI, and a league-leading 28 steals). Frankie's playing career lasted through the 1937 season, but he managed for 16 years, with St. Louis, Pittsburgh, and Chicago, winning 1,138 games.

Second baseman
New York Giants
1919-1925
St. Louis Cardinals
1927-1937

Manager
St. Louis Cardinals
1933-1938
Pittsburgh Pirates
1940-1946
Chicago Cubs 1949-1951
1,138-1,078

Frankie Frisch slides into first under Jack Bentley's tag in a 1925 spring game between the New York Giants' regulars and yannigans.

Major League Totals									
BA	G	AB	R	H	2B	3B	HR	RBI	SB
.316	2,311	9,112	1,532	2,880	466	138	105	1,244	419

KENESAW MOUNTAIN LANDIS
BASEBALL'S FIRST COMMISSIONER
ELECTED, 1920 — DIED IN OFFICE, 1944
HIS INTEGRITY AND LEADERSHIP
ESTABLISHED BASEBALL IN THE
RESPECT, ESTEEM AND AFFECTION
OF THE AMERICAN PEOPLE.

THE HEADLINE IN THE *NEW York Times* in 1920 read "BASEBALL PEACE DECLARED; LANDIS NAMED DICTATOR." Over a decade later, in legal court documents, he was called "legally an absolute despot." Judge Kenesaw Mountain Landis (1866-1944) was everything and more than what the owners who hired him bargained for, a tough, uncompromising man who trusted his own opinion beyond any other.

Landis was born in Millville, Ohio, in 1866. He received his name from a major Civil War battle, during which his father had been wounded at Kennesaw Mountain, Georgia. "Ken" became nationally known in his capacity as a District

This 1925 Sportlife provided the public with a rare glimpse of Landis. Although his public image was one of absolute impartiality, Landis was secretly a Cubs fans, dating from the early part of the century when he became an admirer of Three Finger Brown.

Judge starting in 1907 when he levied a $29,240,000 fine against Standard Oil in a freight rebate case (the ruling was overturned, but drew attention to the violations). He was not only a passionate baseball fan, but when called upon to rule in legal battles arising from the challenge of the Federal League to Major League Baseball, his handling of the affair allowed the Federal League to be absorbed, and worked to the satisfaction of most parties.

Landis is best known for his rulings concerning the 1919 Black Sox, when he banned the eight players accused of throwing World Series games from baseball despite the lack of evidence to convict them in a court of law. He also put an end to barnstorming by making an example of Babe Ruth. Landis suspended Ruth and two others for 40 days in 1922.

Landis was keenly aware of the relationship between baseball and America. He gave himself a pay cut during the Depression, and limited travel, particularly for spring training, during the war years.

Landis never saw eye to eye with American League founder Ban Johnson, and eventually usurped most of Johnson's considerable power. There was also ongoing friction between Landis and Branch Rickey. The Judge foresaw the effect that Rickey's farm system would have on the competitive nature of the minor leagues, which he believed were as entitled to compete to their full powers as were the major leagues. This was one of the few battles he was destined to lose. He championed the collective good of the players in most things, and honesty and square dealings in all things.

Landis was rarely photographed smiling, and the stern, craggy eccentric that his photos capture seem to have been a true picture of the man. When he died in 1944, at the age of 78, he had a year to go on his contract, and had just been voted to a new, seven-year term.

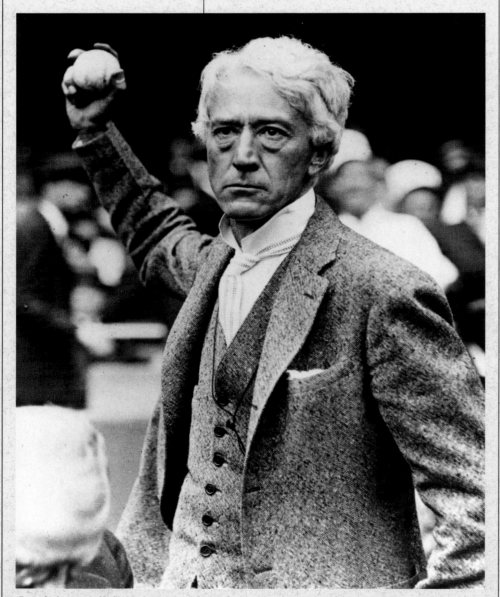

Landis's overall demeanor was that of a man who seemed to know his word was meant to be law.

PIE TRAYNOR

"PIE" TRAYNOR

HAROLD J. (PIE) TRAYNOR
RATED AMONG THE GREAT THIRD BASEMEN
OF ALL TIME, BECAME A REGULAR WITH
THE PITTSBURGH N.L. TEAM IN 1922 AND
CONTINUED AS A PLAYER UNTIL CONCLUSION
OF 1937 SEASON. MANAGED THE PIRATES
FROM JUNE, 1934, THROUGH SEPT. 1939. HOLDS
SEVERAL FIELDING RECORDS AND COMPILED
A LIFETIME BATTING MARK OF .320, ONE OF
FEW PLAYERS EVER TO MAKE 200 OR MORE
HITS DURING A SEASON, COLLECTING
208 IN 1923.

Third baseman
Pittsburgh Pirates
1920-1937

PIE TRAYNOR MAINTAINED HE was given his odd nickname because he was inordinately fond of pie as a boy in Somerville, Massachusetts. Whatever its roots, however, Traynor was never known by any other name.

Originally a shortstop, Harold Joseph Traynor (1899-1972) was a sandlot standout in Somerville, and in 1918 he tried to get a tryout with the Braves but was turned away. He signed his first professional contract in 1920 with Portsmouth of the Virginia League and played well, prompting the Pirates to sign him. He spent 1921 in the Southern Association, batting .336, and was handed the Pirates shortstop post in 1922.

Traynor floundered there for nearly two months until Bill McKecknie was installed as the Pittsburgh manager. One of McKecknie's first moves was to switch Traynor to third base. Pie hit .282 that season. In 1923, he hit .338 with 12 homers and 101 RBI, and he led NL third sackers with 191 putouts and 310 assists. The Bucs won the pennant in 1925, with Pie hitting .320 with 106 RBI. He again led NL third basemen in putouts and assists. The Pirates then beat the Senators in the Series, with Traynor

hitting .346. In the seventh game, he drove in the tying run in the seventh inning on a triple.

In 1927, Pie hit .342 and had 106 RBI, again leading the loop in putouts, as Pittsburgh again took the pennant. In the Series this time, however, the Pirates were swept by the Yankee juggernaut. Pie, however, began a four-year run where his yearly batting average never went below .337, and a five-year stretch of 100-plus RBI seasons.

Pie played with the Pirates his entire 18-year career and also managed the club for five and one-half campaigns. A player-manager when he first took the job, he spent the last four years of his dugout stint as a helmsman only. Traynor could never quite pilot the Pirates to the top of the heap. His greatest disappointment came in 1938 when Pittsburgh lost out to the Cubs on Gabby Hartnett's "Homer in the Gloamin'."

In 1969, Traynor was selected as the game's all-time greatest third baseman by sportswriters. He wouldn't if the same poll were taken today; his reputation has probably suffered more than any other player's during the past 20 years, especially defensively. While he may have been overrated with the glove in past, he was still an excellent third baseman. He led NL third sackers in putouts seven times, chances per game five times, and double plays four times. Traynor was selected for the Hall of Fame in 1948.

Top: The subject of this 1934 Diamond Star card, Traynor assumed the role of player-manager for Pittsburgh halfway through the 1934 campaign. Left: Traynor had feet like violin cases, according to Ed Barrow who scouted Pie in his youth. While he was managing the Red Sox, nevertheless, Barrow attempted to acquire Traynor.

Major League Totals									
BA	G	AB	R	H	2B	3B	HR	RBI	SB
.320	1,941	7,559	1,183	2,416	371	164	58	1,273	158

JOSEPH WHEELER SEWELL
CLEVELAND A. L., NEW YORK A. L.,
1920 – 1933
POSTED LIFETIME .312 BATTING AVERAGE,
TOPPING .300 IN TEN OF 14 YEARS. MOST
DIFFICULT MAN TO STRIKE OUT IN GAME'S
HISTORY. CREATED RECORDS WITH: FEWEST
CAREER STRIKEOUTS (114), FOUR SEASONS
OF FOUR WHIFFS OR LESS IN 500 AT-BATS
AND 115 GAMES IN ROW WITHOUT FANNING.
LED A. L. SHORTSTOPS IN FIELDING TWICE
AND IN PUTOUTS AND ASSISTS FOUR TIMES.

Shortstop; third baseman
Cleveland Indians
1920-1930
New York Yankees
1931-1933

T O THOSE WHO NEVER SAW HIM play, Joe Sewell's Hall of Fame credentials may seem insufficient. Although a steady .300 hitter, he was active during an era when many players hit over .300. It may seem that the chief reason for his enshrinement would seemingly be his incredible proclivity for almost never striking out. The holder of every major season and career record for fewest strikeouts by a batter, Sewell fanned only 114 times in 14 seasons and 7,132 at bats, an average of only one whiff for every 63 plate trips. Sewell was considerably more than the hardest player in history to fan. During his peak years in the mid-1920s, he was also the best fielding shortstop in the game.

Joseph Wheeler Sewell (1898-1990) was born in Titus, Alabama, and was a three-sport athlete. He went to the University of Alabama, where he played football and basketball. Crimson Tide football coach Xen Scott got Sewell a tryout with the Indians in 1920. When Sewell signed with Cleveland in 1920 his future with the club seemed unclear. The Indians already had Ray Chapman, the best shortstop in the American League and only 29 at the time. Sewell was unimpressive in spring training, and was sent to Cleveland's New Orleans farm club.

The Indians were in a tight three-way race for the AL pennant when Chapman was tragically killed in mid-August by a Carl Mays fastball. His replacement, Harry Lunte, injured his leg on Labor Day; Cleveland had no choice but to summon Sewell from New Orleans. Joe hit .329 in the remaining 22 games of the season and otherwise filled the hole Chapman had left so capably that the Indians won the first pennant in Cleveland history.

The following year Sewell was joined on the Tribe by his younger brother, Luke, a catcher. Another brother, Tommy, played one game in the bigs. In his ten full seasons with the Tribe, Joe hit over .300 eight times, had over 90 RBI five times, and scored over 90 runs five times. His slugging percentages were consistently in the .400s. He was moved to third base in 1929, and traded to the Yankees a year later.

In his three seasons with the Yankees, Sewell struck out just 15 times in 1,511 at bats but otherwise continued his general decline. His high point with the Bombers came in 1932 when he fanned a record-low three times in 503 at bats and then hit .333 in the World Series that fall against the Cubs. He was elected to the Hall of Fame in 1977.

Top: *After spending 11 seasons with Cleveland, Sewell played with the Yankees the final three years of his career. In 390 games and 1,511 at bats with the New Yorkers, Sewell fanned only 15 times, while collecting 188 walks.* Right: *Joe and his brother, Luke, played together with Cleveland for nearly a full decade.*

Major League Totals

BA	G	AB	R	H	2B	3B	HR	RBI	SB
.312	1,902	7,132	1,141	2,226	436	68	49	1,051	74

KIKI CUYLER

THERE ARE SEVERAL STORIES of how Hazen Shirley Cuyler (1899-1950) came by his nickname. One is that he stuttered so badly as a toddler whenever he tried to pronounce his surname that it came out "Cuy Cuy." In any case, Cuyler's nickname is one of the more memorable of the era in which he played.

Born of German parents in Harrisville, Michigan, Kiki was a pitcher-outfielder as a youth. He attended West Point for a couple of months after he finished high school. Within a year Cuyler was playing for the Bay City team in the Michigan-Ontario League. A serious spike wound prompted a move from the mound to the outfield.

In his four minor league seasons, interrupted by three short major league trials with Pittsburgh, Cuyler seemed a solid prospect but nothing remarkable. Therefore the Pirates were pleasantly surprised when he debuted in 1924 with one of the finest rookie seasons in history. Cuyler batted .354, the fourth highest average in the National League, cracked 16 triples and swiped 32 bases. When Kiki did even better as a sophomore, hiking his average to .357 and leading the loop in both triples and runs, he was hailed as the game's newest star.

Unfortunately, even though he had a fine career, Cuyler never again ascended to the heights he reached during his first two seasons. His critics felt he had the talent to be as good as any player in the game at the time but lacked the drive to excel that had pushed others, such as Ty Cobb (who, in truth, probably had less ability than Cuyler). Whatever the case, the Pirates grew disenchanted with Kiki midway through the 1927 season. When he clashed with manager Donie Bush, who wanted him to bat second in the order while Cuyler preferred the third slot, Bush began looking for an excuse to bench him. Bush was given it when Cuyler failed to slide into second base in a game on August 6 against the Giants; Bush removed Cuyler from the lineup. In the World Series that fall against the Yankees, Kiki rode the bench the entire way as the Pirates were being swept. Two months later he was traded to the Cubs.

Cuyler enjoyed several banner seasons with the Cubs, helped by batting ahead of such players as Rogers Hornsby. In 1935, Kiki was released by the Bruins and picked up by the Reds. He rallied to have one final good season in 1936, batting .326. Cuyler was named to the Hall of Fame in 1968.

HAZEN SHIRLEY CUYLER
"KIKI"
PITTSBURGH N.L. 1921 TO 1927
CHICAGO N.L. 1928 TO 1935
CINCINNATI N.L. 1935 TO 1937
BROOKLYN N.L. 1938
LED N.L. IN STOLEN BASES 1926, 1928, 1929, 1930. BATTED .354 IN 1924, .357 IN 1925, .360 IN 1929, .355 IN 1930. LIFETIME TOTAL 2299 HITS, BATTING AVERAGE .321. NAMED TO ALL STAR TEAM IN 1925.

Outfielder
Pittsburgh Pirates
1921-1927
Chicago Cubs 1928-1935
Cincinnati Reds 1935-1937
Brooklyn Dodgers 1938

In 1925, Cuyler nearly became one of an elite few players who have totaled 20 or more doubles, triples, and home runs in the same season. He fell two homers short of joining this select company.

An Orbit gum pin of Kiki Cuyler. In 1930, Cuyler and fellow Cubs outfielder Hank Wilson combined to set a NL teammates RBI record with 324.

				Major League Totals					
BA	**G**	**AB**	**R**	**H**	**2B**	**3B**	**HR**	**RBI**	**SB**
.321	1,879	7,161	1,305	2,299	394	157	127	1,065	328

GOOSE GOSLIN

LEON ALLEN GOSLIN
"GOOSE"
WASHINGTON A.L. 1921 TO 1930, 1933, 1938
ST. LOUIS A.L. 1930 TO 1932
DETROIT A.L. 1934 TO 1937

BATTED .344 IN 1924, .334 IN 1925,
.354 IN 1926, .334 IN 1927. LED A.L.
IN BATTING IN 1928 WITH .379 AVERAGE.
RUNS BATTED IN FOR 1924—129.
HIT .300 OR BETTER 11 YEARS.
LIFETIME TOTAL OF 2735 HITS,
BATTING AVERAGE .316.
MADE 37 HITS IN 5 WORLD SERIES.

Outfielder
Washington Senators
    1921-1930; 1933; 1938
St. Louis Browns
    1930-1932
Detroit Tigers 1934-1937

GOOSE GOSLIN WAS THE ONLY American Leaguer between 1921 and 1939 who was on five pennant-winning teams despite never playing for the Yankees or under Connie Mack.

Nicknamed Goose both because of his last name and because of his large nose, Leon Allen Goslin (1900-1971) grew up on a small farm in Salem, New Jersey. Originally a pitcher, he was converted to the outfield when his first professional manager thought that Goose's bat had more promise than his arm.

While in the midst of leading the Sally League in hitting during his second season in the loop, Goslin was bought by Washington for $6,000. A successful trial at the end of the 1921 campaign gave Goose hope of winning a regular job in the nation's capital the following year, but he injured his arm while heaving a shotput during spring training prior to the 1922 season and was never

Few players in Goslin's day had soft drinks named for them. But then few players have had names that stuck as indelibly in the public mind as Goose's.

again able to throw with his old ability. Mediocre defensively even before the injury, Goslin had to work hard to become a competent outfielder.

Goose quickly emerged, though, as a standout slugger. In 1923 he led the American League in triples. A year later he was the loop's RBI king, his 129 ribbies topping even Babe Ruth and preventing the Babe from winning a Triple Crown. Playing in Washington, Goslin had no hope of ever winning a Triple Crown himself. The outfield fences in his home park—Griffith Stadium—were so distant that no Washington player won an AL home run crown until the 1950s when changes were made in the park's contours. Indeed, Goslin hit 17 homers in 1926 on the road and none on his home soil.

The Senators in those years were good enough to win without the long-ball, however, taking back-to-back pennants in 1924 and 1925. When a drought followed, Goslin was dealt to the Browns early in the 1930 season only a year and one-half after he won the AL batting title. Washington owner Clark Griffith almost immediately regretted having let Goose go and worked for two years to get him back.

Reobtained on December 14, 1932, in a six-player trade, Goslin helped the Senators to win their third and last pennant the following summer. Unable to pay Goose what he was worth, the Depression-handicapped Griffith then swapped him to Detroit.

Goslin played on flag winners in each of his first two seasons in the Motor City and produced the hit in the 1935 World Series that brought the Tigers their first World Championship. Goose was selected to the Hall of Fame in 1968.

In 1925, Goslin led the AL champion Washington Senators in every major batting department and placed high among the loop's leaders as well.

Major League Totals

BA	G	AB	R	H	2B	3B	HR	RBI	SB
.316	2,287	8,655	1,483	2,735	500	173	248	1,609	175

DAZZY VANCE

Pitcher
Pittsburgh Pirates 1915
New York Yankees 1915;
    1918
Brooklyn Dodgers
    1922-1932; 1935
St. Louis Cardinals
    1933-1934
Cincinnati Reds 1934

NO PLAYER IN THE HALL OF Fame took longer to make his mark in the major leagues than Dazzy Vance.

Nicknamed by an uncle who noted the way Dazzy idolized a cowboy entertainer who pronounced daisy as dazzy, Clarence Arthur Vance (1891-1961) was born in Orient, Iowa. He began his professional career with Red Cloud of the Nebraska State League in 1912. Nine years later he was still buried in the minors, the owner of an 0-4 record at the major league level.

Already past age 30, Vance had shaved two years off his birthdate early in his career. It paid off when the Dodgers, assuming that he was 29 rather than 31, gave him a long look in 1922 after he won 21 games for New Orleans of the Southern Association. Dazzy responded by winning 18 games in his first full big league test and topping the National League in strikeouts for the first of seven consecutive seasons. Vance's finest mark came two years later in 1924, when he bagged 28 victories for Brooklyn, fanned 262 hitters, and had a loop-leading 2.16 ERA.

Featuring a blistering fastball and an excellent curve, Dazzy walked just 1.8 batters per game in 1928 to pace the National League. A part of Vance's success in baffling hitters came from the tattered undershirt he wore beneath his uniform. The ragged right sleeve gave him what many batters considered to be an unfair advantage and earned vociferous protests. Finally, the success enjoyed by Vance and other hurlers, like Johnny Allen, who sported flapping sleeves, caused a rule to be written prohibiting pitchers from wearing such items as shredded undergarments or white wristbands.

Although never on a pennant winner in Brooklyn, Vance made more money than many stars on contending teams. His salary in 1930, for example, was probably higher than any of the members of the flag-winning Cardinals received, with the possible exception of Frankie Frisch. Ironically, Vance's only postseason experience came with the Cardinals. Nearing the end of the line, he was a reliever and occasional starter for the Gas House Gang team that won the 1934 World Championship. Dazzy's lone fall appearance came in game four when he relieved starter Tex Carleton and fanned three Detroit Tigers in the inning and a third that he worked.

Released the following spring, Vance hooked on with the Dodgers for one last season. He retired to Florida at age 44 with 197 career victories, all of them coming after his 30th birthday.

In 1955, Vance was elected to the Hall of Fame. He died on February 16, 1961.

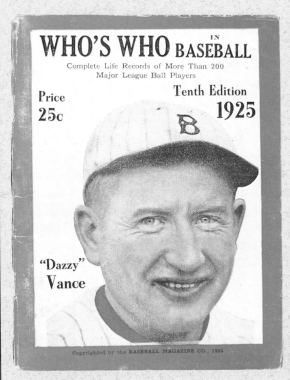

WHO'S WHO IN BASEBALL
Complete Life Records of More Than 200
Major League Ball Players

Price
25¢

Tenth Edition
1925

"Dazzy"
Vance

Copyrighted by the BASEBALL MAGAZINE CO., 1925

Top: *Vance lied about his age in order to receive a second chance in the majors. His deception induced the Dodgers to bring him to training camp in the spring of 1922. Left: He was a natural for the 1925 cover of* Who's Who in Baseball *after he was voted the NL MVP after the previous year.*

			Major League Totals						
W	**L**	**ERA**	**G**	**CG**	**IP**	**H**	**ER**	**BB**	**SO**
197	140	3.24	442	216	2,967	2,809	1,068	840	2,045

JIM BOTTOMLEY

JAMES LE ROY BOTTOMLEY
"SUNNY JIM"
ST. LOUIS N.L., CINCINNATI N.L.,
ST. LOUIS A.L. 1922-1937
SUPERB CLUTCH HITTER. DROVE IN
100 OR MORE RUNS SIX YEARS IN ROW,
1924-1929, LEADING LEAGUE TWICE.
ESTABLISHED RECORD BY BATTING IN
12 RUNS IN ONE GAME. MOST VALUABLE
PLAYER 1928. HIT SEVEN HOMERS
IN SPAN OF FIVE GAMES IN 1929. HAD
LIFETIME .310 BATTING AVERAGE.

First baseman
St. Louis Cardinals
1922-1932
Cincinnati Reds 1933-1935
St. Louis Browns
1936-1937

Top: Bottomley's finest season came in 1928 when he topped the NL in triples, home runs, RBI, and total bases and was second in slugging average.
Right: The October 1928 issue of Baseball Magazine *was on the newsstands when the World Series opened between the New York Yankees and Bottomley's St. Louis Cardinals.*

O N SEPTEMBER 17, 1924, AT Ebbets Field in Brooklyn, in just his second full season in the big leagues, Jim Bottomley had one of the biggest run-producing games in major league history. He drove in a record 12 runs that day, as he went six-for-six with two homers, a double, and three singles. Bottomley was known as "Sunny Jim" because of his disposition, but he was no friend to enemy pitchers, as he posted 2,313 hits, 1,422 RBI, and a .310 career average.

Born in Oglesby, Illinois, James LeRoy Bottomley (1900-1959) was another product of the Cardinals' immense minor league system. He arrived in St. Louis in 1922 and hit .325 in a 37-game trial. He replaced Cardinal first baseman Jack Fournier the next year and held down the position for ten years. Bottomley batted a lofty .371 in 1923 but finished second to teammate Rogers Hornsby, who posted a .384 mark. Besides Bottomley's .367 average in 1925, he smacked 227 hits with a league-leading 44 doubles and 128 RBI. That year he began a string of five consecutive seasons of over 120 RBI.

The Cardinals won the World Series in 1926, with Sunny Jim pacing the team in RBI (120) and homers (19). He hit .345 in the seven-game World Series. He is one of a handful of players

who have hit at least 20 doubles, 20 triples, and 20 homers in a season; in 1928 he had 40 doubles, 20 triples, and tied for the league-lead with 31 homers. He also led the league with 136 RBI and was the choice for the league's Most Valuable Player Award, a distinction that made him the first MVP to rise from a team's own farm system. The Cards returned to the Series that year but lost to the Yankees. Jim and the Cardinals were back in 1930 and 1931, winning another Championship in 1931.

Bottomley's performance began to slide after the second Championship, and he moved to Cincinnati in 1933. He played three seasons with the Reds but never approached the offensive production of his Cardinal years. He finished his 16-year career with the St. Louis Browns in 1936 and '37. Jim replaced Rogers Hornsby as manager of the Browns midway through the '37 season. The team was in the cellar when Bottomley took over and was unable to climb out during his leadership. He was replaced at the helm before the 1938 season.

Jim retired to his cattle ranch in Missouri but returned to baseball as a scout for the Cubs and as a manager in the minor leagues. He died shortly after, in 1959. Bottomley was elected to the Hall of Fame in 1974.

			Major League Totals							
BA	G	AB	R	H	2B	3B	HR	RBI	SB	
.310	1,991	7,471	1,177	2,313	465	151	219	1,422	58	

UNTIL JOHNNY BENCH CAME along, Gabby Hartnett was the greatest catcher in the history of the National League. A prototype catcher, he couldn't run, would talk your ear off—they didn't call him Gabby for nothing—and lasted for years on a lot of bat and a lot more savvy. Burleigh Grimes said that Gabby "had as good an arm as ever hung on a man."

Born in Woodsocket, Rhode Island, Charles Leo Hartnett (1900-1972) grew up in Massachusetts the oldest of 14 children. Gabby's father, Fred, was a semipro catcher, and he taught seven of his children (four boys and three girls) how to catch well enough to play organized ball. Gabby's first pro assignment was with Worcester of the Eastern League, where he caught 100 games and batted .264 in 1921. The Giants rejected the backstop because of his small hands, so the Cubs bought his contract in 1922. Gabby needed a few years to develop his batting, but Bob O'Farrell was able to hold the spot, having his best two years at the plate in 1922 and '23. When Hartnett took over in 1924, he held the position until the late 1930s, save for an injury-plagued 1929.

Gabby became a reliable stickman for several years after taking the position. He batted in the .275 range with some power. After injuring his arm in 1929, he exploded in 1930, hitting .339 with 37 homers and 122 RBI.

In 1935, Hartnett was the National League MVP, though his power stats would not stand with those of the heavy hitters of his day. His .344 average was third in the league, and he led league receivers in assists, double plays, and fielding average as he guided Cub pitchers to 100 wins and a pennant. His last three years with the Cubs were as player-manager.

Hartnett left a host of career fielding records, but is best known for the "Homer in the Gloamin'" in 1938. As player-manager of the Cubs he led his team from nine games out in August to wrest the pennant away from the Pirates. As the *New York Times* reported it: "In the thickening gloom, with the score tied and two out in the ninth inning today, red-faced Gabby Hartnett blasted a home run before 34,465 cheering fans to give his Cubs a dramatic 6-to-5 victory over the Pirates." The Cubs won four pennants during Gabby's time with them: in 1929, 1932, '35, and '38.

Red Smith wrote, "[Hartnett] was so good that he lasted 20 years in spite of the fact that he couldn't run. All other skills were refined in him."

Catcher
Chicago Cubs 1922-1940
New York Giants 1941

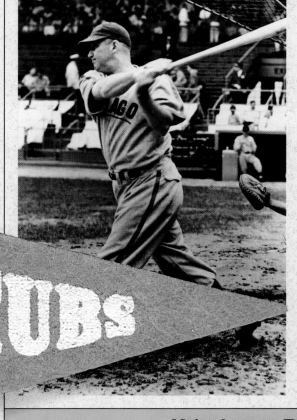

Left: *The 1937 season was the last in which Hartnett caught 100 games. He hit .354 in 110 contests and spurred the Cubs to a second-place finish, three games back of the flag-winning Giants. The following season Hartnett took over the managerial reins in midseason and piloted the club to a pennant.*

Major League Totals

BA	G	AB	R	H	2B	3B	HR	RBI	SB
.297	1,990	6,432	867	1,912	396	64	236	1,179	28

COOL PAPA BELL

JAMES THOMAS BELL
"COOL PAPA"
NEGRO LEAGUES 1922-1950
COMBINED SPEED, DARING AND BATTING
SKILL TO RANK AMONG BEST PLAYERS
IN NEGRO LEAGUES. CONTEMPORARIES
RATED HIM FASTEST MAN ON BASE
PATHS. HIT OVER .300 REGULARLY,
TOPPING .400 ON OCCASION. PLAYED
29 SUMMERS AND 21 WINTERS
OF PROFESSIONAL BASEBALL.

Outfielder
teams include:
   St. Louis Stars,
   Detroit Wolves,
   Kansas City Monarchs,
   Pittsburgh Crawfords,
   Chicago American
   Giants, Homestead
   Grays 1922-1946

COOL PAPA BELL WAS A SWITCH-hitter with the speed to beat out ground balls and to score from second on fly-outs. He also owned the power to hit the long ball righthanded. He was widely recognized as the best outfielder in the Negro Leagues and the fastest man in all of baseball. Long-time teammate Satchel Paige said Bell could turn out the light and be in bed before the room got dark.

James Thomas Bell (1903-1991) at age 17 moved from Starkville, Mississippi, to St. Louis, where his mother felt he would get a better education. The St. Louis Stars signed him in 1922 as a lefthanded knuckleball pitcher. He earned his nickname when he fell asleep before he was supposed to pitch. Even though he was later swiched to the outfield, he was still a "Cool Papa."

Bell was popular in St. Louis, and he remained with the Stars for 10 seasons. He gained his fame with the great Pittsburgh Crawfords team and, later, with the Homestead Grays. He joined the Crawfords in 1933, a team that also raided other ballclubs (including the Steel City rival Grays) for the services of future Hall of Famers

Cuba, 1928

Like other Negro Leaguers, Bell added to his income by playing in Cuba and Mexico.

Satchel Paige, Oscar Charleston, Judy Johnson, and Josh Gibson. Other very good players—such as Sam Bankhead, Sam Streeter, Rap Dixon, Cy Perkins, Leroy Matlock, and Vic Harris—played for the Crawfords at some time from '33 to 1936. It might have been the greatest concentration of talent in baseball at the time.

Cool Papa joined other Negro League stars and went south, playing in both the Dominican Republic and in Mexico. Bell was in such demand that he played for 29 summers and 21 winters. He was still hitting .300, though he couldn't field, when he was age 48. In his day they would at times play three games in three towns in a day, play 200 games in a season, and travel everywhere by bus.

Bell's lifetime average, by available records, was .338, and he hit .395 in exhibition games against major leaguers. He once stole over 175 bases in a 200-game season, but as he remembered, "one day I got five hits and stole five bases, but none of that was written down because they didn't bring the scorebook to the game that day." Bell was elected to the Hall of Fame in 1974.

Monte Irvin said, "The only comparison I can give is—suppose Willie Mays had never had a chance to play big league? Then I were to come to you and try to tell you about Willie Mays. Now this is the way it is with Cool Papa Bell."

Bell slides into third base in a 1943 game at Griffith Stadium. His legendary speed remained intact until the end of his career.

Negro League Stats*

BA	G	AB	H	2B	3B	HR	SB
.338	919	3,952	1,335	203	68	56	173

*Note: Bell's career stats are incomplete.

Shortstop; third baseman
New York Giants
1922-1936

AFTER LEADING THE LEAGUE in errors in 1924, Travis Jackson became one of the best fielders in the league, earning the nickname "Stonewall."

Travis Calvin Jackson (1903-1987) was born in Waldo, Arkansas. His uncle, who lived in Little Rock, was a friend of Kid Elberfeld, a former Yankee shortstop and a manager of the Little Rock team of the Southern League. When young Travis visited Little Rock, he fielded hours worth of ground balls hit at him by Elberfeld. In 1921, when Travis was 17 years old, Elberfeld signed him to a contract to play with Little Rock. While Jackson was playing in 1922 (he finished the season with a .280 average), Elberfeld recommended him to Giants manager John McGraw. Although the Giants had a shortstop, Dave Bancroft, who would later be a Hall of Famer, McGraw signed Jackson.

In 1922, Jackson got in three games with the Giants, a team bound for its second straight World Championship. He played 96 games in 1923, including 60 at shortstop, when Bancroft was out with pneumonia. At the end of that year, McGraw dealt Bancroft and installed Travis as his shortstop.

Jackson was not a heavy hitter by the standards of the day, though he was capable of explosive performances. When he became a regular in 1924, he capped his first full season (which included a .302 average and 81 runs) by hitting two grand slams in a September game, and the Giants went on to win the pennant by a single game. In 1928, he had eight RBI in one game, and in 1929, a double, triple, and two homers in a single contest.

Complemented by a very strong arm, Jackson became a regular league-leader in assists and double plays, and was voted the outstanding major league shortstop by *The Sporting News* in 1927, 1928, and 1929.

Jackson suffered a broken knee in 1932 and didn't resume play as a regular until late in 1933 as a third baseman. He spent his last two seasons at third base. He retired after the 1936 season. He returned to the Giants as a coach for two stints before managing in the minor leagues.

A solid hitter, with a .291 career batting average, Jackson adapted his stroke to fit the Polo Ground's short fences. He topped the .300 plateau six times in his career, reaching a high mark of .339 in 1930. He also pounded 21 homers in 1929. Jackson's glove work and impressive batting stats for a shortstop of his era convinced the Veterans Committee to induct him into the Hall of Fame in 1982. He died on July 27, 1987, in his hometown of Waldo, Arkansas.

Top: *Jackson's highwater mark came in 1930 when he hit .339 and had a .529 slugging average for a Giants club that batted an NL record .319 as a team. Above: A 1931 Jackson card. That season he led all NL shortstops in total chances and fielding average, and he finished seventh in MVP balloting.*

			Major League Totals							
BA	G	AB	R	H	2B	3B	HR	RBI	SB
.291	1,656	6,086	833	1,768	291	86	135	929	71

LOU GEHRIG

HENRY LOUIS GEHRIG
NEW YORK YANKEES·1923-1939
HOLDER OF MORE THAN A SCORE OF
MAJOR AND AMERICAN LEAGUE RECORDS,
INCLUDING THAT OF PLAYING 2130
CONSECUTIVE GAMES. WHEN HE RETIRED
IN 1939, HE HAD A LIFE TIME BATTING
AVERAGE OF 340.

**First baseman
New York Yankees
1923-1939**

ON JUNE 2, 1925, WHEN NEW York Yankees backup first sacker Fred Merkle, who was giving the club's long-time regular Wally Pipp a day off, seemed about to collapse from the heat, manager Miller Huggins called on rookie first baseman Lou Gehrig as a late-inning replacement. Merkle never started another game in the majors and Pipp never got his job back. Gehrig played a record 2,130 consecutive games for the Yankees. He did not always play all nine innings and he was not always stationed at first base, but one way or another his name always appeared on the lineup card before the game was over. Only very rarely did he play for the sole reason of extending his monumental streak. He played because he was the best all-around first baseman in baseball history.

Born in Manhattan, Henry Louis Gehrig (1903-1941) starred in all sports at the High School of Commerce. Upon graduation, he signed a professional baseball contract with Hartford of the Eastern League under the name of Lewis. Regardless of what disguise Gehrig chose, he could not hide his prodigious talent, and the ruse was soon discovered. As a consequence, he was declared ineligible for sports at Columbia University, where he had been counted on to play for both the football and baseball teams.

Gehrig accepted a bonus of $1,500 from the Yankees against his father's wishes and began playing with Hartford under his own name. A two-year apprenticeship in the minors was all he needed before he was ready to take his place among the game's greats. In his first full season, Gehrig hit .295, scored 73 runs, and knocked home 68 teammates. He would never again tally under 100 runs or collect less than 100 RBI in a full season. Gehrig averaged the highest number of runs and RBI per game of any 20th century player.

In 1931, Lou established an American League record when he drove in 184 runs, breaking his own old mark of 175 set in 1927. The following year he became the first player in the 20th century to clout four home runs in a game. He also once had three triples in a game that was rained out in the fourth inning before it became an official contest. When Lou left baseball he had 493 home runs, second at the time only to Babe Ruth.

Gehrig's slugging exploits were only part of the story. He was also both an excellent baserunner and a solid first baseman. He was extremely consistent and, of course, very durable. Twice he was selected the AL's Most Valuable Player, and he was always known for his overall performance.

Above: The Yankees presented this trophy to Gehrig. Right: He always seemed a hair away from the recognition he deserved. For most of his career he played in the shadow of Babe Ruth or Joe DiMaggio. On the day he hit four home runs John McGraw resigned as manager of the Giants.

Gehrig tearfully bids goodbye to baseball in his famous 1939 "Farewell" speech.

This Song was written by FRED FISHER and Mrs. LOU GEHRIG
DEDICATED TO LOU GEHRIG - FAMOUS FIRST BASEMAN
I CAN'T GET TO FIRST BASE WITH YOU

FRED FISHER MUSICAL Music Publisher

A Perfect Marriage: Eleanor and Her Luke

In real life as in the film *The Pride of the Yankees*, Lou and Eleanor had a storybook relationship and loving marriage. It was Eleanor Gehrig who took the shy slugger out of his reticent shell and introduced him to the world beyond baseball. It was through her prodding that the Columbia-educated Gehrig began to read the classics in earnest, attend plays and concerts.

Far from merely enjoying a common love for the arts, the couple also enjoyed a playfulness, with pet names and quiet candlelight dinners at home. During the slugger's two-year battle against amyotropic lateral sclerosis, Eleanor cared for her husband around the clock, keeping his spirits up with her jokes and performing little tasks such as lighting cigarettes and opening mail for him.

Neither Teresa Wright nor Gary Cooper, who were cast in the roles of Eleanor and Lou Gehrig, knew anything about the Gehrigs or baseball in general before being hired to make the film. However, their screen portrayals were viewed approvingly by Eleanor Gehrig.

In 1934, Gehrig won the Triple Crown while copping his only batting title with a .363 mark. Two years later he garnered his final home run crown with 49 four-baggers, tying his own personal high. When Gehrig's batting average slipped to .295 in 1938 and his RBI and homer totals also dipped, it seemed just an off year at first. The strange slump persisted into the next season, restricting him to a meager four singles in his first eight games. When teammates began congratulating him for making routine plays, Lou knew the time had come to step down. On May 2, 1939, he took himself out of the lineup for the first time in nearly 14 years. A few weeks later he entered the Mayo Clinic for tests, which revealed that he had amyotrophic lateral sclerosis—a hardening of the spinal cord. The rare disease has no known cure and is always terminal. Knowing he would soon die, Gehrig retired formally on July 4, 1939, in a special ceremony at Yankee Stadium. Tearfully, he told the packed house, "Today, I consider myself the luckiest man on the face of the earth."

Following the 1939 season, Gehrig took a job with the New York City Parole Commission. He continued to work with youth groups and to play bridge with his wife, Eleanor, and close friends until just a few weeks before his death on June 2, 1941. He was inducted into the Hall of Fame in 1939.

Major League Totals

BA	G	AB	R	H	2B	3B	HR	RBI	SB
.340	2,164	8,001	1,888	2,721	535	162	493	1,990	102

WILLIAM HAROLD TERRY
NEW YORK N.L. 1923 TO 1941
BATTED .401 AND TIED N.L. RECORD FOR
BASE HITS WITH 254 IN 1930. MADE 200 OR
MORE HITS IN SIX SEASONS. RETIRED WITH
LIFETIME BATTING AVERAGE OF .341, A
MODERN N.L. RECORD FOR LEFT-HANDED
BATTERS. MOST VALUABLE PLAYER IN 1930.
SUCCEEDED JOHN McGRAW AS MANAGER IN
1932 AND WON PENNANTS IN 1933-36-37.

First baseman
New York Giants
1923-1936

Manager
New York Giants
1932-1941
823-661

Top: Terry is the last National League player to retire with a career batting average of .340 or better (.341). Right: After appearing on the cover of Baseball Magazine *in June 1933, Bill went on to take the New York Giants to the National League pennant in his first full season as their skipper.*

NEW YORK GIANT FIRST BASEman Bill Terry was the last National League player to hit .400, when he notched a .401 average in 1930.

William Harold Terry (1896-1989) was born in Atlanta and was a pitcher for local teams. He began his pro career in 1915 as a pitcher in the Georgia-Alabama League, where he went 7-1. He was sold to Shreveport of the Texas League, where he pitched for a couple of years. His record was 14-11 with a 3.00 ERA in 1917, and he hit .231. Not happy that he wasn't offered a contract, he moved to Memphis to work for Standard Oil and to play first base for the company's semipro baseball team. John McGraw was tipped off to this hot-hitting first sacker, and in 1922, on one of McGraw's annual trips to Memphis, he signed Terry, but not without Terry arguing for a $5,000 annual salary first.

Bill then ripped up the American Association for a couple of years. But it wasn't until he was age 26 that he joined the Giants in late 1923. He had to bust into an infield that included Travis Jackson, Freddie Lindstrom, Frankie Frisch, and George Kelly, all future Hall of Famers. It was 1927 before Terry established himself as the regular first baseman, waiting for Kelly to be traded. Bill turned in six consecutive seasons of

over 100 runs and 100 RBI and showed good power, from 1927 to 1932.

McGraw turned over the managing duties to Terry in 1932, and "Memphis Bill" led the team to a World Series victory as player-manager in 1933, and two more pennants in 1936 and 1937.

Terry had his greatest year in 1930. He batted .401 with a National League record 254 hits, 77 for extra bases, and posted career highs with 139 runs and 129 RBI. He was among the top MVP vote-getters for the next five years, and his .352 average for the 1930s was the best in the majors. Terry was a standout with the glove as well, generally considered the best of his day. He led the league in fielding average twice, assists and putouts five times each, and total chances per game nine times.

Terry also topped the .340 mark six times in his career and rapped 200-plus hits in a season six times. He carved a .341 career average with 2,193 hits in only 14 years of service, five of those years with the added responsibility of managing the club.

Bill retired after the 1936 season, but continued to manage the Giants until 1941. Despite his fine record as a hitter, fielder, and manager, he had to wait until 1954 before he was inducted into the Hall of Fame.

Major League Totals									
BA	G	AB	R	H	2B	3B	HR	RBI	SB
.341	1,721	6,428	1,120	2,193	373	112	154	1,078	56

TED LYONS

Pitcher
Chicago White Sox
1923-1942; 1946

TED LYONS PITCHED 21 SEASONS with the Chicago White Sox, going 260-230 for a .531 winning percentage. In those years, without Lyons pitching, the White Sox compiled a .447 winning percentage. Ted is the only Hall of Fame pitcher to serve 21 years with the same team without ever playing on a pennant winner.

Theodore Amar Lyons (1900-1986) was a star basketball player and second baseman as a high school player in Vinton, Louisiana. He attended Baylor University with the intention of becoming a lawyer, and he played on the baseball team as an extra-curricular activity. The team had too many infielders, however, so Ted became a pitcher, and was so good that he attracted the attention of the major league clubs.

In 1923, Lyons went straight from the campus to the major leagues with the White Sox. An important reason he signed with the White Sox rather than Cleveland or the Philadelphia A's, both of whom were also courting him, was because Chicago owner Charlie Comiskey pledged that Lyons would not be demoted to the minors until he'd spent at least one full year in the majors.

Lyons had rough seasons in 1923 and '24, but he rebounded in 1925 to tie Eddie Rommell for the American League lead in wins with 21—pretty impressive, since Ted pitched on a team that was 79-75. Two years later, he again

tied for the AL lead with 22 victories, while the ChiSox were 70-83. He also topped the loop in innings pitched and complete games that year. After mediocre seasons in 1928 and '29, he bounced back to go 22-15, leading the loop with 29 complete games and 297²/₃ innings pitched.

Lyons injured his arm during spring training in 1931. Pitching a night exhibition game against the Giants, he tore something in his shoulder. Rather than sit out the year and allow the injury to heal, he tried to pitch through it. When he was ineffective, Lyons resurrected a knuckleball he had discarded earlier in his career.

Judicious use of the knuckler enabled Lyons to extend for 13 more seasons a career that seemed doomed in 1931. Between ages 30 and 40, he won just 107 games and lost 108. In 1942, nearing his 42nd birthday, he topped the American League with a 2.10 ERA while posting a 14-6 record and tossing 20 complete games in 20 starts.

Returning from the Marines in 1946 after a three-year hitch during World War II, Lyons was the oldest player in the majors at 45. On May 25, 1946, Lyons retired as an active player when he was named the White Sox manager. Ted piloted the Pale Hose through 1948. He was elected to the Hall of Fame in 1955.

Top: *This 1934 Diamond Stars card pictures Lyons, who has one of the poorest strikeout-to-walk ratios of any pitcher in the Hall of Fame. Yet he registered a .531 career winning percentage while playing for a team that generally finished well below .500. Left: Lyons shown in his final season as the manager of the White Sox.*

		Major League Totals							
W	**L**	**ERA**	**G**	**CG**	**IP**	**H**	**ER**	**BB**	**SO**
260	230	3.67	594	356	4,161	4,489	1,697	1,121	1,073

HEINIE MANUSH

HENRY EMMET MANUSH
1923-1939
SLUGGING OUTFIELDER
FOR 6 MAJOR LEAGUE CLUBS. BATTING
CHAMPION OF A.L. AT .378 WITH 1926 TIGERS.
LIFETIME AVERAGE OF .330 IN 2,009
MAJOR LEAGUE GAMES. HAD 2,524 HITS.

Outfielder
Detroit Tigers 1923-1927
St. Louis Browns
    1928-1930
Washington Senators
    1930-1935
Boston Red Sox 1936
Brooklyn Dodgers
    1937-1938
Pittsburgh Pirates
    1938-1939

Top: *The ball Manush tagged for his 2,500th career hit, in 1937. Right: Manush is often linked with Goose Goslin, another lefthanded-hitting Hall of Fame outfielder. The two vied for several AL bat titles in the 1920s, were traded for one another in 1930, and played together in 1933 on the last flag-winning Senators team.*

HENRY EMMETT MANUSH (1901-1971) was an outstanding amateur ballplayer as a youth in Tennessee. He had six older brothers, two of whom played professional baseball. The eldest, Frank, vied with Home Run Baker for the Philadelphia A's third base job in 1908.

Originally intending to be a pipefitter, Heinie revised his ambitions when a scout for the Detroit Tigers thought highly enough of him to sign him to a contract in 1921 with Edmonton of the Western Canada League. A pull hitter at the outset of his career, Heinie topped the northern loop in home runs, but it was to be his only four-bagger crown. By the time he reached the majors two years later he had already begun to shorten his swing and punch the ball toward whichever part of the diamond he saw a hole. Manush's adjustment was an unusual one,

especially for a big man—he weighed around 200 pounds. With the lively ball era already in full bloom, power had become the ticket to stardom, but Manush apparently foresaw that his skills would best be served by focusing just on meeting the ball squarely.

Brought up to the Detroit Tigers in 1923, Heinie platooned with Bobby Veach in an outfield that included Ty Cobb and Harry Heilmann. Cobb was the skipper of the Bengals at that time, and Manush said that his production at bat benefitted greatly from his long hours with Cobb.

Heinie won one American League batting crown, in 1926, when he hit .378. After dropping to a .298 batting average in 1927, Manush was traded to the Browns. He narrowly missed another batting crown when Goose Goslin edged him by a single point. Manush also paced the junior circuit in hits and doubles twice and triples on one occasion.

In 1930, Manush came to Washington as part of a swap for Goose Goslin. The deal enabled Heinie to play on his only flag winner three years later when the Senators claimed their final pennant. In game four of the 1933 World Series, he became the first player to be ejected from a postseason contest since 1919 when he argued a close play at first base too vigorously.

Traded to the Red Sox in 1936, Heinie played just one season in Fenway Park before traveling to the National League, where he spent his final three seasons. In his 17-year career, he hit .330. Named to the Hall of Fame in 1964, Manush died seven years later on May 12 in Sarasota, Florida.

Major League Totals

BA	G	AB	R	H	2B	3B	HR	RBI	SB
.330	2,009	7,653	1,287	2,524	491	160	110	1,173	114

132

LEWIS ROBERT WILSON
"HACK"
NEW YORK N.L., CHICAGO N.L.,
BROOKLYN N.L., PHILADELPHIA N.L.,
1923-1934
ESTABLISHED MAJOR LEAGUE RECORD OF 190
RUNS BATTED IN AND NATIONAL LEAGUE HIGH
OF 56 HOMERS IN 1930. LED OR TIED FOR N.L.
HOMER TITLE FOUR TIMES. COMPILED LIFETIME
.307 BATTING AVERAGE AND DROVE IN 100 OR
MORE RUNS SIX YEARS. HIT TWO HOMERS IN
INNING IN 1925 AND THREE IN GAME IN 1930.

Outfielder
New York Giants
1923-1925
Chicago Cubs 1926-1931
Brooklyn Dodgers
1932-1934
Philadelphia Phillies 1934

THERE HAS NEVER BEEN ANY-one in baseball that looked quite like Hack Wilson. Only 5'6" tall, but weighing 200 pounds, Wilson had a huge barrel chest supported by tree-trunk-sized legs, resting on two tiny feet. He wore an 18-inch collar and size six shoes.

Born and raised in Pennsylvania steel country, Lewis Robert Wilson (1900-1948) never made it past the sixth grade and worked throughout his childhood. He developed his enormous upper-body strength by swinging heavy hammers while working in the Baldwin, Pennsylvania, locomotive works. There is debate about where the nickname "Hack" originated, either from the former Chicago Cubs outfielder Hack Miller or from wrestler George Hackenschmidt.

Hack began his pro career in 1921 playing with Martinsville in the Blue Ridge League, and two years later he moved up to the Virginia League. Originally a catcher, he broke a leg sliding and ended up an outfielder. Although he batted .356, .366, and .388 in his three seasons in the minors, leading his league in homers, he was deemed too short by several clubs. John McGraw stood only 5'7" and was a pretty good ballplayer, so he had no problems with signing Wilson. Hack was a part-timer in New York, he hit a solid .295 in 1924, before slumping to .239 in 1925, earning a demotion to the minors, leaving him unprotected. The Cubs grabbed

Hack in the 1925 postseason draft for $5,000.

During the next five years, Hack's worst numbers included a .313 batting average, 21 home runs, and 109 RBI. He won four home run titles in that span (from 1926 to 1928 and 1930) and led the Cubs to the World Series in 1929 when he hit 39 homers and led the league with 159 RBI.

In 1930, Wilson rode the crest of an offensive wave that swept through baseball to heights never reached before or since. He hit 56 home runs, the NL record, and drove in 190 runs, the major league record. Hack was named MVP, but it was his last good year. In 1931, he fell to .261 with 13 homers and 61 RBI, prompting the trade that sent him to the Cardinals, who in turn traded him to Brooklyn prior to the '32 season.

Alcohol proved to be Wilson's downfall. His bad temper grew worse, he got in fights on and off the field, and he showed up for games drunk or hungover. Though he played in four more seasons he hit just 51 more homers. With the Dodgers in 1932, he rallied for a season, and then was out of baseball after 1934. When he died in 1948 he was broke. In 1979, 31 years after his death, Wilson was elected to the Hall.

The
SPORTING
NEWS
RECORD BOOK for 1931

LEWIS (HACK) WILSON
Chicago Cubs

Published by
CHARLES C. SPINK & SON
···ST. LOUIS. MO.···
Price: Ten Cents the Copy

Top: *After his outburst in 1930, Wilson sagged to just 13 homers and 61 RBI in '31.* Above: *Ideally suited for the cover of the 1931* Sporting News Record Book, *he was coming off a 1930 season in which he set the NL home run record with 56 and the all-time record with 190 RBI.*

Major League Totals

BA	G	AB	R	H	2B	3B	HR	RBI	SB
.307	1,348	4,760	884	1,461	266	67	244	1,062	52

MARTIN DIHIGO
"EL MAESTRO"
NEGRO LEAGUES 1923-1947
MOST VERSATILE OF NEGRO LEAGUE STARS.
PLAYED IN BOTH SUMMER AND WINTER
BALL. MOST OF CAREER REGISTERED MORE
THAN 260 VICTORIES AS PITCHER. WHEN NOT
ON MOUND HE PLAYED OUTFIELD OR INFIELD.
USUALLY BATTING WELL OVER .300. ALSO
MANAGED DURING AND AFTER PLAYING DAYS.

**Outfielder; pitcher;
infielder; catcher;
manager**
teams include:
 Cuban Stars;
 Homestead Grays;
 Philadelphia Hilldales;
 Baltimore Black Sox;
 New York Cubans
 1923-1945

SINCE THE NEGRO LEAGUE teams obtained such slender profit margins, often teams carried only 14 to 18 players. The most valuable player to a team was usually the one who could play several positions adequately. Martin Dihigo could pitch and play all the infield and outfield positions at an All-Star quality level.

Born in Matanzas, Cuba, Martin Dihigo (1905-1971) began his pro career in 1923 in the Cuban Winter League as a 17-year-old strong-armed but weak-hitting outfielder. There is a legend that he won a distance-throwing contest against a jai alai player who was allowed to use his wicker-basket cesta. He is compared very favorably to Roberto Clemente by those who saw both players throw from the outfield. Like the American-born Negro League players, Martin crossed and recrossed the 90 miles of water between the two countries to ply his trade; he also played in Puerto Rico, Mexico, and Venezuela. From the time he came to America in 1923 through 1936, he made only occasional forays to the pitching mound, having some success with his good fastball and control.

Dihigo pitched more often when he was in the Latin American countries. His pitching stats

include an 18-2 record and an 0.90 ERA in 1938, and a 22-7 record and a 2.53 ERA in 1942. He twirled the first no-hitter in Mexican League history. According to the albeit unsubstantiated records found by historians thus far, he probably won 256 games while dropping only 136.

From his early troubles at the plate, Martin developed into a great hitter by age 20. He made his lasting impression with his bat in the United States. He was a fine hitter—he hit over .400 three times and led two different leagues in batting average—and he hit a 500-foot round-tripper in Pittsburgh in 1936. At 210 pounds Dihigo led his league in homers at least twice, in 1926 and in 1935. He tossed runners out at home plate with frightening regularity.

He posted a .316 career batting average in the Negro Leagues. He often left the outfield to pitch relief, especially when he was managing. Dihigo was a manager for the New York Cubans, in Mexico, and in Cuba until 1950. He also played all nine positions in one game on several occasions.

After his retirement, Dihigo became a broadcaster and the Minister of Sport in Cuba. He died in 1971 one of Latin America's most admired players. Martin is the only player to be in the Cuban, Mexican, and American halls of fame.

Top: *Dihigo was the first Cuban to be selected for the Hall of Fame.* Right: *Early in his career, he was hamstrung by curveball pitchers. Once he matured, he became not only one of the top pitchers in the Negro Leagues but a outstanding hitter. It was not uncommon for him to be a league leader in a pitching and a batting department in the same season.*

Negro League Stats*

BA	G	AB	H	2B	3B	HR	SB
.316	415	1,435	453	53	18	64	32

W	L	G	CG	IP	H	BB	SO
27	21	50	32	309	235	61	126

*Note: Dihigo's career stats are incomplete.

NEVER FLAMBOYANT AND THE possessor of an almost Sphinx-like demeanor, Charlie Gehringer might have gone virtually unnoticed on the baseball diamond but for one remarkable quality. He gave the same quietly outstanding performance day in and day out. Gehringer's unceasing excellence led to his being nicknamed "The Mechanical Man." Mickey Cochrane, after managing Charlie for two years in Detroit, said of him, "He says hello on opening day and goodbye on closing day, and in between he hits .350."

Charles Leonard Gehringer (born in 1903) was raised about 60 miles north of Detroit in the small farming town of Fowlerville. After starring as an athlete in high school, he played both football and baseball for one year at the University of Michigan and then decided his future lay in professional baseball. On the recommendation of former Tigers outfielder Bobby Veach, Gehringer was given a tryout by none other than the great Ty Cobb, then the Detroit player-manager.

Signed by the Tigers in 1924 as a third baseman, Gehringer was soon moved to second base and became the club's regular there in 1926. For the next 16 years Charlie broke the hearts of all the other keystone aspirants in the Detroit organization. After hitting .277 as a rookie, he batted over .300 every other season but one until he began to fade in 1941.

Gehringer's high-water mark came in 1937 when he batted .371 to win the American League

Second baseman
Detroit Tigers 1924-1942

batting crown. At age 34, he was the oldest first-time winner of a hitting title in history. Before 1937, Gehringer had also paced the junior loop on several occasions in runs, hits, doubles, triples, and stolen bases. His play in all departments was of such high caliber that he was voted the AL second baseman for the first All-Star game in 1933. Gehringer played in six All-Star games altogether and hit a combined .500 with ten hits in 20 at bats. He displayed the same steady brilliance in his three World Series appearances with the Tigers. In 81 at bats, Charlie hit .321, one point higher than his overall career batting mark of .320.

Reduced to a utility role by 1942, Gehringer retired at the end of the season even though he still had enough of his old batting skill left to lead the AL in pinch hits. Following three years in the Navy during World War II, Gehringer went to work for an auto dealer in Detroit. Two years after he was elected to the Hall of Fame in 1949, Charlie returned to the Tigers as general manager. He subsequently served as a Tigers vice president until 1959.

Top: *Co-authored by Gehringer and Billy Herman, the two top second basemen of their day, this book appeared in 1941.* Left: *Gehringer holds the all-time record for the most doubles in a season by a second baseman—60 in 1936—and the AL second-sackers record for the most runs in a season (144) and the most total bases (356).*

				Major League Totals					
BA	G	AB	R	H	2B	3B	HR	RBI	SB
.320	2,323	8,860	1,774	2,839	574	146	184	1,427	182

ALOYSIUS HARRY SIMMONS
PLAYED WITH 7 MAJOR LEAGUE CLUBS 1924-
1944. STAR WITH PHILA.(A.L.). BATTED
.305 TO .392 FROM 1924 TO 1934. LEADING
BATTER .381 IN 1930, .390 IN 1931. MOST
HITS BY A.L. RIGHT-HANDED BATTER WITH
253. LED LEAGUE RUNS BATTED IN, RUNS
SCORED, HITS AND TOTAL BASES SEVERAL
SEASONS. HIT 5 HOME RUNS, JULY 15, 1932.
LIFETIME BATTING AVERAGE .334.

Outfielder
Philadelphia Athletics
   1924-1932; 1940-1941;
   1944
Chicago White Sox
   1933-1935
Detroit Tigers 1936
Washington Senators
   1937-1938
Boston Braves 1939
Cincinnati Reds 1939
Boston Red Sox 1943

Top: This 1933 Delong card portrays the stature Simmons was expected to assume for the White Sox. He did pace the Sox in every major batting department in 1933 and 1934. Right: In the twilight of his career, he began the 1939 season with the lowly Braves but was picked up by Cincinnati in time to play in the World Series.

AL SIMMONS'S CAREER .334 batting average made mincemeat of critics who believed that he would never be able to hit good pitching with his peculiar penchant for striding toward third base when he swung rather than toward the mound. The unorthodox batting style caused him to be tagged "Bucketfoot Al."

Born Aloys Szymanski (1902-1956) in a Polish section of Milwaukee, Wisconsin, Simmons never wanted to be anything but a baseball player. In 1922, he signed his first professional contract with the Milwaukee Brewers of the American Association. When Al hit .398 for Milwaukee in a 24-game trial at the end of the 1923 campaign, the Brewers found themselves with a hot property on their hands and were able to sell him to the Philadelphia Athletics for around $50,000.

In 1924, his rookie year with the A's, Simmons batted .308 and knocked home 102 runs. The following year, he collected a league-leading 253 hits and hiked his average to .384. Moreover, he became the first player in American League history to drive in 100 or more runs in each of his first two seasons in the majors.

Not only an outstanding hitter, he was also an able outfielder with a strong throwing arm. The addition of Ty Cobb in 1927 helped Al to develop even further as a hitter. Like Harry Heilmann, another great righthanded hitter during the 1920s, Simmons found it remarkably easy to befriend the much shunned Cobb. In his single-minded dedication to becoming the best player he possibly could be, Simmons himself acquired the reputation for not being overly personable.

When the A's copped their first of three consecutive pennants in 1929, Al enjoyed the first of five straight seasons in which he collected 200 or more hits, at the time an American League record. The following year he won the first of two consecutive batting crowns and was generally regarded as the American League's most valuable player.

Simmons was traded to the Chicago White Sox in 1933 when A's manager Connie Mack began to break up his dynasty for economic reasons. Later in his career Al played for Detroit, Washington, and Boston before spending one season in the National League. He returned to the A's in 1944 before retiring.

A coach for the A's during the late 1940s, Simmons also acted as the club's unofficial manager when Connie Mack grew too old to serve as anything more than a dugout ornament. In 1953 Al was elected to the Hall of Fame.

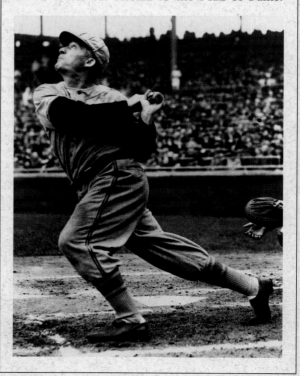

Major League Totals

BA	G	AB	R	H	2B	3B	HR	RBI	SB
.334	2,215	8,761	1,507	2,927	539	149	307	1,827	87

CHARLES HERBERT RUFFING
"RED"
BOSTON, A.L. 1924-1930
NEW YORK, A.L. 1930-1946
CHICAGO, A.L. 1947
WINNER OF 273 GAMES.
WON 20 OR MORE GAMES IN EACH OF FOUR
CONSECUTIVE SEASONS. LED IN COMPLETE
GAMES 1928. TIED IN SHUTOUTS 1938-1939.
WON 7 OUT OF 9 WORLD SERIES DECISIONS.
SELECTED FOR ALL STAR TEAMS
1937-1938-1939

Pitcher
Boston Red Sox 1924-1930
New York Yankees
    1930-1942; 1945-1946
Chicago White Sox 1947

ON MAY 6, 1930, RED RUFFING had a 39-96 career won-lost record and a .289 winning percentage. Over the next 15 seasons he won 231 games and posted a .651 winning percentage. More tellingly than any other pitcher in history, Ruffing proved what can happen when a good hurler buried on a miserable team is traded to a contender.

Charles Herbert Ruffing (1904-1986) was born in Granville, Illinois, the son of a coal miner. Red left school at age 15 to join his father in the mines. Red was an excellent outfielder on the company team until he lost four toes on his left foot in a mining accident shortly after arriving at the mines. His dream of being a big league outfielder was dashed, but when the company pitcher was injured, Red took the mound and found a new calling.

Signed in 1923 by Danville of the Three-I League, Red was purchased by the Red Sox toward the end of that season. Upon joining Boston for keeps in 1925, Ruffing found himself on the worst club in the majors. The Red Sox in the late 1920s had so little punch that Red was often the best hitter in the lineup on the days he pitched. His fortunes changed dramatically after he was traded in May 1930 to the Yankees. Two years later Ruffing bagged 18 victories as the

Yankees copped their first flag under Joe McCarthy.

Before Red was done he pitched on seven pennant winners in New York and had a glittering 7-2 record in World Series play. Four times a 20-game winner, he served in addition as the Yankees' chief righthanded pinch-hitter for several seasons. Ruffing's career highpoint came in 1938 when he led the American League with 21 wins and a .750 winning percentage.

Red spent over two years in the Army during World War II before rejoining the Yankees in June 1945. Although age 41, he won 12 of his first 16 decisions after his return but then broke his ankle early in the 1946 season. Released by the Yankees, he pitched part of the 1947 campaign for the Chicago White Sox before a knee injury forced his retirement.

Red's main assets were his excellent control, baffling changeup, and ability to work well over 200 innings year after year. Although he posted a career 3.80 ERA, the highest of any pitcher currently in the Hall of Fame, he retired with the most career wins of any pitcher in Yankee history. His mark has since been broken by Whitey Ford, but he remains the club's top righthanded winner. In 1967, Ruffing was named to the Hall of Fame.

CHARLEY
"RED"
RUFFING

Top: Ruffing won 20 games for the first time in 1936. That same year he rapped .444 as a pinch-hitter. He was valued nearly as much for his bat as his arm. His first pinch-hit came in 1928 and his last 19 years later when he was 43. Left: The topic of this 1934 Diamond Stars card had his finest season to date that year, winning 19 games.

			Major League Totals						
W	L	ERA	G	CG	IP	H	ER	BB	SO
273	225	3.80	624	335	4,344	4,294	1,834	1,541	1,987

EARLE BRYAN COMBS
NEW YORK YANKEES 1924-1935
LEAD-OFF HITTER AND CENTER FIELDER OF YANKEE CHAMPIONS OF 1926-27-28-'32. LIFETIME BATTING AVERAGE .325, 200 OR MORE HITS THREE SEASONS. LED LEAGUE WITH 231 HITS IN 1927 WHILE BATTING .356. PACED A.L. IN TRIPLES THREE TIMES AND TWICE LED OUTFIELDERS IN PUTOUTS. BATTED .350 IN FOUR WORLD SERIES.

Outfielder
New York Yankees
1924-1935

WHEN ONE THINKS OF THE 1927 Yankees, such names as Ruth and Gehrig come to mind. The man who had the most hits, though, was center fielder Earle Combs. While the Babe pounded 60 home runs, Earle hit .356, collected 231 hits, scored 137 runs, and led the league in triples with 23. "The Kentucky Colonel" spent his entire career with the Yankees, during the glory years of Murderers' Row.

Earle Bryan Combs (1899-1976) grew up on a farm in eastern Kentucky. He attended Eastern Kentucky State Teachers' College, where he patrolled center field for the baseball squad. He became a teacher after his graduation in 1921, but soon quit to play ball for a company team. He moved up in 1922 to the Kentucky Colonels of the American Association, managed by Joe McCarthy. In 1923, Earle led the loop in batting, and was purchased by the Yankees. He started 1924 as the Bombers center fielder, but broke his ankle early in the year. He returned in 1925 to play his first full season in major league ball.

Combs's average of .342 in 1925 is one of the highest in history for a rookie. Since he walked a fair amount and almost never struck out, Combs led off for the Yanks, scoring more than 100 runs in eight straight seasons. Although Earle didn't have a home run stroke, he led the league in triples three times (1927, 1928, and 1930), once hitting three in a single game.

After three pennants in the early 1920s, the Yankees machine ran low in 1924 and 1925. In 1925, Combs and Lou Gehrig became regulars, and in 1926, with rookie Tony Lazzeri, the Yanks resumed their hold on the American League. They lost the '26 Series in seven games, but won in 1927 and 1928, sweeping each fall classic in four games, though an injured hand forced Earle to miss almost the entire '28 Series.

Connie Mack's powerful A's displaced the Yankees for a few years. In 1932, with Joe McCarthy at the helm, the Bronx Bombers were back, again winning in four games. In 16 games in four World Series, Combs compiled a .350 average, amassed 21 hits, and scored 17 runs. His .350 average in World Series play is one of the highest ever.

Not having the strongest arm in the league, Combs's greatest asset was his speed as a fly hawk. He led AL outfielders in putouts several years. In 1934, while chasing down a deep fly, Earle crashed into the fence at Sportsman Park, fracturing his skull and limiting him to just 63 games. Able to make a remarkable comeback, he retired after the 1935 season. Combs was elected to the Hall of Fame in 1970.

Top: Combs was the first in a long tradition of great Yankees center fielders. He was followed by first Joe DiMaggio and then Mickey Mantle. In the short hiatus between Combs's departure and DiMaggio's arrival, Ben Chapman and Jake Powell filled the center spot in Yankee Stadium. Right: A Combs autographed baseball.

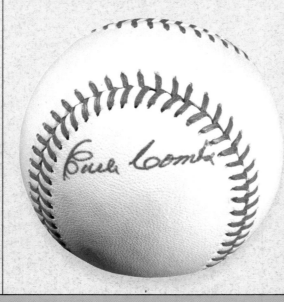

Major League Totals

BA	G	AB	R	H	2B	3B	HR	RBI	SB
.325	1,454	5,748	1,186	1,866	309	154	58	629	96

Outfielder
St. Louis Cardinals
1924-1931
Cincinnati Reds
1932-1935; 1937

PLAGUED THROUGHOUT HIS career by poor health and weak eyesight, Chick Hafey played over 100 games in a season on just seven occasions and garnered only 1,466 hits and 833 RBI. Rogers Hornsby, however, called Hafey the greatest righthanded hitter he ever saw.

A native of Berkeley, California, and a star athlete at Berkeley High, Charles James Hafey (1903-1973) had a chance to go to the University of California but opted instead to journey to Florida in the spring of 1923 to try out for the Cardinals as a pitcher. Unimpressive on the mound, he seemed destined for a trip home. However, a good day at the plate prompted Cardinals manager Branch Rickey to reconsider and offer Chick a contract, provided he become an outfielder.

Hafey started his pro career with Fort Smith in the Western Association in 1923. Fort Smith was one of the first minor league clubs that Rickey bought in developing a farm system for the Cardinals. Hafey hit .284 in his first year as an outfielder, and the Cards were so pleased that they moved Chick up to Houston of the Texas League for the 1924 season. There, he hit .360 with 90 RBI in 126 games. A major league club offered Houston $35,000 for Hafey, and the president of the Houston team had the right to sell his players—despite the fact that the Cardinals owned 59 percent of the team. However, Rickey matched the bid. The Cardinals only paid $14,350 for Chick, since the other $20,650 (or

59 percent) ended up back in the St. Louis coffers.

Although Hafey joined the Cardinals to stay early in the 1925 season, injuries and poor health prevented Chick from playing a full season until 1928. That year he hit .337 and collected 111 RBI. A poor showing in the '28 World Series helped convince Hafey to try playing with glasses the following season.

Having conquered the stigma of playing with "cheaters," Hafey upped all of his offensive marks in 1929 and also enjoyed a good season the following year. In 1931, Chick had his finest campaign. He won the National League batting title in the closest three-way batting race in history. Hafey checked in at .3489, Bill Terry of the Giants was at .3486, and Chick's St. Louis teammate Jim Bottomley batted .3482.

A contract dispute with Rickey prior to the start of the 1932 season brought about a trade that sent Hafey to the Reds. Illness and sinus problems plagued Hafey during his stint in Cincinnati. Quitting the Reds in June 1935, Hafey was induced by Cincinnati to return in 1937, but he batted only .261. He then retired for good. Hafey was inducted into the Hall of Fame in 1971.

Top: *Even though he was paid more by the Reds than he ever made as a member of the St. Louis Cardinals, Hafey never really adjusted to playing in Cincinnati. Left: Hafey leaps for a ball in Crosley Field after joining the Cincinnati Reds in 1932.*

Major League Totals									
BA	G	AB	R	H	2B	3B	HR	RBI	SB
.317	1,283	4,625	777	1,466	341	67	164	833	70

FRED LINDSTROM

FREDERICK CHARLES LINDSTROM
NEW YORK N.L., PITTSBURGH N.L.,
CHICAGO N.L., BROOKLYN N.L.,
1924 - 1936
COMPILED LIFETIME .311 BATTING MARK,
INCLUDING SEVEN SEASONS OF .300 OR
BETTER. ONE OF ONLY THREE PLAYERS TO
AMASS 230 OR MORE HITS A YEAR TWICE.
AS YOUNGEST PLAYER (AGE 18) IN WORLD
SERIES HISTORY, HE TIED RECORD WITH
FOUR HITS IN GAME IN 1924. EQUALLED
MAJOR LEAGUE RECORD BY COLLECTING
NINE HITS IN 1928 DOUBLEHEADER.

Infielder; outfielder
New York Giants
**   1924-1932**
Pittsburgh Pirates
**   1933-1934**
Chicago Cubs 1935
Brooklyn Dodgers 1936

Top: *In 1924, Lindstrom
became the youngest World
Series starter in history.* Above:
*He holds the NL records for the
most hits (231) and the highest
average (.379) in a season by a
third baseman.*

THE SAYING GOES THAT FIRST
impressions are hard to erase. If so, then
Fred Lindstrom's arrival at Cooperstown was
the culmination of an uphill journey.

In 1924, the Giants had to rush an 18-year-old
Lindstrom up to the big club because third
baseman Heinie Groh suffered a knee injury late
in the season. The Giants were on their way to
winning their fourth consecutive NL pennant,
and they needed Fred for World Series duty.
Considered a good gloveman at third base during
his career, Lindstrom is best remembered for two
ground balls that he didn't field in the 1924
World Series. With the Series tied at three
games each, the Giants led 3-1 in the bottom of
the eighth inning of game seven. Then a ground
ball hit to Lindstrom bad-hopped off a pebble
and bounced over his head. Two runs raced
home to tie it up. In the 12th inning, disaster
struck again. Muddy Ruel doubled, and then
Earl McNeely's grounder hit the same pebble,
or another just like it — so the legend goes. The
ball skipped over Lindstrom again, and the
Senators won the World Championship. He
wasn't charged with an error on either play,
nevertheless, and he hit .333 in the Series.

Frederick Charles Lindstrom (1905-1981)
was a pitcher in hometown Chicago when he was
growing up. Fred's high school coach was Jake
Weimer, a former major leaguer and another
of John McGraw's many informants. McGraw
liked what he heard and signed Lindstrom upon
Fred's high school graduation in 1922.

A .311 lifetime hitter, "Lindy" topped the
.300 plateau seven times, and twice slapped out
over 230 hits. An accomplished place-hitter,
he was quickly dubbed "The Boy Wonder" by
Giants fans. Lindstrom's most productive years
were his nine-year stint with the Giants. Freddie
led the league in hits in 1928 with 231 while
batting an impressive .358. In 1930, he again
collected 231 hits and pounded a career-high 22
homers, while driving home 106 runs — eye-
opening numbers, even without his .379 batting
average. Unfortunately, due to a plethora of
lofty averages in a year in which the composite
NL batting average was .303, Freddie's .379
mark was good for only fifth. Teammate Bill
Terry led the league at .401.

When McGraw stepped down in 1932,
Lindstrom hoped to succeed McGraw, but when
the job went to Bill Terry instead in 1933,
Lindstrom asked to be traded and was obliged.
He played in four more seasons with three teams,
making it back to the World Series with the
Cubs when they lost to Detroit in 1935.

After his major league career, Lindstrom
managed in the minor leagues and at Northwestern University in the 1950s. He was inducted
to the Hall of Fame in 1976.

Major League Totals

BA	G	AB	R	H	2B	3B	HR	RBI	SB
.311	1,438	5,611	895	1,747	301	81	103	779	84

Bucky Harris talks with Lou Boudreau prior to a 1942 game at Griffith Stadium.

BUCKY HARRIS EARNED HIS fame early, as "The Boy Manager" of the Washington Senators, and earned his Cooperstown credentials as one of the longest-running management acts in history. He won 2,157 games and guided five teams during his 29-year career.

Stanley Raymond Harris (1896-1977) was raised in Pittson, Pennsylvania. His father, Thomas, was a semipro baseball player and former teammate of Hughie Jennings. Jennings, a Scranton resident, was impressed when he saw young Bucky play baseball and got him a tryout with the Tigers in 1916, but Harris failed to impress and was jettisoned to the minors. After several unsatisfactory seasons, Bucky hit .282 with Buffalo of the International League. Washington owner Clark Griffith saw Harris and signed him. Bucky broke in with the Senators in 1919, becoming a glove wizard and an annual double-play champ.

Washington went nowhere under a succession of managers. In 1924, Griffith installed Harris as manager, and with young star Goose Goslin and seasoned veteran Walter Johnson, the Senators pulled away from the Yankees with a great stretch drive. Harris and the Senators were the talk of baseball and were going against John McGraw's New York Giants. In game seven, Harris started righty hurler Curly Ogden and

replaced him with lefthander George Mogridge after two batters, forcing McGraw to start young star lefty hitter Bill Terry then to replace him in the sixth inning. Harris hit a pebble-ball that bounced over Giants third baseman Fred Lindstrom's head, as the Senators won their only World Series.

The Senators won another pennant in 1925—though they lost the Series to the Pirates—and Harris continued to play for and manage the team until 1928. Harris then began his managerial travels in 1929, managing in Detroit, Boston, back in Washington, and in Philadelphia in the next 15 seasons, only twice finishing as high as fourth.

As a manager, Harris was a hard man. He only had one taste of success after his first years in Washington. In 1947, he took over the Yankees and promptly won his second World Series. When the team finished third in 1948 Harris was sacked. He managed for seven more years in Washington and Detroit, never finishing higher than fifth.

Despite his losing record, Harris drew praise for his management. His clubs generally lacked talent, and he got the best out of them by inspiring intense loyalty. Goose Goslin called Bucky "the best manager I ever played for." Harris was inducted in the Hall of Fame in 1975.

STANLEY RAYMOND HARRIS
"BUCKY"
SERVED 40 YEARS IN MAJORS AS PLAYER, MANAGER AND EXECUTIVE, INCLUDING 29 AS PILOT. SLICK SECOND SACKER EARNED TAG OF "BOY WONDER" BY GUIDING WASHINGTON TO 1924 WORLD TITLE AS 27-YEAR-OLD IN DEBUT AS PLAYER-PILOT. WON A.L. FLAG AGAIN IN 1925. LED 1947 YANKEES TO WORLD TITLE. MANAGED DETROIT, BOSTON RED SOX AND PHILADELPHIA PHILLIES.

Manager
Washington Senators
    1924-1928; 1935-1942;
    1950-1954
Detroit Tigers 1929-1933;
    1955-1956
Boston Red Sox 1934
Philadelphia Phillies 1943
New York Yankees
    1947-1948

LEADER OF 'EM ALL   A TASTY BIT THAT MAKES A HIT

"BUCKY" HARRIS

5¢ A SURE HIT   BAR

MANUFACTURED BY
WILKES-BARRE MAID CANDY CO. INC.
WILKES-BARRE, PENNA.

Life was never again as tasty for Bucky Harris as it was in his first two seasons as a major league pilot.

Major League Managing Totals				
W	L	T	PCT	G
2,157	2,218	31	.493	4,408

ROBERT MOSES GROVE
PHILADELPHIA A.L. 1925-1933
BOSTON A.L. 1934-1941
WINNER OF 300 GAMES IN THE MAJORS
OVER A SPAN OF 17 YEARS. LED A.L. IN
STRIKEOUTS SEVEN CONSECUTIVE SEASONS.
WON 20 OR MORE GAMES EIGHT SEASONS.
IN 1931, WHILE WINNING 31 GAMES AND
LOSING FOUR, COMPILED A WINNING STREAK
OF 16 STRAIGHT. WON 79 GAMES FOR THE
THREE TIME PENNANT WINNING
ATHLETICS TEAM OF 1929-30-31.

Pitcher
Philadelphia Athletics
1925-1933
Boston Red Sox 1934-1941

Top: *Grove (left) shakes hands with Dizzy Dean. The two mound greats were both on the downsides of their careers when this picture was taken. Earlier each had a 30-win season.* Above: *Lefty is on the cover of Ted Oliver's classic 1945 book.*

GENERALLY ACKNOWLEDGED to be the greatest lefthanded pitcher ever, Lefty Grove is considered by many authorities to be the greatest pitcher, period. The holder of the highest career winning percentage among pitchers who posted 300 or more career victories, Grove in addition compiled a 112-39 record in the minors to give him a combined winning percentage of .696, which is far and away the highest of any pitcher in organized baseball history.

Born in Lonaconing, Maryland, Robert Moses Grove (1900-1975) quit school in the eighth grade to work in a coal mine. Later an apprentice glass blower and railroad worker, Lefty was age 20 before he decided that baseball might offer a brighter future. After six games with Martinsburg in the Blue Ridge League, he was purchased by Jack Dunn, owner of the Baltimore Orioles in the International League.

For the next four and one-half years, Grove was trapped in Baltimore, unable to move up to the majors because International League teams at that time were exempt from the draft system and allowed to retain their stars for as long as they wished. Although Grove was paid better by Dunn than he would have been by several major league owners, he was nevertheless impatient to leave Baltimore. Finally, after the 1924 season, Connie Mack of the Philadelphia A's agreed to pay Dunn $100,000 for Grove's contract, plus an extra $600 to make the purchase higher than the amount the Yankees paid the Red Sox for Babe Ruth.

For all his minor league training, Grove was still not quite ready to become a major league star. The control problems that had beset him in Baltimore persisted during this first two seasons with the A's. But in 1927, Grove for the first time in his career gave up less than three walks per game. Not coincidentally, he also won 20 games for the first time in the majors that season.

The following year, Lefty topped the American League in wins for the first of four occasions. In 1929, he paced the AL in winning percentage for the initial time, a feat he was to repeat on five occasions. That year Grove also led the loop in strikeouts for the fifth of what would soon be seven straight seasons. It was his stinginess with runs that was Grove's greatest forte, however. On nine separate occasions he topped the AL in ERA.

Grove had his finest season to date in 1930 when he won 28 of 33 decisions and led the AL in winning percentage, ERA, and strikeouts. It seemed that he had surely reached his pinnacle, but incredibly his 1931 season was better. That year, Lefty had a 31-4 mark and an .886 winning percentage, the highest in history by a 30-game winner. The real topper, though, was his 2.06 ERA that was 2.32 runs per game below the league average of 4.38. As a consequence of his scorching performance, Grove received the first AL MVP Award voted upon by the Baseball Writers' Association of America.

Traded to the Red Sox by the A's after the 1933 season when Connie Mack wanted to unload his high salary players, Grove was never again the game's most dominant hurler, although he collected four ERA crowns and one winning percentage crown with Boston. In his later years, Lefty developed a great curveball when arm trouble reduced his blazing speed. After winning his 300th game in 1941, he officially retired that fall on the day that Pearl Harbor was attacked. Although his retirement announcement was overshadowed as result, little else he did during his career escaped notice. Elected to the Hall of Fame in 1947, Lefty devoted himself for years to working with young players and financially supporting youth leagues. He died in Norwalk, Ohio, of a heart attack on May 22, 1975.

The A's purchased Grove after he was 26-6 for Baltimore in 1924. He won just 23 of 49 decisions in his first two seasons in the bigs. For the remaining 15 years of his career, however, he had a .707 winning percentage.

Burning Determination and Raw Anger

Lefty Grove glowed with a combination of burning determination and raw anger both on and off the mound while forging one of the great careers in baseball history. Stories of his temper tantrums are legendary.

In August 1931 while attempting to win a record 17th straight game, he lost to the lowly St. Louis Browns by a score of 1-0 due to a dropped fly ball by a rookie outfielder who had replaced injured Hall of Famer Al Simmons. Following the game, Grove proceeded to lay waste to the visitor's clubhouse at Sportsmans Park. First he tried to tear his locker door off its hinges and, failing that, he splintered it with a swift kick. He then pulled his uniform off and tore it to pieces. Following this epic tantrum Grove didn't speak to anyone for nearly a week, and never really forgave Simmons for not playing. Teammates dreaded facing Grove after making an error in the field behind him as his tongue lashings were especially harsh.

Major League Totals

W	L	ERA	G	CG	IP	H	ER	BBI	SO
300	141	3.06	616	300	3,940.2	3,849	1,339	1,187	2,266

GORDON "MICKEY" COCHRANE
PHILADELPHIA A.L. 1925-1933
DETROIT A.L. 1934-1937
FIERY CATCHER COMPILED A NOTABLE
RECORD BOTH AS A PLAYER AND MANAGER,
THE SPARK OF THE ATHLETICS CHAMPIONSHIP
TEAMS OF 1929-30-31, HAD AN AVERAGE
BATTING MARK OF .346 FOR THOSE THREE
YEARS. LED DETROIT TO TWO LEAGUE
CHAMPIONSHIPS AND A WORLD SERIES
TITLE IN 1935.

Catcher
Philadelphia Athletics
1925-1933
Detroit Tigers 1934-1937

Top: Cochrane was still learning his trade as a catcher when he joined the Philadelphia A's. He was so raw defensively that several A's hurlers complained to manager Connie Mack. Mack stood by Cochrane and was soon vindicated, though. Below: He dives to tag a runner.

MICKEY COCHRANE WAS THE first major leaguer to play a full season on a pennant-winning team managed by Connie Mack and then later manage a pennant winner himself.

In the spring of 1923, Gordon Stanley Cochrane (1903-1962) signed his first professional contract in the Eastern Shore League under the name Frank King. Mickey used an alias not to protect his college eligibility—he had already graduated from Boston University, where he had been a five-sport star—but to guard against failure.

However, Cochrane did well at Dover, although it took him several weeks to learn his true position was behind the plate. Once he became a catcher, he caught the eye of Connie Mack. So certain was Mack of Cochrane's future greatness that he took over Portland in the Pacific Coast League in order to give Mickey a place where he could hone his skills without danger of the A's losing him.

Joining the Mackmen in 1925, Cochrane caught a rookie-record 134 games, while hitting .331. Despite his good offensive numbers Mickey was still a long way from being a polished maskman. Some felt that he never did fully master his trade. When Pepper Martin ran wild for the Cardinals against the A's in the 1931 World Series, Philadelphia pitcher George

Mickey COCHRANE

Gabby HARTNETT

Earnshaw publicly blamed Cochrane for the embarrassment; others felt that the responsibility belonged to the A's hurlers.

Mickey laid claim throughout his career to being the best-hitting catcher in baseball. His .320 batting average and .419 on-base percentage are both career records for a catcher, and his .478 slugging average is an AL record. Cochrane also had an exceptional batting eye—he walked four times as often as he struck out.

Cochrane played on five pennant winners, three in Philadelphia and two more after he was traded to Detroit following the 1933 season. He had early success as a pilot—Cochrane won flags in 1934 and '35, his first two seasons at the Detroit helm. In 1937, Mickey was beaned on May 25 by Bump Hadley of the Yankees and hovered near death for more than a week before recovering. Cochrane was eager to get back into action as soon as he was out of danger, but Detroit owner Walter Briggs would not permit it, especially since doctors had warned that a second beaning could prove fatal. Through as a player, Mickey managed the Tigers another season and a half. He coached under Connie Mack in 1950 and later served in the front offices of the A's and Tigers. Cochrane was named to the Hall of Fame in 1947.

Major League Totals

BA	G	AB	R	H	2B	3B	HR	RBI	SB
.320	1,482	5,169	1,041	1,652	333	64	119	832	64

Outfielder
New York Giants 1926-47

MEL OTT STOOD OUT EVEN IN an era of great sluggers, for his youth, his stance, and his consistent performance over nearly two decades.

Melvin Thomas Ott (1909-1958) was born in Gretna, Louisiana, and was a three-sport star at Gretna High. At age 16, Mel tried out for New Orleans in the Southern Association but was rejected as too small. He played semipro ball that summer for a team owned by Harry Williams, who was another in John McGraw's vast scouting network.

Williams tipped McGraw, who gave Ott a tryout. Immediately impressed with his hitting ability, McGraw signed Ott despite the fact that Mel had an odd batting technique. McGraw refused to send him down to the minors to develop, fearing that a farm skipper would alter Ott's stance, thereby "ruining" him. Under the wing of McGraw, who knew when to use the carrot as well as the stick, Ott emerged as a star.

Ott's stance was one of the most unique in baseball. He lifted his front foot before swinging, his hands held low, almost below his belt. The result was a level swing with terrific power, amply announced in his first season as a regular, in 1929, when he hit 42 home runs with 152 RBI. He also led the league with 113 walks, a sign of the discipline that would lead to a lifetime on-

base average of .414. He was only 20 years old, and his youthful appearance and size (he was a compact 5'7", 160 pounds) reinforced the impression of youth that was to stay with him throughout his career.

Ott was a fine outfielder with perhaps the best arm of his day. Though he was not slow he had a way of running on his heels that caused him some leg problems, but he managed to circle the bases 1,859 times, one of history's highest totals. Ott did benefit greatly from his home park, hitting "only" 187 road homers—out of 511 total. Though he missed out on McGraw's pennant winning teams, he was a World Series hero when Bill Terry managed the club in 1933, hitting .389 with two homers, one winning the final game in the tenth inning. He returned to the Series twice more, coming up empty against the Yankees both times.

Mel became player-manager of the Giants in 1942 but failed to win a pennant. For a man known for his sweet disposition, he was a hard taskmaster as a manager, and helped the careers of such players as Johnny Mize. Ott was inducted to the Hall of Fame in 1951.

Top: *Normally an outfielder, Ott was moved to third base by the Giants in 1938. In his lone season as a regular at the hot corner, Ott set records for the most home runs and the highest slugging average by a third baseman.* Above: *Ott touts a brand of pipe tobacco popular with sportsmen during the 1930s and 1940s.*

	Major League Totals									
BA	**G**	**AB**	**R**	**H**	**2B**	**3B**	**HR**	**RBI**	**SB**
.304	2,734	9,456	1,859	2,876	488	72	511	1,861	89

JAMES E. (JIMMY) FOXX
PHILADELPHIA A.L. 1925-35
BOSTON A.L. 1936-42, CHICAGO N.L. 1942-44
PHILADELPHIA N.L. 1945

NOTED FOR HIS BATTING, PARTICULARLY AS A
HOME RUN HITTER, COLLECTED 534 HOME RUNS
IN 2,317 GAMES. HAD A LIFETIME BATTING
AVERAGE OF .325 AND IN THREE WORLD
SERIES COMPILED A MARK OF .344. APPEARED
IN SEVEN ALL-STAR GAMES IN WHICH HE
BATTED .316. PLAYED FIRST AND THIRD BASES
AND ALSO WAS A CATCHER.

First baseman
Philadelphia Athletics
1925-1935
Boston Red Sox 1936-1942
Chicago Cubs 1942; 1944
Philadelphia Phillies 1945

Top: *Foxx won one Triple Crown during the 1930s. Had the modern rule for determining batting leaders been in effect in 1932, he would have bagged a second Triple Crown. He lost the bat title that year by three points to Dale Alexander, who had just 392 at bats.* Right: *Foxx's burly physique tended to conceal his remarkable athleticism. Early in his career, he played catcher and third base before settling down at first base.*

IN AN ERA OF BIG HITTERS, JIMMIE Foxx won four home run titles and two batting titles. As well, he was the first American Leaguer to win consecutive MVP awards and the first man to win the award three times.

James Emory Foxx (1907-1967) grew up on a farm in rural Maryland. He enjoyed both high school track and baseball, and through his athletic ability and immense home runs he became celebrated. Frank "Home Run" Baker—the former Athletics and Yankees third baseman who was the manager for Easton, Maryland, of the Eastern Shore League—scouted Foxx pitching in both high school and semipro games. In 1924, Baker sent Jimmie a penny postcard reading, "Would you be interested in becoming a professional ballplayer? If you are, contact me." Jimmie signed a contract at age 16, and Baker, short of catchers, put Foxx behind the plate. He caught 76 games, batting .296 with 10 homers.

Both the Yankees and Athletics were interested in Foxx, but Baker steered Jimmie to the A's as a favor to Connie Mack. Foxx joined Philadelphia in 1924, sitting on the bench next to Mack to learn the American League. Jimmie began the 1925 season in Philadelphia, but was optioned soon to Providence of the International League.

He hit .327 there, though curiously he had only one home run in 101 at bats. He was back in Philadelphia in 1926, and from '26 to 1928, he was a utility player, backing up Mickey Cochrane at catcher and playing first and third.

By the time Foxx became the regular first baseman in 1929, the A's were a powerhouse. "Double X" formed with Al Simmons and Lefty Grove the heart of Mack's last great team, and appeared in three consecutive World Series from 1929 to 1931. Foxx and Simmons combined for 192 home runs and Grove was 79-15 in those three years. Jimmie won consecutive MVPs in 1932 and '33. He had 169 RBI and 58 homers in 1932, and he earned the Triple Crown in 1933 with 48 homers, 163 RBI, and a .356 average. The A's won two Championships before bowing to St. Louis in seven games in 1931. That was to be Foxx's postseason swan song—he hit .344 and slugged .609 in 18 World Series games.

Because Connie Mack suffered economically during the Depression, he sold Foxx to Boston in 1936. Ted Williams said, "Jimmie Foxx with all those muscles, hitting drives that sounded like gunfire. *Crraack.* A hell of a lot louder than mine sounded." Jimmie hailed his arrival by hitting 41 homers and 143 RBI in '36.

Foxx is the only player to hold the single-season homer record for two teams. In 1932, he set the A's mark with 58 dingers; in '38, he gained the BoSox record with 50.

The Eloquent Rebuttal of 1938

Before the 1938 season, Boston sportwriters began knocking Jimmie Foxx by suggesting his career was starting to slide. Their columns claimed he was spending too much time at any number of Boston taverns and not enough time working on baseball. Foxx's eloquent rebuttal to these attacks was to win the American League MVP Award with one of his greatest seasons.

Fenway Park has never seen a righthanded power-hitting display over a prolonged period to match Foxx's 1938 season. The powerfully built first baseman set a league record by driving in 104 runs in home games only. He also batted .405 at Fenway and socked 35 of his 50 homers at home. For the second time in his career Foxx totaled 50 homers.

For his efforts, Foxx captured a then unprece-dented third MVP Award. He also made the Boston press sing his praises and probably pick up more than a few of his bar tabs.

Though Foxx's career began to be affected by his drinking, he had enough left for a final burst. After "slumping" to 36 homers, 127 RBI, and a career-low .285 average in 1937, he bounced back in 1938. Foxx hit 50 homers and led the league in RBI and average, winning his third MVP Award. Appendicitis shortened his terrific 1939 season, and 1940 was his last decent year. When he retired only Ruth had more home runs, and Jimmie slammed more homers than anyone in the 1930s. He had three seasons with slugging averages of over .700. His eyes failed him, however, and he laid down his bat after 1945. Foxx was inducted in 1951.

Major League Totals

BA	G	AB	R	H	2B	3B	HR	RBI	SB
.325	2,317	8,134	1,751	2,646	458	125	534	1,921	88

JOE CRONIN

JOSEPH EDWARD CRONIN
PITTSBURGH N.L. 1926-1927
WASHINGTON A.L. 1928-1934
BOSTON A.L. 1935-1945
NAMED ALL-STAR SHORTSTOP SEVEN
SEASONS. MOST VALUABLE PLAYER A.L.
1930. LED A.L. SHORTSTOPS IN FIELDING
1935-1932. MOST PUTOUTS AND DOUBLE
PLAYS 1930-31-32. LIFETIME BATTING
AVERAGE .302. WON PENNANT IN 1933 IN
FIRST SEASON AS MANAGER WASHINGTON
A.L. AT AGE 26. TRADED TO BOSTON 1934 FOR
REPORTED RECORD PRICE OF $250,000.

Shortstop
Pittsburgh Pirates
 1926-1927
Washington Senators
 1928-1934
Boston Red Sox
 1935-1945

Manager
Washington Senators
 1933-1934
Boston Red Sox 1935-1947

AT AGE 20 IN 1926, JOE CRONIN sat on the bench in Pittsburgh, was farmed out and then sold. In 1959, he became president of the American League. Between, he turned in a Hall of Fame career as one of the best hitting shortstops in history.

Joseph Edward Cronin (1906-1984) was born in San Francisco a few months after the great earthquake. Coming from a low-income background, Joe grew up an all-around athlete. He won a city-wide tennis championship as a youngster, and in high school he played soccer and basketball, along with baseball. He played semipro baseball after graduation. A Pittsburgh Pirates scout signed Joe in 1925, and he played one good season for Johnstown, Pennsylvania, in the Mid-Atlantic League. Promoted to the Pirates the next year, he sat behind Glenn Wright in Pittsburgh for two seasons.

After his trials in the National League, Cronin finally landed in Washington in the American League in 1928. As the regular shortstop in 1929, he had a decent season, and followed it up with a year that was to earn him *The Sporting News* Most Valuable Player Award in 1930, when he hit .346 with 127 runs and 126 RBI. Joe reached the 100-RBI mark in eight seasons,

Joe Cronin, the likable leader of the Red Sox

THE POWER OF THE PRESS IN BASEBALL - F. C. Lane   THE WRECKING CREWS OF 1934 - F. Scheible
THE BIG BAD GIANTS - R. Rennie   BASEBALL CLIPPINGS - C. Bordynel   SPEAKING OF SPATS - J. M. Gould

remarkable for a shortstop with his fielding ability. Cronin compiled a lifetime .301 batting average by hitting over .300 in 10 seasons. He socked 51 doubles in 1938 and hit 515 in his career. He was a fine defensive player and was named the outstanding major league shortstop by *The Sporting News* seven times.

Cronin was active in an era when player-managers were common, and he served a long term in that role, as skipper of the Washington club in 1933 and 1934, and bossing the Red Sox for 13 years after his sale to the Boston club in 1934. His rookie year as a manager produced a pennant in 1933, and Cronin hit .318 as Washington lost to the Giants in the World Series. Ted Williams said when Cronin quit playing he was "the greatest manager I ever played for." Cronin also had many doubts about his double duty and tried to resign after his first season. He didn't finish first again until 1946, the year he stepped down as a player, when he brought Boston its first pennant since 1918. A broken leg finally took him out of the lineup for good.

In 1959, Joe was elected president of the American League, the first former player to be so honored, remaining in the office until 1973. He was inducted in the Hall of Fame in 1956.

Top: *Featured on the February 1935 cover of* Baseball Magazine, *Cronin marked his first season as the Boston Red Sox player-manager that year by leading the Sox to their first above-.500 finish since 1919. Right: Cronin was probably the best all-around shortstop in the majors between 1930 and World War II.*

Major League Totals										Major League Managing Totals				
BA	G	AB	R	H	2B	3B	HR	RBI	SB	W	L	T	PCT	G
.301	2,124	7,579	1,233	2,285	515	118	170	1,424	87	1,236	1,055	24	.540	2,315

148

JOE McCARTHY

Manager
Chicago Cubs 1926-1930
New York Yankees
1931-1946
Boston Red Sox 1948-1950

JOE McCARTHY'S .615 MANAGE-rial career winning percentage and his .698 World Series winning percentage are both the best of all time.

Joseph Vincent McCarthy (1887-1978) was born and raised in Philadelphia, and he attended Niagara University for two years. He left in 1907 after signing with Wilmington of the Tri-State League. There he showed enough talent to move up to the high minor leagues for four years as a utility infielder. In 1913, Wilkes-Barre of the New York State League made Joe a player-manager. He guided them into second place while hitting .325. That offense got him back to the high minors for five more seasons—as a second baseman only.

In 1919, Joe was with Louisville of the American Association, when in midseason they made him player-manager. He guided the team into third place, and he stayed with Louisville for six more years, winning two pennants. Louisville won 102 games in 1925, while the Cubs won 68, and Chicago signed McCarthy.

McCarthy's first action with the Cubs was cutting Grover Alexander, establishing a reputation as a disciplinarian. But "Marse Joe" was very much a man behind the scenes, and was partly remarkable for his low profile, despite the great success of his teams. Joe improved the Cubs each year, and the acquisition of Rogers Hornsby in 1929 gave Chicago the final

ingredient needed to win the pennant. The Cubs were destined for second the next year, but McCarthy left the club with four games to play and Hornsby took over. McCarthy assumed control of the Yankees, skipperless after the death of Miller Huggins.

Babe Ruth wanted the Yankee manager job very badly, and it is a tribute to McCarthy's ability that he was able to deflect the Babe's resentment and make the team his own. The Yankees finished second in 1931, but in 1932 the Yanks beat McCarthy's old Chicago team in the World Series. Three second-place finishes followed, then in 1936 Joe DiMaggio joined the team, and the Yankees won four straight Series, winning 16 games while losing just three. In 1941, they won it all again.

McCarthy was one of the first to get significant pitching help from his bullpen, and the 1941 team had no 20-game winner. He brought them to the Series again in 1942 and 1943, winning his final championship in 1943.

McCarthy left the Yankees in 1946 for health reasons, and in 1948 went to Boston. Ted Williams felt the two heartbreaking second-place finishes in 1948 and '49 took the heart out of Joe. "He finally quit during the '50 season, I think out of his own extreme disappointment," Williams said.

McCarthy was inducted into the Hall of Fame in 1957.

Major League Managing Totals				
W	L	T	PCT	G
2,125	1,333	26	.615	3,487

Top: McCarthy was hired as manager of the Red Sox when Joe Cronin moved up to the club's front office in 1948. During Joe's first two seasons Boston became the only team in history to lose two consecutive pennants on the last day of the campaign. Left: Accusations that he was no more than a "push-button" manager only amused the Yankee players.

PAUL GLEE WANER
(BIG POISON)
PITTSBURGH·BROOKLYN·BOSTON, N.L.
NEW YORK, A.L.
1926-1945
LEFT HANDED HITTING OUTFIELDER BATTED
.300 OR BETTER 14 TIMES IN NATIONAL
LEAGUE. ONE OF SEVEN PLAYERS EVER TO
COMPILE 3,000 OR MORE HITS. SET MODERN
N.L. RECORD BY COLLECTING 200 OR MORE
HITS EIGHT SEASONS. MOST VALUABLE PLAYER
IN 1927 AND FOUR TIMES SELECTED FOR
ALL STAR GAME.

Outfielder
Pittsburgh Pirates
    1926-1940
Brooklyn Dodgers 1941;
    1943-1944
Boston Braves 1941-1942
New York Yankees
    1944-1945

Top: *In 1926, Waner had the highest average of any NL player with more than 400 at bats (.336). Below: Having the Waner brothers connected with it made a moderate seller of a board game that would otherwise probably have died during the '30s.*

BECAUSE PAUL WANER AT 5'9", 150 pounds, was bulkier than his brother Lloyd, he was called "Big Poison" and Lloyd "Little Poison." The nicknames supposedly were Brooklynese for the word "person" and stemmed from a moment early in their careers when a Dodgers fan, bemoaning the frequent pastings the Waners gave Brooklyn pitchers, said something like: "There goes that big and little poison again."

Paul Glee Waner (1903-1965), left East Central Teachers' College in Oklahoma against his father's advice to pursue a professional baseball career in 1923. Originally a pitcher, he switched to the outfield when he hurt his arm while training that spring with the San Francisco Seals of the Pacific Coast League. In his third year with the Seals, Waner paced the PCL with a .401 batting average and 75 doubles.

Sold to Pittsburgh along with infielder Hal Rhyne for $100,000 and three players, Paul began immediately to demonstrate that he was cheap even at that enormous price, one of the largest ever paid for a minor leaguer to that time. In 1926, his rookie season, he hit .336, higher than any other National League regular that year, but missed the batting crown when it was awarded to Cincinnati catcher Bubbles Hargrave, who had only 326 at bats. Waner's performance spurred the Pirates to buy his

younger brother Lloyd. The two combined to amass a sibling record 460 hits in 1927, but more important, their offensive production helped bring Pittsburgh the National League pennant. That year, Paul led the NL with a .380 average, 237 hits, 17 triples, and 131 RBI, winning the MVP Award.

Paul developed into one of the finest hitters in National League history. He not only won three hitting titles but led the NL at one time or another in every major batting department except home runs and walks. En route to accumulating 3,152 career hits, he set an NL record by tabulating 200 or more hits in a season on eight separate occasions. He was an outstanding right fielder, combining a center fielder's speed with one of the strongest arms in the league.

An imbiber, Waner one year foreswore liquor. When his average hovered at .250, his manager brought Paul to the nearest tavern and bought him a drink. Named to the Hall of Fame in 1952, Waner returned to the game in 1957 as a hitting instructor with the Braves. Later he served in a similar capacity with the Cardinals and the Phillies. One of the few great hitters who could convey his secrets to young players, Waner wrote a book on hitting in the early 1960s that was well received.

				Major League Totals					
BA	**G**	**AB**	**R**	**H**	**2B**	**3B**	**HR**	**RBI**	**SB**
.333	2,549	9,459	1,626	3,152	603	190	112	1,309	104

LOYD WANER WAS ONE OF THE smallest men to achieve star status. At 5'9" and just 135 pounds when he came up, he was even smaller than his diminutive older brother Paul. Lloyd played center field in the Pirates outfield alongside Paul in right for 14 campaigns. The brothers' nicknames "Big Poison" and "Little Poison" are Brooklynese for "big and little person." He may not have been the hitter his big brother Paul was, but Lloyd compiled some impressive stats.

Lloyd James Waner (1906-1982) was born in Harrah, Oklahoma, where he emulated his older brother, Paul. Paul in 1924 hit .365 for the San Francisco Seals in the Pacific Coast League and garnered a tryout for Lloyd. Lloyd made the Seals in 1925, mostly as a defensive replacement, but was dropped early in 1926. Lloyd's brother Paul was signed by Pittsburgh in 1926, where he promptly sold Pirates owner Barney Dreyfuss on Lloyd. Lloyd hit .345 at Columbia in the South Atlantic League in '26, and wowed Pirate skipper Donie Bush in spring training in 1927. The Pirates were in the process of replacing Hall of Fame outfielders Max Carey and Kiki Cuyler at the time, so Bush may have been primed to be impressed.

Lloyd's first three seasons were by far his best, as he hit .355, .335, and .353, and collected over 200 hits and scored 120-plus runs each season. His 198 singles in his 1927 rookie season still stand as a record, as do his 223 rookie hits. He missed most of the 1930 season because of a

CLOSE COVER BEFORE STRIKING MATCH

bout with appendicitis, but rebounded in 1931 to post a .314 average and collect 214 hits. Though he never sustained production like that again, he was a high average hitter and one of the game's fastest men and best outfielders for years. Lloyd led all NL flyhawkers in putouts four times, though he had below average arm strength.

He had very little power, hitting just 28 homers in his career, though he led the league in triples in 1929 with 20. Lloyd was one of the toughest batters to fan, with just 173 strikeouts in 7,772 at bats, or about once every 45 at bats. The Waner boys' only World Series appearance was their 1927 ill-fated run-in with the Yankees whose '27 team is legendary, yet Lloyd did his part, hitting .400 and scoring five runs in the four games.

Little Poison retired after playing in only 100 games with the 1942 Phillies. He staged a comeback during the war years of 1944 and '45 with the Dodgers and finally the Pirates, but was used sparingly as a pinch-hitter. He retired after the 1945 season. In 1967, the Veterans Committee elected Lloyd to the Hall of Fame.

Outfielder
Pittsburgh Pirates
1927-1941; 1944-1945
Boston Braves 1941
Cincinnati Reds 1941
Philadelphia Phillies 1942
Brooklyn Dodgers 1944

Top: *Waner established several records in his rookie season of 1927. Among them are the marks for the most runs (133) and the most hits (223) by a frosh player in the 20th century.* Left: *This Diamond matchbook cover pictures "Little Poison."*

Major League Totals									
BA	G	AB	R	H	2B	3B	HR	RBI	SB
.316	1,992	7,772	1,201	2,459	281	118	28	598	67

ANTHONY MICHAEL LAZZERI
"POOSH 'EM UP TONY"
NEW YORK, A.L. 1926-1937
CHICAGO, N.L. 1938
BROOKLYN, N.L. 1939
NEW YORK, N.L. 1939
FEARED CLUTCH HITTER WITH LONG BALL POWER.
PLAYED SECOND BASE WITH QUIET PROFICIENCY
ON FAMED MURDERER'S ROW YANKEE TEAMS WITH
RUTH AND GEHRIG. A .300 HITTER FIVE TIMES WITH
CAREER .292 MARK. DROVE IN OVER 100 RUNS
SEVEN TIMES. SET A.L. SINGLE GAME RECORD WITH
2 GRAND SLAMS AND 11 RBIS, 5/24/36. BELTED 60
HOMERS FOR SALT LAKE CITY (PCL) IN 1925.

Second baseman
New York Yankees
  1926-1937
Chicago Cubs 1938
Brooklyn Dodgers 1939
New York Giants 1939

Top: *Lazzeri's uniform while he was with the Dodgers in 1939. The patch on the left sleeve commemorates baseball's 100th anniversary and the year that the Hall of Fame opened.*
Right: *Playing with Salt Lake City of the Pacific Coast League, in 1925 he became the first player to belt 60 home runs in a season. Two years later he was a teammate of the first player to do it in the majors, Babe Ruth.*

Tony LAZZERI WAS A HARD-hitting second baseman on the great Yankee teams of the 1920s. He received his nickname, "Poosh 'Em Up," for his habit of getting clutch hits with men on base.

Anthony Michael Lazzeri (1903-1946) was born in San Francisco, and got his start in pro ball in 1922. He hit only .248 at Peoria in 1923, but he also showed good power with 14 homers. The next season, he moved up to Lincoln of the Western League, where he batted .329 with 28 homers. He became one of the few players in history to hit 60 home runs in a season when he had 60, with 222 RBI and 202 runs scored in 197 games for Salt Lake City of the Pacific Coast League in 1925. New York Yankee scout Bill Essick bought Lazzeri from Salt Lake City for $75,000 after the 1925 season.

The 1925 Yankees were disappointing, finishing seventh in the AL in both record and scoring. Manager Miller Huggins, looking to improve his offense for 1926, replaced shortstop Pee Wee Wanninger and second baseman Joe Dugan with Mark Koening and Lazzeri, respectively. That move helped the Yanks score 847 runs in '26 (Tony had 114 RBI, second in the loop) and presented a powerful lineup to face the St. Louis Cardinals in the fall classic.

With the Series tied at three games each, Redbird hurler Jesse Haines allowed the Yankees to load the bases in the seventh inning of game seven with Lazzeri at bat. The Cardinals brought in Pete Alexander, who pitched complete game wins in games two and six. Alexander struck Tony out on four curveballs to end the threat in one of the most famous pitcher-batter confrontations in Series history. Both Alexander and Lazzeri, curiously, suffered from epilepsy.

Lazzeri had over 100 RBI in seven seasons from 1926 to 1937 as the Yankee second sacker. He reached the .300 level in five seasons. In 1933, he was chosen as the league's second baseman in the first All-Star Game.

After Lazzeri fell to a .247 batting average in 1937, and with Joe Gordon waiting in the wings, Yankees owner Jake Ruppert allowed Tony to make his own deal with a team that wanted him. Lazzeri chose the Cubs, and in 1938 he later played in his last World Series as Chicago won the NL flag. He played with both Brooklyn and the Giants in 1939 before ending his major league career. He returned to the minor leagues, serving as a player-manager until 1943. Lazzeri suffered from an epileptic seizure and died from the resulting injuries in 1946. He was named by the Veterans Committee to the Hall of Fame in 1991.

Major League Totals

BA	G	AB	R	H	2B	3B	HR	RBI	SB
.292	1,739	6,297	986	1,840	334	115	178	1,191	148

CARL HUBBELL WAS A WINNER. He had to be to earn a nickname like "The Meal Ticket." In his 16 years with John McGraw's Giants, Hubbell won 253 games and lost 154, while posting a remarkable 2.97 earned run average.

Carl Owen Hubbell (1903-1988) grew up on a pecan farm in Oklahoma. He started pitching for an oil company team after high school and pitched well enough to get signed by Cushing of the Oklahoma State League in 1923. He made it to Oklahoma City of the Western League by 1925, going 17-13. Hubbell threw a screwball, breaking toward lefty batters, unlike a curve, which broke away from lefty batters. Carl was sold to the Tigers in 1925, who did not permit him to use his screwball, fearing it would ruin his arm. His performance was inferior, he was optioned to the minors, and his confidence collapsed shortly thereafter.

After two seasons of mediocre pitching in minor league ball, Hubbell received his outright release from Detroit in 1928 and began pitching in the Texas League. Giants scout Dick Kinsella was a delegate to the Democratic national convention in Houston that year and took in a Texas League game. He discovered Hubbell, and Giants skipper John McGraw paid $30,000 for the hurler, a record for that loop.

Hubbell put the league on alert, tossing the league's only no-hitter in 1929, but his big years didn't begin until 1933. He registered five straight 20-plus victory seasons starting in 1933. That season, King Carl pitched a record 18-inning shutout against the Cardinals, won two games in

Pitcher
New York Giants
1928-1943

the World Series, pitched 20 Series innings without allowing an earned run (he tossed a Series record eleven-inning shutout), and was chosen the league's Most Valuable Player.

The following season he had his most famous moment. In the second All-Star game in 1934, Hubbell fanned Babe Ruth, Lou Gehrig, Jimmie Foxx, Al Simmons, and Joe Cronin in succession, electrifying the fans and prompting fellow All-Star Gabby Hartnett to call down to the AL dugout, "We gotta look at that all season."

Hubbell won the MVP again in 1936 when he turned in one of the best pitching records in history at 26-6. The Giants returned to the World Series that year and in 1937, losing to the Yankees both times. Hubbell had finished 1936 with 16 straight wins, and won his first eight in 1937, for a 24-game winning streak. Throwing his screwball for so many years had turned his left arm around, and he underwent elbow surgery after the 1938 season. He never was the same, although he won 11 games each from 1939 to 1942. Carl was inducted into the Hall of Fame in 1947.

Top: *Hubbell's bread-and-butter pitch was a wicked screwball. Expected to take a quick toll on his arm, it instead enabled him to hurl until he was past age 40.* Left: *As this board game suggests, Hubbell could deal the Ks. He fanned better than 100 hitters for ten consecutive years.*

Major League Totals									
W	L	ERA	G	CG	IP	H	ER	BB	SO
253	154	2.97	535	258	3,589.1	3,463	1,184	724	1,678

WILLIAM MALCOLM DICKEY
NEW YORK A.L. 1928-1946
SET RECORD BY CATCHING 100 OR MORE
GAMES 13 SUCCESSIVE SEASONS. PLAYED
WITH YANKEES, CHAMPIONS OF 1932-36-37-
38-39-41-42-43, WHEN CLUB WON 7 WORLD
SERIES TITLES. HOLDS NUMEROUS WORLD
SERIES RECORDS FOR CATCHERS, INCLUDING
MOST GAMES, 38. PLAYED ON 8 ALL-STAR
TEAMS FROM 1932 TO 1946. LIFETIME
BATTING AVERAGE OF .313 IN 1789 GAMES.

Catcher
New York Yankees
  1928-1943; 1946
Manager
New York Yankees 1946
57-48

UNTIL YOGI BERRA CAME along, Bill Dickey was not only known as the greatest Yankee catcher but one of the greatest catchers of all time.

Born in Bastrop, Louisiana, in 1907, William Malcolm Dickey grew up in Arkansas. After playing the infield in high school, he attended Little Rock College in 1925, where he was a pitcher and catcher. Lena Blackburne, manager for Little Rock in the Southern Association, spotted Dickey and signed him that year. For several seasons thereafter, Bill played with both Little Rock and their associate teams in the lower minors. Since Little Rock was an unofficial tributary team for the White Sox, most major league teams took little notice of him. Of course the Yankees scouted him, and when their investigation proved worthwhile, purchased him in 1928. He caught in ten games at the end of that season, joining one of the greatest teams of all time.

In 1929, Dickey's first full season, he batted .324 and completed the outstanding lineup. He was Lou Gehrig's roommate, and they were a matched set—quiet and consistent. Dickey was

a steady .300 hitter, ten times topping the .300 mark. His mark of .362 in 1936 was a record for backstoppers. Over the four-year period from 1936 to 1939, the lefthanded Dickey took advantage of the short right field porch in Yankee Stadium to pop 20-plus homers a year and drive in 100-plus runs.

A hard worker and a fierce competitor, Dickey handled Yankee pitching staffs on eight World Series teams, winning seven championships. His 17-year career spanned the era from Ruth to DiMaggio. Bill caught 100 or more games for 13 consecutive seasons, a record that would stand until Johnny Bench appeared. At the time of Dickey's retirement, he held the records for putouts and fielding average.

A quiet leader and generally calm on the field, Bill lost his cool one day in 1932 and received a one-month suspension and a fine after he broke baserunner Carl Reynolds's jaw with one punch after a collision at home plate. After catching only 71 games during the 1943 season, Dickey hit a two-run homer in the fifth and final game of the World Series that fall against the Cardinals to propel the Yanks to the championship.

Bill enlisted in the Navy at age 36, missing the 1944 and 1945 seasons. He returned but played in only 54 more games to finish his career in 1946. When the Bombers were working with a young kid named Berra, Bill was called in to show the youngster the way to do it. Dickey was named to the Hall of Fame in 1954.

Top: *This* Baseball Magazine *is from August 1936. That year, Dickey set an all-time record for the highest batting average by a catcher with more than 400 at bats when he stroked .362 for the New York Yankees.* Right: *In the eight World Series the Yankees participated in while he was with the club, Dickey caught every inning of every game.*

Major League Totals

BA	G	AB	R	H	2B	3B	HR	RBI	SB
.313	1,789	6,300	930	1,969	343	72	202	1,209	36

BORN IN INDIANAPOLIS, Indiana, Charles Herbert Klein (1904-1958) worked in a local steel mill and played semipro ball until he was in his early 20s. A broken leg threatened to end his career in 1927 after only 14 games with Evansville of the Three-I League, but Klein recovered to sock 26 homers in the first 88 games he played for Fort Wayne of the Central League the following year.

On the recommendation of manager Burt Shotton, the Phillies purchased Chuck from the Indiana club for $7,500 and immediately put him into Philadelphia livery. In his rookie season, Chuck tattooed and eye-opening 91 hits in just 64 games and batted .360. As a sophomore, Klein hit .356 and topped the National League with 43 home runs, a new loop record. In 1930, his third season, Chuck set another modern NL record that still stands when he scored 158 runs and also bagged 59 doubles, then a senior loop record. In addition, he batted .386, pounded out 250 hits, and collected 170 RBI. Klein did not exactly go on vacation while he was in the field that year, either. He set a 20th century record for outfielders when he amassed 44 assists and led all NL gardeners with 10 double plays.

During the next three seasons, Klein continued to decimate pitchers as he topped the NL on each occasion in home runs and slugging average.

CHARLES KLEIN
Chicago "Cubs"

CLOSE COVER BEFORE STRIKING MATCH

His apex came in 1933 when he won the Triple Crown. A year earlier he had become the only player since the end of the dead-ball era to lead his loop in both home runs and stolen bases. Many wondered what the southpaw-slugging Klein would do with a contender, and in 1934 they got their answer when he was traded to the Cubs by the financially strapped Phils.

Bothered by a series of hamstring pulls and a growing drinking problem, Klein played just 115 games for Chicago in 1934 and 119 in 1935. Although he posted decent numbers in both seasons, they were nowhere near what Cubs officials had expected from him. Shortly after the 1936 season began, Chuck was sent back to the Phillies. On July 10, a few weeks after his return, he hit four home runs in a game—not at the cozy Baker Bowl but at Pittsburgh's spacious Forbes Field where only one player, Babe Ruth, had previously hit as many as three in a contest.

After retiring from the game in 1944, he ran a bar for awhile in Philadelphia and then drifted back to Indianapolis. Under siege for years to name Klein to the Hall of Fame, the Veterans Committee finally relented in 1980.

CHARLES HERBERT KLEIN
"CHUCK"
PHILADELPHIA N.L., CHICAGO N.L.,
PITTSBURGH N.L., 1928-1944
ONLY PLAYER IN 20TH CENTURY TO COLLECT
200 OR MORE HITS IN EACH OF FIRST FIVE
FULL MAJOR LEAGUE SEASONS. ATTAINED
.320 CAREER AVERAGE AND 300 HOME RUNS.
LED N.L. IN HOMERS AND TOTAL BASES FOUR
TIMES AND IN RUNS SCORED AND SLUGGING
PCT. THREE EACH. SET LEAGUE RECORD FOR
MOST EXTRA BASE HITS IN SEASON--107 IN 1930.
VOTED MOST VALUABLE PLAYER IN 1932.

Outfielder
Philadelphia Phillies
    1928-1933; 1936-1939;
    1940-1944
Chicago Cubs 1934-1936
Pittsburgh Pirates 1939

Top: *In his first six seasons, Klein was the best all-purpose hitter in the major leagues, bar none.* Left: *Klein on a 1936 Diamond matchbook. No satisfactory explanation has ever been given for why his skills declined so dramatically after he joined the Cubs.*

Major League Totals

BA	G	AB	R	H	2B	3B	HR	RBI	SB
.320	1,753	6,486	1,168	2,076	398	74	300	1,202	79

CHAPTER FOUR

Home Front
America's Pastime at War

BASEBALL OPENED THE 1940s WITH ONE EYE on the growing conflict in Europe and another on its new legion of stars. Cleveland's Bob Feller began the decade with an Opening Day no-hitter over the White Sox. Shortly thereafter, however, many of the game's top stars were wearing military uniforms. An Army-Navy exhibition game played in Cleveland in mid-1942 drew 62,094 fans, because Feller was pitching for Mickey Cochrane's Great Lakes Naval Training team.

In January 1942, President Franklin D. Roosevelt asked commissioner Kenesaw Mountain Landis not to suspend play. "I honestly feel it would be best for the country to keep baseball going," the President wrote. The green-light letter did not save most major-leaguers from military service, but it did create major league jobs for more than 200 men who had been classified 4-F. Things got so desperate that the Cardinals actually advertised for players in 1943; other clubs followed suit. Within four years of the bombing of Pearl Harbor, the armed forces had taken all but 400 of the 5,800 men in professional baseball at the time of the attack.

In 1946, baseball picked up where it had paused four years earlier. Feller won 26 games, Ted Williams batted .342, and Stan Musial led the NL in six offensive categories. The minor leagues had also recovered from a wartime situation that required many to suspend operations. One league, the International League, had a new batting champion: Jackie Robinson of the Montreal Royals.

A hot start in 1939 got Joe DiMaggio the cover of Life *magazine. DiMaggio hit .381 that season to gain both his first AL batting crown and MVP Award. DiMaggio was the most popular ballplayer in the 1940s.*

Opposite page: *Bob Feller lost four years to the war, and still managed to win 266 games in his career.* Below: *Al Lopez was the era's most durable catcher before he turned his attention to managing. In addition to his durability, one of his main attributes was speed. Lopez snagged 46 career stolen bases, a relatively high number for a catcher of his day.*

JAY HANNA (DIZZY) DEAN
ST. LOUIS (N.L.) 1932-1937
CHICAGO (N.L.) 1938-1941
ONE OF FOUR N.L. PITCHERS TO WIN 30 OR
MORE GAMES UNDER MODERN REGULATIONS.
PITCHED IN 1934 (ST.L.) 1938 (CHICAGO)
WORLD SERIES. LED LEAGUE IN STRIKEOUTS
1932-33-34-35. SINGLE GAME RECORD WITH
17, JULY 30, 1933. FIRST PITCHER TO MAKE
TWO HITS IN ONE INNING IN WORLD SERIES.
MOST VALUABLE N.L. PLAYER IN 1934.

Pitcher
St. Louis Cardinals 1930;
    1932-1937
Chicago Cubs 1938-1941
St. Louis Browns 1947

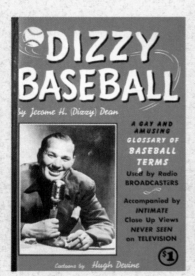

Top: *Dean was traded by St. Louis to the Cubs in 1938. His ailing wing restricted him to just 13 appearances that season, but he had a glittering 7-1 record with a 1.81 ERA.*
Above: *Dean seemed to take a delight in mangling the past tenses of verbs. A typical Deanism: "He must've thunk he would be out unless he slud."*
Right: *Dean visits Jim Konstanty before the 1950 World Series.*

ONE OF THE MOST ENTERTAINing players in the history of baseball, and a member of the overpowering Gashouse Gang of the old St. Louis Cardinals, Dizzy Dean blazed across the baseball sky for five seasons. He was the last pitcher to win 30 games in a season before Denny McLain in 1968. Diz was the league's Most Valuable Player in 1934 and finished second in the voting in 1935 and 1936.

Jay Hanna Dean (1911-1974) was born in Arkansas to an itinerant farm worker, and the Dean family traveled the Southwest. Diz and his brothers (his kid brother Paul was also a pitcher) went to work in the fields at early ages. Jay picked up his nickname and his knowledge of pitching while in the Army. After serving, he moved to Texas and pitched for a company team. A Cardinals sleuth spotted him and signed him to a St. Louis organization contract for the 1930 season. He had a combined 25-10 record that year in the minor leagues before pitching a three-hit shutout for the Cardinals on the final day of the season. After winning 26 games in 1931 at Triple-A Houston, he was called up to stay for the 1932 campaign. Dizzy won 18 games and led the NL in shutouts, innings pitched, and strikeouts, the first of four consecutive strikeout titles he would earn.

Dizzy was a shrewd negotiator. Once, he staged a holdout during the 1934 championship season for his brother Paul, whom Diz felt was underpaid. Despite missing some starts during the holdout, the elder Dean went 30-7, and rookie Paul was 19-11.

The Dean brothers won four World Series games as the Cards beat the Tigers. While pinch-running in game four, Dizzy was beaned in the forehead while breaking up a double play. It was feared that he would miss the remainder of the Series until the headlines the next day ran "X-Ray of Dean's Head Reveals Nothing." Dizzy ended up pitching a shutout and scoring the only run he would need in the seventh game.

During the 1937 All-Star game, a line-drive off the bat of Earl Averill broke Dizzy's toe. He tried to come back too soon, which altered his motion and, as a result, injured his right arm. He never fully recovered and never again won more than eight games in a season. He retired in 1941 at age 30.

Dizzy became a popular broadcaster in St. Louis with a unique gift for memorable malapropisms. He was elected to the Hall of Fame in 1953.

Major League Totals										
W	L	ERA	G	CG	IP	H	ER	BB	SO	
150	83	3.02	317	154	1,967.1	1,925	660	453	1,163	

First baseman; outfielder
Detroit Tigers 1930;
1933-1941; 1945-1946
Pittsburgh Pirates 1947

Top: *Despite losing nearly five seasons to military duty during World War II, Greenberg cracked 331 home runs and bagged 1,276 RBI.* Above: *Leading the American League in home runs and RBI in 1935 earned Hank Greenberg the cover of the World Series issue of* Baseball Magazine.

O F THE MANY PLAYERS WHO lost playing time and had their career totals diminished by World War II, Hank Greenberg may have lost the most. He was active for only nine and one-half seasons, serving in the Army for four and one-half years, but was able to produce Hall of Fame numbers.

Henry Benjamin Greenberg (1911-1986) was raised in the Bronx, and the Yankees offered the 18-year-old a contract in 1929. With Lou Gehrig at first base for the Yanks, Greenberg chose to sign with the Tigers. In his first two farm seasons, he was a .300 hitter with average power. In the Texas League in 1932, though, he hit 39 homers with 139 RBI. These numbers pushed him into the role of Tiger first baseman in 1933.

In 1934, Greenberg led the league with 63 doubles and drove in 139 runs. In 1935, the Tigers won a World Championship, as Hank won his first MVP Award, leading the league with 36 homers and 170 RBI. For the next four years the Tigers vainly chased the Yankees before sinking to the second division. High RBI totals became his obsession and his special gift. His 183 in 1937 is the third highest total in history, and Greenberg's career rate of .92 RBI per game is matched only by Gehrig in this century. Greenberg challenged Babe Ruth's single-season home run record by clubbing 58 in 1938.

In 1940, Hammerin' Hank led the Tigers to a pennant as he grabbed his second MVP Award as he led the league in doubles, homers, and of course, RBI. He also made the shift from first base to left field in order to accommodate Rudy York, and the originally apprehensive Greenberg found the outfield to his taste. Though Hank hit .357 and drove in six runs, the Tigers bowed to Cincinnati in seven games, and Greenberg played in only 19 games in 1941 before going to war.

He returned to lead the Tigers to the World Championship in 1945, cracking a grand-slam home run on September 30 to clinch the pennant. He hit .304 in the Series as Detroit ousted the Cubs. In 1946, he led the league in home runs and RBI, but it was to be his last good season.

A salary dispute sent Greenberg to Pittsburgh in 1947. He promptly retired, but Pittsburgh officials were desperate for his drawing power (the club had just been sold to a group that included Bing Crosby). The Pirates met Greenberg's every demand, and Hank played one more year before retiring. While with the Pirates he worked extensively with Ralph Kiner. Hank also encouraged Jackie Robinson; Greenberg withstood his share of prejudice, being the greatest Jewish star of his day.

Major League Totals										
BA	G	AB	R	H	2B	3B	HR	RBI	SB
.313	1,394	5,193	1,051	1,628	379	71	331	1,276	58

HOWARD EARL AVERILL
"ROCK"
CLEVELAND A.L. DETROIT A.L.
BOSTON N.L. 1929-1941
COMPILED .318 CAREER BATTING AVERAGE
AND HIT 238 HOME RUNS. TWICE MADE
MORE THAN 200 HITS IN SEASON, PACING
LEAGUE WITH 232 IN 1936. DROVE IN
100 OR MORE RUNS FIVE TIMES. RAPPED
FOUR HOMERS, THREE CONSECUTIVELY
IN FIRST GAME AND BATTED IN 11 RUNS
IN 1930 TWIN-BILL.

Outfielder
Cleveland Indians
    1929-1939
Detroit Tigers 1939-1940
Boston Braves 1941

R AISED ON A SMALL RANCH IN Snohomish, Washington, Howard Earl Averill (1902-1983) — known all his life by his middle name — was nicknamed the "Earl of Snohomish" by sportswriters soon after he began his professional career. Among fellow players, though, he was more commonly called "Rock."

A severe arm injury in high school made Averill give up dreams of a baseball career. He worked and played semipro ball. Spotted by a bird dog of the San Francisco Seals of the Pacific Coast League, Earl was convinced to give pro baseball a whirl in 1926, at the rather advanced age of 24. Averill became an immediate sensation but seem destined never to rise above the high minors, partly because of his age but more because San Francisco was under no obligation to sell him to a major league team unless made an offer that was too attractive to refuse. In 1928, such an offer came from Billy Evans, business manager of the Cleveland Indians. Evans had journeyed to San Francisco to scout two other Seals outfielders, but he paid $50,000 for Averill.

At that time, $50,000 was a huge sum for an unproven minor leaguer, but the gamble reaped a quick dividend when Averill became the first

player in American League history to homer in his first major league at bat and went on to hit .331 for the Indians and compile 199 hits and 97 RBI. In addition, his 18 home runs established a Cleveland record to that point.

For more than a decade, Averill continued his onslaught on American League pitchers. Selected to play in the first All-Star game in 1933, he singled as a pinch-hitter against Carl Hubbell of the Giants. Four years later, in an All-Star game at Washington, Averill lined a shot back at Dizzy Dean, fracturing Dean's big toe. When Dean tried to return to duty too early, he injured his arm and was never again the same pitcher.

Ironically, Averill himself was seriously ailing at the time of the 1937 All-Star game. Just a week earlier his legs had mysteriously become momentarily paralyzed when he attempted to leave the Cleveland clubhouse for a pregame workout. Rushed to a hospital and X-rayed, Averill was found to have a congenital malformation of the lower spine. In order to continue playing, he had to alter his hitting style and become more of a spray hitter. With his power diminished and his average slipping, Rock was little more than an average player for the remaining four years of his career. In 1939, Averill was traded to Detroit, for which he played in his only World Series the following year.

Averill saw his son Earl follow him into the major leagues. The elder Earl was chosen to the Hall of Fame in 1975.

Top: *In 1936, Averill, featured in* Baseball Magazine, *hit .378 and paced the AL with 232 hits. Right: Between 1929 and 1933, Cleveland unveiled four rookies who had Hall of Fame potential. Three — Wes Ferrell, Joe Vosmik, and Hal Trosky — were derailed in midcareer. Averill survived a near midcareer derailing and eventually was selected for Cooperstown.*

				Major League Totals					
BA	**G**	**AB**	**R**	**H**	**2B**	**3B**	**HR**	**RBI**	**SB**
.318	1,669	6,358	1,224	2,020	401	128	238	1,165	69

LEFTY GOMEZ

VERNON LOUIS GOMEZ
"LEFTY"
NEW YORK A.L. 1930-1942
WASHINGTON A.L. 1943
WON 20 OR MORE GAMES FOUR TIMES IN
HELPING YANKEES TO WIN SEVEN
PENNANTS. LED A.L. WITH 26-5 RECORD,
2.33 EARNED RUN AVERAGE IN 1934 AND
WITH 21 VICTORIES AND 2.33 ERA IN
1937. PACED A.L. IN WINNING PCT. TWICE,
STRIKEOUTS THREE TIMES. SET WORLD
SERIES MARK BY WINNING 6 GAMES
WITHOUT A LOSS.

Pitcher
New York Yankees
1930-1942
Washington Senators 1943

Top: *The Gomez bat was not a big seller. There were worse-hitting pitchers, but not many.* Below: *Gomez coined the line, "I'd rather be lucky than good."*

ONCE LEFTY GOMEZ WAS ASKED why they called him "Goofy." He said: "I'm something like the Old Soak who never knew whether his wife told him to take one drink and come home at 12, or take 12 and come home at one." He was a top pitcher for the 1930s Yankees and was at his best in the big games.

Vernon Louis Gomez (1908-1989) was born in Rodeo, California. At a slim 6'2", 150 pounds in high school, he was a fireballing lefty. The San Francisco Seals of the Pacific Coast League signed him in 1928, and optioned him to Salt Lake in the Utah-Idaho League, where he went 12-14. Pitching for San Francisco in 1929, he was 18-11 and led the league with a 3.44 ERA.

The Yankees bought Gomez in 1929, and it took Lefty two years to become a winner. Gomez knew the value of playing for a powerhouse (his secret to success was "clean living and a fast outfield"), but he was capable of smothering teams on his own, as the possessor of a wicked fastball and a fine curve. Although he was plagued by arm ailments throughout his career, he changed his style and repertoire of pitches as he got older, perfecting a baffling slow curveball. He compiled a career 189-102 won-loss record.

Although his career is interspersed with mediocre seasons, he was the top winner on the Yanks in six of his ten full seasons with them, and twice led the league in wins and ERA. In 1934 he was 26-5, leading the league in ERA, strikeouts, shutouts, and complete games. In 1932, when the Yankees finally broke through against the Athletics, who had won three straight pennants, Gomez won 24 games and beat Philadelphia seven times, a spectacular clutch performance.

Gomez has the greatest World Series record in history, winning six games without a loss and winning five World Championship rings. He also won a record three All-Star games while losing just one.

When Joe DiMaggio was a rookie in 1936, he played a very shallow center field. When Gomez advised his rookie roommate to play deeper, DiMaggio said, "Don't worry. I'm going to make them forget about the great Tris Speaker." After an opponent tripled over DiMaggio's head, Gomez said to him, "Roomie, if you don't back up a little, you're going to make them forget about the great Lefty Gomez." Elected to the Hall of Fame in 1972, Lefty continued to delight fans as a broadcaster. After his heart operation in 1980, he said "Just had a triple bypass operation. Only triple I ever got."

Major League Totals

W	L	ERA	G	CG	IP	H	ER	BB	SO
189	102	3.34	368	173	2,503	2,290	929	1,095	1,468

JOSHUA (JOSH) GIBSON
NEGRO LEAGUES 1930-1946
CONSIDERED GREATEST SLUGGER IN NEGRO
BASEBALL LEAGUES, POWER-HITTING CATCHER
WHO HIT ALMOST 800 HOME RUNS IN LEAGUE
AND INDEPENDENT BASEBALL DURING HIS
17-YEAR CAREER. CREDITED WITH HAVING
BEEN NEGRO NATIONAL LEAGUE BATTING
CHAMPION IN 1936-38-42-45.

Catcher
teams include: Homestead Grays, Pittsburgh Crawfords, 1930-1946

Top: Gibson was Buck O'Neil's obvious choice at catcher for his all-time Negro League All-Star team. O'Neil said of Gibson, "He was our Babe Ruth." Below: Gibson, rounding third, was an all-around athlete.

POSSIBLY THE BEST KNOWN OF the Negro League sluggers, Josh Gibson's tape measure home runs rattled off the seats at a rate that could not be ignored.

Joshua Gibson (1911-1947) was born in Buena Vista, Georgia. Josh's father, wishing to give his children a better chance in life, moved the family to Pittsburgh, where Josh grew up. Gibson maintained that the greatest gift his father gave to him was to let him grow up in Pittsburgh. An outstanding athlete, he won medals as a swimmer before turning full attention to baseball. Working at an air-brake factory at age 16, he was a star for an all-black amateur team.

Josh was playing semipro ball by 1929. He was watching a Homestead Grays game when their catcher injured a finger. They pulled Gibson, who had already acquired some small fame for his long hits, out of the stands and put a Grays uniform on him. Within two years he was one of the team's biggest stars. Though he was barely in his 20s, Gibson was hitting around 70 home runs a year. He was lured to the Pittsburgh Crawfords in 1932, where he caught Satchel Paige for five years.

Gibson had always been a catcher, but he was not polished during the early stages of his career. Since he played more than 200 games a year, with

summer in the States and winter in either Mexico or the Dominican Republic, Josh became a veteran backstop in little time. Walter Johnson said Gibson was a better receiver than Bill Dickey. "He catches so easy he might as well be in a rocking chair," said the Big Train. Roy Campanella, though, called Gibson "not only the greatest catcher but the greatest ballplayer I ever saw."

Gibson reached distances in major league parks undreamed of by the white players who played in them regularly. He is credited with hitting a ball out of Yankee Stadium, and his longest hits are variously estimated between 575 and 700 feet. His career total is uncertain, but even the lowest estimates put him ahead of Hank Aaron, with 800 to 950 career homers. Gibson's lifetime average is the highest in the Negro Leagues, at .354 or .440 depending on your source. Against major league pitching in 16 exhibition games, he hit .424 with five homers.

Gibson went back to the Grays in 1936, but began to suffer from headaches, and drinking more than was his habit, partly in a search for relief from what was finally diagnosed a brain tumor. He died in 1947, age 36, after Jackie Robinson played his first game for Montreal in the Dodger farm system.

			Negro League Stats*					
BA	**G**	**AB**	**H**	**2B**	**3B**	**HR**	**SB**
.354	439	1,820	644	110	45	141	17

*Note: Gibson's career stats are incomplete.

JOSEPH FLOYD VAUGHAN
"ARKY"
PITTSBURGH N.L. 1932-1941
BROOKLYN N.L. 1942-1948
AMONG HALL OF FAME SHORTSTOPS, HIS .318
LIFETIME BATTING AVERAGE IS SECOND ONLY TO
HONUS WAGNER'S .329. LED LEAGUE WITH .385 IN
1935. HOMERED TWICE IN 1941 ALL-STAR GAME.
FANNED ONLY 276 TIMES IN 6622 CAREER AT-BATS.
POLISHED FIELDER AND ACCOMPLISHED BASE
RUNNER, LEADING N.L. WITH 20 STOLEN BASES IN
1943.

Shortstop
Pittsburgh Pirates
1932-1941
Brooklyn Dodgers
1942-1943; 1947-1948

A NINE-TIME ALL-STAR, ARKY Vaughan was one of the greatest offensive shortstops in baseball history. He led the NL three times in walks, triples, runs, and on-base percentage. He also led the loop in putouts and assists thrice, proving that he was no slouch with the glove.

Born in Clifty, Arkansas, Joseph Floyd Vaughan (1912-1952) was raised in Fullerton, California, where he received his nickname. After he played a few years in semipro ball, he was signed in 1931 by Wichita of the Western Association, where he hit .338 with 21 homers and 145 runs scored. The Pirates made Arky their starting shortstop in 1932.

Vaughan retired with a .318 career batting average, the second highest in history by a shortstop. It is also the second highest by a shortstop on the team for which he played most of his career. Because he broke in with Pittsburgh, Arky invited immediate comparison to Honus Wagner, a comparison that he and every other shortstop could not but suffer for the making. Although never Honus's equal in the field, Arky gave Wagner a close run offensively. Vaughan's .385 season in 1935 not only achieved the National League batting crown but set a 20th century loop record for the highest average by a shortstop. A year later, he garnered 118 walks to carve out another senior circuit record.

In the 1941 All-Star game at Briggs Stadium in Detroit, Vaughan became the first player to hit two home runs in a midsummer classic when he rapped a two-run clout in the seventh inning and then repeated his feat in the eighth. Vaughan's second four-bagger put the National League ahead 5-2 and seemed to cement his effort to be the game's hero. With two out in the ninth inning, however, Ted Williams socked a three-run homer to give the American League a 7-5 win.

In 1943, Vaughan paced his loop in stolen bases. After being traded to the Dodgers the previous year, Vaughan was just age 31 and still at his peak. He could not abide having to play for Brooklyn manager Leo Durocher, nonetheless. Unable to get the Dodgers to trade him, the mild-mannered Vaughan opted to retire quietly. He sat out all of the next three seasons, returning only in 1947 when Durocher was suspended for the year. After slumping to .244 in 1948, he retired again, this time for good.

In 1952, Vaughan drowned in a fishing mishap off the coast of Eagleville, California. Noted for giving preference to living former stars, the Veterans Committee passed over Vaughan again and again until he was finally selected in 1985.

FLOYD VAUGHAN

Top: Vaughan's .406 career on-base percentage is the highest in history by a shortstop. Left: This 1933 Goudey baseball card of Vaughan was issued on the heels of a rookie season that saw him hit .318 but lead all NL shortstops in errors.

				Major League Totals					
BA	G	AB	R	H	2B	3B	HR	RBI	SB
.318	1,817	6,622	1,173	2,103	356	128	96	926	118

LUCIUS BENJAMIN APPLING
CHICAGO A.L. 1930-1950
A.L. BATTING CHAMPION IN 1936 AND 1943.
PLAYED 2,218 GAMES AT SHORTSTOP
FOR MAJOR LEAGUE MARK.
HAD 2,749 HITS.
LIFETIME BATTING AVERAGE OF .310.
LED A.L. IN ASSIST 7 YEARS.
HOLDS A.L. RECORD FOR CHANCES
ACCEPTED BY SHORTSTOP 11,569.

Shortstop
Chicago White Sox
1930-1943; 1945-1950

L UKE APPLING WAS A BATSMAN second to none, hitting over .300 sixteen times in his 20-year career. He had outstanding command of the strike zone, once fouling off 19 pitches in a single at bat.

Lucius Benjamin Appling (1909-1991) grew up in Atlanta and was an all-city shortstop in high school. He attended Atlanta's Oglethorpe University, where, despite weighing 155 pounds, he was a football player as well as a baseball star. In 1930, after his sophomore year, he was signed by Atlanta in the Southern Association. After hitting .326, Luke was purchased by the White Sox and debuted that year. He batted .308 in six games and showed the Chicago South Side what a generation could expect from a shortstop at bat.

Defensively, though, Appling didn't adjust to major league standards. He became the full-time shortstop in 1933 and won the first of his two batting titles in 1936 when he hit .388, his career high. He had 204 hits and 128 RBI that season. He was also named the outstanding major league shortstop by *The Sporting News*, an honor he was to receive twice more in his career.

Luke hit .317 in 1937, but in 1938 he broke his leg, robbing him of some speed and range. He still managed to hit over .300 that year. In

1940, he lost the batting crown to Joe DiMaggio by four points, .352 to .348. Appling won another batting title in 1943 with a .328 average, but in 1944 he was gone to war, missing the entire season and playing in just 18 games in 1945.

Pushing 40, Appling hit over .300 each year from 1946 to 1949. He always seemed to have a knee or back problem, and he always seemed to make sure the whole team understood that, so much so that his nickname was "Old Aches and Pains." In 1949, he hit .301 in 142 games, and when his average slipped to just .234 the following year, he retired.

When Luke retired he left behind all-time records for major league shortstops in games and double plays, as well as American League records for putouts, assists, and total chances. The records lasted 23 years until fellow South-Sider Luis Aparicio broke them. Appling remained in baseball as a scout, coach, and manager for many years, and awakened memories of his greatness when he hit a home run in the first Crackerjack Old Timers Game in Washington, D.C., in 1985, when he was 78 years old. Luke never got the chance to play in a World Series, but he sustained a remarkable level of performance for an astounding length of time, and was one of the best-hitting shortstops in history.

Top: Appling is the only shortstop to have won two AL batting titles. Luke also once held the AL career records for both the most putouts and most assists by a shortstop. **Right:** *This is one of the many uniforms Luke wore during his long tenure with the Chicago White Sox. Appling's career spanned from 1930 to 1950.*

Major League Totals

BA	G	AB	R	H	2B	3B	HR	RBI	SB
.310	2,422	8,857	1,319	2,749	440	102	45	1,116	179

BILLY HERMAN

UNTIL ROD CAREW RETIRED IN 1985, Billy Herman was the last player to appear in 1,000 or more games at second base and retire with a career batting average above .300. During his 15 major league seasons, he participated in ten All-Star games and played on four pennant winners.

Born in New Albany, Indiana, William Jennings Bryan Herman (born in 1909) barely played enough in high school to earn a letter. Not until he graduated did he develop enough upper body strength to attract the interest of professional scouts. He was signed by Vicksburg of the Cotton States League in 1928, and hit .332. He advanced to Dayton of the Central League in 1929, and finally to Louisville of the American Association in 1930. When he hit .350 for the Colonels in 1931, he was brought up by the Cubs for a late-season trial. Billy played so well that Chicago player-manager Rogers Hornsby decided to turn his second base post over to the rookie in 1932.

In his first full big league campaign, Herman tied for the National League lead in games played with 154, batted .314, and collected 206 hits. After suffering a slight case of the sophomore jinx in 1933, Billy rebounded in 1934, hitting .303 and playing in his first All-Star Game.

In 1935, Billy collected 57 doubles, a record for National League second basemen, and then tied his own mark the following season. He topped NL second basemen in putouts a record seven times and ranked as the best all-around keystone sacker in the senior loop for nearly a decade.

Herman remained the linchpin of the Cubs infield until 1941 when he was traded to the Dodgers, where he sparked Brooklyn to their first flag in 21 years. Teaming with shortstop Pee Wee Reese, Billy gave Brooklyn one of the top keystone combinations in the game.

After hitting a hefty .330 in 1943 and driving in a career high 100 runs on just two homers, Billy spent the next two seasons in the Navy. He returned from World War II to hit .298 in 1946, most of which he spent with the Boston Braves after an early season trade. Dealt to Pittsburgh at the close of the 1946 campaign, he was named player-manager of the Pirates. Unprepared for the job, Herman was fired after a cellar finish in 1947. Given the Boston manager's job in 1965, he lasted two seasons before being replaced by Dick Williams.

Named to the Hall of Fame in 1975, Billy last worked in baseball with San Diego. From 1976 through 1979 he served as the Padres' minor league hitting coach and special assignment scout.

Second baseman
Chicago Cubs 1931-1941
Brooklyn Dodgers
  1941-1943; 1946
Boston Braves 1946
Pittsburgh Pirates 1947

BILLY HERMAN
CHICAGO "CUBS"
67

Top: *Herman was the last major leaguer to play 1,500 or more games at second base and retire with a .300-plus career batting average. Left: Orbit gum offered pins of only the top players in the game during the early 1930s. Herman made his Orbit debut in 1933 after hitting .314 and collecting 206 hits as a Cubs rookie in '32.*

Major League Totals									
BA	G	AB	R	H	2B	3B	HR	RBI	SB
.304	1,922	7,707	1,163	2,345	486	82	47	839	67

WILLIAM BOYD McKECHNIE
MANAGER OF
PITTSBURGH N.L. 1922-1926
ST. LOUIS N.L. 1928-1929
BOSTON N.L. 1930-1937
CINCINNATI N.L. 1938-1946
ONLY N.L. MANAGER TO WIN PENNANTS
WITH THREE DIFFERENT CLUBS-PITTSBURGH
1925; ST. LOUIS, 1928; CINCINNATI, 1939, 1940
WON WORLD SERIES 1925 AND 1940. NAMED
NO. 1 MAJOR LEAGUE MANAGER 1937 AND
1940. ACTIVE IN BASEBALL AS MANAGER,
COACH, PLAYER, 1906 TO 1953.

Manager
Newark Peppers 1915
Pittsburgh Pirates
    1922-1926
St. Louis Cardinals
    1928-1929
Boston Braves (Bees)
    1930-1937
Cincinnati Reds 1938-1946

R AISED IN WILKINSBURG, Pennsylvania, William Boyd McKechnie (1886-1965) was a member for 25 years of the Wilkinsburg Methodist Church choir. His background accounted in part for his nickname of "Deacon," but his managerial skills were equally responsible.

That McKechnie's record is not even more remarkable than it is can be traced largely to the fact that he never had the luck to obtain the reins of a great team. Indeed, his experience was often quite the opposite. In 1935, McKechnie had the misfortune to be at the helm of the worst team in modern National League history, a Boston Braves outfit that won just 38 of 153 games. Within two years, however, the Deacon had rebuilt the club and was named Manager of the Year.

McKechnie's first managerial test in the majors came in 1915 when he took charge of the Newark team in the Federal League while still an active player. Seven years later, he got his second chance as a major league manager when the Pirates fired George Gibson in July and gave Bill the job. After two successive third-place finishes, in 1925 McKechnie skippered Pittsburgh to its first pennant since 1909. A year later, though, he was ousted following an internal revolution on the club that pitted him against coach Fred Clarke. Bill was hired by Branch Rickey in 1928 to manage the Cardinals and promptly won a

McKechnie, featured in the October 1925 Baseball Magazine, delivered a World Championship to Pittsburgh that year.

pennant. A devastating loss to the Yankees in the '28 World Series and a slow start in 1929, however, cost him another job within a year after he had won a pennant.

Hired in 1930 to reverse the fortunes of the lowly Boston Braves, McKechnie remained in the Hub through 1937. Then in 1938, he took an offer of $25,000 to pilot Cincinnati. Following a fourth-place finish in his initial season with the Reds, Bill won back-to-back pennants in Cincinnati with a team that for many years held the record for being the only club in modern major league history to cop consecutive pennants despite not having a player judged worthy of selection to the Hall of Fame. In 1986, that distinction was lost when Ernie Lombardi was enshrined.

McKechnie's triumph with the Reds made him the first manager ever to win pennants with three different major league teams. Some analysts consider him later to have won a flag with yet a fourth club. In 1948, although Lou Boudreau was officially Cleveland's player-manager and McKechnie his chief coach, Bill made many of the field decisions that resulted in the Tribe capturing the AL flag. Deacon Bill was named to the Hall of Fame in 1962.

McKechnie won pennants as a pilot with three different teams—Pittsburgh, Cincinnati, and the St. Louis Cardinals. He skippered the Braves to two consecutive first-division finishes in 1933 and 1934, a remarkable achievement considering that Boston had only once before in the 20th century finished in the top half of the NL two years in a row.

Major League Managing Totals				
W	L	T	PCT	G
1,899	1,724	28	.524	3,651

ERNIE LOMBARDI

ERNIE LOMBARDI RETIRED with the fourth highest career batting average in history among players who appeared in over 1,000 games as a catcher. Those who saw him play insist his .306 mark would have been 50 points higher if he had even average speed. Lombardi was so slow afoot that infielders customarily played him back on the outfield grass, thus cutting off many screeching line drives that otherwise would have been hits.

Born in Oakland, California, Ernesto Natali Lombardi (1908-1977) drove a delivery truck for his father's fruit and vegetable business in the Bay area and played baseball on the sandlots. When he was 18 years old, he was signed by the local Oakland Oaks in the Pacific Coast League, in 1926. Ernie didn't get many at bats that year, and he was sent to Ogden of the Utah-Idaho League, where he batted .398. Oakland brought Ernie back in 1928, and over the next three years he batted .377, .366, and .370.

The Dodgers bought the 6'3", 230 pound catcher after the 1930 season for $50,000 and several players. Ernie played there one year, but with Al Lopez holding down the Dodger backstop job, Brooklyn traded Lombardi to Cincinnati prior to the 1932 season. Ernie hit .303 in his first year of regular duty and collected nine triples.

From 1934 to '37, Lombardi hit .305, .343, .333, and .334, with about 60 RBI a season. In 1938, he became the first receiver in major league history to win an undisputed batting crown when

Catcher
Brooklyn Dodgers 1931
Cincinnati Reds 1932-1941
Boston Braves 1942
New York Giants
 1943-1947

he hit .342 for the Reds in 489 at bats. Bubbles Hargrave had been awarded the National League batting crown in 1926 despite batting fewer than 400 times, and Lombardi himself took a second hitting title in 1942 with only 309 at bats.

With Lombardi behind the plate and a pitching tandem of Paul Derringer and Bucky Walters, in 1939 the Reds grabbed their first pennant since 1919. Ernie's poor Series performance culminated in a home plate collision with Yankees outfielder Charlie Keller in the final game of a New York sweep. The collision left Lombardi dazed and sprawled beside the plate while three Yankees runs scored.

Cincinnati then repeated the following year, with Ernie batting .319. A late-season injury held him to just three at bats in the 1940 World Series, however. When Lombardi slipped to a .264 batting average in 1941, he was traded to the Boston Braves. After he rebounded to win the hitting crown in 1942, the Braves sent him to the New York Giants, where he spent his final five seasons in the majors as a backup catcher and a pinch-hitter. In 1986, nearly nine years after his death, the Veterans Committee selected Ernie for the Hall of Fame.

Top: Lombardi palms seven baseballs. He not only had mammoth hands, every physical aspect of him was gargantuan. Left: When Lombardi topped the National League in 1938 with a .342 batting average, it marked the first time that a backstopper with over 400 at bats had finished the season as his loop's leading hitter.

Major League Totals									
BA	G	AB	R	H	2B	3B	HR	RBI	SB
.306	1,853	5,855	601	1,792	277	27	190	990	8

JOE MEDWICK

JOSEPH MICHAEL MEDWICK
"DUCKY WUCKY"
ST. LOUIS N.L. 1932 TO 1940, 1947, 1948
NEW YORK N.L. 1943 TO 1945—BOSTON N.L. 1945

LED N.L. IN BATTING IN 1937 WITH .374
AVERAGE, BATTED .353 IN 1935, .351 IN 1936,
.332 IN 1939. LIFETIME TOTAL 2471 HITS.
BATTING AVERAGE .324. NAMED TO ALL STAR
TEAMS 1935-6-7-8-9. MOST VALUABLE PLAYER
N.L. 1937. LED N.L. IN RUNS BATTED IN
AND TWO BASE HITS 1936-7-8.
BATTED .300 OR MORE 15 TIMES.

Outfielder
St. Louis Cardinals
1932-1940; 1947-1948
Brooklyn Dodgers
1940-1943; 1946
New York Giants
1943-1945
Boston Braves 1945

EARLY IN HIS CAREER JOE Medwick tried to get the baseball public to call him Mickey. Anything seem preferable to "Ducky Wucky," the nickname given to him for his ducklike walk. Finally the sobriquet was shortened to Ducky, and Medwick eventually learned to live with it—or at least not to fight fellow players who referred to him by it.

Joe was never one to back off from an altercation on or off the field. It was no accident that he was an instigator in one of the most famous World Series incidents. In the seventh game of the 1934 classic between the Tigers and Medwick's Cardinals, Joe slid hard into Detroit third baseman Marv Owen. Too hard, thought partisan Detroit fans, who began to pelt him with fruit and refuse when he tried to take his position in left field at the bottom of the inning. Finally, so much debris had been hurled onto the field that Commissioner Landis ordered Medwick to be removed from the game for his own safety. Since the Cardinals were cruising to an 11-0 victory, Joe departed without argument.

Born in Carteret, New Jersey, Joseph Michael Medwick (1911-1975) was one of the greatest

Medwick played for four NL teams, but St. Louis received most of his best work.

all-around athletes in the Gem State's history. He was a high school star in track, football, basketball, and baseball. After high school, Joe turned down a football scholarship to Notre Dame to sign with the Cardinals organization. His first season in pro ball, in 1930, was a huge success. He batted .419 with 22 homers in 75 games for Scottsdale of the Middle Atlantic League. He then played two years for Houston of the Texas League, batting .305 with 19 homers and 126 RBI in 1931, and .354 with 26 dingers and 111 RBI in 1932.

Medwick was deemed ready to replace defending batting crown winner Chick Hafey in the St. Louis lineup late in 1932. Joe hit .300 every year from 1933 to 1942. He had over 100 RBI from 1934 to 1939. He reached his peak in 1936 when he led the National League in hits and RBI and set a new loop record with 64 doubles. The following year he became the last player in National League history to win a Triple Crown. Even though Medwick hit .332 in 1939, he was dispatched early the next season to Brooklyn.

Medwick played for the Dodgers until he was sold to the Giants in July 1943. Two years later he was traded to the Braves and then released by them prior to the 1946 season. After a year with Brooklyn, Joe spent two more seasons with the Cardinals. Medwick was elected to the Hall of Fame in 1968.

Medwick tallies a run for Brooklyn in 1942 against Pittsburgh and its catcher Al Lopez. Medwick batted .300 for the Dodgers that year.

Major League Totals

BA	G	AB	R	H	2B	3B	HR	RBI	SB
.324	1,984	7,635	1,198	2,471	540	113	205	1,383	42

RAY DANDRIDGE

RAYMOND EMMETT DANDRIDGE
NEGRO AND MEXICAN LEAGUES
1933 - 1948
FLASHY BUT SMOOTH THIRD BASEMAN. DEFENSIVELY,
A BRILLIANT FIELDER WITH POWERFUL ARM.
OFFENSIVELY, A SPRAY HITTER WITH OUTSTANDING
BAT CONTROL. PLAYED FOR DETROIT STARS, NEWARK
DODGERS, NEWARK EAGLES AND NEW YORK CUBANS
IN NEGRO LEAGUES AND FOR VERACRUZ AND MEXICO
CITY IN MEXICAN LEAGUES. AMERICAN ASSOCIATION
MVP IN 1950 WITH .311, 11 HOME RUNS AND
80 RBI'S PLAYING FOR MINNEAPOLIS MILLERS.

Third baseman
teams include: Detroit Stars, Nashville Elite Giants, Newark Dodgers, Newark Eagles, New York Cubans

ONE OF THE GREATEST FIELD-ing third basemen in baseball history, Ray Dandridge was a high average hitter who at age 36 batted .362 in the American Association.

Raymond Dandridge was born in 1913 in Richmond, Virginia. He was a Golden Glove amateur boxer as a young man. He was playing with his hometown sandlot team when it played the barnstorming Detroit Stars in 1933. The Stars were led by Candy Jim Taylor, and when he saw Ray's quickness in the outfield, Taylor knew that he had a potential great infielder on his hands.

At bat, Ray used a very light bat and swung for the fences. Taylor gave Dandridge a lesson in contact hitting, using a heavy bat, making contact, and placing the ball. Ray compiled a .335 lifetime average in the Negro Leagues, using the best data available, and hit .347 against white major leaguers during the course of his career.

Defensively, Ray had terrific reflexes and a fine arm, and Taylor put Dandridge first at shortstop, the position that Taylor played. It was not until Ray was with the Newark Dodgers that he was moved to third base—by Dick Lundy, another shortstop. Ray was unequaled at third, with a glove often compared to Brooks Robinson's, but a better arm. Ray was a familiar sight at second base as well—and any fan could recognize the bowlegged Dandridge.

Dandridge played in the Negro Leagues from 1933 to 1938. In 1939, he took a higher offer to play at Vera Cruz in the Mexican League. His manager, shortstop Willie "Devil" Wells, moved Ray to second base because Ray was hard of hearing on his left side and he couldn't hear the instructions from his skipper. Ray made good money for his time, as one of the star players in Mexican baseball.

While in Mexico, Dandridge had been approached by Cleveland about joining their system, but would not go without a bonus. Alex Pompez, the owner of the New York Cubans and a scout for the Giants, signed him for the Minneapolis Millers of the American Association, in 1949. Dandridge could hardly have played better. He narrowly missed the batting title with a .362 average, and was voted the loop's Rookie of the Year in 1949. In 1950, he hit .311 and won the MVP Award. He also became a mentor to teammate Willie Mays. But Dandridge was never called up. Ray was inducted into the Hall of Fame in 1987.

Top: Dandridge was age 36 when he joined the Minneapolis Millers of the American Association in mid-1949. He amassed 144 hits in 99 games and posted a .362 batting average. He was thought to be too old to play in the majors by the time the color line was broken, but his record in the high minors discredits that judgment. Left: He played for nearly a decade with teams south of the U.S. border.

Negro League Stats*

BA	G	AB	H	2B	3B	HR	SB
.335	229	824	276	40	13	4	1

*Note: Dandridge's career stats are incomplete.

EDWARD GRANT BARROW
CLUB EXECUTIVE, MANAGER, LEAGUE
PRESIDENT IN MINORS AND MAJORS FROM
1894 TO 1945. CONVERTED BABE RUTH FROM
PITCHER TO OUTFIELDER AS MANAGER BOSTON
A.L. IN 1918. DISCOVERED HONUS WAGNER
AND MANY OTHER GREAT STARS. WON WORLD
SERIES IN 1918. BUILT NEW YORK YANKEES INTO
OUTSTANDING ORGANIZATION IN BASEBALL
AS BUSINESS MANAGER FROM 1920 TO 1945,
WINNING 14 PENNANTS, 10 WORLD SERIES.

Top: A relaxed Barrow is seen on the March 1947 cover of Baseball Magazine. Below: Babe Ruth is the most famous personage the Yankees acquired at bargain-basement rates from the Boston Red Sox, but Barrow may have been the most important acquisition.

THE BASEBALL PLAYING DAYS of Iowa-bred Edward Grant Barrow (1868-1953) came to a halt in his late teens due to arm trouble. Forced to drop out of high school in his sophomore year as his father's poor health rendered him the breadwinner of the family, Barrow turned to sportswriting. It was while working for the Des Moines *Blade* in 1889 that Barrow discovered Fred Clarke, a soon-to-be star outfielder.

From then on, Barrow was gradually drawn into a career in baseball. In 1894, he operated the concession stands at Exposition Field in Pittsburgh. The following year, he managed a minor league team in Wheeling, West Virginia. He next purchased the Paterson, New Jersey, club of the Atlantic League. One of his first acts as owner was to sign a rawboned youth named Honus Wagner. Midway through the 1897 season, Barrow peddled Wagner to Louisville in the National League for $2,100.

From the Atlantic League, where he also served as president for three years, Barrow moved

to the position of manager and part owner of the Toronto franchise in the Eastern League. The club captured the circuit's flag in 1902. Named manager of the Detroit Tigers, Barrow lasted just a year and one-half in the Motor City before resigning after a dispute with Frank Navin, the club's new owner.

In 1905, while managing Indianapolis in the American Association, Barrow passed up a chance to buy Ty Cobb for $500 (he always considered it to be his greatest error in judgment).

During the early 1910s, Barrow served as president of the Eastern League. Asked to take a salary cut in 1917 owing to the lagging wartime economy, he instead quit to become the manager of the Boston Red Sox. The club promptly won the 1918 World Championship, and Barrow had a large hand in converting Babe Ruth from a pitcher to an outfielder.

After the 1920 season, Barrow was appointed business manager of the Yankees, a job he held for the next 27 years. It proved to be his true calling. More than any other man, Barrow was responsible for developing the Yankees into the greatest dynasty in professional sports history. He combined a keen eye for recognizing talent with consummate front office savvy. Among his many contributions to the Yankees regime were putting numbers on the backs of players' uniforms, hiring George Weiss to develop a farm system, and, perhaps most significantly, selecting Joe McCarthy to manage the club in 1931. Barrow was elected to the Hall of Fame in 1953.

BUCK LEONARD

BUCK LEONARD WAS A LEFT-handed power-hitting first baseman who was often compared to Lou Gehrig. Buck was a key ingredient to the domination of the Homestead Grays in the 1930s.

Walter Fenner Leonard (born in 1907) was born to a railroad fireman in Rocky Mount, North Carolina. Buck also worked on the railroad until the Depression forced him out of a job. He played semipro baseball with clubs in North Carolina and Virginia until 1933, when the Baltimore Stars signed him. He traveled with the team until it ran out of money in New York and disbanded. Stuck in New York, he was lucky to find a position with the Brooklyn Royal Giants for the rest of the season. Leonard stopped in a New York bar owned by Joe Williams, a retired player who had starred on Cumberland Posey's Homestead Grays. Williams now had his eye open for talent, because the Grays had been all but wiped out by player raids and retirement.

Leonard had a tryout, and he signed to play first base for the Grays. The team began to regain respectability, and when Josh Gibson came aboard in 1937, the Grays caught fire, winning nine consecutive flags. But when Gibson jumped ship to play in Mexico in 1940, it was Leonard who carried the club, hitting .392 in 1941 to lead the Negro National League. He had already won a pair of home run titles in his long career and at age 39 won another batting title, hitting .395.

First baseman
teams include: Baltimore Stars, Brooklyn Royal Giants, Homestead Grays 1933-1950

Buck was fairly well paid for his services. The Homestead Grays were based both in Pittsburgh and Washington, playing games in Forbes Field when the Pirates were out of town and in Griffith Stadium when the Senators were on the road. Since the Grays were able to fill both stadiums, they were able to pay their stars more than other Negro League teams. The lure of Mexican baseball was also a boon to Leonard. The Grays were forced to match the salary that he was being offered to play south of the border, and he was able to command over $1,000 per month in 1942, and even more later, good amounts for the Negro Leagues. He stayed with the Homestead Grays for his entire career, instead of jumping to other teams as other Negro League stars had done.

Buck played in Mexico, Cuba, Puerto Rico, and Venezuela in the winter, and he also barnstormed with Satchel Paige's all-stars. He played in Mexico in the early 1950s after he retired from the Grays. In 1972, Leonard was selected for the Hall of Fame.

Top: Leonard takes a pregame swing. Buck O'Neil, himself a fine Negro League first baseman, rated Leonard as the best first baseman ever to play in the black circuits. Left: Buck was nearly 40 by the time the color line was finally dissolved. Even though he was too old to play in the majors, however, he performed both with and against many black players who went on to major league stardom, including Jackie Robinson and Roy Campanella.

	Negro League Stats*						
BA	G	AB	H	2B	3B	HR	SB
.324	382	1,587	514	85	33	71	10

*Note: Leonard's career stats are incomplete.

LELAND STANFORD MacPHAIL
"LARRY"

DYNAMIC, INNOVATIVE EXECUTIVE MADE HIS MARK AS PROGRESSIVE HEAD OF THREE CLUBS CINCINNATI REDS, BROOKLYN DODGERS AND NEW YORK YANKEES FROM 1933 TO 1947. WON CHAMPIONSHIPS IN BOTH LEAGUES WITH DODGERS IN 1941 AND YANKEES IN 1947. PIONEERED NIGHT BALL AT CINCINNATI IN 1935, ALSO INSTALLED LIGHTS AT EBBETS FIELD AND YANKEE STADIUM. ORIGINATED PLANE TRAVEL BY PLAYING PERSONNEL AND IDEA OF STADIUM CLUB. HELPED SET UP EMPLOYEE AND PLAYER PENSION PLANS.

Top: *MacPhail combined with Del Webb and Dan Topping to buy the Yankees and return them to the top in 1947.* Below: *He took over the floundering Brooklyn franchise in the late 1930s. In 1941, the club won its first pennant since 1920.*

LEO DUROCHER ONCE SAID about Larry MacPhail: "There is no question in my mind but that Larry was a genius. There is a thin line between genius and insanity, and in Larry's case it was sometimes so thin that you could see him drifting back and forth."

Leland Stanford MacPhail (1890-1975) was born in Cass City, Michigan. He was an athlete as well as a scholar, and he received his law degree at age 20. By age 24, he was the president of a department store in Nashville, Tennessee. MacPhail led a group of officers into Holland after the World War I Armistice was signed in a nearly successful attempt to kidnap Kaiser Wilhelm. MacPhail kept the Kaiser's ash tray on his desk as a reminder of the attempt.

Larry bought the declining Columbus, Ohio, franchise in the American Association in 1930. It took him three years to revive it. In 1934, he became general manager of the nearly bankrupt Cincinnati Reds. He introduced night baseball and air travel to the major leagues, and he also

built the foundations of pennant winners in 1939 and 1940.

MacPhail moved to the Dodger organization by 1938 before he could enjoy the fruits of his success with Cincinnati. He and Durocher won a pennant in 1941. In addition, Larry put lights in Ebbets Field, and also brought in Red Barber to broadcast Dodger games — breaking an informal agreement among the three New York ballclubs. Larry solidified a reputation as a slick trader and as a power. When Kenesaw Mountain Landis died in 1944, MacPhail was able to use his considerable clout to have Happy Chandler named the new commissioner.

MacPhail served in World War II, and when he got out he became part-owner of the New York Yankees, with a 10-year contract to run the team. As president and general manager he helped build what would become the most successful team in baseball history.

A big, hard-drinking man, MacPhail almost made an alcohol-induced trade with Boston owner Tom Yawkey — Joe DiMaggio for Ted Williams one-for-one. Sober, neither had the nerve to go through with the deal. Larry installed lights in The House Ruth Built, and the Yankees won the World Series in 1947. His celebration of the event included a drunken brawl that prompted his partners to buy him out and fire him. Larry's son Lee became American League President, and his grandson, Andy, is general manager of the Minnesota Twins. MacPhail was named to the Hall of Fame in 1978.

BOB FELLER WAS PROBABLY harmed more than any other great pitcher by World War II. While serving in the Navy he lost nearly four full seasons just as he was entering his prime. Had Feller's career been allowed to proceed without interruption, he might now be considered the greatest pitcher in history.

Born in 1918 at Van Meter, Iowa, Robert William Andrew Feller was signed by Cleveland while still a 16-year-old high school student, in 1935. The signing was illegal according to the rules of the time and would have cost the Indians the rights to Feller had commissioner Kenesaw Mountain Landis not feared a gargantuan bidding war among the other teams if Feller was made a free agent. For even as a teenager, he was renown for the blazing fastball that would soon gain him the nickname "Rapid Robert."

No one could have taught Feller what he possessed when he debuted with Cleveland in a July 1936 exhibition game against the Cardinals. Though only 17, Feller was already so swift that he fanned eight Redbirds in the three innings he hurled, causing home plate umpire Bob Ormsby to label him the fastest pitcher Ormsby had ever seen, Walter Johnson included.

All did not come easy, though, for Bob. Batters quickly learned that while he was virtually unhittable, they could nevertheless reach base

Pitcher
Cleveland Indians
1936-1941; 1945-1956

simply by waiting for walks. In 1938, he topped the major leagues with 240 strikeouts and also set a modern single-game record when he fanned 18 Tigers in his last start of the season. Notwithstanding his remarkable feat, Feller lost the contest, due in part to walks. Along with his record-shattering strikeout performance, Rapid Robert also set a new modern mark for bases on balls in 1938 when he gave up 208 free passes.

His control slowly improving, Feller paced the American League in wins during each of the next three seasons and then went into the Navy. His prewar high and low points both came in 1940. That year Feller tossed the first Opening Day no-hitter in AL history but then ended the season with a 1-0 loss to Detroit that killed Cleveland's hope for its first pennant since 1920.

Returning from the war, Feller had his finest season in 1946 when he won 26 games and logged 348 strikeouts. An arm injury in 1947 curtailed Bob's fastball thereafter, but he continued to be one of the game's top hurlers until 1955. He was the author of three career no-hitters and 12 one-hit games. Feller was selected to the Hall of Fame in 1962.

Top: *When he joined Cleveland in 1936 as a flame-throwing 17-year-old Iowa schoolboy, Feller was instantly compared to Walter Johnson.* Left: *Feller knew the value of not only his pitching arm but also his name. One of the best-paid players of his day, Feller made an additional bundle in endorsements.*

Major League Totals										
W	L	ERA	G	CG	IP	H	ER	BB	SO
266	162	3.25	570	279	3,827	3,271	1,384	1,764	2,581

JOE DiMAGGIO

JOSEPH PAUL DI MAGGIO
NEW YORK A.L. 1936 TO 1951

HIT SAFELY IN 56 CONSECUTIVE GAMES FOR MAJOR LEAGUE RECORD 1941. HIT 2 HOME-RUNS IN ONE INNING 1936. HIT 3 HOME-RUNS IN ONE GAME (3 TIMES). HOLDS NUMEROUS BATTING RECORDS. PLAYED IN 10 WORLD SERIES (51 GAMES) AND 11 ALL STAR GAMES. MOST VALUABLE PLAYER A.L. 1939, 1941, 1947.

Outfielder
New York Yankees
1936-1942; 1946-1951

Top: *DiMaggio announces his retirement in 1951. Below: Joe displays the AL MVP Award he won in 1947 by a controversial one vote over Ted Williams. Ted won the Triple Crown while DiMaggio failed to finish among the top five in either batting or homers.*

IF JOE DiMAGGIO WASN'T THE greatest all-around player in baseball history, he almost certainly was the most majestic.

Joseph Paul DiMaggio (born in 1914) was a native of San Francisco, where he and his brothers Vince and Dom played baseball on the sandlots hour after hour. Joe left high school early to work in a cannery and to play semipro baseball. At age 17, he signed with the San Francisco Seals (for whom brother Vince played) at the end of the 1932 season. Joe played in three games and batted .222. The next season, he had a .340 batting average, 28 homers, and 169 RBI in 187 games. Joe was a local hero.

DiMaggio batted .341 in 1934, but he suffered a knee injury that scared some big league clubs away from him, especially at the price that the Seals were demanding. The Yankees had no such qualms; with their superior financial position, the Bombers were able to risk the $25,000 and five minor league players for Joe. The Yankees assigned him back to San Francisco for the 1935 season, and he had a .398 average, 34 homers, and 154 RBI — raising the hopes of Bronx fans.

DiMaggio lived up to even tough New York standards, joining with Lou Gehrig to power the Yankees to the first of four consecutive World Championships in his 1936 rookie season. Although he was severely hampered by Yankee Stadium's cavernous left field, The Yankee Clipper twice led the league in home runs and twice in slugging. He hit only 148 of his 361 lifetime home runs at home.

DiMaggio was an outstanding and graceful defensive outfielder. He played center with ease and threw the ball with terrific power. He led the league in assists with 22 his rookie year, and had 21 and then 20 before the league apparently got wise and stopped running on him.

Joltin' Joe won his first Most Valuable Player Award in 1939, when he had his career-best .381 batting average. When he won his second MVP in 1941 he had 76 walks and only 13 strikeouts. He also hit in a record 56 consecutive games, a feat considered the greatest by some observers. No other hitter has ever hit in more than 44. He almost never struck out — his high was 39, his rookie year — and actually came close to having more lifetime homers than Ks, with 369 strikeouts to his 361 round-trippers.

If Yankee Stadium depressed his career totals, World War II was even more of a factor as Joe lost three seasons. He won his third MVP and the Yankees won another Championship in 1947 (it was Joe that hit the drive that made Al

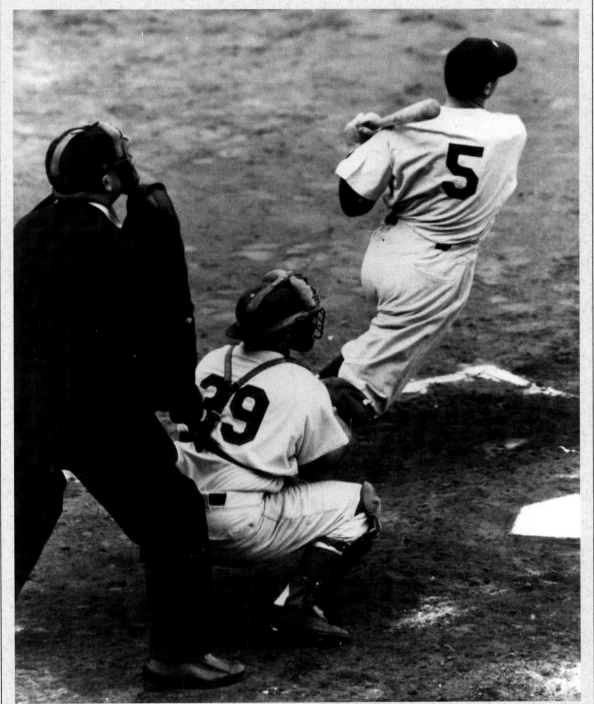

DiMaggio rips one in the 1949 World Series as Brooklyn catcher Roy Campanella watches unhappily. The Yankees star managed just two hits in 18 at bats in that fall classic, however.

The Brothers DiMaggio

Baseball has had many famous brother combinations, but none are more famous than Vince, Dominic, and Joe DiMaggio. Raised by immigrant parents near the docks of San Francisco, the brothers played baseball against their parents wishes.

Vince began playing for the hometown San Francisco Seals, where he made his reputation as a superb fielder though he had a penchant for striking out. It was during his career with the Seals that he introduced brother Joe to team management. Before long, Vince would hurt his arm, forcing his trade to the Hollywood Stars and setting the stage for Joe to take his place in center field. By 1937, Joe and Vince were in the majors, while Dominic was just beginning his pro career with the Seals.

All three were playing in the majors in 1940. With a lifetime .298 batting average, Dom's career was in the neighborhood of his immortal brother's. Of Vince, Casey Stengel probably said it best when he remarked of the trio that "Joe is the best hitter, Dom the best fielder, and Vince the best singer."

Gionfriddo famous), but a heel injury slowed Joe in 1948, and he couldn't return to the lineup until June of 1949. His return was memorable, as he was 5-for-11 with four homers and nine RBI in a double-header. Another World Championship followed, the first of five straight for the Yanks, but DiMaggio would only stick around for three of them. Injuries and the grind of the road drove Joe into retirement after the 1951 season. He was succeeded in center by Mickey Mantle.

With the passing of time, Joe's legend continued to grow to an enormous magnitude.

Ernest Hemingway used Joe as a symbol in *The Old Man and the Sea*. Musicians from Les Brown to Paul Simon wrote about DiMaggio in songs. Marilyn Monroe married Joe. He became a spokesman for a national product, Mr. Coffee, that became part of the American vocabulary. DiMaggio was a joy to watch, and loved to play the game. DiMaggio was inducted into the Hall of Fame in 1955.

Major League Totals									
BA	G	AB	R	H	2B	3B	HR	RBI	SB
.325	1,736	6,821	1,390	2,214	389	131	361	1,537	30

BILL VEECK

OWNER OF INDIANS, BROWNS AND WHITE SOX. CREATED HEIGHTENED FAN INTEREST AT EVERY STOP WITH INGENIOUS PROMOTIONAL SCHEMES, FAN PARTICIPATION, EXPLODING SCOREBOARD, OUTRAGEOUS DOOR PRIZES, NAMES ON UNIFORMS. SET M.L. ATTENDANCE RECORD WITH PENNANT-WINNER AT CLEVELAND IN 1948; WON AGAIN WITH "GO-GO" SOX IN 1959. SIGNED A.L.'S FIRST BLACK PLAYER, LARRY DOBY IN 1947 AND OLDEST ROOKIE, 42 YEAR OLD SATCHEL PAIGE IN 1948.
A CHAMPION OF THE LITTLE GUY.

BILL VEECK WAS NOT THE FIRST owner to realize that baseball was more than a sport to the players or a business to the owners. He believed that it was an entertainment. Due to this he did more than other owners during his time to entertain the fan. The other owners belittled his promotions as travesties but eventually used his ideas and went beyond them.

William Veeck Jr. (1914-1986) was born to Chicago sportswriter William Veeck Sr. The elder Veeck was named the Cubs general manager when Bill Jr. was four years old. Junior grew up performing odd jobs at Wrigley Field, and often claimed to have planted the ivy that covers the outfield walls.

When Senior died, in 1933, Junior quit college and went to work full-time for the Cubs. He quit in 1941 after buying the Milwaukee franchise in the American Association. He revived the franchise with various gimmicks, and sold the franchise in 1945. In 1943, he put together a partnership to buy the Phillies. It was Bill's plan to stock the team with Negro Leagues stars, but commissioner Kenesaw Mountain Landis nixed the deal.

While fighting in the South Pacific theater in World War II, Veeck had to have his left leg amputated, but that never quenched his spirit. He put another partnership together and bought the Cleveland Indians in 1946. The attendance

"I lived in Milwaukee, I ought to know...

Blatz is Milwaukee's Finest Beer!"

Blatz is Milwaukee's **First Bottled Beer!**

increased from 558,182 in 1945 to 1,057,289 the next year. In 1948, the Tribe drew 2,620,627, a franchise record. Bill signed the first African-American to play in the American League, Larry Doby, in 1947. In 1948, Veeck signed Negro League legend Satchel Paige. During Paige's first start in Cleveland, he attracted 78,382 people — the largest crowd ever at a night game.

Veeck sold Cleveland in 1949 and bought the St. Louis Browns, the major leagues' most pitiful franchise. His most famous stunt was in late 1951 when the Browns sent Eddie Gaedel, a 3'7", 65 pound entertainer, up to bat. Eddie wore the number ⅛ and walked on four pitches. The baseball establishment was *not* amused. Losing money, Veeck tried to move the Browns to Baltimore in 1953, only to be blocked by the AL owners. Veeck sold, and the club moved to Baltimore in 1954.

After several years of nonbaseball-related promoting, Bill bought the White Sox in 1958, and promptly introduced the exploding scoreboard. Forced by his doctors to sell in 1961, Bill wrote his autobiography, *Veeck as in Wreck*. In 1975, a group of Seattle investors tried to buy the ChiSox, and Veeck came back to buy the team, selling five years later at a profit. Veeck could be found from that time in the bleachers of Wrigley, shirtless and with a beer, among the people he loved the best, the fans. Veeck was inducted into the Hall of Fame in 1991.

Right: Veeck at work. The package of Beechnut and the open-necked sport short were among Veeck's trademarks.
Top: Veeck was a regular guy. The idea of watching his teams play from a private box would have mortified him. Even while he was an owner, Veeck frequently doffed his shirt and sat in the bleachers.

JOHNNY MIZE

HARD-HITTING FIRST BASEMAN Johnny Mize was a link from the great 1930s Cardinals teams to the great Yankees dynasty of the 1950s.

John Robert Mize was born in 1913 in Demorest, Georgia. He played a good deal of basketball as a youngster, because his hometown was small enough to make gathering enough players for baseball difficult. He played baseball well enough while in high school to sign with Greensboro of the Piedmont League in 1930. In 1933, while at Rochester of the International League, he suffered painful leg cramps that would haunt him for the next several years. In 1935, he underwent surgery to remove a growth on his pelvis. Thus cured, he moved up to the St. Louis Cardinals.

Mize joined the Cards in 1936, batted .329, and clubbed 19 home runs, a total he was to increase each year for the next four years. He surpassed the .300 mark for the next eight years, peaking at .364 in 1937. In 1939, Johnny led the league in homers (28) and batting average (.349). In 1940, "The Big Cat" walloped 43 dingers to top the senior circuit and drove home 137 runs, also the league lead. He finished second in the MVP voting to Frank McCormick. Mize led the NL with three consecutive seasons of .600-plus slugging percentages—1938 to 1940.

First baseman
St. Louis Cardinals
  1936-1941
New York Giants 1942;
  1946-1949
New York Yankees
  1949-1953

Traded to the New York Giants prior to the 1942 season, Mize led the NL that season with a .521 slugging percentage and 110 RBI. He served three years in the Navy during World War II. He returned from the service to top the NL twice in home runs, including 51 round-trippers in 1947—a mark that still stands for NL lefties—tying Ralph Kiner for the league's top spot. Mize, however, paced the loop in RBI (138) and runs scored (137).

He seemed to get better with age, but Mize was slowing down, and toward the end of the '49 season the Yankees acquired him for $40,000. He went 2-for-2 in the 1949 World Series with two RBI. The Yanks were champs and looked like geniuses. Mize was even a bigger hero in the 1952 Series. In a wild battle with the Dodgers, he hit .400 with six RBI and three homers in 15 at bats, grabbing the Series MVP honor. A part-time first sacker and pinch-hitter, Johnny led the AL in pinch hits from 1951 to 1953.

In all, "The Big Cat" won five World Series rings with the Yanks. He retired after the 1953 season, at age 40. The only slugger in history to hit three home runs in a game six times, Mize was named to the Hall of Fame in 1981.

Top: *Mize was the defending NL batting and home run champ in 1940 when this advertisement appeared. After he slumped to just 16 homers in 1941, he was swiftly traded to the Giants. Mize promptly showed St. Louis its mistake by pacing the NL in both RBI and slugging average in 1942. Left: Mize was the last Cardinals home run champion.*

			Major League Totals							
BA	**G**	**AB**	**R**	**H**	**2B**	**3B**	**HR**	**RBI**	**SB**
.312	1,884	6,443	1,118	2,011	367	83	359	1,337	28

BOBBY DOERR

ROBERT PERSHING DOERR
BOSTON, A.L., 1937–1951

QUIET LEADER OF RED SOX DURING 1940's. CONSISTENT SECOND BASEMAN, TOP DOUBLE PLAY MAN AND FINE CLUTCH HITTER. LIFETIME BATTING AVERAGE OF .288 WITH SIX SEASONS OF OVER 100 RBI's. HELD A.L. RECORD FOR 2B BY HANDLING 414 CONSECUTIVE CHANCES WITHOUT ERROR. LED A.L. 2B IN DOUBLE PLAYS FIVE TIMES, PUTOUTS FOUR TIMES AND ASSISTS ON THREE OCCASIONS. BATTED .409 IN 1946 WORLD SERIES.

Second baseman
Boston Red Sox
1937-1944; 1946-1951

B OBBY DOERR WAS A GREAT-hitting second baseman who drove in over 100 runs six times as the Red Sox finished first or second in seven of his 14 seasons. His name is eternally linked with that of Ted Williams. They played together in San Diego in 1936, and it was when Eddie Collins of the Red Sox came to scout Doerr that Williams was discovered.

A Los Angeles native, Robert Pershing Doerr (born in 1918) was a star on his American Legion team and well known throughout the Los Angeles area. The 1934 Hollywood Stars in the Pacific Coast League had a hole at second base and desperately wanted Bobby to patrol the keystone. After persuading his father, the Stars were able to sign the 16-year-old Doerr. He spent three years in the PCL, leading the loop in hits with 238 in 1936 and 504 assists at second base.

Signed by the Boston Red Sox as a 19-year-old rookie in 1937, Doerr's first season wasn't

memorable. One year later Bobby was the Red Sox starting second baseman, a spot he would hold for the next 12 years. The righthanded-hitting Doerr was able to take advantage of Fenway Park's peculiarities to hit for terrific power. He led the league in slugging in 1944 with a career-high .528 mark, while posting a career-high .325 batting average. The next year he was off to World War II, returning in 1946 and picking up just where he left off.

Doerr appeared in his only World Series in '46. Although the Red Sox lost, Doerr did his part with a Series-leading nine hits and a .409 average in six games.

Although he played with Ted Williams, one of the most scientific hitters who ever lived, and one of Bobby's best friends, Doerr was primarily a guess hitter with terrific intuition. A solid .288 lifetime hitter, Doerr collected 2,042 hits, 223 home runs, and 1,247 RBI. In 1950, Doerr led the league in triples, hit 27 dingers, and drove home 120 runs. It was his last productive year, and he was out of baseball by 1952 due to a severe sacroiliac attack during the 1951 season.

A solid fielder, Bobby remains in the all-time top lists for putouts and assists for second basemen, even though many second sackers have played much longer. In the 1948 near-pennant year, Doerr accepted 414 chances without an error—almost three months. After his retirement, Doerr served as a coach for the Red Sox and later was a coach for the Toronto Blue Jays until 1981. The Veterans Committee elected Bobby Doerr to the Hall of Fame in 1986.

Top: A chronic back problem permanently sidelined Doerr in 1951 when he was still among the top second basemen in the game. In his 14 seasons with the Red Sox, Doerr averaged 16 home runs and 89 RBI per year. Right: An autographed postcard of Bobby. In 1948, he and shortstop Junior Stephens combined for 268 RBI, the most ever by a keystone pair.

Major League Totals

BA	G	AB	R	H	2B	3B	HR	RBI	SB
.288	1,865	7,093	1,094	2,042	381	89	223	1,247	54

Boudreau was so revered by Cleveland fans he received a standing ovation the first time he appeared there with the Red Sox.

MANY ARGUE THAT NO DEC-ade in this century has had more great shortstops than the 1940s. Of the great ones, most analysts rate Lou Boudreau the best.

Louis Boudreau (born in 1917) grew up in Harvey, Illinois, and was a three-time all-state basketball player. He played basketball and baseball for the University of Illinois in 1936 and '37. The Indians signed him to an agreement in 1938, and Big Ten Conference officials ruled Lou ineligible. He joined the Indians' Cedar Rapids farm club that year and also played pro basketball.

In 1939, Boudreau was in Cleveland to stay. In 1940, his initial year as a regular, he hit .295 and drove in 101 runs. The next season he topped the AL in doubles. In 1944, Lou copped the AL bat crown and seemed headed for a repeat win the next season before a broken ankle sidelined him.

Before the 1942 campaign, although just age 24, Lou applied for and was given the Cleveland manager's post, thus becoming the youngest skipper to open the season at the helm of a major league team. Known as the "Boy Manager," Boudreau quickly showed he was mature beyond his years. Among his many leadership qualities were a remarkable self-confidence and a willing-ness to experiment.

Boudreau created the famous "Williams Shift" in 1946 to combat lefty pull-hitter Ted Williams. Lou moved to the right side of second base, challenging Ted to hit the other way. Lou also moved the strong-armed Bob Lemon from a third baseman to a pitcher.

When Bill Veeck took over as Cleveland owner in 1946, he at first wanted Boudreau to give up the manager's reins and concentrate solely on playing. The torrential protests of Cleveland fans made Veeck reconsider. His change of mind paid off when the Indians won the World Championship in 1948. The 1948 AL MVP, during the regular season Lou hit .355, and in the playoff game he belted two homers.

Owing to weak ankles, Boudreau was one of the slowest infielders in the game, and he had a mediocre arm. Lou was so thoroughly schooled, however, that he almost never errored on a routine play and had an unerring sense of anticipation. Between 1940 and 1948, Boudreau led the AL in fielding every year but one.

Released by Cleveland in 1950, Lou signed with the Red Sox as a player, and took over in the Red Sox dugout in 1952. He later managed the Athletics and the Cubs. He then became a long-time fixture in the Cubs' broadcast booth. Boudreau was elected to the Hall of Fame in 1970.

LOUIS BOUDREAU
CLEVELAND A.L. 1938-1950
BOSTON A.L. 1951-1952

LED A.L. SHORTSTOPS IN FIELDING EIGHT SEASONS. SET MAJOR LOOP MARK FOR DOUBLE PLAYS BY SHORTSTOP (134) AND WON BATTING TITLE 1944. PACED A.L. IN DOUBLES THREE TIMES. MOST VALUABLE PLAYER 1948 WHEN HE BATTED .355 TO LEAD INDIANS TO PENNANT AS PLAYER-PILOT. LIFETIME BATTING AVERAGE .295

Shortstop
Cleveland Indians
   1938-1950
Boston Red Sox 1951-1952
Manager
Cleveland Indians
   1942-1950
Boston Red Sox 1952-1954
Kansas City Athletics
   1955-1957
Chicago Cubs 1960
1,162-1,224

Boudreau is with three members of the Tribe's 1948 Championship team. From left are Joe Gordon, Bob Lemon, Boudreau, and Gene Bearden.

Major League Totals

BA	G	AB	R	H	2B	3B	HR	RBI	SB
.295	1,646	6,030	861	1,779	385	66	68	789	51

ENOS BRADSHER SLAUGHTER
"COUNTRY"
ST. LOUIS N.L. 1938-1953
NEW YORK A.L. 1954-1955, 1956-1959
KANSAS CITY A.L. 1955-1956 MILWAUKEE N.L. 1959
HARD-NOSED, HUSTLING PERFORMER WHO PLAYED
THE GAME WITH INTENSITY AND DETERMINATION.
FLAT, LEVEL SWING MADE HIM A LIFETIME .300
HITTER WHO INVARIABLY CAME THROUGH IN
CLUTCH SITUATIONS. EXCELLENT OUTFIELDER WITH
STRONG ARM. DARING BASERUNNER FAMOUS FOR
HIS MAD DASH HOME TO WIN 1946 WORLD SERIES
FOR CARDINALS. BATTED .291 IN 5 WORLD SERIES.

Outfielder
St. Louis Cardinals
   1938-1942; 1946-1953
New York Yankees
   1954-1955; 1956-1959
Kansas City Athletics
   1955-1956
Milwaukee Braves 1959

Slaughter steals home in the 1946 World Series. It set the tone for his brazen dash around the bases in the Series finale that sunk the Sox.

WHILE PLAYING FOR THE Columbus, Georgia, Redbirds of the South Atlantic League in 1936, Enos Slaughter was walking in from the outfield, brooding about his hitting, when manager Eddie Dyer reprimanded Enos for not hustling in. At that moment Slaughter vowed never to walk on a ballfield again. And he didn't. For the next 23 years Slaughter was the epitome of hustle, a quality that permeated all facets of his game.

Enos Bradsher Slaughter was born in 1916 in Roxboro, North Carolina. He was discovered playing semipro ball and was signed in 1935. Enos proved he was ready for the big leagues in 1937, when he led the American Association with a .382 batting average, 147 runs, and 245 hits.

Slaughter won the right field job with the Cards in 1938, and fans around the circuit soon discovered that he meant business while on the ballfield. He batted .320 in 1939, scoring 95 runs. He hit .306 in 1940 with 96 runs scored, and batted .311 in 1941.

A .300 lifetime hitter, "Country" topped the .300 mark ten times. He collected 2,383 hits in 19 years. Had he not missed three years due to

A Slaughter autographed baseball. Losing three of his prime seasons to World War II cost him some 500 hits and 300 RBI.

World War II, he would have been within striking distance of 3,000. Slaughter led the senior circuit in hits in 1942 (188), in RBI in 1946 (130), in doubles in 1939 (52), and in triples twice, in 1942 and '49. Enos also worked hard on his defense, overcoming a reputation for wildness by developing a strong and accurate throwing arm.

A member of two World Championship Cardinal teams, Slaughter led the 1942 Cards to the pennant with a .318 average, 13 home runs, and 98 RBI, although he hit only .263 in the World Series. He redeemed himself in the '46 fall classic against the Boston Red Sox, batting .320 and scoring five runs—the last on what has come to be known as the "Mad Dash." In game seven, with the score tied 3-3 in the eighth inning, Enos had a leadoff single. Two outs later, he broke for second base while Harry Walker singled over Boston shortstop Johnny Pesky. Running all the way, Slaughter rounded third as Pesky hesitated after he took the relay throw. Pesky may have had a play, but Slaughter hustled all the way to the plate, easily sliding in for the winning run.

After 13 years with the Cardinals, Slaughter was traded to the New York Yankees for the 1954 season, where he played as a part-timer and pinch-hitter. A brief stint with Kansas City ended in midseason 1956, when he returned to the Yankees. In all, Enos played on three pennant-winning teams with New York (1956, '57, '58). In 1955, he led the AL with 16 pinch-hits. Slaughter was elected to the Hall of Fame in 1985.

Major League Totals

BA	G	AB	R	H	2B	3B	HR	RBI	SB
.300	2,380	7,946	1,247	2,383	413	148	169	1,304	71

RICK FERRELL

WHEN RICK FERRELL RETIRED, he had toiled behind the plate for more games than any previous American League catcher, and he was one of the most respected receivers in baseball history. He played in over 18 seasons for three teams. He never won a pennant or a batting title, but he lasted because of his defense and his ability to handle pitchers.

Born in 1905 in Durham, North Carolina, Rick was one of seven brothers. Some of the boys wanted to be hurlers and designated Rick to be the catcher. He and one brother, Wes, formed a battery that dominated the county in which they were raised. Rick was also a professional boxer, winning the state championship in the lightweight division. He played baseball at Guilford College in North Carolina, and signed with the Detroit organization in 1926. While his defense was up to major league standards, he didn't show that he could hit big league pitching immediately. Detroit wasn't overly enthusiastic about his chances.

By 1928, Ferrell had improved enough at bat to become an American Association All-Star and notch a .333 batting average for Columbus. The Tigers were pleased with Rick's development, and wanted him to challenge Al Wingo as the backup catcher to Pinky Hargrave. Detroit tried to hide Ferrell by making a verbal agreement

to lend him to Columbus without putting him on their draft lists. Commissioner Kenesaw Mountain Landis, called in to resolve the matter, ruled that Ferrell was a free agent. He signed with the St. Louis Browns, who finished third in the AL in 1928 (Detroit finished sixth), and had 39-year-old Wally Schang at catcher.

Ferrell hit over .290 eight times, and had some doubles power when he was younger, though the trials of catching robbed him of his speed later. His brother, Wes, won 20 games six times, and they formed a battery for four years when they both played for Boston and Washington. Wes was one of the best-hitting pitchers ever, and in 1933 the brothers each connected for home runs in the same game. They had another brother, George, who played in the minor leagues for 20 years.

With Washington, Rick faced his biggest challenge, as he caught four knuckleballers in the rotation. He led the league in various defensive categories 11 times. He was a small man for a catcher, at 170 pounds, but he was able to withstand the rigors of catching for 1,806 games, an AL record that stood for more than 40 years, until Carlton Fisk topped it. Ferrell was inducted in 1984.

RICHARD BENJAMIN FERRELL
ST. LOUIS A.L. 1929-1933; 1941-1943
BOSTON A.L. 1933-1937
WASHINGTON A.L. 1937-1941; 1944-1947
CAUGHT MORE GAMES (1,806) THAN ANY OTHER
AMERICAN LEAGUER. DURABLE DEFENSIVE STAND-OUT
WITH FINE ARM. EXPERT AT HANDLING PITCHERS.
MET CHALLENGE OF 4 KNUCKLE-BALLERS IN SENATORS
STARTING ROTATION. OFTEN FORMED BATTERY WITH
BROTHER, WES. HIT OVER .300 4 TIMES. SECOND
ONLY TO DICKEY IN A.L. CAREER PUTOUTS AT
RETIREMENT.

Catcher
St. Louis Browns
  1929-1933; 1941-1943
Boston Red Sox 1933-1937
Washington Senators
  1937-1941; 1944-1945;
  1947

Top: Ferrell was spending his first full season with the Red Sox in 1934 when this Diamond Stars card of him was issued. Left: Ferrell was among the American League's steadiest and most durable catchers for 18 seasons. Pictured here in a St. Louis Browns uniform, he served two separate stints in the Mound City.

Major League Totals

BA	G	AB	R	H	2B	3B	HR	RBI	SB
.281	1,884	6,028	687	1,692	324	45	28	734	29

Above: McGowan was regarded as the best umpire in the American League. His nickname was "No. 1." Players, managers, and fellow umpires alike used that moniker to refer to Bill. Top right: Indicators became common during McGowan's era.

BILL McGOWAN'S CAREER AS AN American League umpire began in 1925, and during his tenure, he developed such a reputation for fairness, accuracy, and integrity that he earned the nickname, "No. 1."

A native of Wilmington, Delaware, William Aloysius McGowan (1896-1954) began his career as an arbiter in the Virginia League in 1915. He also served in the New York State League, the International League, and the Blue Ridge League all before serving in World War I. He returned to the International League in 1919, and he stayed there until 1922, when he moved to the Southern League for the 1923 campaign.

McGowan's vigorous style of umpiring attracted enough attention to earn him a promotion to the American League in 1925. Among his many noted calls, he cost Yankee first baseman Lou Gehrig sole possession of the loop's 1931 home run crown. After hitting the ball over the center field fence at Washington's Griffith Stadium on April 26, Gehrig was well into his home run trot when teammate Lyn Lary—on third base at the time—mistakenly thought that the ball was caught and proceeded directly to the dugout rather than completing the circuit to home plate. Gehrig, who didn't notice Lary's blunder, was called out by McGowan for passing Lary on the basepaths. Credited with a triple instead of a home run, Lou finished the year with 46 homers, tying Babe Ruth.

McGowan was chosen to work in eight World Series and four All-Star games, including the initial midsummer classic at Chicago's Comiskey Park in 1933. Bill also was chosen to work behind the plate in the AL's first pennant playoff, between the Cleveland Indians and the Boston Red Sox in 1948.

Regarded as the best and most colorful umpire of his day, McGowan was called, "the greatest umpire I've ever seen," by Clark Griffith. AL president Will Harridge said Bill was "one of the all-time greats of his profession." Ted Williams, who sat on the Veterans Committee that elected Bill (in 1992) said he "made the right call 99.99 percent of the time." McGowan was tough enough to work every inning of 2,541 consecutive games before a bout with neuritis forced him to miss a game on September 3, 1940. He also operated the Bill McGowan School for Umpires in Florida, which opened its doors as the second such institute in 1939. He retired from the American League in August 1954 because of a heart disorder.

HAL NEWHOUSER

Pitcher
Detroit Tigers 1939-1953
Cleveland Indians
1954-1955

HAL NEWHOUSER WAS A Detroit native who made good with the hometown Tigers. Though he was age 13 before he began playing baseball, Harold Newhouser (born in 1921) blossomed into such a star American Legion player that the Tigers signed in 1938 him at age 17. He received $400 to sign with the Tigers. Detroit secured his contract moments before the Cleveland Indians offered $15,000 and a new car. A year later, in 1939, he pitched in his first major league game, and the 6'2" lefty spent 15 of his 17 major league seasons with the Bengals.

Early in his career, Newhouser had difficulty with control. Plagued by streaks of wildness and a volcanic temper, he alienated both managers and teammates. His fortunes changed, however, with the 1943 arrival of catcher Paul Richards in Detroit.

Richards helped the talented but erratic Newhouser develop into the American League's premier pitcher during the war years. Newhouser wanted to serve in the armed forces during the war, but a congenital heart disorder kept him at home, and for a while even threatened his baseball career. Hal had a 29-9 record with a 2.22 ERA in 1944, winning his first Most Valuable Player Award. He went 25-9 with a 1.81 ERA in 1945 to earn his second MVP, as the Tigers won the pennant and beat the Chicago Cubs in the World Series. Hal was 2-1 with a 6.10 ERA in that tourney.

Newhouser paralyzed opponents with an arsenal that included a fastball, curveball, and changeup. He led the league in victories three times and strikeouts and ERA twice each. With 152 wins by age 27, Hal seemed certain to challenge Eddie Plank's record (since broken) of victories by a lefthanded pitcher. Pitching with one day's rest on the last day of the 1948 campaign, Newhouser beat Cleveland star Bob Feller—forcing the Indians into a one-game pennant playoff with Boston. Nevertheless, the victory—the league-leading 21st for Hal—had its price. Newhouser started to experience the shoulder pain that eventually would shorten his career. He won 18 games in 1949—and after winning 15 games in 1950, he never again won in double figures in a season.

Released by Detroit at age 32 after the 1953 season, Hal received a tryout with Cleveland. The general manager of the Indians at the time, Hank Greenberg, was a teammate of Newhouser's in Detroit. The Indians were short of lefthanded pitching, and they found Hal a welcome addition. He hurled for the Tribe in 1954, but he hung up his spikes after two games in 1955. Newhouser was inducted into the Hall of Fame in 1992.

Top left: Newhouser joined the Tribe in 1954, and he won seven games and saved seven to help Cleveland win the pennant that year. Above: Hal was at the end of his term with the Tigers when this 1953 Topps card was manufactured. Left: After Newhouser notched a complete-game victory over the Cubs in game five of the 1945 World Series, he returned two days later and won game seven 9-3.

Major League Totals

W	L	ERA	G	CG	IP	H	ER	BB	SO
207	150	3.06	488	212	2,992.2	2,674	1,016	1,249	1,796

CHAPTER FIVE

Equal Opportunity

Robinson Erases the Line

AFTER STARRING IN THREE SPORTS AT UCLA AND serving as an Army lieutenant, Jackie Robinson was selected by Branch Rickey of the Brooklyn Dodgers in 1946 to break baseball's color line. Rickey told Robinson that he required a talented player "with guts enough not to fight back."

Once the gifted but outspoken Robinson agreed, Rickey sent him to the Dodgers' top Triple-A farm club in Montreal for a year of physical and mental preparation. In 1947, when Robinson was placed on the Brooklyn roster, several teammates circulated a petition protesting his presence. Members of the Phillies and Cardinals undertook to strike—until commissioner Happy Chandler threatened lifetime suspensions for anyone who participated.

Though deluged with taunts from rival dugouts, Robinson kept his word and his cool. He not only survived the abuse but proved so talented as a hitter, runner, and fielder that he was named Rookie of the Year in 1947. Two years later, he was the National League's Most Valuable Player. Robinson's arrival opened the door for others. Larry Doby of the Cleveland Indians became the American League's first black player later in 1947, and Satchel Paige, Roy Campanella, Don Newcombe, Monte Irvin, and Hank Thompson soon followed.

In 1953, the Braves changed the baseball map for the first time in 50 years by moving from Boston to Milwaukee. The Braves' immediate success convinced other clubs in two-team towns to seek greener pastures. The St. Louis Browns became the Baltimore Orioles in 1954, and the Philadelphia Athletics moved to Kansas City a year later.

Above: *Satchel Paige's 1953 Topps baseball card. The previous year, he pitched for part of the campaign under manager Rogers Hornsby, whom Paige had faced in exhibition contests more than 20 years earlier while Hornsby was still active.* Opposite page: *Jackie Robinson crosses the plate after slugging a homer in the 1952 All-Star Game.*

Roy Campanella was featured on this Time *magazine cover. In 1953, he set a record with 41 home runs and 142 RBI generated by a player who served at no other position but catcher.*

SATCHEL PAIGE

LEROY ROBERT PAIGE
"SATCHEL"
NEGRO LEAGUES   1926-1947
CLEVELAND A.L.   1948-1949
ST. LOUIS A.L.   1951-1953
KANSAS CITY A.L.   1965
PAIGE WAS ONE OF THE GREATEST STARS
TO PLAY IN THE NEGRO BASEBALL LEAGUES.
THRILLED MILLIONS OF PEOPLE AND WON
HUNDREDS OF GAMES. STRUCK OUT 21 MAJOR
LEAGUERS IN AN EXHIBITION GAME. HELPED
PITCH CLEVELAND INDIANS TO THE 1948
PENNANT IN HIS FIRST BIG LEAGUE YEAR
AT AGE 42. HIS PITCHING WAS A LEGEND
AMONG MAJOR LEAGUE HITTERS.

Pitcher
Negro League teams
    include: Chatanooga
    Black Lookouts,
    Birmingham Black
    Barons, Nashville Elite
    Giants, Cleveland Cubs,
    Pittsburgh Crawfords,
    Kansas City Monarchs'
    "B" team, Kansas City
    Monarchs, St. Louis
    Stars, Philadelphia Stars
    1926-1947; 1950
Major League teams
Cleveland Indians
    1948-1949
St. Louis Browns
    1951-1953
Kansas City Athletics 1965

SOMETIMES IT SEEMS THAT Satchel Paige was more a mythological being than a flesh-and-blood man. He was the most popular baseball player in the Negro Leagues. After Jackie Robinson and Larry Doby integrated the major leagues, Paige was still baseball's biggest draw. He was ageless, could do anything with a baseball, and few who faced him could help but acknowledge his greatness.

Leroy Robert Paige (1906-1982) was born in Mobile, Alabama, one of 11 children. His birthday is recorded as July 7, 1906, but even that is shrouded in the mists of legend. Negro League star Ted "Double-Duty" Radcliffe, who was born in Mobile 1902, said that he was younger than Paige. Satchel got his nickname because he worked as a porter at the train station when he was a boy. In 1918, at age 12, he was sent to a state reform school, where he learned to pitch.

Released from the reform school in 1923, Paige was signed by the semipro Mobile Tigers in 1924 at age 18. His reputation spread, and by 1926 he was hurling for the Chattanooga Black Lookouts. He jumped to the Birmingham Black Barons in 1927, all the while pitching exhibition games and in the Caribbean and Mexico in the winter. He stayed with Birmingham until 1930.

Paige had two fastballs that were overpowering: one nicknamed "Long Tommy," which was supersonic, and the other called "Little Tommy," which was merely unhittable. He also threw his "bee ball," named because it would "be where I want it to be."

Paige gained fame when he joined the Pittsburgh Crawfords in the early 1930s, with others such as Josh Gibson. Crawfords owner Gus Greenlee would hire Paige out to semipro clubs that needed an attendance boost for a day. When Paige barnstormed around the country or pitched in the Dominican Republic, he was so popular that fans would not come to see his teams unless he pitched, so he would pitch every day. He would promise to fan the first nine men he faced, and often delivered. He also regularly got the best of the likes of Dizzy Dean and Bob Feller, proving that he could pitch against the best in the major leagues. Paige would walk hitters to get to Joe DiMaggio. DiMaggio said Satchel "was the best I ever faced." Paige was fantastically well paid for the times, earning close to $50,000 a year.

Paige offers tips to several Kansas City A's pitching teammates in 1965. Paige came out of retirement that season to start a game for the A's at age 59 against the Red Sox. In his three-inning stint he surrendered just one hit and no runs.

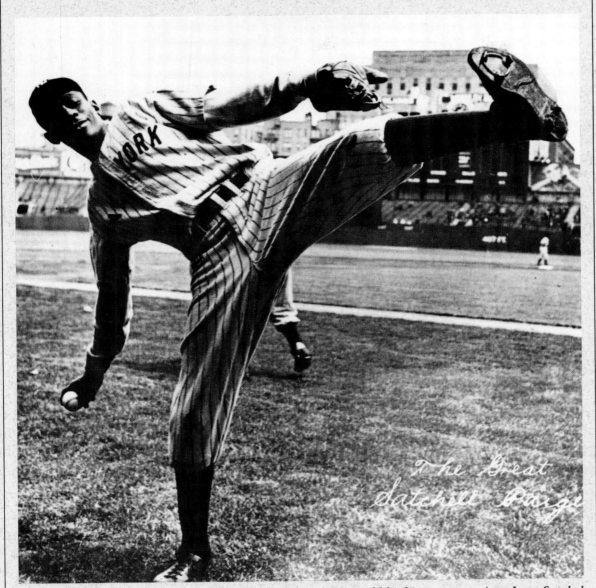

According to Buck O'Neil, Paige had "uncanny control. He could hit his spot every time. I saw Satchel beat Feller and Dean and Hubbell before the War. What a treat that was."

Beating the Major Leaguers

Long before Jackie Robinson broke the color barrier for major leaguers, the only opportunity afforded African-American ballplayers to compete with their white major league counterparts was in exhibition games. No pitcher made quite as dramatic a mark in these games as Satchel Paige.

In two memorable contests played at Los Angeles' Wrigley Field in 1947, Paige outdueled Indians legend, future teammate, and fellow Hall of Famer Bob Feller. Over five innings pitched, Paige struck out 15.

Paige wrote that he beat major league barnstorming teams in 17 straight games during the 1930s. This string was broken in December 1935 in Oakland, when he lost to a team of Bay area major leaguers led by then minor leaguer Joe DiMaggio, who made the game-winning hit. In later years, DiMaggio said that Paige was the toughest pitcher he ever faced.

All those innings in all those games gave Satchel a sore arm, and by 1939 the fastballer looked to be through as a dominant hurler. J.L. Wilkinson, the owner of the Kansas City Monarchs, signed Paige primarily as a gate attraction to pitch for the Monarchs' traveling "B" team. During that year, Satchel developed several off-speed pitches. He also used several hesitation deliveries that were so convincing that hitters were helpless. When his arm recovered the next season, he was a better pitcher than he had ever been in the 1930s. Satchel pitched for the Monarchs in the 1940s, but he was more an independent operator than a team member.

Finally, in 1948, Bill Veeck, longing for more talent, signed Paige to a contract. He asked Indians manager Lou Boudreau to take some swings against Paige, and when Boudreau failed to get good wood on the ball, he became enthusiastic. Paige was 6-1, pitching before packed houses, as the Browns won the pennant.

Satch was disappointed that he didn't get a start in the World Series, which Cleveland won, though he did pitch two scoreless innings. Many who had cried that Veeck was pulling a publicity stunt were forced to eat their words.

Paige's last big league appearance came in 1965 at age 59. He continued to pitch well in the minor leagues for years. He was a colorful speaker and original thinker; his six rules for "How to Stay Young" became famous, the sixth being "Don't look back. Something might be gaining on you." Paige was inducted into the Hall of Fame in 1971.

Negro League Stats*							
W	L	G	CG	IP	H	BB	SO
123	79	279	122	1,584	1,142	241	1,177

Major League Stats									
W	L	ERA	G	CG	IP	H	ER	BB	SO
28	31	3.29	179	7	476.0	429	174	183	290

*Note: Paige's Negro League career stats are incomplete.

CAL HUBBARD

ROBERT CAL HUBBARD
UMPIRE
AMERICAN LEAGUE 1936-1951
ONE OF MOST RESPECTED, EFFICIENT AND
AUTHORITATIVE UMPIRES IN HISTORY OF
MAJORS. GENTLE GIANT BOASTED SPECIAL
KNACK FOR DEALING WITH SITUATIONS ON
FIELD. WORKED FOUR WORLD SERIES AND
THREE ALL-STAR GAMES. SERVED AS LEAGUE'S
ASSISTANT UMPIRE SUPERVISOR IN 1952 AND AS
UMPIRE SUPERVISOR FROM 1953 TO 1969.

TED WILLIAMS ONCE SAID THAT umpire Bill Summers "was like Cal Hubbard. He took complete charge of a game." Hubbard was perfectly capable of taking complete charge; at 265 pounds, the former football star backed down from no one.

Robert Cal Hubbard (1900-1977) was born in Keytesville, a small town in north-central Missouri. He was raised on a farm, and as a youngster played baseball, though he was not considered very good. He enrolled at Centenary College in 1922, because his boyhood idol, Bo McMillan, was the football coach there. Cal played football there two years, and was always the dominant player on the gridiron. Cal also played baseball at Centenary, but again was not considered very good. When McMillan left to coach at Geneva College in 1924, Hubbard went with him.

Hubbard played well enough to be named an All-American in 1926. He joined the New York Giants in the National Football League in 1927. A five-time all pro, Hubbard played tackle both ways, and after being granted a requested trade to the Green Bay Packers, helped the team to three consecutive championships. His skills on the gridiron earned him election to both the College Football Hall of Fame and the Pro Football Hall of Fame. He was also voted the NFL's greatest tackle for the league's first 50 years.

In 1928, Hubbard started umpiring in both the Piedmont and the Southeastern Leagues. He also worked in the South Atlantic League. By 1931, he had moved up to the Triple-A International League. He put in eight minor league seasons before joining the American League in 1936, which was his last as a pro football player. He was such a good umpire, with an uncanny knowledge of the rule book, that he worked his first World Series by 1938—he worked four All-Star games and three World Series in his career. His size had its advantages. Once, while working behind the plate, he warned a catcher to quit arguing balls and strikes. "If you don't shut up," Cal said, "I'm gonna hit you so hard on the top of your head it'll take a derrick to get you back to ground level." Most catchers shut up.

A hunting accident in 1951 impaired the vision in Cal's right eye, forcing him to retire. He was named the assistant supervisor of AL umpires that year, and moved up to supervisor in 1954. He remained in that position until 1969, the same year he was elected to Cooperstown.

While playing tackle for the NFL champion Green Bay Packers in the early 1930s, Hubbard was simultaneously learning his craft as an umpire in the minor leagues.

WILLIAM HARRIDGE WAS THE American League president for 28 years, yet his is one of the least-recognized names of baseball's short list of administrators. He was a man behind the scenes.

William Harridge (1881-1971) was born in Chicago to British parents. He learned stenography as a young man, and got a job for the Wabash Railroad. One of his duties was to process the incredible amount of paperwork generated by the rail travel of baseball teams. Ban Johnson, the president of the American League, recognized the organizational skills that Will brought to his railroad work. In 1911, Ban hired Will as his personal secretary, increasing Harridge's salary from $90 a month to $200 a month.

Harridge helped Johnson keep the growing American League together for 16 years, until Johnson was forced to take a leave of absence in 1927. After a few months, Ban came back to find Harridge still working and was furious. After Johnson resigned, Harridge continued as secretary under Ernest Barnard for four more years. After Barnard died, in 1931, White Sox owner Charles Comiskey pushed Harridge's nomination through, and Will became the AL president.

By 1932, Harridge had proved that he was tough enough to take on some of the strong-willed owners. He suspended Yankee catcher Bill Dickey for a month for punching another player — challenging the most powerful owner in

the circuit, the Yankees' Jacob Ruppert. Ruppert was furious initially, but within a few years was a strong supporter.

Harridge worked quietly to promote league attendance and enforce the rules. He championed the All-Star game, and after initial opposition, night baseball. He disliked stunts, however, and quickly put a stop to Bill Veeck after Eddie Gaedel, a 3'7" performer, managed to enter a game as a pinch-hitter in 1951. Will fined one of his favorite players, Ted Williams, when the Splinter's feud with fans and press, expressed through spitting, became an issue. Yet Harridge encouraged Williams when fans accused him of draft-dodging in 1942. In one of his less far-sighted moves, Harridge fired umpire Ernest Stewart for unionizing in 1948, though at the same time, Will worked hard to end umpire-baiting at the hands of players and managers.

Harridge stepped down as president in 1958, remaining chairman of the board of the American League until he died in 1971. Will was named to the Hall of Fame in 1972.

Top: *Harridge was about to begin his fourth season as the American League president when he made the cover of* Baseball Magazine *in February 1934.* Below: *Harridge, the third president of the AL, served the junior circuit for 28 years without a written contract.*

GEORGE WEISS

GEORGE MARTIN WEISS
MASTER BUILDER OF CHAMPIONSHIP TEAMS.
WAS CLUB EXECUTIVE IN MINORS AND
MAJORS FROM 1919 TO 1966.
DEVELOPED BEST MINOR LEAGUE CHAIN
IN GAME AS NEW YORK YANKEE FARM
MANAGER, 1932-1947. GENERAL MANAGER
OF THE YANKEES FROM 1947-1960 WHICH
WON 10 PENNANTS AND 7 WORLD SERIES
DURING THIS PERIOD.
PRESIDENT OF THE NEW YORK METS
1961-1966.

The trio that propelled the '50s Yankees: Weiss (left) masterminded the club's front office for manager Casey Stengel (center) and outfielder Hank Bauer.

FROM 1932 TO 1947, GEORGE Weiss developed talent to outfit a New York Yankees club that won nine pennants and eight World Series.

Not athletic as a child, George Martin Weiss (1894-1972) became manager of his New Haven, Connecticut, high school team when he was a senior, in 1912. In 1914, while attending Yale, he organized then managed a semipro team, which played on Sunday, something pro teams were forbidden to do in the state. To gain attendance, he once lured Ty Cobb to a game, with Cobb insisting on being paid $350. After the game, George handed Cobb $800, and when the Tigers were playing in New York or Boston, Cobb would thereafter travel to New Haven to play for George's team.

At age 24, Weiss bought a team in New Haven in the Eastern League, in 1919, eventually

Weiss was given many awards by his peers; he kept salaries low and profits high.

earning a reputation as a developer of big league talent. He moved to Baltimore of the International League in 1929, bringing financial success to the team through the sale of prospects. Yankee owner Colonel Jake Ruppert, eager for the same success he was seeing in Branch Rickey's St. Louis Cardinal farm system, hired Weiss in 1932 to create and direct a Yankee minor league organization.

Some of the players that came up through Weiss's system included Joe Gordon, Charlie Keller, Phil Rizzuto, and Yogi Berra. In 1947, Weiss was named general manager, and he hired Casey Stengel in 1949. The duo led the Yanks to a record five straight World Championships. Weiss's ability to acquire such pennant insurance as Johnny Mize and Enos Slaughter was uncanny. Weiss stole Roger Maris from Kansas City. And his farm system produced Mickey Mantle and Whitey Ford. Weiss also raised an estimated $2 million in player sales.

The Yanks won ten pennants and seven championships before Weiss was fired, in 1960. He and Stengel were both cut loose after the Pirates shocked the Yankees and the world in the Series. The Yankee juggernaut staggered on for two more years on stored talent, before collapsing after 40 years of excellence. Weiss and Stengel were told that they were "too old."

Weiss was hired to build the expansion Mets — with Stengel as manager. History has well recorded the futility of the early Mets, but Weiss knew his business, and he laid the groundwork for the first World Championship ever won by an expansion team, the '69 "Miracle" Mets. George was inducted into the Hall of Fame in 1971.

FORD FRICK

AS PRESIDENT OF THE NATION-al League, Ford Frick used the power of his office to guarantee that Jackie Robinson would be able to break the color line in 1947. Frick also furthered the idea behind the Baseball Hall of Fame in Cooperstown and administered baseball's expansion.

Born in Indiana, Ford Christopher Frick (1894-1978) worked as a sportswriter in the 1910s to pay his way through DePauw University. After graduation, he moved to Colorado, continuing as a sportswriter. Some of his clippings were sent to the publisher of the New York *American*, who hired Frick to become a baseball writer, and he covered the Giants and Yankees from 1922 to 1934. He was Babe Ruth's ghostwriter from 1924 to 1932. He also became a prominent figure in sportscasting in the 1920s.

In 1934, Frick became a publicist for the National League. He was elevated to circuit president only nine months later. As NL president for 17 years, Frick was a prime mover in the creation of the Hall of Fame in Cooperstown.

At the start of his tenure, Frick was not a force behind the National League's moving toward integration. He had said that "baseball is biding its time and waiting for the social change

Frick was featured in January 1935, a few months after he was named NL president.

which is inevitable." Later, he was far more instrumental in making integration stick. Perhaps his finest hour arrived when word came to him that the Cardinals were organizing a boycott of games that Jackie Robinson participated in. Frick told St. Louis owner Sam Breadon, "If you do this you will be suspended from the league. I do not care if half the league strikes. This is the United States of America and one citizen has as much right to play as another."

In 1951, "Happy" Chandler was removed as commissioner, and the field for a successor was wide open. After 16 votes, Frick was named, beating out, among others, General Douglas MacArthur. Frick served two seven-year terms. He oversaw the expansion or movement of many franchises, starting with the Boston Braves to Milwaukee in 1953 and the Dodgers and Giants to California. He was active during the end of the reserve clause and the birth of free agency. He also predicted the death of baseball from excessive TV broadcasting (he later negotiated a $13 million deal with ABC).

Frick may be best remembered for trying to hang an asterisk on Roger Maris's single-season home run record, because Maris needed more games than Ruth had the opportunity to play in to break record; the ruling was never enforced. Frick was inducted into the Hall of Fame in 1970.

The rabbit ball controversy arose several times while Frick was the NL president.

THEODORE SAMUEL WILLIAMS
"TED"
BOSTON RED SOX A.L. 1939~1960
BATTED .406 IN 1941. LED A.L. IN BATTING
6 TIMES; SLUGGING PERCENTAGE 9 TIMES;
TOTAL BASES 6 TIMES; RUNS SCORED 6 TIMES;
BASES ON BALLS 8 TIMES. TOTAL HITS 2654
INCLUDED 521 HOME RUNS. LIFETIME BATTING
AVERAGE .344; LIFETIME SLUGGING AVERAGE
.634. MOST VALUABLE A.L. PLAYER 1946 & 1949.
PLAYED IN 18 ALL STAR GAMES. NAMED PLAYER
OF THE DECADE 1951~1960.

Outfielder
Boston Red Sox 1939-1942; 1946-1960

Below: *Williams hits the dirt in 1949. To Williams baserunning was like fielding: a necessary but less-than-thrilling part of the game. Though he had better than average speed, he pilfered just 24 bases in his 19-year career.* Top: *Williams never wore any major league uniform but that of the Red Sox.*

TED WILLIAMS ONCE SAID THAT he had a dream of walking down the street and having people point to him and saying "There goes Ted Williams, the greatest hitter who ever lived." Some baseball historians support that claim. Williams holds the distinction of working harder at hitting than anyone.

Born in 1918 in San Diego, Theodore Samuel Williams spent most of his solitary, difficult childhood playing baseball on the sandlots. His renown in that city swelled to the point that, in 1936, Williams signed with his hometown San Diego Padres of the Triple-A Pacific Coast League despite having no pro experience and being only 17 years old. He hit .271 that year and batted .291 with 23 homers in 1937. Signed by the Red Sox, the brash, young Williams in the 1938 spring training alienated the veteran BoSox outfielders. When Ted was sent down to Minneapolis, he responded, "Tell them I'm going to make more money in this game than all three of them put together." He then won the American Association Triple Crown with a .366 average, 43 homers, and 142 RBI.

Williams made an immediate impact in Boston. He finished his rookie 1939 season with a .327 average, 31 homers, and a league-leading 145 RBI. He led the AL with 134 runs scored while batting .344 in 1940. In 1941 he hit .406, the last man to hit over .400. Going into the last day

of the year, he was at .39955. Manager Joe Cronin gave Ted the opportunity to sit out the double-header to save his average, which would have rounded up to .400, but Williams played both games and went six-for-eight to raise his mark to .406. In 1942, Williams produced his first major league Triple Crown, with a .356 average, 36 home runs, and 137 RBI, yet lost out on the MVP to Yankees second baseman Joe Gordon.

Early in his career he became disenchanted with the Boston press and fans. Disenchantment turned to antagonism when, in 1942, he was labeled a slacker for filing for military deferment because he was the sole supporter of his mother. He often went public with his anger at times, spitting and making obscene gestures.

Williams spent three years as a pilot in World War II, returning in 1946 to lead Boston to its only pennant during his years, and winning his first MVP Award. That year he first encountered "The Williams Shift," a defensive scheme invented by Indian manager Lou Boudreau that loaded the defense against Williams pulling the ball, forcing him to hit the other way. Teddy Ballgame captured his second Triple Crown in 1947 (with a .343 batting average, 32 home runs, and 114 RBI) but was denied the MVP, losing to Joe DiMaggio. Ted won the batting crown in 1948 (.369 average), and another MVP in 1949—hitting .343 with a league-leading 43 homers, 159 RBI, 150 runs, and 162 walks. In 1950, he fractured his elbow and played only a half a year, totaling just 28 homers and 97 RBI.

In 1952, when Ted was 34 years old, he was recalled for the Korean War, where he flew 39 missions, missing most of two more seasons. Back from Korea, he missed out on two more batting titles in 1954 and 1955 because requirements for the league crown counted at bats and not plate appearances. He got two more batting

Nothing could distract Williams from his main passion in life—hitting a baseball.

The "Other" Final Home Runs

Ted Williams smashed his 521st home run in 1960 on his last at bat, ending his career sensationally. However, he also hit two not so famous "last" home runs in his "final" major league at bats before the blast that eventually ended his career in 1960.

On April 30, 1952, the Red Sox staged a special day for Williams in celebration of his recall to service by the Marines and his imminent service in the Korean War. In the seventh inning of a tie game, he blasted his 324th career home run off a Dizzy Trout curve and, for all his fans and teammates knew, ended his 14-year career in memorable fashion.

In 1954, Williams announced in spring training that he would retire following the end of the season. In his last game of the season, in his second to last at bat, he hit career home run No. 366 off Constantine Keriazakos of the Senators. Although Williams returned to Boston in May 1955 after missing spring training, no player before or since has ever matched his penchant for dramatic exits.

crowns when he hit .388 (with 38 homers) in 1957 when he was 39 years old, and .328 in '58 at age 40. At age 41, he hit a career-low .254 and was urged to retire by almost everyone, even owner Tom Yawkey. Williams was too proud to retire with such a bad final season, and returned in 1960, hitting .316 with 29 home runs, including one in his last at bat.

Despite missing five years to military duty, his career numbers are astounding: the highest on-base average in history at .483, with five seasons when he got on base over half the time (his high was .551 in 1941); the second-highest slugging average at .634; the second-highest number of walks at 2,019; and he hit 521 home runs. Hitting was a science to Williams, who wrote a highly regarded book on the subject. The Thumper was elected to the Hall of Fame in 1966. He managed the Washington Senators from 1969 to 1974.

Major League Totals

BA	G	AB	R	H	2B	3B	HR	RBI	SB
.344	2,292	7,706	1,798	2,654	525	71	521	1,839	24

CHARLES DILLON STENGEL
"CASEY"
MANAGED NEW YORK YANKEES 1949-1960.
WON 10 PENNANTS AND 7 WORLD SERIES WITH
NEW YORK YANKEES. ONLY MANAGER TO WIN
5 CONSECUTIVE WORLD SERIES 1949-1953.
PLAYED OUTFIELD 1912-1925 WITH BROOKLYN,
PITTSBURGH, PHILADELPHIA, NEW YORK AND
BOSTON N.L. TEAMS. MANAGED BROOKLYN
1934-1936, BOSTON BRAVES 1938-1943,
NEW YORK METS 1962-1965.

Manager
Brooklyn Dodgers
    1934-1936
Boston Braves 1938-1943
New York Yankees
    1949-1960
New York Mets 1962-1965

Dodgers manager Chuck Dressen joins Stengel (to the right of Dressen) and the rest of the Yankees in their victory celebration of the 1952 World Series.

RENOWNED FOR HIS UNIQUE misuse of the English language, Casey Stengel was as smart a field general and judge of talent as baseball ever produced.

Born in Kansas City, the city that provided him his nickname, Charles Dillon Stengel (1890-1975) signed his first pro contract in 1910. He played his way to Brooklyn by 1912, and he was a part-time outfielder for 14 years. He launched two game-winning homers for John McGraw's New York Giants in 1923, after which McGraw promptly sold him to the Braves. Casey said, "if I'd hit three homers McGraw might've sent me clear out of the country."

In 1925, Stengel was hired as president, manager, and outfielder for Worcester of the Eastern League. After the season, Stengel the president released Stengel the outfielder and fired Stengel the manager, and then resigned. He moved to Toledo of the American Association in 1926, staying for six years. He coached in Brooklyn for two seasons, and got his first major league managing stint in 1934 with the Dodgers. Casey managed Brooklyn from '34 to 1936, finishing in the second division each year. In 1938, the Boston Braves hired him, and again he had no first-division finishes from 1938 to 1943. By 1944, Stengel was managing back in Triple-A, where he stayed for five years.

Casey won Sport's kudos in 1953 after his fifth straight World Championship.

In 1949, Yankees general manager George Weiss surprisingly hired Casey to run a Yankee team with Yogi Berra and Joe DiMaggio, and with Mickey Mantle and Whitey Ford waiting in the wings. Even that collection of talent couldn't account for the Yankee stretch of five straight World Series wins. Stengel was largely responsible for the revival of platooning, out of favor for almost two decades. He always wanted to get big years out of as many players as possible. In his 12 years with the Bombers they won 10 pennants and seven World Series, success unmatched in professional ball. The Yankees job came to an end when they lost the World Series in 1960. "I commenced winning pennants when I came here but I didn't commence getting any younger" said "The Old Perfesser," age 70.

George Weiss hired Casey to run the Mets in 1962. That year the Mets lost 120 games, but Stengel took it with a smile. Stengel had a way with words that can't be imitated, dubbed "Stengelese" by the press. He saw the bottom and the top, and as he said himself, "There comes a time in every man's life and I've had plenty of them." He was inducted into the Hall of Fame in 1966.

Major League Managing Totals				
W	L	T	PCT	G
1,905	1,842	19	.508	3,766

Irvin was past age 30 before he signed his first organized baseball contract.

"MOST OF THE BLACK BALL-players thought Monte Irvin should have been the first black in the major leagues. Monte was our best young ballplayer at the time. He could hit that long ball, he had a great arm, he could field, he could run. He could do everything." Cool Papa Bell spoke for the black stars of his day—many felt that Irvin was the best.

Monford Merrill Irvin was born in 1919 in Columbus, Alabama, but he grew up in Orange, New Jersey. He was one of the greatest all-around athletes that the state ever produced, winning All-State honors in four sports in high school. After graduation, he attended Lincoln University in Pennsylvania, while playing pro ball for the Newark Eagles under the assumed name "Jimmy Nelson" to protect his amateur status.

Irvin was a star in the Negro Leagues. It was acknowledged that he was the batting leader in 1940 and 1941. "My only wish," said Irvin, "is that major league fans could've seen me when I was at my best." In 1942, in Mexico he hit .398 with power. He was drafted late in 1942, and missed most of the next three seasons while he was serving in the armed forces. He came back to Newark for full seasons in 1946 to '48. He was signed by the Dodgers after the Eagles folded in 1948. The owner of the defunct Eagles demanded $5,000 for Irvin, so the Dodgers relinquished the contract. The New

York Giants paid the sum, however, and signed the 29-year-old Irvin.

In 1949, Irvin hit .373 for Jersey City of the International League. He had his first taste of big league ball late that year. In 1950, he returned to Jersey City, where he was hitting .510 with 10 homers in just 51 at bats, and back up he came, hitting .299 with 15 homers for the Giants. Willie Mays joined the team for the 1951 "Miracle at Coogan's Bluff," but manager Leo Durocher called Irvin "my best hitter." Monte hit .312 and led the league with 121 RBI. The Giants ran down the Dodgers, beat them in a playoff (Bobby Thomson's famous home run), and faced the Yankees in the World Series. Though they lost, Irvin hit .458. He called that season "the high point of my life."

Monte hit over .300 in '52, but a broken ankle sidelined him for most of the season. He bounced back in 1953, hitting .329 with 21 home runs and 97 RBI. Late in the 1953 season, he reinjured his ankle, and it bothered him for the rest of his career. He retired after the 1956 season. Irvin was inducted into the Hall of Fame in 1973.

Outfielder
Negro League team
Newark Eagles 1938-1942;
 1945-1949
Major League teams
New York Giants
 1949-1955
Chicago Cubs 1956

Before his ankle problems, Irvin (sliding into second) added speed to his package of skills.

Negro League Stats*

BA	G	AB	H	2B	3B	HR	SB
.346	224	908	314	54	10	34	26

Major League Totals

BA	G	AB	R	H	2B	3B	HR	RBI	SB
.293	764	2,499	366	731	97	31	99	443	28

*Note: Irvin's Negro League career stats are incomplete.

PEE WEE REESE

HAROLD HENRY "PEE WEE" REESE
BROOKLYN N.L. 1940-1957
LOS ANGELES N.L. 1958
SHORTSTOP AND CAPTAIN OF GREAT DODGER TEAMS
OF 1940's AND 50's. INTANGIBLE QUALITIES OF SUBTLE
LEADERSHIP ON AND OFF FIELD, COMPETITIVE FIRE
AND PROFESSIONAL PRIDE COMPLEMENTED DEPENDABLE
GLOVE, RELIABLE BASE-RUNNING AND CLUTCH-HITTING
AS SIGNIFICANT FACTORS IN 7 DODGER PENNANTS.
INSTRUMENTAL IN EASING ACCEPTANCE OF JACKIE
ROBINSON AS BASEBALL'S FIRST BLACK PERFORMER.

Shortstop
Brooklyn Dodgers
1940-1957
Los Angeles Dodgers 1958

Reese was an excellent bunter, and his 2,170 career hits were topped only by Luke Appling among shortstops of that era.

PEE WEE REESE WAS THE leader of the 1940s and 1950s Brooklyn Dodgers. He was an outstanding shortstop who, despite his short stature, stood so tall among his teammates that he was able to silence a team revolt against Jackie Robinson in 1947.

Harold Henry Reese was born in Louisville in 1918. He was a city marbles champion at the age of 12, and was tagged with the Pee Wee nickname. He was a very good player on the same church-league team that sent Billy Herman to professional ball. Pee Wee was signed by the Louisville club of the American Association in 1938, and spent two solid seasons there. The Red Sox owned the rights to Reese, and when they were not ready to purchase him, Branch Rickey of the Dodgers spent $75,000 to obtain him.

Dodger manager Leo Durocher said, "Pee Wee was 20 years old when I first saw him in spring training and he looked 12. I took one look at him and I said to myself, 'Leo, you can rest your aching tootsies.'" While Pee Wee wasn't a great player immediately, he became important

Reese was the only Dodger player who spanned from the MacPhail era to L.A.

to the Dodgers, as a hitter, a fielder, and a leader. In 1941, Pee Wee took the first misstep in the legendary Dodger-Yankee rivalry, when he was caught stealing in the World Series, killing a Dodger rally. It was the first of five Series losses to the hated Yanks.

Reese spent three years in the Navy during World War II, but returned to the Dodgers to become the old man of the Boys of Summer, the "Little Colonel" of the team that won six pennants in Reese's 12 postwar seasons. Though his batting stats don't indicate a big hitter, he was a three-time league leader, once in runs, once in walks, and once in stolen bases. He was a complete player, who despite limited power, helped make the offense go and was an anchor on defense. His play won him top ten mention in MVP voting eight times.

Reese's teammates were lavish in their praise. Though at first he was among the many to request a trade upon the signing of Jackie Robinson, Reese quickly changed his mind. When the rebellion continued, Pee Wee befriended Jackie, and the other Dodger players fell in line. Robinson and the other pioneer black Dodgers continually name Pee Wee as one of the men who helped them on their difficult road. Reese was inducted into the Hall of Fame in 1984.

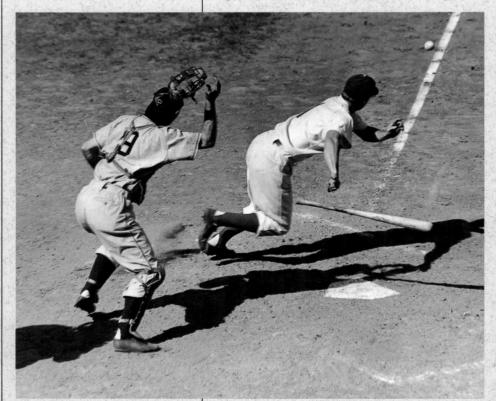

Major League Totals

BA	G	AB	R	H	2B	3B	HR	RBI	SB
.269	2,166	8,058	1,338	2,170	330	80	126	885	232

196

AL BARLICK

ALONG WITH BILL SUMMERS, Al Barlick holds the record for working the most All-Star games, seven, which is perfectly appropriate. As umpire schools became all but mandatory, umpires became more uniform and interchangeable, but Barlick stood out as an All-Star in his own right.

Albert Barlick (born in 1915) started his umpiring career on the sandlots of Springfield, Illinois, in 1935. He moved to the Class-D Northeast Arkansas League in 1936. Other circuits that he worked included the Piedmont League, the Eastern League, and the International League.

By age 26, Barlick joined the National League in 1940, when the legendary Bill Klem was forced from the field due to illness. Barlick was immediately recognizable to fans due to his flamboyant, and loud, strike calls, and "out" gestures that even fans in the cheap seats couldn't miss. He was a hustling umpire who inspired respect among managers; they could never accuse him of not "bearing down." In 1943, he joined the Coast Guard, serving on a submarine in the Atlantic Ocean. He resumed his career in 1946. He worked the World Series that year, when Enos Slaughter made his mad dash home to win the fall classic for the Cardinals. In 1947, he worked first base during the first game that Jackie Robinson played for the Brooklyn Dodgers.

The Giants felt joy and anguish during two of the World Series in which Barlick was an umpire. Al worked the 1954 fall classic, when Willie Mays made his over-the-shoulder grab of Vic Wertz's line drive nearly 460 feet from home plate. Mays twirled and fired a perfect throw to hold the baserunners at first and third. Al was also the arbitrator in the 1962 World Series, when Yankee second baseman Bobby Richardson speared Willie McCovey's liner to end the Giants' comeback bid.

Barlick's most memorable call was in 1949, when he ruled that Chicago Cub Andy Pafko trapped a ball in the outfield after a 220 foot pop. A riled Pafko argued the call, while the batter wheeled around the bases for one of the shortest inside-the-park home runs in history. Barlick had heart trouble and sat out the 1956 and 1957 seasons, returning in 1958. He took such pride in his profession that when voted Best National League Umpire in 1961, he spurned the honor because it was not voted on by umpires.

Barlick retired from active duty in 1971, after 30 distinguished years in the majors. Along with his seven All-Star calls, he worked in seven World Series. His most memorable midseason classic was in 1970, when he was working the plate as Pete Rose flattened catcher Ray Fosse. That year, Barlick was again voted Umpire of the Year. He accepted the award, as it was based on a vote among his fellow arbiters. He was inducted into the Hall of Fame in 1989.

After he retired, Barlick worked for the National League as a consultant and a scout. He surveyed the Triple-A American Association and the Pacific Coast League, looking at the quality of umpires in those two circuits.

Prior to 1961 most umpires were former professional players. Barlick was an exception. He began umpiring in the minor leagues in 1936 when he was just 21 years old and was already working in the National League by the time he was 26.

197

STAN MUSIAL

STANLEY FRANK MUSIAL
"THE MAN"

ST. LOUIS CARDINALS 1941-1963
HOLDS MANY NATIONAL LEAGUE RECORDS;
AMONG THEM: GAMES PLAYED 3026; AT
BAT 10972 TIMES; 3630 HITS; MOST RUNS
SCORED 1949; MOST RUNS BATTED IN 1951;
TOTAL BASES 6134, LED N.L. IN TOTAL
BASES 6 YEARS, SLUGGING PERCENTAGE
6 YEARS, MOST VALUABLE PLAYER 1943-
1946-1948. PLAYED IN 24 ALL-STAR GAMES.
LIFETIME BATTING AVERAGE .331.

Outfielder; first baseman
St. Louis Cardinals
1941-1944; 1946-1963

*Top: Musial tags his 3,000th
career hit. Had he not lost a
year to military service during
World War II, he would
probably have collected well
over 3,800 hits. Below: Many
young players used Musial
model bats, but none with any
sense tried to emulate The
Man's bizarre batting stance.*

S TAN "THE MAN" MUSIAL starred for the St. Louis Cardinals for 22 seasons and was the first National League player to win three Most Valuable Player awards.

Stanley Frank Musial was born in 1920 in Donora, western Pennsylvania, an area which produced many great athletes. When Musial was a youngster he was the batboy for a local team, until they gave him the opportunity to pitch and he rang up 13 Ks in six innings. When he was just 18 years old, in 1938, he went to see the Pirates play the Giants, and he turned to his friend and said that he thought that he could hit big league pitching. That year, Musial joined the Cardinals organization as a pitcher.

Assigned to Daytona Beach in the Florida State League in 1940, Stan was pitching very well and hitting over .300. He played in the outfield on the days that he didn't pitch, on one of those days he attempted a diving catch and injured his left (pitching) shoulder so badly that his career on the mound was over. The Cards, aware of his great athletic talent, moved him to the outfield full time, and he performed so well that he was in the majors by the end of 1941.

In 1942, the emerging Cardinal powerhouse won the first of three straight pennants and the

World Series as the rookie Musial hit .315. In 1943, he won his first MVP Award, leading the league with a .357 batting average, 220 base hits, 48 doubles, and 20 triples. He again led the NL in hits and doubles in 1944.

Musial had good home run power, terrific doubles power, and for his time, was a spectacular triples hitter. He was terrifically fast—one of his nicknames was "The Donora Greyhound." He was also a fine fielder, in left and later as a first baseman. Though he never led the league in homers, he won six slugging titles and in 1954 hit five round-trippers in a double-header. His unique batting corkscrew stance, described by Ted Lyons as "like a kid peeking around the corner to see if the cops are coming," resulted in seven batting crowns. He posted a lifetime .416 on-base average, scoring at least 105 runs in 11 straight seasons.

After leaving the Navy in 1945, Stan the Man came back to win his second MVP in 1946 as the Cards won another World Championship. He led the league with a .365 batting average, 50 doubles, 20 triples, and 124 runs scored. He won his third Most Valuable Player trophy in 1948. He missed the Triple Crown by a single home run, hitting a career-

Musial shows off his lumber. He clubbed 475 regular season home runs, the most of any player who was never a league four-bagger king.

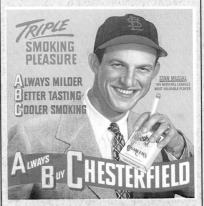

From the Mound to the Outfield

Like many great hitters, Stan Musial began his career as a pitcher. Fortunately Stan was goaded from the mound by a combination of injury and the sage advice of Daytona Beach manager and former White Sox ace hurler Dickie Kerr.

Following his 1938 signing with the Cardinals, Musial fashioned an impressive three-year minor league pitching career. He was 18-5 at Daytona Beach in the Florida State League in 1940. Musial also played part time as an outfielder, batting .311. In late August of that season, he injured his left shoulder while attempting to make a catch. By the time he arrived at spring training in 1941, the injury had still not healed.

Dickie Kerr encouraged Stan to make the full transition to the outfield. In 87 games with Springfield, West Virginia, Musial batted .379 with a Western Association-leading 26 home runs. By season's end he was called up to St Louis. Musial maintained a lifetime friendship with Kerr, whom Stan considered his baseball mentor. Musial purchased Kerr a home in Houston as a retirement gift.

high 39 to Johnny Mize's and Ralph Kiner's 40. He had a .376 average (the NL's highest since Bill Terry hit .401 in 1930), 230 base hits, 46 doubles, 18 triples, 131 RBI, and 135 runs scored, all of which led the NL.

Several of the other NL organizations gained ground on St. Louis and its farm system by the early 1950s. Even though Stan won batting crowns from 1950 to 1952 (with averages of .346, .355, and .336), the Cardinals could finish no better than third. Stan won his final batting title in 1957 when he was age 37, and the Redbirds finished second. But while Stan maintained his excellence, St. Louis from 1953 to '59 would get no closer than fourth place or 17 games out at the end. Musial hit .330 in 1962, when he was 42 years old. In his final season, 1963, he hit a home run in his first at bat after becoming a grandfather. Musial was voted the Player of the Decade in 1956 for the period from 1946 to 1955. Stan the Man was elected to the Hall of Fame in 1969.

Major League Totals

BA	G	AB	R	H	2B	3B	HR	RBI	SB
.331	3,026	10,972	1,949	3,630	725	177	475	1,951	78

EARLY WYNN
"GUS"
WASHINGTON A.L.,CLEVELAND A.L.,
CHICAGO A.L. 1939 - 1963
WINNER OF 300 MAJOR LEAGUE GAMES, SET
RECORD BY PITCHING 23 YEARS IN MAJORS.
GAINED 20 OR MORE VICTORIES FIVE TIMES
AND LED A. L. IN EARNED-RUN AVERAGE IN
1950. LEADER IN INNINGS PITCHED THREE
SEASONS AND IN STRIKEOUTS TWICE. TIED
FOR MOST VICTORIES WITH 23 IN 1954 AND
LED LEAGUE WITH 22 WINS AT AGE 39 IN
1959 TO EARN CY YOUNG AWARD.

Pitcher
Washington Senators
   1939; 1941-1948
Cleveland Indians
   1949-1957; 1963
Chicago White Sox
   1958-1962

I T TOOK EARLY WYNN EIGHT tries to win his 300th game. The Chicago White Sox released him after the 1962 season when he had 299 wins. He was not picked up in 1963 until June, when his former club, the Cleveland Indians, contacted him. He started five games for the Indians, winning his 300th game on July 13. He retired after that season.

Early Wynn was born in Hartford, Alabama, in 1920. His father was an area semipro ballplayer. Early helped lift 500 pound bales of cotton for a dime an hour after school. At age 17, he signed a pro contract with the Senators after attending a tryout camp. He worked often in the minor leagues, though he wasn't overly impressive. Although he pitched three games for the Senators in 1939, he didn't stay in the bigs until 1941. He produced one good year with Washington, 1943, when he went 18-12 with a 2.91 ERA.

After nine frustrating years in Washington, compiling a 72-87 record, Wynn joined the Cleveland Indians in 1949, and changed the course of his career. In 1951, he won 20 games for the first time. He then won 23 in 1952, a league-leading 23 in 1954, and 20 in 1956.

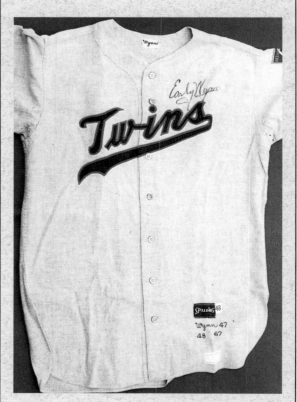

With the Indians he was to become a member of a legendary pitching staff, as he joined with Bob Lemon, Mike Garcia, Art Houtteman, and Bob Feller on the 1954 Indians. Wynn won Cleveland's record 111th game, carrying a no-hitter into the ninth, and led the league with 23 wins, his third 20-win season in four years. The frustrated Senators' pitcher had become a star. Wynn had nine winning records in the ten years he pitched in Cleveland.

Wynn was among the meanest head-hunters in the game; calling home plate his office, he would not hesitate to move batters off the plate. "Gus" would also throw at a man on first base if he felt the need, disguising the beanball as a pick-off throw. He once said he would knock down his own grandmother if she dug in against him. In Cleveland he learned control, pitching patterns, and a curveball from Mel Harder. Wynn's strikeout totals rocketed, and his 1,544 were the most Ks in the 1950s. He was still wild though, and may have been an even bigger winner if he hadn't retired with a then-record for most career free passes.

Wynn went to the White Sox in 1958 and was 1-1 for the Sox in the 1959 World Series. He helped them get there with his last outstanding season, going 22-10. Wynn was elected to the Hall of Fame in 1972.

Top: *Wynn was a coach for the Twins from 1964 to 1966.*
Right: *He won his 100th, 200th, and 300th victories in a Cleveland Indians uniform. On the day he turned 30, Wynn had an 83-94 career record. He finished with an even 300 victories and a .551 winning percentage.*

Major League Totals

W	L	ERA	G	CG	IP	H	ER	BB	SO
300	244	3.54	691	290	4,564	4,291	1,795	1,775	2,334

Conlan played in the minor leagues for more than a decade.

JOCKO CONLAN WAS THE FIRST umpire from the modern era to be selected to the Hall of Fame. Known for his trademark polka-dot bow tie, he had a quick wit and a sharp tongue, and was one of the most respected umpires of all time.

John Bertrand Conlan (1899-1989) was born in Chicago. The son of a policeman, he played baseball on the sandlots in the shadow of Comiskey Park. He was the envy of other South Side boys when he served as a Sox batboy at ages 13 and 14. He was a good outfielder and played in the minors from 1920 to 1933, reaching Triple-A but never getting a call to the bigs. He retired before the 1934 season. In 1934, however, the White Sox had lost several outfielders to injury and signed Jocko to fill in. He did well enough to come back in '35 as a reserve.

Umpire "Red" Ormsby suffered heat prostration during a double-header in St. Louis in 1935, and Jocko, sitting out the game with a sprained thumb, volunteered for duty on the bases. There were only two umpires a game then, and Browns manager Rogers Hornsby surprisingly agreed to let Conlan work the second game. He worked the game in his White Sox uniform, and he even called teammate Luke Appling out trying for a triple. Jocko did such a good job he decided to make it his only job.

After four years in the minors as an ump, Conlan returned to the bigs in 1941. He established his authority quickly, ejecting 26 men in that first season. Conlan had a favorite target for ejection: Leo Durocher. In 1961, Durocher kicked dirt on Conlan after an ejection, and the two got into a kicking match. Jocko was wearing shin guards and steel-toed shoes, however. Durocher said, "Every time Jocko kicked me, he raised a lump on my shins; every time I kicked him I bruised my toes."

Jocko was struck in the larynx by a foul tip, and although the other National League umpires used inside chest protectors, afterwards he was allowed to wear the outside chest protector to protect his throat. He officiated for 27 seasons, arbitrating six All-Star games, six World Series, and four playoffs, before retiring in 1967. Jocko was inducted into the Hall of Fame in 1974.

Off the field, Conlan was ebullient; between the lines, he was tough.

ROBERT GRANVILLE LEMON
CLEVELAND A.L.
1941-1942 AND 1946-1958
GAINED COVETED 20-VICTORY CLASS SEVEN
TIMES IN NINE-YEAR SPAN. BECAME ONLY
SIXTH PITCHER IN 20TH CENTURY TO POST
20 OR MORE WINS IN SEVEN SEASONS. HAD
207-128 RECORD FOR CAREER. PACED A.L.
OR TIED FOR LEAD IN VICTORIES THREE
TIMES, SHUTOUTS ONCE, INNINGS PITCHED
FOUR SEASONS AND COMPLETE GAMES FIVE
YEARS. HURLED NO-HITTER IN 1948

Pitcher
Cleveland Indians
1941-1942; 1946-1958

Top: *Lemon turned to pitching in 1946 as a last resort. His mound career spanned only 13 years, but he led the AL in complete games five times.* Below: *After his playing career was over, Lemon was affiliated with the Angels for seven years.*

BOB LEMON IS THE ONLY 20TH century player in the Hall of Fame who began his major league career as a hitter and subsequently became a pitcher. Initially a third baseman, Lemon played center field for Cleveland on Opening Day in 1946 before beginning a transition to the mound that resulted in seven 20-win seasons and a stellar .618 career winning percentage.

Raised in Long Beach, California, Robert Granville Lemon (born in 1920) was a star shortstop and pitcher as a youngster. He spent five years in the Cleveland farm system before his career was interrupted by World War II. Upon returning from the Navy, he was moved to center field to shore up a club weak spot. When Lemon's batting average still lagged below .200 several weeks into the season, player-manager Lou Boudreau decided to try him as a relief hurler.

Lemon spent over a year in the Tribe bullpen before getting a chance to crack the starting rotation on July 31, 1947. He responded by winning ten consecutive games and finished with an 11-5 mark. The following year, his first as a full-time starter, Lemon won 20 games and topped the American League with 293⅔ innings, 20 complete games, and 10 shutouts. In addition, he tossed a no-hitter against the Tigers on June 30. When Cleveland won its first pennant in 28 years in 1948, Lemon was given two starting

assignments in the World Series that fall against the Boston Braves. He won both as Cleveland copped the Championship in six games.

Frequently used as a pinch-hitter, Lemon hammered a total of 37 home runs, including seven in 1949 alone. In addition, his experience as a third baseman helped make him the top-fielding pitcher of his era. Often a league leader in putouts, assists, and total chances accepted, he set a major league record in 1953 that still stands when he participated in 15 double plays as a moundsman.

In 1950, Bob led the AL with 23 wins, 170 strikeouts, and 288 innings pitched. He also led the league in victories in 1954, with 23, and complete games with 21. Again in 1955 he was tops in the AL with 18 wins.

Only the fourth pitcher in American League history to win 20 games in a season as many as seven times, Lemon spent his entire playing career with Cleveland. Afterwards, he worked for a number of years as a scout and a pitching coach. Later, Bob managed the Royals, White Sox, and the Yankees. Replacing Billy Martin midway through the 1978 season, Lemon guided the Yankees to a World Championship. He was elected to the Hall of Fame in 1976.

Major League Totals										
W	L	ERA	G	CG	IP	H	ER	BB	SO
207	128	3.23	460	188	2,850	2,559	1,023	1,251	1,277

WARREN SPAHN

WARREN EDWARD SPAHN
BOSTON N.L.,MILWAUKEE N.L.,
NEW YORK N.L.,SAN FRANCISCO N.L.,
1942-1965
BECAME FIFTH BIGGEST WINNER IN MAJORS
HISTORY WITH 363 VICTORIES. MOST
VICTORIES FOR A LEFT-HANDER. WON 20
OR MORE GAMES IN A SEASON, SIX IN A ROW.
SET ALL-TIME RECORDS FOR YEAR'S LEADING
LEAGUE IN VICTORIES (8) AND COMPLETE
GAMES (9). ALSO N.L. CAREER HIGHS WITH
665 GAMES STARTED; 5,526 INNINGS;
2,653 STRIKEOUTS. PITCHED NO-HITTER
IN 1960, ANOTHER IN 1961.

Pitcher
Boston Braves 1942;
1946-1952
Milwaukee Braves
1953-1964
New York Mets 1965
San Francisco Giants 1965

WARREN SPAHN WON MORE than 20 games in 13 of the 18 years in which he had at least 30 starts, on his way to winning more games than any lefty in history. He was the best, and often the only good pitcher, on two decades of Braves teams, from Boston to Milwaukee, as he led the league in wins a record eight times, and complete games a record nine times.

Born in Buffalo in 1921, Warren Edward Spahn's father was an avid amateur baseball player. Warren grew up as a first baseman, but he was unable to win the first base job in high school, so he switched to pitching. Signed by the Braves in 1940, he struck out 62 Class-D batters in 66 innings. In 1941, he moved up to Evansville and led the Three-I League with 19 wins and a 1.83 ERA in 1941.

Spahn was called up to Boston in 1942 and did not win in four appearances that year. When he failed to knock down Pee Wee Reese in a game, Braves manager Casey Stengel said, "Young man, you've got no guts." Spahn was off to war for the next three years, where he earned a Bronze Star and a Purple Heart.

Warren returned in 1946 and went 8-5 with a 2.94 ERA. He bloomed in 1947, winning 21 and leading the NL with a 2.33 ERA. In 1948, he teamed with Johnny Sain in the famous "Spahn and Sain and pray for rain" rotation. Sain won 24 games to lead the league, Warren went 15-12, and the Braves won the pennant, losing to Cleveland in the Series.

In 1949, Spahn led the NL with 21 wins, 25 complete games, 302⅓ innings, and 151

strikeouts. He led the NL with 21 wins and 191 Ks again in 1950. He won 22 games in 1951, a league-leading 23 in 1953, 21 in 1954, and 20 in 1956. He began to lose some velocity on his fastball in the early 1950s, but he compensated with developing new pitches and researching the league's batters.

The Braves, with Eddie Mathews, Lew Burdette, and Hank Aaron, were a pennant-caliber team in the late 1950s, and they won the World Series while Spahn went 21-11 on the season. They returned to the fall classic in 1958 (with Spahn going 22-11), and he pitched beautifully (a 2-1 record with a 2.20 ERA). 1957 would be Warren's only World Series win, and '58, his last appearance. He won more than 20, though, in 1959, 1960, '61, and '63.

"You don't make concessions," Spahn once said. "If you concede one little thing, pretty soon you find yourself conceding another, then another." He retired in 1965, finishing in the top ten for career wins, innings pitched, and shutouts. Warren was elected to the Hall of Fame in 1973.

Top: This LP record featured an LP pitcher. Spahn pitched 21 years in the majors and won a southpaw-record 363 games. Were it not for a three-year interruption during World War II, Spahn probably would have collected almost 400 victories.
Left: Spahn almost literally made them tear the uniform off him before he would quit pitching.

Major League Totals

W	L	ERA	G	CG	IP	H	ER	BB	SO
363	245	3.09	750	382	5,243.2	4,830	1,798	1,434	2,583

GEORGE KELL

GEORGE CLYDE KELL
PHILADELPHIA A.L. 1943-1946
DETROIT A.L. 1946-1952
BOSTON A.L. 1952-1954
CHICAGO A.L. 1954-1956
BALTIMORE A.L. 1956-1957
PREMIER A.L. THIRD BASEMAN OF 1940'S AND
1950'S. SOLID HITTER AND SURE-HANDED FIELDER
WITH STRONG, ACCURATE ARM. BATTED OVER
.300 9 TIMES, LEADING LEAGUE WITH .343 IN
1949. LED A.L. THIRD BASEMEN IN FIELDING
PCT. 7 TIMES, ASSISTS 4 TIMES AND PUTOUTS
AND DOUBLE PLAYS TWICE.

Third baseman
Philadelphia Athletics
1943-1946
Detroit Tigers 1946-1952
Boston Red Sox 1952-1954
Chicago White Sox
1954-1956
Baltimore Orioles
1956-1957

Top: A's fans gloated in 1946 when the Mackmen traded Kell to Detroit for Barney McCosky. Three years later—with McCosky shelved for the season by a back problem—they groaned in Philly when Kell hit .343 to cop the AL batting title. Right: In his early years, Kell offered little indication that he would mature as well as a hitter.

GEORGE KELL WAS A PIVOTAL player in the evolution of third basemen, displaying outstanding glovework while blazing the way for a new breed of third sackers who could also hit. He helped change the perception of third basemen from a sort of "second shortstop" in terms of hitting.

George Clyde Kell (born in 1922 in Swifton, Arkansas) was signed by the Brooklyn organization in 1940 and was assigned to Newport of the Northeast Arkansas League. Despite leading that league in base hits in 1941, he was dropped at the end of the season. Recently married, George was ready to take a construction job when his bride urged him to give the game another try. He hooked on with Lancaster of the Inter-State League, and announced his readiness for the bigs by leading the league in runs, hits, and doubles in 1943. His .396 batting average was tops in organized baseball that year.

Connie Mack brought George to Philadelphia in 1943, and kept him for the 1944 and '45 seasons. Both of those seasons were solid, but Mack wasn't sure if Kell would be able to compete with the rest of the league when the stars and regulars returned from World War II. Needing a center fielder, Mack traded Kell to Detroit for Barney McCosky in 1946.

Kell played up to the new level in the major leagues, beginning a string of eight straight .300 seasons in 1946. While not a power hitter, he

George Kell

was able to smack line drives into the gaps. His 56 two-baggers in 1950 is one of history's highest totals and beat the league runner-up by 19. Kell won a batting title in 1949, edging Ted Williams by two-tenths of a point, .3429 to .3427. In 1950, he led the league in base hits, smacking 218. He was one of the few players in modern baseball history to drive in more than 100 runs without hitting 10 homers in that season. He also led the AL with 191 base hits in 1951.

Kell was renowned for his glove as well, retiring with a .969 fielding average—a record that stood for 20 years. He was a Gold Glove winner and a regular All-Star, but though he played for five teams in his 15-year career, he never saw postseason play. He was one of the very best third basemen of his era, and paved the way for even better hot-corner men to follow. After his retirement, George entered the Tiger broadcasting booth. He was joined by Al Kaline in 1976. When Kell was inducted into the Hall of Fame in 1983, Kell and Kaline were the first Hall of Famers to team up to broadcast baseball.

				Major League Totals						
BA	G	AB	R	H	2B	3B	HR	RBI	SB
.306	1,795	6,702	881	2,054	385	50	78	870	51

204

RED SCHOENDIENST

Second baseman
St. Louis Cardinals
1945-1956; 1961-1963
New York Giants
1956-1957
Milwaukee Braves
1957-1960

ONE OF THE BEST SECOND basemen in the 1950s, Red Schoendienst teamed with shortstop Marty Marion to form one of baseball's best-ever double-play combinations.

Albert Fred Schoendienst was born in 1923 in Germantown, Illinois. In 1942 he went to a tryout at Sportsman's Park in St. Louis when he was 19 years old, and the Cardinals liked his potential. He spent most of that season with Albany of the Georgia-Florida League, batting .269. In 1943, he reported to Rochester of the Triple-A International League. Rochester manager Pepper Martin took one look at Red and moaned that the Cardinals were sending him babied-faced kids to make up his roster. Schoendienst impressed Martin and the Cardinals by leading the league with a .337 batting average and 438 assists from the shortstop position that season.

When Red returned from World War II in 1945, he was called to St. Louis and used at shortstop, second base, third base, and the outfield for a few seasons. By 1947, he played mostly second base. He scored 80 or 90 runs a season each season in St. Louis save for 1948, and provided often spectacular keystone sack play.

Schoendienst had five seasons hitting better than .300. In 1957, he led the league with 200 hits, becoming only the second man to ever do so after being traded during the season (the other was Piano Legs Hickman in 1902). Red reached a career-high batting average of .342 in 1953. Despite contracting tuberculosis in 1958, he returned to play parts of five more seasons. Although Red led the league in steals with 26 his rookie year, he never again was a serious threat to run, though he had good speed and was a fine doubles hitter. In 1950, he shocked the American League with a game-winning home run in the 14th inning of the All-Star Game in his only at bat, a precursor to his fine pinch-hitting.

The Cardinals won the World Series in 1946, and Schoendienst returned to the Series with Milwaukee in 1957 and 1958. His trade to the Braves in 1957 was considered a key in putting the eventual World Champions over the top—he hit .310 for them in 93 games—and he finished third in the MVP voting. After the 1960 season Red returned to St. Louis, and was one of the game's top pinch-hitters in 1962, leading the league in pinch-hit at bats and hits. He retired as a player in 1963, continuing his baseball career as a coach and manager, and won a World Series in St. Louis in 1967. Inducted in 1989, he had 2,449 career hits and 1,223 runs scored.

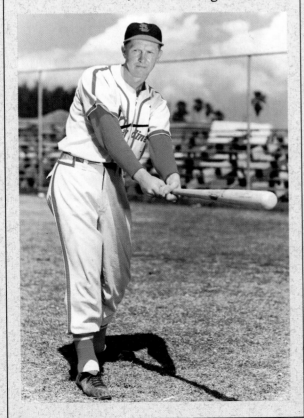

Top: *In one capacity or another, Schoendienst has worn a St. Louis Cardinals uniform almost continuously since 1945. He ranks first on the club in point of overall service. Left: Red gave three National League clubs steady work at second base and spread his significant offensive accomplishments over a 17-year span.*

Major League Totals									
BA	G	AB	R	H	2B	3B	HR	RBI	SB
.289	2,216	8,479	1,223	2,449	427	78	84	773	89

JACKIE ROBINSON

Second baseman
Negro League team
Kansas City Monarchs
   1945
Major League team
Brooklyn Dodgers
   1947-1956

Top: *This Jackie Robinson bank box encouraged young fans of his to save their money. Among the many jobs he held after leaving baseball was working for a bank. Below: Robinson pilfers home. Playing in an era when anyone who swiped over 10 bases in a season was considered a speed demon, he bagged 197 career thefts.*

DURING THE FIRST HALF OF this century a color line excluding African-Americans extended to nearly every significant field of endeavor. There was a great inertia that needed to be overcome in order to create the integrated society promised in the Constitution. That first, high-profile integration came on a baseball diamond, and the first black man to cross the white lines was Jackie Robinson.

Jack Roosevelt Robinson (1919-1972) grew up in Pasadena, California, in a poor neighborhood. His brother, Mack, participated in the 1936 Summer Olympics in Berlin and Jackie was an outstanding athlete as well. He went to UCLA and starred in four sports. He broke the Pacific Coast Conference record in the broad jump and twice was the PCC's leading scorer in basketball. He lead the nation in yards per carry in football and was a baseball star. In 1941, he played with the Los Angeles Bulldogs pro football team. After the Pearl Harbor attack, Jackie attended Officer Candidate School in Kansas, making it to second lieutenant. In 1944, he was threatened with a court martial, because he refused to sit in the back of an army bus; he instead received an honorable discharge.

Robinson joined the Kansas City Monarchs of the Negro League after his discharge. At $100 per week, it was the best paying job he could get. When he was approached by Dodgers general manager Branch Rickey's representative, Clyde Sukeforth, Jackie was initially disbelieving and disinterested. "Suddenly I became dis-

gusted with myself," Robinson said. "Why the reluctance? Why the hesitancy? After all, it was a gamble; you don't get anyplace in life if you don't take a risk once in a while." Rickey chose Robinson to be the first African-American in the major leagues for many reasons, but aside from being an outstanding athlete and baseball player, he had many character strengths. Rickey impressed upon Jackie the need to turn the other cheek. From the beginning, Jackie was everything Rickey wanted.

Robinson first broke the color line with Montreal of the International League in 1946, and led the league with a .349 batting average and 113 runs scored as his team won the Little World Series.

With the Dodgers in 1947, Robinson was Rookie of the Year. He said that the lowest day of his rookie year was his first visit to Philadelphia, when he could "scarcely believe my ears. Almost as if it had been synchronized by some master conductor, hate poured forth from the Phillies dugout." Jackie said he was never closer to quitting. "How could I have thought that barriers would fall, that my talent could triumph over bigotry?"

Jackie was also combative after the most overt racism had faded. He refused to be someone he was not, refused to conform to an image of a man who "knew his place." It is important to his memory that he not only took the first step to integrate the majors, but he took the next step, too. He was not afraid to let his talent speak for itself, and to be himself.

Jackie won a batting title in 1949 at .342 on the way to being named the league's Most Valuable Player. Though he played just 10 seasons, he helped the Dodgers to six World Series, winning one; the Dodgers were often the victims of the Yankee buzz saw. Robinson was

Because Eddie Stanky had a lock on the second base job in 1947, Brooklyn switched Robinson to first base.

The April 1945 Tryout with the Red Sox

In 1959, the Boston Red Sox became the last major league team to integrate. But in April 1945, the Red Sox gave Jackie Robinson and two other African-Americans, outfielder and future Boston Brave Sam Jethroe and Marvin Williams, a tryout at Fenway Park. The trial was the result of political pressure exerted on the team by Boston City Councilor Isadore H.Y. Muchnick, who vowed to fight the renewal of the club's permit to play Sunday baseball at Fenway Park unless they gave a tryout to black players. Through the efforts of sportswriter Wendell Smith of the *Pittsburgh Courier*, an audition was arranged for Robinson, Jethroe, and Williams at Fenway.

In later years, Robinson was convinced the Red Sox never had any intention of becoming the first team to break the color line.

the most devastating baserunner of his day and a fine base stealer. He had dangerous home run power and was exceptionally difficult to strike out, fanning only 291 times in over 5,000 plate appearances. He played his first season for the Dodgers at first base, an unfamiliar position, and set a record for rookie double plays that still stands. Later he became one of the very best second basemen in history. Robinson retired in 1957, and was inducted into the Hall of Fame in 1962.

Negro League Stats*

BA	G	AB	H	2B	3B	HR	SB
.387	47	163	63	14	4	5	13

Major League Totals

BA	G	AB	R	H	2B	3B	HR	RBI	SB
.311	1,382	4,877	947	1,518	273	54	137	734	197

*Note: Robinson's Negro League career stats are incomplete.

WESLEY BRANCH RICKEY
ST. LOUIS A.L. 1905-1906 1914
NEW YORK A.L. 1907
FOUNDER OF FARM SYSTEM WHICH HE
DEVELOPED FOR ST. LOUIS CARDINALS
AND BROOKLYN DODGERS. COPIED BY ALL
OTHER MAJOR LEAGUE TEAMS,
SERVED AS EXECUTIVE FOR BROWNS,
CARDINALS, DODGERS AND PIRATES.
BROUGHT JACKIE ROBINSON TO BROOKLYN
IN 1947.

THE RULES OF BASEBALL HAVE remained relatively stable throughout this century. Off the field, however, revolutionary changes have taken place, and no man had a greater impact on what happened to baseball outside the white lines than Branch Rickey. His biggest fight was the campaign to integrate baseball.

Born to fundamentalist Methodist parents, the early life of Wesley Branch Rickey (1881-1965) was characterized by three themes: education, organization, and baseball. He received several bachelor's degrees, and a law degree from Michigan, where he also coached baseball. His playing career was undistinguished; he started in the low minor leagues in 1900 and finished for the New York Highlanders in 1907. While coaching at Michigan, he was hired as manager of the St. Louis Browns in 1913. Unsuccessful, he moved to the St. Louis Cardinal front office in 1917. He also managed the Redbirds from 1919 to 1925. His managing career was less distinguished than his playing career. Rickey was a seriously religious man who wouldn't play or attend games on Sundays, no doubt hurting both ventures. It was as a club operator that Rickey was peerless. He had a keen eye for talent and was a man able to take advantage of his times.

With the Cardinals in the 1920s, Rickey began to acquire minor league clubs from which the Cardinals could obtain talent. He saw the value of owning his own source of players, both to stock the Cards and to provide trade bait. "The Mahatma" maintained, however, that the farm system was borne of necessity. By the time the Cards won their first pennant in 1928, they owned 10 clubs, and by 1938 they were an established power, owning or controlling 38 clubs and the contracts of hundreds of players. Commissioner Kenesaw Mountain Landis, who opposed farm systems, ordered the release of 74 Cardinal minor leaguers in 1940. Under the control of Rickey, the Cardinals won pennants in 1926, 1928, 1930, '31, '34, and 1942.

Moving to Brooklyn in 1942, Rickey is best remembered for bringing Jackie Robinson to "organized" baseball, first in the minors and then with the Dodgers. With the support of unsung hero commissioner Happy Chandler, and the infinite patience and considerable talent of Robinson, the color line was broken in 1947. Rickey also signed Roy Campanella and Don Newcombe out of the Negro Leagues, providing Brooklyn with three awesome talents that helped the Dodgers dominate the National League in the 1950s.

Rickey's last venture in baseball was an attempt to launch a third major league in 1960, spurring the major league expansion in the early 1960s. He was inducted into the Hall of Fame in 1967.

Top: Rickey was a brilliant innovator for much of his career as a manager and an executive. Among other things, he helped to introduce sliding pits, batting cages, and blackboard drills. Right: In 1906, Rickey hit the first grand slam by a St. Louis Brown.

HAPPY CHANDLER'S TENURE as commissioner of baseball, from 1945 to 1951, was marked by wide extremes of strong action, inaction, and questionable action, all of which helped lead to his ouster at the end of his single term. His were difficult times in baseball, but he left a rich legacy of his stewardship.

Albert B. Chandler (1907-1991) was born in Corydon, Kentucky. He attended Transylvania University in Lexington, where he played baseball, and earned a law degree from the University of Kentucky. The former governor was serving in the U.S. Senate at the time of Kensaw Mountain Landis's death, and Happy felt that World War II was all but over and that he could in good conscience leave his legislative duties to take over the reins of baseball.

At the top of the list of Chandler's accomplishments stands the integration of baseball. Without his approval, Branch Rickey may not have been able to proceed with his plan to open the doors to black players. Landis had stopped Bill Veeck's earlier plans to hire African-Americans. In doing so, Chandler defied all 15 other owners and made sure that there would be no more talk about "when the time is ripe."

When some players jumped to the Mexican League in 1946, Chandler suspended them for five years. It was a strong action, but it also opened the door for successful challenges to the reserve clause, a result that could not please the owners. He gave a blanket amnesty in 1949. A

ALBERT BENJAMIN CHANDLER
"HAPPY"
BASEBALL'S SECOND COMMISSIONER, 1945-1951. UNITED STATES SENATOR (1939-1945). GOVERNOR OF KENTUCKY (1935-39, 1955-59). IRON-WILLED AND HONEST, HE WAS KNOWN AS A "PLAYER'S COMMISSIONER" BECAUSE OF HIS BROAD CONCERN FOR ALL PHASES OF THE GAME.

lawsuit filed by one of the players, Danny Gardella, was successfully appealed, and baseball had to settle out of court. Some feel that the court challenge led to Chandler's undoing as commissioner.

Chandler served the players in many ways. He supported the Players Association, helped fund the pension plan by allowing them to share in broadcast revenues, and worked toward a minimum salary. He suspended Leo Durocher from baseball for one year, for alleged association with gamblers and "conduct detrimental to baseball." Some felt that Chandler was trying to bolster his image as a strong leader, and respond to fresh reports of fixed games in the minors.

In the end, Chandler was sent packing. Only nine of the required 12 owners voted for his reinstatement as commissioner. Red Smith wrote: "Chandler operated so effectively as a regulatory agency over the owners that the owners marked him incompetent and kicked him, bawling for just one more chance, into the street." Happy was elected to the Hall of Fame in 1982.

Top: Chandler stood tall when the hard questions were presented to him. Left: Chandler stands in the middle of the AL and the NL representatives at the 1949 World Series. The others are, from left: AL president Will Harridge, Yankees manager Casey Stengel, Dodgers manager Burt Shotton, and NL president Ford Frick.

RALPH McPHERRAN KINER
PITTSBURGH, N. L. CHICAGO, N. L.
CLEVELAND, A. L. 1946-1955

HIT 369 HOME RUNS AND AVERAGED BETTER
THAN 100 RUNS BATTED IN PER SEASON IN
TEN-YEAR CAREER. ONLY PLAYER TO LEAD HIS
LEAGUE OR SHARE LEAD IN HOMERS SEVEN
YEARS IN A ROW, 1946-1952. TWICE HAD
MORE THAN 50 IN SEASON. SET N.L. MARK
OF 101 FOUR-BAGGERS IN TWO SUCCESSIVE
YEARS WITH 54 IN 1949 AND 47 IN 1950.
LED N. L. IN SLUGGING PCT. THREE TIMES.

**Outfielder
Pittsburgh Pirates
    1946-1953
Chicago Cubs 1953-1954
Cleveland Indians 1955**

RECOGNIZED AS THE GREATEST slugger in those years immediately after World War II, Ralph Kiner had a National League record seven straight home run titles. Only Babe Ruth has a career home run ratio that is better than Kiner's.

Ralph McPherran Kiner (born in 1922) was a renowned semipro baseball player in Alhambra, California, as both a pitcher and a hitter. After he graduated from high school in 1940, he was approached by several ballclubs, who all wanted him to sign with a Class-D affiliate. Instead, Ralph signed with the Pittsburgh Pirates, who offered to start him in Class-A. He played in the minors for two and one-half seasons, making it to the Triple-A International League before joining the Navy in mid-1943.

After his release in December 1945, Ralph said, "I began preparing for spring training, and I got myself into just sensational shape. Sure enough, I had a spring training like no one's ever had." In 1946, Kiner became the Pirates left fielder, and he hit 23 home runs to lead the league.

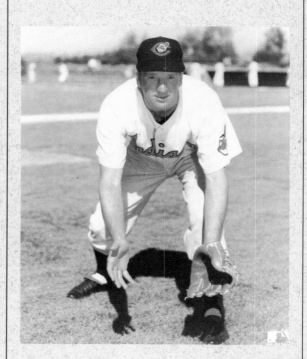

In 1947, Pittsburgh acquired Hank Greenberg, and the Pirates moved the left field fence in from 365 feet to 335 feet (an area known as "Greenberg's Garden"). Kiner's 23 homers began to look like small potatoes. Ralph hit 51 homers in 1947, while he found a mentor in Greenberg. Hank retired after the '47 season, and left field became "Kiner's Korner." Ralph slugged 40 homers in 1948, and 54 in 1949. Though his slugging was aided by Forbes Field, he twice set road home run records. He walked 100 times or more in six straight seasons to post an excellent lifetime on-base average of .397, which in turn helped him to six seasons of at least 100 runs scored. The Pirates were usually in the cellar during Kiner's tenure, but he was recognized as one of the game's greatest stars.

Kiner was a hard and innovative worker. "I remember back in 1941 or 1942, I obtained a filmstrip of Babe Ruth's swing, broken down frame by frame, which I copied carefully and practiced whenever I got the chance," he said. He later had films taken of his own swing in order to spot flaws, and took hours of extra batting practice. Though he had a weak arm, he was a four-time *Sporting News* All-Star. He was also a prime mover in the players' movement, which led to the pension plan and eventually the financial bonanza of modern players. Later, Ralph would become an immensely popular broadcaster for the Mets. He was inducted into the Hall of Fame in 1975.

Top: Kiner never got to play for a contending team until 1955, his final season, when he was dealt to Cleveland. Right: In Kiner's heyday, comic books like this one were still only a dime and sluggers were still expected to keep their strikeout totals relatively modest. After fanning 109 times as a rookie in 1946, Kiner never again topped 100 Ks.

Major League Totals										
BA	G	AB	R	H	2B	3B	HR	RBI	SB
.279	1,472	5,205	971	1,451	216	39	369	1,015	22

YOGI BERRA

YOGI BERRA WAS A MAINSTAY of the most dominating baseball team in history, the New York Yankee team that played from the end of World War II until the early 1960s. Although he never led the league in a single major offensive category, he was just the third man to win three Most Valuable Player awards, and he played in fourteen World Series.

Lawrence Peter Berra (born in 1925) grew up in a largely Italian neighborhood in St. Louis. One of his neighbors was Joe Garagiola, and they played sandlot and American Legion baseball together. When both went to a Cardinal tryout in 1943, the Redbirds offered Garagiola $500 to sign, and they offered Yogi less. His pride hurt, Berra refused, eventually signing with the Yankees for the $500. He played in the Piedmont League until he joined the Navy. He saw action in the Normandy Invasion of 1944.

In 1946, Berra was discharged and played for Newark, hitting .314 with 15 homers. He was called up to the Yankees that season, where he would star until 1963.

Berra captured the imagination of baseball fans with his malapropisms. "It ain't over till it's over" has become a rallying cry for anyone trailing in a game. He was stocky, short, with a broad face and a well-publicized penchant for comic books and a natural quality that fans found amusing and endearing. He was also one of the most dangerous hitters in the American League.

Yogi didn't become the Bombers' No. 1 catcher until 1949. In 1950, he batted .322, with 28 homers and 124 RBI. Although his 1951 season wasn't as impressive (a .294 batting average, 27 home runs, and 88 RBI), he won his first MVP Award. His 1952 or 1953 seasons weren't much different than his 1954 (a .307 average, 22 homers, 125 RBI) and his 1955 (a .272 average, 27 homers, 108 RBI), but he won consecutive MVPs in 1954 and '55. It was a tribute to his consistency that his three MVP seasons were not necessarily his best years. He had 90 RBI in nine seasons, and 20 homers in 11 seasons.

Berra worked to become a fine defensive catcher, and in 1958 fielded a perfect 1.000. He was a wonderful handler of pitchers and a wizard, for a catcher, at the double play. Although he played with Mickey Mantle and Whitey Ford, Berra's teams were not stocked like the 1927 Yankees, yet they won five consecutive World

Catcher
New York Yankees
1946-1963
New York Mets 1965

Top: *Berra was almost unquestionably the best-hitting catcher in American League history.* Below: *Berra fails in his bid to score from third base on a sacrifice fly in a 1957 World Series game. He caught every one of the seven contests in a losing cause and hit .320—after batting just .251 during the regular season, a career low to that point.*

Series. Berra owns a host of World Series records, he was named an All-Star from 1948 to 1962, and he had perhaps the greatest career of any catcher in baseball history. He also managed the Yankees and the Mets to pennants. He was inducted in 1972.

Major League Totals									
BA	G	AB	R	H	2B	3B	HR	RBI	SB
.285	2,120	7,555	1,175	2,150	321	49	358	1,430	30

MICKEY MANTLE

MICKEY CHARLES MANTLE
NEW YORK A.L. 1951-1968
HIT 536 HOME RUNS. WON LEAGUE HOMER TITLE
AND SLUGGING CROWN FOUR TIMES. MADE
2415 HITS. BATTED .300 OR OVER IN EACH
OF TEN YEARS WITH TOP OF .365 IN 1957.
TOPPED A.L. IN WALKS FIVE YEARS AND
IN RUNS SCORED SIX SEASONS. VOTED
MOST VALUABLE PLAYER 1956-57-62. NAMED
ON 20 A.L. ALL-STAR TEAMS. SET WORLD
SERIES RECORDS FOR HOMERS, 18; RUNS, 42;
RUNS BATTED IN, 40; TOTAL BASES, 123;
AND BASES ON BALLS, 43.

Outfielder
New York Yankees
1951-1968

MICKEY MANTLE WAS THE most feared hitter on the most successful team in history, and overcame great pain in his quest to satisfy his fans, his father, and himself.

Mickey Charles Mantle was born in 1931 in Spavinaw, Oklahoma, the son of Mutt Mantle, a lead miner who had dreams of a good life for Mickey. Mickey (named after Mickey Cochrane) was a standout schoolboy player, but a serious football injury nearly derailed his career—and his life. He suffered from osteomyelitis, a condition that weakened his left leg, and could have lost his leg if Mickey's mother had not procured a then-new treatment with the revolutionary drug, penicillin.

The Yankees signed Mickey to a contract in 1949, and the Class-B shortstop hit .313 that year, and committed 47 errors. The next year he led the Western Association with a .383 batting average, 141 runs scored, 199 base hits, and 55 errors at shortstop in 137 games. His 26 homers and 136 RBI led Casey Stengel to proclaim Mickey the top prospect in baseball.

Mickey opened the 1951 season in right field (after extensive defensive tutoring by former Yankee outfielder Tommy Henrich). He did not live up to his advance billing, and was sent to the American Association in midseason.

Discouraged, he wanted to quit, but it was Mutt that goaded Mickey's pride.

Mantle had enormous forearms and blazing speed, and he became a superb center fielder, taking over for Joe DiMaggio in 1952. Mantle was possibly the fastest man in the game during his early years. In his best seasons, and there were many, Mantle was simply a devastating player. He could run like the wind and hit tape measure homers, like his famous 565-footer in Washington in 1953. He led the Yanks to 12 fall classics in 14 years, and seven World Championships. He still owns records for most homers, RBI, runs, walks, and strikeouts in World Series play. He led the AL with 129 runs in 1954, and got his first home run title in 1955 with 37. He was a free-swinger who struck out often, but could also take a walk, drawing at least 100 ten times.

In 1956, Mantle had one of the greatest seasons ever at the plate. He hit 52 homers with 130 RBI and a .353 average to win the Triple Crown. He also led the league with 132 runs and a .705 slugging percentage. He had 112 walks and won the first of three Most Valuable Player awards. He won the MVP again in 1957, hitting .365 with 34 homers, 94 RBI, 121 runs scored, and 146 bases on balls.

Bobby Kennedy adds his presence to the festivities on "Mickey Mantle Day" at Yankee Stadium in 1965. The many injuries Mantle sustained over the course of his career first began to take their toll that season. In 122 games, the Mick collected just 46 RBI and hit .255.

Mantle is greeted by Yogi Berra (upper left) and two other Yankees teammates after one of his two home runs in the 1953 World Series.

Mickey Mantle Pencil Set

25¢

The Tape Measure Home Run

Mickey Mantle invented the "Tape Measure" home run on April 17, 1953, while facing Senator lefty Chuck Stobbs at Washington's Griffith Stadium.

Mickey was using a bat he borrowed from reserve Loren Babe, and he bludgeoned Stobbs's second pitch (a slightly high fastball in the middle of the plate) over the bleachers; the ball ticked the corner of a beer sign and vanished. Yankee publicist Red Patterson found the baseball in the hands of a 10-year-old, who showed him where he had found the ball—more than 100 feet from the park, making it a 565-foot shot.

Mantle notched homer crowns in 1958 and 1960, then got into a duel with Roger Maris in 1961 to break Babe Ruth's single-season home run mark. While Maris's 61 was the winner, Mick led the league with a .687 slugging percentage, 132 runs scored, and 126 bases on balls. Mick won an MVP Award in 1962 with a .321 average, 20 homers, and 89 RBI.

Mantle's high school leg injury, torn knee cartilage in 1951, and many other injuries he suffered after that, shortened his career and were a constant source of pain and injury. After two painful seasons in 1967 and 1968, The Mick retired. He said, "If I miss anything today it's the atmosphere of the clubhouse." Mickey was a lively companion, and he and soul-mate Whitey Ford painted many towns red. Mantle was not generous with the press or fans; the difficulties of being a star often overwhelmed him. He was voted the greatest switch-hitter in history by the Society of American Baseball Researchers. Mantle was inducted in 1974.

Major League Totals

BA	G	AB	R	H	2B	3B	HR	RBI	SB
.298	2,401	8,102	1,677	2,415	344	72	536	1,509	153

ROY CAMPANELLA

ROY CAMPANELLA
"CAMPY"

BROOKLYN N. L. 1948 - 1957
MOST VALUABLE PLAYER N.L. 1951-1953-1955
ESTABLISHED RECORDS FOR CATCHER'S MOST
HOME-RUNS IN A SEASON 41; MOST RUNS
BATTED IN 142. SET N.L RECORD FOR CHANCES
ACCEPTED BY CATCHER, FOR MOST CONSECUTIVE
YEARS 6; TIED RECORD FOR MOST YEARS IN
PUTOUTS 6; CAUGHT 100 OR MORE GAMES FOR
MOST CONSECUTIVE YEARS 9; LED IN FIELDING
AVERAGE FOR CATCHERS 1949-1952-1953-1957.

Catcher
Negro League team
Baltimore Elite Giants
    1937-1942; 1944-1945
Major League team
Brooklyn Dodgers
    1948-1957

Commissioner Ford Frick is forced to hit the deck as Campy chases a pop foul into the stands.

ROY CAMPANELLA—ALONG with Jackie Robinson and Don Newcombe—was a pioneering black ballplayer who boosted a Dodger organization that to this day is acknowledged as one of the top teams in baseball history.

Born in 1921 in Philadelphia, as a youngster Roy Campanella decided to become a catcher because no one else had signed up for that position in school. He played well enough that in 1937, the 15-year-old backstop was catching on the weekends for the semipro Bacharach Giants. He moved to the Baltimore Elite Giants, with whom he played most of his career in the Negro Leagues. By the mid-1940s, Campy challenged Josh Gibson as the best catcher in the Negro Leagues.

Campanella was approached about signing with the Brooklyn organization late in 1945 but was unwilling, because he thought that he would be playing with the Brooklyn Brown Dodgers Negro League team. Eventually, Campanella was convinced to sign and played the 1946 season with Class-B Nashua, where he was the

Campanella donned the tools of his trade in at least 103 games in every season but his rookie year of 1948.

Eastern League MVP. In 1947, he was the International League MVP while with Montreal.

Campy was a success from the day he arrived in Brooklyn in mid-1948. The stocky catcher had a rocket for an arm, a powerful bat, and guided a legendary pitching staff to five pennants in 10 years. Campanella was a prime reason the 1950s Dodgers were the exceptional team in the National League. In 1951, Campanella won the first of three Most Valuable Player awards, a feat accomplished by only a tiny group of stars. He batted .325 with 33 homers and 108 RBI. His 1953 MVP season was among the best ever recorded by a catcher, as he led the league with 142 RBI, clubbed 41 homers, scored 103 runs, and batted .312.

In spring training of 1954, Campy chipped a bone in his left hand, which caused nerve damage; and he hit only .207 in 111 games that year. He rebounded in 1955 to win his third MVP by batting .318, with 32 homers and 107 RBI. Starting in 1956, the hand injury of 1954 began to cause him more trouble, and his hitting suffered further decline in 1957. He hoped for a return to form in 1958, but it never happened. Campanella was paralyzed in a car crash during the winter between the 1957 and 1958 seasons, and never played again. Confined to a wheelchair, he eventually went to work for the Los Angeles Dodgers. Inducted in 1969, Campy summed up his love for the game by saying, "You got to be a man to play baseball for a living, but you got to have a lot of little boy in you, too."

Negro League Stats*

BA	G	AB	H	2B	3B	HR	SB
.334	188	631	211	41	12	18	10

Major League Totals

BA	G	AB	R	H	2B	3B	HR	RBI	SB
.276	1,215	4,205	627	1,161	178	18	242	856	25

*Note: Campanella's Negro League career stats are incomplete.

DUKE SNIDER

THERE WAS AN UNPRECE- dented concentration of talent playing center field in New York in the 1950s. The Yankees had Mickey Mantle, the Giants had Willie Mays, and in Brooklyn, Duke Snider was king. In the four years the three played together, Duke took a back seat to no one. From 1954 to 1957, Snider had the most homers and RBI of the three, and he totaled more home runs and had more RBI than any player in the 1950s.

An outstanding athlete as a youth in Compton, California, Edwin Donald Snider (born in 1926) signed with the Dodgers in 1944 after high school, leading the Piedmont League in home runs. He served in the Navy in 1945 and part of 1946, coming back to the Texas League for part of that season.

The Duke played his first game for the Dodgers on the same day in 1947 that Jackie Robinson did. Snider, though a good minor league hitter, was batting only .241 with 24 strikeouts in 83 at bats at Brooklyn before he was sent down to St. Paul. In 1948, Snider spent most of the season in Montreal rather than Brooklyn. Branch Rickey put Duke through a strict regime, having him stand and watch pitch after pitch go by without swinging, learning the strike zone.

Outfielder
Brooklyn Dodgers
1947-1957
Los Angeles Dodgers
1958-1962
New York Mets 1963
San Francisco Giants 1964

When he mastered the strike zone, Snider became the lefthanded power for the Boys of Summer. He hit .292 with 23 homers in 1949, and led the NL with 199 base hits while getting 31 homers in 1950. He led the league in runs scored in 1953, '54, and '55. He joined Babe Ruth and Ralph Kiner as the only men to ever hit at least 40 homers in five straight seasons (from 1953 to 1957). Snider's streak ended when in 1958 the Dodgers moved to the L.A. Coliseum with its vast right field.

The Duke was a regular on six Dodger pennant winners, turning in awesome World Series performances. He hit four homers twice in World Series competition—once in the Dodgers' first World Championship when they beat the hated Yankees in 1955. He was an outstanding center fielder with an amazingly powerful arm. He ranks fourth on the all-time World Series home run list with 11.

Duke played in the 1959 World Series, but he injured his knee and was reduced to part-time play in 1960. In 1961, he broke his elbow, and he was never again a dominating player. He spent a year with the Mets in 1963, enjoying his familiar New York but not enjoying the Mets, and retired after a year with the Giants in 1964. He was inducted in the Hall of Fame in 1980.

Top: In 1957, Snider became the first slugger in history to slug 40 homers without totaling at least 100 RBI. That deed has since become relatively common. The 1957 campaign was the fifth consecutive year that Snider belted at least 40 home runs. Left: Lengthy drills designed to teach him the strike zone made Snider more willing to wait for his pitch.

Major League Totals

BA	G	AB	R	H	2B	3B	HR	RBI	SB
.295	2,143	7,161	1,259	2,116	358	85	407	1,333	99

ROBIN EVAN ROBERTS
PHILADELPHIA N.L., BALTIMORE A.L.,
HOUSTON N.L., CHICAGO N.L.,
1948 - 1966
WON 286 GAMES THOUGH USUALLY PITCHING
FOR SECOND-DIVISION TEAMS. GAINED 20 OR
MORE VICTORIES SIX YEARS IN A ROW,
1950-1955, AND TOPPED LEAGUE OR TIED
FOR LEAD IN VICTORIES FOUR SUCCESSIVE
SEASONS. LED N.L. FIVE CONSECUTIVE
YEARS IN INNINGS PITCHED, 1951-1955,
AND COMPLETE GAMES, 1952-1956. LED IN
SHUTOUTS AND STRIKEOUTS TWICE EACH.

Pitcher
Philadelphia Phillies
1948-1961
Baltimore Orioles
1962-1965
Houston Astros 1965-1966
Chicago Cubs 1966

ROBIN ROBERTS WON 20 OR more games each season from 1950 to 1955. He pitched in the majors for 19 years, and never failed to win at least 10 games in any of the 14 seasons in which he had at least 30 starts.

Robin Evan Roberts (born in 1926) was raised in Springfield, Illinois, and was a good high school basketball player. He attended Michigan State University on a basketball scholarship in 1945 after his discharge from the Air Force. He found his way to the diamond, and eventually dominated. He threw two no-hitters at MSU and by 1948 was the subject of a bidding contest. The Phillies offered him a $25,000 bonus, and Robin signed.

Roberts spent just part of the 1948 season in the Inter-State League, giving up only 82 hits plus walks in 96 innings, and fanning 121 for a 9-1 record. Late that season, he joined a Phillies team that was on the rise. They had finished sixth in '48, third in '49, and first in 1950.

In that first-place season, Roberts was 20-11 and was among the league leaders in nearly every significant category. His 20-win season that year was the first of six consecutive 20-plus win seasons as the "Whiz Kids"—so known because of youthful stars Roberts, Curt Simmons, and Richie Ashburn—bowed to the Yankees in the World Series. Roberts gave up just one run in

the first nine innings of his sole start, losing to a Joe DiMaggio homer in the tenth. It was to be Robin's only shot at a championship, as his teams only twice finished as high as third during the rest of his career.

In 1952, Roberts was 28-7, the leader of the league by 10 wins, and recorded the most National League wins in 50 years. From 1953 to 1955, he led the NL with 23 wins a year. He led the league in games started from '50 to '55, and complete games from 1952 to '56. He also led the NL with 198 strikeouts in 1953 and 185 Ks in 1954. He had outstanding control and extraordinary durability, leading the league in innings in four straight seasons but allowing very few walks. The poor quality of his teams and the constant managerial changes that accompany failure did not dim his ardor for pitching. Although he led the NL in losses in 1956 and 1957, he was a good pitcher from 1958 to 1965, save for the 1961 season.

Roberts later said "I had a fine right arm and a great delivery, but I pitched too much and wore myself down." He became a driving force in the Players Association, swaying the organization to pick Marvin Miller as its head. Roberts was inducted into the Hall of Fame in 1976.

Top: Roberts was on top of the world as a Phillies pitcher in the 1950s. He collected 179 wins before he turned 30 and seemed a safe bet to join the coveted 300-victory club. Right: On the final day of the 1950 season, he became the first Phillies hurler since 1917 to notch 20 victories.

Major League Totals

W	L	ERA	G	CG	IP	H	ER	BB	SO
286	245	3.41	676	305	4,688.2	4,582	1,774	902	2,357

WHITEY FORD

T HE "CHAIRMAN OF THE Board," Whitey Ford was the ace pitcher for the 1950s Yankees. His .690 winning percentage is the best of any modern 200-game winner, as his teams won 11 pennants and six World Series. Ford captured 15 Series records, including a streak of 33 scoreless innings.

Born in 1926, Edward Charles Ford grew up in New York City. He started pitching only as a senior in high school. The Yankees discovered him in 1946 playing in the sandlot Queens-Nassau League after high school, but they had to out-bid the Red Sox and the Dodgers to the tune of $7,000 for Ford's services. He started his minor league career in 1947 by notching a 13-4 record; he was 16-8 in 1948, and he led the Eastern League with a 1.61 ERA while going 16-5 in 1949.

Ford was summoned to New York in mid-1950 after a 6-3 start in the American Association. He teased New York fans with a brilliant 9-1 record in 12 starts, and a near shutout in the World Series. He then served two years in the military, leaving behind the greatest of expectations. When he returned in 1953 he more than measured up, with a record of 18-6 as the Yankees won their fifth straight Championship.

Whitey didn't just win, he won spectacularly. During his first 14 seasons, only twice did he post a record that was as low as three games over .500, and in 12 seasons he was at least six games

SPALDING CONSULTANT

Whitey Ford

EDWARD CHARLES FORD
"WHITEY"
NEW YORK A.L. 1950-1967
POSTED BEST WINNING PERCENTAGE (.690) AMONG TWENTIETH CENTURY PITCHERS WITH 200 OR MORE DECISIONS. HAD 236 VICTORIES AND 106 LOSSES. LIFETIME EARNED RUN AVERAGE 2.74. PACED A.L. IN VICTORIES AND WINNING PCT. THREE TIMES AND IN EARNED-RUN AVERAGE AND SHUTOUTS TWICE. WON CY YOUNG AWARD IN 1961. SET WORLD SERIES STANDARDS FOR GAMES PITCHED, 22; INNINGS, 146; WINS, 10, AND STRIKEOUTS, 94, AND WITH 33 2/3 CONSECUTIVE SCORELESS INNINGS.

Pitcher
New York Yankees 1950;
1953-1967

over .500. He led the AL with 18 wins and 18 complete games in 1955. In 1956, he had the league's best ERA at 2.47. Manager Casey Stengel didn't let Ford pitch more than 250 innings a season, using him mostly against first-division teams.

When Ralph Houk took the Yankees reins in 1961, he unleashed Whitey, and he went an AL-top 25-4 with a league-high 39 starts and 283 innings pitched, winning the Cy Young Award. He had a 24-7 record in 1963, again leading the AL with 37 starts and 269 1/3 innings pitched.

Ford was a superb craftsman with excellent control. He used several pitches. Although some weren't legal, the threat that he fixed some balls kept hitters guessing, helping him more than actually throwing doctored balls.

Whitey, his best buddy Mickey Mantle, Billy Martin, and some of the other Yankees were well known about town. "When Whitey pitched he always felt like unwinding that night after the ballgame," Mickey Mantle said. He added that he was ready to celebrate if Whitey won the game. "Lucky for both of us, he won 236 games when he was pitching for the Yankees." Ford was inducted into the Hall of Fame in 1974, the same year as the Mick.

Top: Ford, who knew something about fixing a baseball, was a consultant to Spalding. After his election to the Hall of Fame, Ford revealed that he had sometimes doctored a baseball with a sticky home-made substance and a specially made "rasping" ring. Left: He pitched for 11 pennant winners in his first 13 seasons.

			Major League Totals							
W	**L**	**ERA**	**G**	**CG**	**IP**	**H**	**ER**	**BB**	**SO**
236	106	2.75	498	156	3,170.1	2,766	967	1,086	1,956

WILLIE HOWARD MAYS, JR.
"THE SAY HEY KID"
NEW YORK N.L., SAN FRANCISCO N.L.,
NEW YORK N.L., 1951-1973
ONE OF BASEBALL'S MOST COLORFUL AND
EXCITING STARS; EXCELLED IN ALL PHASES OF
THE GAME. THIRD IN HOMERS (660), RUNS (2,062)
AND TOTAL BASES (6,066); SEVENTH IN HITS
(3,283) AND RBI'S (1,903). FIRST IN PUTOUTS
BY OUTFIELDER (7,095). FIRST TO TOP BOTH
300 HOMERS AND 300 STEALS. LED LEAGUE IN
BATTING ONCE, SLUGGING FIVE TIMES, HOME
RUNS AND STEALS FOUR SEASONS. VOTED N.L.
MVP IN 1954 AND 1965. PLAYED IN 24
ALL-STAR GAMES - A RECORD.

Outfielder
Negro League team
Birmingham Black Barons
 1947-1950
Major League teams
New York Giants
 1951-1952; 1954-1957
San Francisco Giants
 1958-1972
New York Mets 1972-1973

Top: *Mays eludes Cardinals catcher Bill Sarni's tag to score for the Giants. Below: Besides this big stick, Mays also used a very different type of bat on occasion early in his career. At times, he would join in a stickball game on the New York streets after a Giants contest, using a broom handle.*

FEW PLAYERS HAVE COMBINED grace, popularity, and accomplishment like Willie Mays. He was a beautiful fielder, a tremendous power hitter, an outstanding thrower, a canny base-runner, a huge drawing card, and durable champion.

Born in 1931 in Westfield, Alabama, Willie Howard Mays was so advanced that he competed with the men on his father's steel mill team when Willie was 14 years old. He played semipro ball at age 16, and was on the Birmingham Black Barons by 1947. He was one of the last players, and likely the best, to come from the Negro Leagues to the big leagues. In 1950, the Giants signed him and sent him to the Inter-State League, where he batted .353. In 1951, he was batting .477 at Minneapolis of the American Association when the Giants promoted him. The New York front office published an apology in the Minneapolis paper, understanding the impression Willie had made on Millers fans.

Leo Durocher demanded that Mays be promoted after the Giants started at 6-20. Although Willie started out 0-for-12, he had a galvanizing effect on the Giants. They came from 13½ games back to force a playoff with the front-running Dodgers, beating them on Bobby Thomson's home run (Willie was on deck) in

the culmination of "The Miracle on Coogan's Bluff." Mays hit 20 homers, perfected center field play, and won the Rookie of the Year Award. He also won the hearts of teammates and fans alike for his enthusiasm, good humor, squeaky voice, and incredible play. Leo said, "What can I say about Willie Mays after I say he's the greatest player any of us has ever seen?"

Mays was in the Army for most of 1952 and all of 1953. With those years, Willie is almost certain to have broken Babe Ruth's lifetime home run record. In 1954, Willie returned to win the MVP Award, led the league with a .345 average and a .667 slugging percentage, and hit 41 homers. His catch of a Vic Wertz drive in the Giants' World Series victory has become one of baseball's most admired moments.

Willie led the NL in homers with 51 in 1955. He hit over 35 homers in 10 seasons, 40 homers six times, twice topping 50, and won five slugging crowns. In addition to his power, average, arm, and defense, add speed—he won four stolen base and three triples titles. His biggest victory came over the skeptical San Francisco fans. When the Giants moved out to the West Coast in 1958, Bay Area fans remembered Joe DiMaggio and the old San Francisco Seals. Willie melted all resistance by his spectacular play.

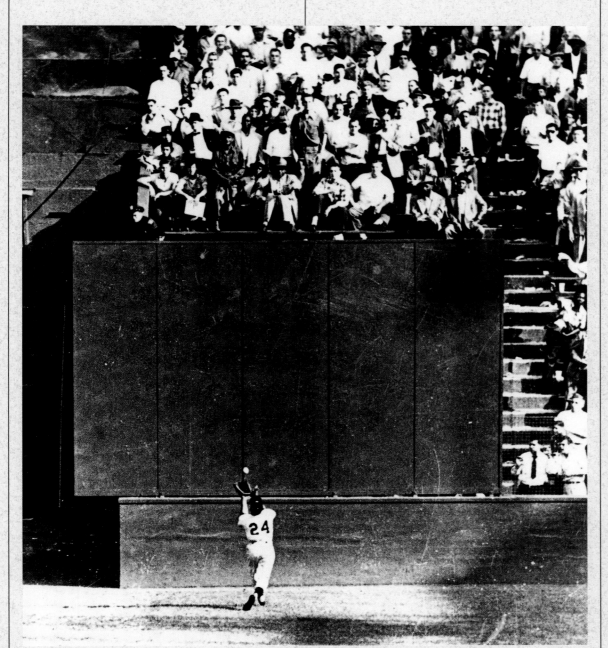

Mays is about to make the most famous catch in World Series history, robbing Cleveland's Vic Wertz of a cinch triple in game one of the 1954 fall classic.

Rookie Blues

When Willie Mays was called up to the Giants in May 1951, he had notched an incredible .799 slugging average while batting .477 for the Minneapolis Millers of the American Association. All that Giant manager Leo Durocher asked of Mays was that he bat .250 and play the brand of center field he had in the minors. Mays jumped at the chance to prove himself.

Mays had only one hit, a homer, in his first 26 major league at bats. He sought out Durocher and, with tears streaming down his cheeks, said "Send me back, I told you I couldn't hit this pitching." To Durocher's everlasting credit he admonished Mays to pull his pants up in order to decrease his strike zone, predicting he'd get two hits the next day if he did and also told the young star that he would continue to be the Giants center fielder no matter how long his slump persisted.

By season's end Mays had socked 20 home runs while batting .274 as he captured *The Sporting News* National League Rookie of the Year honors.

In 1962, Mays and the Giants again found themselves in a tie with the talented Dodgers. Willie led a powerhouse team to another playoff victory, scoring four runs in the ninth to earn the right to face the Yankees in the World Series. It was one of Willie's best seasons, as he hit 49 homers and drove in 141 runs. In 1965, he won his second MVP by batting .317 with 52 homers and 112 RBI. Mays finished among the top six in MVP voting an amazing 12 times.

Mays won a dozen Gold Gloves in a row for his outfield play, from 1957 to 1968. Mickey Mantle, the man Mays would be compared to most often, said "You have to work hard to be able to make things look as easy as Willie makes them look." Willie retired with records for games, putouts, and chances for center fielders.

Willie Mays, the "Say Hey Kid," showed true greatness in his longevity. At age 40 he led the league in walks, hit 18 homers, and was 23 for 26 as a basestealer. Though he hit as high as .290 only once in his final eight seasons, his lifetime average remained above .300. He spent his final two seasons back with the New Yorkers who missed him, with the Mets. He was a near-unanimous selection to the Hall of Fame in 1979.

			Negro League Stats*					
BA	**G**		**AB**	**H**	**2B**	**3B**	**HR**	**SB**
.263	130		460	121	10	2	5	3

				Major League Totals					
BA	**G**	**AB**	**R**	**H**	**2B**	**3B**	**HR**	**RBI**	**SB**
.302	2,992	10,881	2,062	3,283	523	140	660	1,903	338

*Note: Mays's Negro League career stats are incomplete.

CHAPTER SIX

Manifest Destiny
Baseball's Changing Map

AFTER YEARS OF STATUS QUO, BASEBALL franchises began to shift in the 1950s. Air travel made cities across America accessible. With that in mind, in 1958 the Dodgers moved to Los Angeles and Giants to San Francisco.

In an effort to thwart Branch Rickey's proposed upstart Continental League, the American League awarded a new franchise to Washington (after the original Senators moved to Minnesota) and placed another in Los Angeles for the 1961 season. The National League returned to New York with a 1962 expansion team and moved to Houston. Each new franchise cost its owners $2 million.

In the mid-1960s, the Houston Colt .45s changed their nickname to Astros after occupying the Astrodome, baseball's first domed ballpark, which featured artificial turf—and the Milwaukee Braves moved to Atlanta. In 1968, pitchers had become so dominating that batting averages fell, home run production was off, and there were sharp increases in the number of low-scoring games. Baseball executives, viewing those trends with alarm, decided to narrow the strike zone and lower the mound.

There was another round of expansion in 1969. Kansas City, which had lost the Athletics to Oakland in 1968, returned to the AL with the Royals while a new team was awarded to Seattle. The National League assigned a team to San Diego, and went international by adding the Montreal Expos. Both leagues agreed to split into divisions, with divisional champions in a best-of-five playoff to determine World Series participants.

Above: Brooks Robinson's famous No. 5. The Baltimore Orioles began to assert themselves in 1966, and the top-fielding third baseman of all-time, Robinson, was inducted into the Hall of Fame in 1983.

Below: An advertising tab features righthander Don Drysdale, one-half of the lefty-righty duo that the Dodgers used to clobber the opposition with in the 1960s. Sandy Koufax was the lefthanded part of the duo. Opposite page: Henry Aaron, the top home run hitter of all time, was an all-around force for the Braves. In his 21 years with the franchise, he led the NL in batting average twice, slugging average four times, doubles four times, and runs scored three times.

HENRY "HANK" L. AARON
MILWAUKEE N.L., ATLANTA N.L.,
MILWAUKEE A.L., 1954-1976

HIT 755 HOME RUNS IN 23-YEAR CAREER TO BECOME MAJORS' ALL-TIME HOMER KING. HAD 20 OR MORE FOR 20 CONSECUTIVE YEARS. AT LEAST 30 IN 15 SEASONS AND 40 OR BETTER EIGHT TIMES. ALSO SET RECORDS FOR GAMES PLAYED (3,298), AT-BATS (12,364), LONG HITS (1,477), TOTAL BASES (6,856), RUNS BATTED IN (2,297). PACED N.L. IN BATTING TWICE AND HOMERS, RUNS BATTED IN AND SLUGGING PCT. FOUR TIMES EACH. WON MOST VALUABLE PLAYER AWARD IN N.L. IN 1957.

Outfielder
Milwaukee Braves
    1954-1965
Atlanta Braves 1966-1974
Milwaukee Brewers
    1975-1976

ON APRIL 23, 1954, HANK AARON hit the first of his 755 major league home runs, more than any player in major league history.

Henry Louis Aaron (born in 1934) grew up one of eight children in Mobile, Alabama. He used to haul 25-pound blocks of ice as a child, and he learned baseball by hitting bottle caps with a broomstick. He started playing semipro ball in Mobile at age 16. By 1951, the Indianapolis Clowns of the Negro Leagues signed him as a shortstop. He was a cross-handed hitter for awhile, but switched to a conventional grip on a scout's advice and hit two home runs in his first game with the new grip.

The Braves signed Aaron in 1952 and sent him to Eu Claire of the Northwest League, where he batted .336. In 1953, he was one of three players to integrate the South Atlantic League. He led the circuit with a .362 batting average, 125 RBI, and 115 runs scored. Bobby Thomson, the Braves left fielder, broke his ankle early in 1954, and Hank had a job in Milwaukee.

Aaron endured the bigotry and segregation of the major leagues at that time with poise and

Top: One of the uniforms Aaron wore while a member of the Milwaukee Braves. Aaron was originally signed by the Braves franchise in 1952 while the club was still based in Boston. Right: The trophy Hank received for breaking Babe Ruth's career home-run mark on April 8, 1974.

Henry Aaron's 715th
lifetime home run,
April 8, 1974

silence. In his early years in the majors, he was an enigma to most players and fans. He let his bat do the talking for many years, and only gradually did his image evolve from that of a hitting machine to an intelligent, forceful man, who could set seemingly impossible goals and achieve them.

Hank had an all-around game that was second to none. He became one of the top outfielders in the game after coming up as an infielder. He was consistent, careful, and deadly. His quick wrists were the stuff of legend. He led the NL with a .328 batting average in 1956. In 1957, he won the National League MVP Award with a .322 batting average, 44 home runs, and 132 RBI. The Braves won the pennant that year, and then went on to defeat a powerful Yankee team in the World Series. Hank hit .393 in the seven games with three home runs. Although the Braves remained a strong team for many years, it was to be Aaron's only World Championship. The Yankees repaid the Braves in the 1958 Series, although Aaron hit .333 in the Series.

The Braves moved to Atlanta from Milwaukee in 1966, and Aaron, who had been succeeding for years in one of the very worst parks for hitters in baseball, was granted a reprieve; Fulton County Stadium proved to be a great hitter's park. He hit 245 home runs after turning 35 years old, a

The camera captures Aaron as he launches his record-shattering 715th career home run. Hank went on to hit only 20 homers that year, the fewest since his rookie campaign.

The Burden of the Home Run Record

When Hank Aaron was in the process of breaking Babe Ruth's major league career home run record in 1974, he involuntarily became a lightning rod for intolerance. To millions of fans, Aaron's achievement was a moment to savor. Unfortunately, to some this same moment was an affront, both because of Aaron's race and the fact that he was now surpassing the record of America's most celebrated and beloved sports hero. Although Aaron made it clear to the public that he sincerely believed no one could replace the Babe, he was still viewed in some quarters as a villain.

At the time of the record-breaking 715th, talk of such treatment was kept to a minimum. In ensuing years, Aaron hasn't been reticent in describing how he, his parents, and his children received many racially motivated death threats, abusive phone messages, and stacks of hate mail. Many of the letters and calls were investigated by the FBI, and the slugger was assigned an Atlanta police escort. Never has an athlete endured more hatred as the result of breaking a record.

record. He hit .357 with three homers in the 1969 National League Championship Series, the only other postseason appearance of his long career.

On April 8, 1974, Aaron broke Babe Ruth's lifetime home run record. Racism and fans' misguided reverence for the Babe added to the difficulty of that monumental task. Always a quiet, serious professional, Henry withstood the burden and scrutiny of an all-out media assault with cool and restraint. "Thank God it's over," he said after the record-breaking game.

Aaron won a record eight total-bases titles, en route to the all-time record of 6,856 total bases. He slugged over .500 eighteen times, and batted .300 fourteen times. He scored 100 runs in 13 consecutive seasons and 15 times in all. He totaled an all-time best 2,297 runs batted in. He hit 30 or more homers in 15 seasons. When he retired, he played in more games and had more at bats than any player in history, and he had taken all those swings as perhaps the greatest righthanded hitter in history. Pitcher Curt Simmons said, "Throwing a fastball by Henry Aaron is like trying to sneak sunrise past a rooster." Aaron was inducted in 1982.

Major League Totals

BA	G	AB	R	H	2B	3B	HR	RBI	SB
.305	3,298	12,364	2,174	3,771	624	98	755	2,297	240

EDWIN LEE MATHEWS
BOSTON N.L., MILWAUKEE N.L.,
ATLANTA N.L., HOUSTON N.L.,
DETROIT A.L. 1952-1968
BECAME SEVENTH PLAYER IN MAJOR LEAGUE
HISTORY TO HIT 500 HOME RUNS. FINISHED
CAREER WITH 512. HIT 30 OR MORE HOMERS
NINE YEARS IN ROW, 1953-1961. REACHING
40 MARK FOUR TIMES. ESTABLISHED RECORD
FOR HOMERS IN SEASON BY THIRD BASEMAN
WITH 47 IN 1953. LED N.L. IN HOME RUNS
TWICE AND IN WALKS FOUR TIMES. HAD FIVE
SEASONS OF 100 OR MORE RUNS BATTED IN.

Third baseman
Boston Braves 1952
Milwaukee Braves
1953-1965
Atlanta Braves 1966
Houston Astros 1967
Detroit Tigers 1967-1968

Top: *Mathews holds the NL single-season record for the most RBI (135) and the most total bases (363) by a third baseman. Both marks were established in 1953 when he also clubbed 47 home runs, a record for third basemen that stood until 1980 when Mike Schmidt hit 48. Below: Mathews's uniform.*

EDDIE MATHEWS IS BEST RE-membered as teaming with Hank Aaron to form the Braves' one-two punch that dominated the National League in the 1950s and early 1960s.

Edwin Lee Mathews (born in 1931) was a muscular high school baseball and football star in 1949 in Santa Barbara, California. He was pursued by the Brooklyn Dodgers, who offered a $10,000 contract, although signing a free agent for more than $6,000 meant that he had to stay on the major league roster for two seasons. He was also courted by the Boston Braves, who offered $6,000. Eddie researched the rosters, and decided that the Braves would give him the best opportunity to start quickly, and that he didn't want to sit on a major league bench for two years. Mathews batted .363 with 17 homers in 1949 in his first season in pro baseball, and he had 32 homers and 106 RBI for Atlanta of the Southern League in 1950.

Mathews was promoted to Boston in 1952, and though he fanned a league-high 115 times his rookie season, he also cracked 25 homers. The next season, the franchise's first in Milwaukee, he won his first homer title, hitting 47. He provided power the next three seasons, getting 37 or more homers and 95 or more RBI from 1954 to '56. In 1957, he batted .292 with 32

homers and 94 RBI, as the Braves won the World Championship. He hit .251 with 31 homers as the Braves won the pennant in 1958. Eddie won the homer crown in 1959 with 46 round-trippers.

Mathews hit at least 30 homers in nine seasons, four times hitting over 40. He led the league in walks four times, had 90 or more bases on balls nine times, and scored at least 95 runs in ten straight seasons. One reason he scored so much was that he batted ahead of Aaron. Playing with Henry may have obscured Mathews's performance, but while together, they hit 863 home runs, more than Babe Ruth and Lou Gehrig. Mathews was Aaron's manager in 1974, the year he broke Ruth's career home run record.

When Mathews joined the Boston Braves in 1952, he played the hot corner poorly, but he matured into a capable third baseman. He led the NL in putouts twice, assists three times, and fielding average once. He is in the top ten among third sackers in career double plays.

In 1962, Mathews injured his shoulder. He continued to play, but his ability gradually declined. After one year in Atlanta in 1966, he was traded to the Astros. He also played with the Tigers before retiring. Eddie was inducted into the Hall of Fame in 1978.

Major League Totals

BA	G	AB	R	H	2B	3B	HR	RBI	SB
.271	2,388	8,537	1,509	2,315	354	72	512	1,453	68

FOR 40 YEARS, AL LOPEZ HELD the major league record with most games as a catcher, with 1,918. He applied the lessons he learned behind the plate to become one of the best managers in history.

Alfonso Raymond Lopez (born in 1908) got his first taste catching big leaguers by catching Walter Johnson in an exhibition game in 1925. Lopez turned professional in 1926, and he made it to Brooklyn by 1930. He was a natural leader and often found himself named team captain. He was a well-respected defender, field leader, and handler of pitchers. He also had the opportunity to have as major league managers six men who became Hall of Famers (Al would join them in 1977).

Al went to Indianapolis of the American Association as a player-manager in 1948 and won 100 games and a pennant in his first season. He also guided Indianapolis to second-place finishes in 1949 and 1950. He was moved up to Cleveland under difficult circumstances, being hired by Bill Veeck and Hank Greenberg to replace the popular Lou Boudreau.

Lopez finished first or second in each of his first nine seasons as a major league skipper. He drove the Indians to second in '51. The Tribe again finished in second place in 1952 and 1953 to the Yankee juggernaut.

In 1954, however, Lopez steered Cleveland and its dominating rotation of Early Wynn, Bob Lemon, Mike Garcia, and Bob Feller to an AL record 111 wins. Relievers Ray Narleski and Don Mossi closed the door. The Cleveland offense featured Al Rosen and Larry Doby. The heavily favored Indians were swept in the Series, however, by a good Giants squad. Little-known New York pinch-hitter Dusty Rhodes hit two homers—and Willie Mays made "The Catch," an over-the-shoulder snare of a 460-foot drive by Cleveland's Vic Wertz.

Lopez managed the Indians to two more second-place finishes and resigned. In 1957, however, his friends Veeck and Greenberg were running the White Sox, and they persuaded Al to manage in Chicago. He immediately drove the ChiSox to replace the Indians as the runner-up to the Yankees, again by using strong pitching. With pitchers Billy Pierce and Dick Donovan on staff, the Sox added Wynn from the Indians, Bob Shaw, and Turk Lown to topple the Yankees in 1959. The "Go-Go" Sox offense included Luis Aparicio and Nellie Fox. Nonetheless, another unknown knocked off a Lopez-led team in the Series: Dodgers reliever Larry Sherry. Lopez managed for part of eight more seasons, retiring from the helm with 1,410 victories for a .584 winning percentage in 17 seasons.

Catcher
Brooklyn Dodgers 1928;
   1930-1935
Boston Braves 1936-1940
Pittsburgh Pirates
   1940-1946
Cleveland Indians 1947

Manager
Cleveland Indians
   1951-1956
Chicago White Sox
   1957-1965; 1968-1969

Top: Lopez tracks a pop fly. Lopez went behind the plate in 1,918 major league games, a record that stood until it was broken by Bob Boone. Left: Lopez was the only AL manager apart from Casey Stengel to win a pennant between 1949 and 1965. He took Cleveland to a flag in 1954, then led the '59 White Sox to their only pennant since 1919.

Major League Managing Totals				
W	L	T	PCT	G
1,410	1,004	11	.584	2,425

Major League Totals									
BA	G	AB	R	H	2B	3B	HR	RBI	SB
.261	1,950	5,916	613	1,547	206	42	52	652	46

WARREN CRANDALL GILES
DEVOTED 50 YEARS TO BASEBALL AS CLUB AND LEAGUE EXECUTIVE, INCLUDING 33 IN MAJOR LEAGUES. HEADED CINCINNATI REDS FROM 1937 TO 1951, CAPTURING PENNANTS IN 1939-40. NATIONAL LEAGUE PRESIDENT LONGER THAN ANY OTHER MAN - 18 YEARS FROM 1951 THROUGH 1969. PRESIDED OVER FRANCHISE SHIFTS TO PACIFIC COAST AND EXPANSION TO 12 CLUBS AND INTO CANADA AS N. L. ENJOYED UNPRECEDENTED PROSPERITY.

WARREN GILES SERVED AS National League president from 1951 to 1969. He was intimately involved in the development of the farm system, and later, the scouting and signing of African-American and Latin American players.

Warren Giles (1896-1979) was a native of Moline, Illinois, and a three-sport athlete in high school. He was an Army offer and was wounded in World War I. When he returned from the war, he went to a meeting of the stockholders of the Moline club in the Three-I League. The other shareholders at the meeting were so impressed by his aptitude that they named him president of

The gavel Giles wielded as National League president.

the club; Moline won a pennant in 1921. Cardinals president Branch Rickey admired Giles and hired him in 1925 to be the president of the Syracuse club in the International League. Giles worked for minor league teams in the St. Louis farm system for 11 seasons, winning four pennants and two championships.

In 1937, Giles was hired to replace Larry McPhail as the general manager of the cellar-dwelling Cincinnati Reds. His first task was hiring Bill McKechnie, and together they guided Cincy to a first-place finish in 1939 and a World Championship in 1940. Giles also restored the team to financial strength during his 16-year stint.

When commissioner Happy Chandler's term expired in 1952, the owners were deadlocked over a successor, either NL president Ford Frick or Warren. Giles withdrew his name in the interest of unity, and took Frick's vacant post as National League president.

Giles oversaw the moving west of the Boston Braves to Milwaukee in 1953. While that shift created some debate, it was nothing like the turmoil created in 1957 when the Dodgers moved from Brooklyn to Los Angeles and the Giants moved from New York to San Francisco. When Giles's old boss, Branch Rickey, proposed creating a rival Continental League with a franchise in New York, Giles moved to expand the NL and created the New York Mets and the Houston Astros.

Giles also tried his best to eliminate the bean ball, though little was accomplished. In 1965, Giles had to suspend Giants star pitcher Juan Marichal for eight days and fine him $1,750 for clubbing, with his bat, Dodger catcher Johnny Roseboro on the head. Many new stadiums and new stars entered the National League during Giles's administration. His support of Latin scouting gave the NL a huge boost in the acquisition of talent. Warren was inducted into the Hall of Fame in 1979.

Giles (right) served as National League president for 18 years. A frequent critic of umpires while with the Reds, Giles became a staunch defender of arbiters after he assumed his new duties.

HOYT WILHELM BLAZED THE way for the modern relief specialist, and was the first career reliever to enter the Hall of Fame. He got into more games than any pitcher in history, and retired with more relief wins than any other major leaguer.

James Hoyt Wilhelm (born in 1923) was a native of Huntersville, North Carolina. He grew up listening to radio broadcasts of the Senators, and he became a fan of Washington pitcher Dutch Leonard, who was one of the first pitchers to rely almost exclusively on the knuckleball. Wilhelm studied a 1939 newspaper article describing the mechanics of throwing the pitch and eventually became a master. He was successful in his first pro season with Mooresville in the North Carolina League in 1942, but World War II intervened. Wilhelm served three years and saw action in the Battle of the Bulge.

A winner of the Purple Heart, Wilhelm returned to Mooresville in 1946, had two good seasons, and moved to the South Atlantic League in 1948. He was bombed, but returned the next season and mastered the circuit. He moved up to Minneapolis of the American Association in 1950. He stayed for two seasons, had a .500 record, and allowed four and one-half runs a game.

In 1952, Hoyt made the Giants as a reliever. He burst out of nowhere to lead the National League with 71 games pitched, 15 relief wins, a 2.43 ERA, and an .833 winning percentage. He had 11 saves that season. On April 23, during the first at bat in his career, he smashed a home run. In his second at bat, he smacked a triple. When he retired 21 seasons later, he had totaled one career home run and one career triple. He led the league in appearances in 1953, and he notched 15 saves. In 1954, he had a 2.10 ERA and a league-best 12 relief wins as the Giants won the World Series. Wilhelm recorded a save in the Series, the only postseason appearance in his career.

Wilhelm stayed in the majors until he was age 49. From 1962 to 1968, he posted ERAs below 2.00 six times. In his long career he had just 52 starts, most of which came with Baltimore from 1959 to 1960. He had a no-hitter in 1958 and led the AL with a 2.19 ERA as a starter in 1959. He had a career-high 27 saves for the 1964 White Sox.

Like many pioneers, Wilhelm's career save totals and other career records are likely to be eclipsed by those who follow him. But it will be only the outstanding relievers who can follow him into the Hall of Fame. He was inducted in 1985.

Pitcher
New York Giants
    1952-1956
St. Louis Cardinals 1957
Cleveland Indians
    1957-1958
Baltimore Orioles
    1958-1962
Chicago White Sox
    1963-1968
California Angels 1969
Atlanta Braves
    1969-1970; 1971
Chicago Cubs 1970
Los Angeles Dodgers
    1971-1972

Top: In 1952, Wilhelm became the first hurler in major league history to win an ERA crown without pitching a single complete game. Wilhelm paced the NL that season with a 2.43 ERA that was fashioned in 71 mound appearances, all of them in relief. Seven years later he won an AL ERA crown as a starting pitcher. Left: The Atlanta uniform worn by Wilhelm in 1970.

			Major League Totals						
W	L	ERA	G	SV	IP	H	ER	BB	SO
143	122	2.52	1,070	227	2,254.0	1,757	632	778	1,610

Shortstop; first base
Negro League team
Kansas City Monarchs
1950; 1953
Major League team
Chicago Cubs 1953-1971

ERNIE BANKS'S REPUTATION AS a goodwill ambassador should not obscure his great playing ability. He was a fine fielding shortstop and a power hitter who had an unbridled enthusiasm for the game of baseball.

Born in 1931, Ernest Banks was a four-sport athlete in high school, but it was his play in a church-sponsored softball league that induced a scout for the semipro Amarillo Colts to sign Ernie at age 17, in 1948. Within two years, he made it to the Kansas City Monarchs, one of the strongest teams in the Negro Leagues. He played one season before he was drafted into the Army for a two-year stint.

After his discharge, Ernie played the 1953 season for the Monarchs. The major league teams were interested in Banks, but Monarchs owner Tom Baird refused to sell Ernie's rights to a minor league club, insisting that Banks go directly to the bigs. The Cubs relented, and Ernie, the first African-American on the Cubs, played in 10 games for Chicago that year.

Banks was the everyday shortstop in 1954, hitting .275 with 19 home runs and 79 RBI. In 1955, he batted .295 and clubbed 44 home runs, with five grand-slams, a single-season record he shares with Jim Gentile. Banks hit .285 with 43 homers in 1957. He was the first player from a sub-.500 team to be voted the league's Most Valuable Player, when he led the league with 47 home runs (the most ever by a shortstop) and 129 RBI in 1958. The following year he became the first player in the National League to win back-to-back MVP awards. Banks again led the league in RBI (143) and had 45 round-trippers. He led the NL with 41 homers in 1960.

Banks was a fine shortstop for nine seasons, winning a Gold Glove in 1960. His 105 double-play total in 1954 is still a rookie record. He was a nine-time All-Star. His move to first base in 1962 was brought on by knee injuries, not defensive shortcomings. He had 37 homers and 104 RBI that year.

Banks hit over 40 homers five times, and had over 100 RBI in eight seasons. He had over 80 RBI in 13 seasons. Although the Cubs failed to win a pennant during Ernie's 19-year career, he earned the title "Mr. Cub." He was well known for his love of the game, and his credo, "Nice day for baseball. Let's play two," has become part of baseball lingo. He remained a hero in Chicago after his retirement as a player, as he took up a new career in the Cubs' front office. Banks was inducted in 1977.

Top: Few noticed that Banks led all NL shortstops in assists and fielding average in 1959. It was Banks's slugging that captured everyone's attention. By notching 143 RBI, he set his second all-time slugging mark for shortstops in two seasons. Right: Banks's uniform. He played his entire career with the Cubs, but never saw postseason action.

Negro League Stats*

BA	G	AB	H	2B	3B	HR	SB
.255	53	196	50	11	1	1	3

Major League Totals

BA	G	AB	R	H	2B	3B	HR	RBI	SB
.274	2,528	9,421	1,305	2,583	407	90	512	1,636	50

*Note: Banks's Negro League career stats are incomplete.

AL KALINE

THERE IS A STORYBOOK QUAL-ity to the career of Al Kaline, who joined the Detroit Tigers as an 18-year-old boy and retired a 40-year-old legend. He hit for average, hit for power, was a near-perfect defensive player with an arm like a rocket. He is among the brightest—and best loved—in a galaxy of Detroit stars.

Albert William Kaline (born in 1934) was raised to be a baseball player; his grandfather, father, and uncles had all been semipro players. Al played on so many extracurricular teams that he would play three or four games on any given Sunday, changing uniforms in the car. All of that extra work paid off, though, because he hit .488 in his senior year in high school. Every team was interested in obtaining him, but he chose to sign with the Detroit Tigers, for $30,000.

Al never played an inning of minor league ball, since the bonus rule required that he stay on the big league roster for at least two years. He was tossed into his first big league game as a pinch-hitter the day he signed, right out of high school. He was a big league defender from day one, and he knew it: "The first time I went out to play with the outfielders I said, 'Hey, I'm as good as any of these guys. I can throw better than anybody here, and I can go get the ball with any of them.'"

Outfielder
Detroit Tigers 1953-1974

In Kaline's second full season, 1955, he proved he was also a major league hitter. He won the batting title that season, hitting .340 with a league-high 200 hits and 27 home runs. He established himself as a premier player, and finished a close second in the MVP vote to Yogi Berra. Al batted .314 in 1956, with 194 base hits, 27 homers, and a career-high 128 RBI.

As good as Kaline was—and he had some good teammates, too, like Norm Cash, Jim Bunning, and Rocky Colavito—the Tigers were only a mediocre team. In-season management changes were a regular occurrence. From 1957 to 1967, Kaline batted from .280 to .300, with 18 to 25 homers and 70 to 100 RBI.

The Tigers jelled in 1968, winning the pennant, but Kaline broke his leg and played in only 102 games. In the World Series, Tiger manager Mayo Smith gambled that outfielder Mickey Stanley could handle shortstop so Al could play right field. The gamble paid when Kaline batted .379, slugged .655, and drove in eight runs as the Tigers won their first World Championship since 1945. Kaline was inducted into the Hall of Fame in 1980.

Top: *Al's uniform. In 1955, Kaline became the youngest player in AL history to take the batting title when his .340 batting average paced the circuit.* Left: *Kaline is the only member of the 3,000-hit club who achieved all of his personal batting highs before he turned 25. As a fielder, however, Kaline only seemed to get better the longer he played.*

Major League Totals

BA	G	AB	R	H	2B	3B	HR	RBI	SB
.297	2,834	10,116	1,622	3,007	498	75	399	1,583	137

HARMON KILLEBREW

HARMON CLAYTON KILLEBREW
WASHINGTON A.L. 1954-1960
MINNESOTA A.L. 1961-1974
KANSAS CITY A.L. 1975
MUSCULAR SLUGGER WITH MONUMENTAL HOME RUN AND RBI SUCCESS. HIS 573 HOMERS OVER 22 YEARS RANK FIFTH ALL-TIME AND SECOND ONLY TO RUTH AMONG A.L. HITTERS. TIED OR LED A.L. IN HOME RUNS 6 TIMES, BELTED OVER 40 ON 8 OCCASIONS AND IS THIRD IN HOME RUN FREQUENCY. DROVE IN OVER 100 RUNS 9 TIMES. A.L. MVP IN 1969.

First baseman; third baseman; outfielder
Washington Senators
1954-1960
Minnesota Twins
1961-1974
Kansas City Royals 1975

This '54 Topps baseball card to the contrary, Killebrew's first position in the major leagues was second base.

THE TOP RIGHTHANDED HOME run hitter in AL history, Harmon Killebrew had over 40 home runs in eight seasons and over 100 RBI in ten seasons.

Born in 1936, Harmon Clayton Killebrew was an All-State quarterback in Idaho and semipro baseball star. When he was age 17, he was recommended to Clark Griffith of the Senators by Idaho Senator Herman Walker, who wanted to see his young constituent in the majors. Killebrew blasted a 435-foot homer for scout Ossie Bluege, who found out that Harmon was batting .847 with half of the hits being home runs. Bluege signed "Killer" immediately.

Killebrew was a bonus baby, and didn't get a chance to play full-time until 1959. Under the rules of the time, the Senators had to keep him in the bigs for two years, and he sat on the bench in 1954 and 1955, getting in only 47 games, and then spent most of the next three seasons in the minors. He was a third baseman when he came back up, and though he eventually played more games at first base than third, he had significant playing time at the hot corner until 1971. He eventually earned outstanding AL left fielder, third baseman, and first baseman honors from *The Sporting News.*

Killebrew's career high batting average as a regular came in 1961, an expansion year, when he hit .288.

Killer was ready when he played as a regular in 1959, leading the league with 42 home runs during his first full season, and hit 31 the next year, after which the Senators became the Minnesota Twins. A dead pull hitter, he hit 46 for his new fans in 1961, but that year Roger Maris went on his spree. Killebrew led the league in 1962, 1963, and '64, hitting 142 in the three seasons, and driving in 333 runs. The Twins rocketed to first place in 1965 with 102 wins, though Killer had one of his poorest years due to an elbow injury, and the Twins lost the World Series.

Killebrew had established himself as a major star with his consistent slugging, and won the AL MVP Award in 1969 when he hit 49 homers and drove in 140 runs, and drew 145 walks, leading the league with a .430 on-base average. His walk totals were impressive, and though he drew criticism for his less-than-impressive batting averages, his on-base averages were usually among the best in the league.

The Twins won the AL West its first two years of existence, but failed to return to the World Series. Knee problems began to slow Harmon, and after a final year with Kansas City as a designated hitter, he retired after the 1975 season. Harmon was inducted into the Hall of Fame in 1984.

HARMON KILLEBREW *1st base* WASHINGTON NATIONALS

			Major League Totals							
BA	**G**	**AB**	**R**	**H**	**2B**	**3B**	**HR**	**RBI**	**SB**
.256	2,435	8,147	1,283	2,086	290	24	573	1,584	19

WALTER ALSTON WAS AT THE helm of the Dodgers from their mid-1950s battles with the Yankees to their mid-1970s races with the Big Red Machine. Alston managed the Dodgers for 23 years, winning seven pennants and four World Series.

Walter Emmons Alston (1911-1984) was an infielder who played for Miami University in Ohio. He was signed by general manager Branch Rickey's Cardinal organization after he graduated in 1935, and he played two years before getting a single at bat at the end of the 1936 season with St. Louis. It was Alston's only major league at bat. He started his managerial career while still a player, with Portsmouth of the Mid-Atlantic League in 1940. Rickey hired Walt into the Dodger organization in 1944. Branch brought Alston along like he did players, allowing him to experience success at higher and higher levels. In 1946, Rickey chose Alston as one of two managers to manage black players by placing Don Newcombe and Roy Campanella on his Nashua, New Hampshire, team. From 1948 to 1953, Walt managed at the Triple-A level.

After winning two pennants in 1952 and '53 as the Brooklyn manager, Chuck Dressen was fired after demanding a multiyear contract. Alston

WALTER EMMONS ALSTON
SOFT-SPOKEN, LOW-PROFILE ORGANIZATION MAN WHO MANAGED THE DODGERS FOR 23 YEARS, LEADING TEAM TO ITS ONLY WORLD CHAMPIONSHIP IN BROOKLYN IN 1955 AND TO PENNANT IN 1956 BEFORE TEAM MOVED TO WEST COAST. IN LOS ANGELES HIS CLUBS WON WORLD TITLES IN 1959, 1963 AND 1965 AND PENNANTS IN 1966 AND 1974; AND ONLY JOHN McGRAW, WITH 10, TOPPED ALSTON'S SEVEN N.L. PENNANTS. TEAMS FINISHED IN FIRST DIVISION 18 TIMES, WINNING 2,040 GAMES.

Manager
Brooklyn Dodgers
1954-1957
Los Angeles Dodgers
1958-1976

was the surprise choice as Dressen's replacement, and Walt accepted one-year contracts for the next 23 years. In contrast to the other New York managers of the 1950s — Dressen, Leo Durocher, and Casey Stengel — Alston was a quiet, business-like man. As a field general, he was in control. He was a devotee of bunts, the hit-and-run, intentional passes, stolen bases, platooning, and pinch-hitters — involving his entire roster.

The Dodgers finished second in Alston's first season, 1954, and then won the pennant in 1955. For the first time in five tries, the Brooklyn nine finally beat the Bombers in the Series. The Dodgers also won the NL pennant in 1956. In 1958, the Dodgers first year in Los Angeles, the team finished seventh. O'Malley hired Dressen as a coach, and speculation flourished about Alston's imminent demise. Walt did his best managing job in '59, driving an insufficiently talented Dodger team to the championship.

Alston helped to rebuild the Dodgers along the lines of a team that he wanted to manage, emphasizing speed, defense, pitching, and more pitching. With Sandy Koufax and Don Drysdale taking the mound, the Dodgers won the World Championship in 1963 and again in '65, and the NL pennant in 1966. His teams went into a slight decline, rebounded by 1970, and challenged for the NL West crown each year until he retired in 1976. The Dodgers won the NL pennant in 1974. Alston was inducted in 1983.

Top: From 1950 through 1953, Alston piloted the Montreal Royals, the top Brooklyn farm team. He then moved up to the parent club in 1954. It was to be Alston's last stop after nearly 30 years of knocking around the minors. Left: He turned to managing in 1940 at age 28 when it grew clear to him that his progress as a player had ground to a halt.

Major League Managing Totals

W	L	T	PCT	G
2,040	1,613	5	.558	3,658

Pitcher
Brooklyn Dodgers
1955-1957
Los Angeles Dodgers
1958-1966

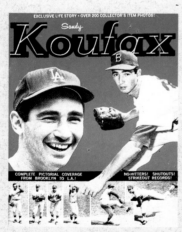

Koufax garnered his first NL winning percentage crown in 1964, the year this picture book of his career appeared. He also collected the third of his record five consecutive ERA titles.

SANDY KOUFAX PUT TOGETHER one of the most dominating stretches of pitching in baseball history. Over a five-year span, he led the NL in ERA five times and compiled a 111-34 record. However, arthritis forced him to retire at age 30.

Sanford Koufax was born in Brooklyn in 1935, and while he liked baseball, he was very interested in basketball. In 1953, he went to the University of Cincinnati on a basketball scholarship. He also pitched for the baseball team, and he had tryouts with several clubs interested in a lefty with such a great fastball. Late in 1954, he signed with his hometown Dodgers for $25,000, even though the Braves offered more. He knew that as a bonus baby he would have to serve his apprenticeship in the majors, and he thought he would more easily adjust at home.

Koufax started only five games in 1955, showing bursts of brilliance surrounded by intervals of wildness. His schooling continued for the next two seasons, when he got 10 and 13 starts and received much of his work out of the bullpen. The Dodgers moved to Los Angeles before the 1958 season, and Koufax posted an 11-11 mark with a 4.40 ERA in 26 starts and 40 appearances. He had 23 starts, an 8-6 mark, and a 4.05 ERA in 1959. He was 8-13 with a 3.91 ERA in 1960.

In spring training of 1961, catcher Norm Sherry advised Koufax to slow his delivery, to throw changeups and curveballs, and to relax. Following that advice, Sandy recorded his first record over .500, going 18-13 and leading the league in Ks with the eye-popping total of 269. In 1962, the Dodgers moved to Dodger Stadium. Sandy developed a frightening numbness in his left index finger. He could make just 26 starts; had he gone on he very well could have lost the finger. He was 14-7 with a league-leading 2.54 ERA that year, and pitched a no-hitter.

The 1963 season was his triumph. Sandy went 25-5, leading the NL with 25 wins, a 1.88 ERA, 11 shutouts, and 306 strikeouts. He won both the MVP and Cy Young awards. He tossed his second no-hitter, and won two games in the Dodgers' World Series victory. In 1964,

Koufax leaps for joy after recording the final out in the 1963 World Series. The Dodgers swept the Yankees in four games.

he was 19-5 with a league-best 1.74 ERA. That year, a deteriorating arthritic condition in his left arm first became conspicuous. He continued to pitch with the help of cortisone shots and ice for two more seasons, winning Cy Young awards in 1965 and '66. He had league-best ERAs of 2.04 and 1.73, and he won 26 and 27 games. He also tossed two more no-hitters, including a perfect game. He was inducted in the Hall of Fame in 1972.

Major League Totals

W	L	ERA	G	CG	IP	H	ER	BB	SO
165	87	2.76	397	137	2,324.1	1,754	713	817	2,396

DON DRYSDALE COMBINED A wicked fastball with a fierce demeanor to be one of the most intimidating hurlers of the period. He teamed with Sandy Koufax to form one of the most dominating strikeout duos in National League history, and one of the top lefty-righty duos of all time.

Donald Scott Drysdale (born in 1936) grew up in Van Nuys, California. He did not become a pitcher until he was a senior in high school because his father (who coached him in American Legion baseball) wanted to save his arm. He signed with the Dodgers in 1954, and he pitched two years in the minors, going 8-5 in the California League in 1954 and 11-11 in the International League in 1955.

Endorsement offers began to flood Drysdale after he led the majors in wins in 1962 with 25 and bagged the Cy Young Award.

Drysdale joined the Dodgers in 1956, where he was tutored in the fine art of pitching inside by Sal "The Barber" Maglie. Drysdale felt that "You've got to keep the ball away from the sweet part of the bat. To do that the pitcher has to move the hitter off the plate." The lesson took, and in 1957, he was 17-9 with a 2.69 ERA. The Dodgers moved to Los Angeles before the 1958 season, and Don fell to a 12-13 record with a 4.17 ERA. The next two seasons, he led the NL in strikeouts, notching 242 in 1959 and 246 in 1960.

There was an immediate impact on Don when in 1962 the Dodgers moved from the Los Angeles Coliseum to Dodger Stadium. He had been a good pitcher for three years, but in Chavez Ravine, he was a great pitcher. He went 25-9, leading the league in wins and strikeouts and earning the Cy Young Award. From 1962 to '65, he averaged over 21 wins per year as the Dodgers won two World Championships. "Big D" pitched some outstanding Series games, including a three-hit shutout in 1963, with nine Ks and just one walk. In 1965, Don not only went 23-12, but hit .300 with seven home runs, tying the NL record for pitchers.

During those four years, Koufax won three consecutive Cy Young awards, and he teamed with Drysdale in an unprecedented joint salary battle after the 1965 season. The two aces reportedly asked for over $1 million for a three-year contract that was to be split evenly between them, which would have made them each the highest paid players in baseball. They eventually settled for less money.

After 1965, Drysdale became less effective, and he retired after the 1969 season. In 1968, he hurled a record 58 2/3 consecutive scoreless innings. Don was elected to the Hall of Fame in 1984.

DONALD SCOTT DRYSDALE
BROOKLYN N.L. 1956-1957
LOS ANGELES N.L. 1958-1969
HARD-THROWING SIDE-ARMER NOTED FOR INTIMIDATING STYLE AND DURABILITY. HAD 209-166 RECORD WITH 2.95 ERA AND 2,486 STRIKEOUTS. LED N.L. IN STRIKEOUTS 3 TIMES AND HURLED 49 SHUTOUTS. WAS 25-9 IN 1962 AND WON CY YOUNG AWARD. THREW 6 SHUTOUTS IN A ROW IN 1968, SETTING RECORD WITH 58 CONSECUTIVE SCORELESS INNINGS. PITCHED IN RECORD 8 ALL-STAR GAMES.

Pitcher
Brooklyn Dodgers
1956-1957
Los Angeles Dodgers
1958-1969

In 1968, Drysdale hurled six straight shutout wins and 58 consecutive scoreless innings. He was in the broadcast booth when Orel Hershiser broke his record in 1988.

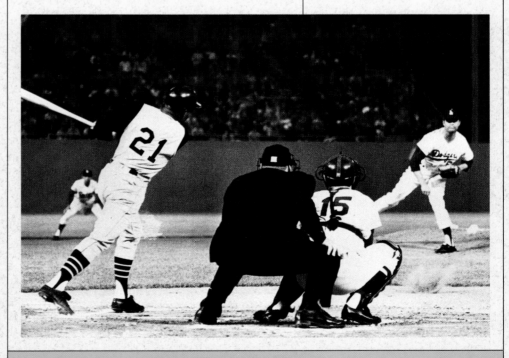

Major League Totals									
W	L	ERA	G	CG	IP	H	ER	BB	SO
209	166	2.95	518	167	3,432.1	3,084	1,124	855	2,486

ROBERTO WALKER CLEMENTE
PITTSBURGH N. L. 1955-1972

MEMBER OF EXCLUSIVE 3,000-HIT CLUB. LED
NATIONAL LEAGUE IN BATTING FOUR TIMES.
HAD FOUR SEASONS WITH 200 OR MORE HITS
WHILE POSTING LIFETIME .317 AVERAGE AND
240 HOME RUNS. WON MOST VALUABLE PLAYER
AWARD 1966. RIFLE-ARMED DEFENSIVE STAR
SET N.L. MARK BY PACING OUTFIELDERS IN
ASSISTS FIVE YEARS. BATTED .362 IN TWO
WORLD SERIES, HITTING IN ALL 14 GAMES.

Outfielder
Pittsburgh Pirates
1955-1972

ROBERTO CLEMENTE TOOK being a role model seriously, sending out 20,000 autographed pictures a year to kids. He had one of the strongest outfield arms in history, won four batting titles, and notched 3,000 base hits. On December 31, 1972, he was on a cargo plane from Puerto Rico airlifting emergency relief supplies, bound for earthquake-torn Nicaragua. The plane crashed a mile off of the Puerto Rico coast and there were no survivors. Clemente left behind his wife, three young sons, and millions of fans. He was elected to the Hall

This is the bat model that produced four National League hitting crowns in an seven-year period between 1961 and 1967.

of Fame in an extraordinary special election held just 11 weeks after his death; he was named on 93 percent of the ballots.

Roberto Clemente y Walker (1934-1972) grew up near San Juan, Puerto Rico. He developed his strength as a youngster by unloading grocery trucks and by squeezing a rubber ball. He started playing for a pennant-winning Santurce team in 1952. By age 19 his outfield mate was Willie Mays. In 1954, Clemente signed with the Dodgers, who attempted to hide him by assigning him to their top minor league club in Montreal and playing him sparingly. The Pirates unearthed him and drafted him in 1955.

Clemente joined the Pirates that year, and he was a good player for several years. By 1960, he began to emerge as a star, achieving personal bests in runs, home runs, RBI, and batting average. He hit .310 as the Pirates beat the Yankees in the World Series. He raised his game another notch in 1961, hitting .351, the first of five times he was to hit above .340.

No one who saw Clemente throw the ball could forget the power and accuracy of those throws. His arm was a deadly weapon that he could unleash from impossible angles and distances. He won Gold Gloves every year from 1961 through 1972.

Roberto won four batting titles, hit 240 homers, and was the National League Most Valuable Player in 1966. He has perhaps the greatest defensive reputation of any right fielder in history, playing more games in right field than any player in National League history.

Although Clemente was troubled by a bad back, bone chips, and shoulder troubles throughout his career, he posted the highest batting average for the decade of the 1960s with a .328 mark. Clemente hit .312 in 1972, at age 38, and rapped his 3,000th hit on September 30, becoming just the 11th man to reach that level. Clemente felt a duty to his fans, particularly his countrymen. He once said, "A country without idols is nothing." Clemente was an idol for many people in many countries.

Clemente hammers a home run off Baltimore's Jim Palmer in game six of the 1971 World Series. Clemente led all hitters in the affair with a .414 batting average and 12 hits.

Major League Totals

BA	G	AB	R	H	2B	3B	HR	RBI	SB
.317	2,433	9,454	1,416	3,000	440	166	240	1,305	83

BROOKS CALBERT ROBINSON, JR.
BALTIMORE A.L. 1955-1977
ESTABLISHED MODERN STANDARD OF EXCELLENCE
FOR THIRD BASEMEN, SETTING MAJOR LEAGUE
RECORDS AT HIS POSITION FOR SEASONS (23),
FIELDING PCT. (.971), GAMES (2,870), PUTOUTS
(2,697), ASSISTS (6,205), AND DOUBLE PLAYS (618),
HIT 268 CAREER HOME RUNS. NAMED TO 18
CONSECUTIVE ALL STAR TEAMS. MVP OF 1970
WORLD SERIES. AMERICAN LEAGUE MVP IN 1964.

Third baseman
Baltimore Orioles
1955-1977

BROOKS ROBINSON REVOLU-tionized the third base position. He was a soft-handed, accurate-armed man who did with reflexes and intelligence what can't be accomplished with just quickness and a strong arm. He won the Gold Glove 16 times and earned 15 straight All-Star Game starting assignments. Upon his retirement, Robinson held almost every major fielding record for third basemen, including most games (2,870), highest fielding average (.971), most putouts (2,697), most assists (6,205), and most double plays (618).

Born in Little Rock, Arkansas, in 1937, Brooks Calbert Robinson was discovered while playing second base in a church league. The Orioles signed him in 1955 and brought him up after he hit .331 in the Piedmont League. He hit .091 with Baltimore that year. He split several more seasons between Baltimore and the minors, and by 1960 was the regular Oriole third baseman. For the next four years, he was not a stellar offensive performer, but a very respectable one, hitting for decent average and some power. He had a .303 batting average and 23 home runs in 1962.

In 1964, Robinson batted .317 with a career-high 28 homers and a league-leading 118 RBI. His offensive production, as well as his sterling glove work that year, earned him AL MVP honors, though the Orioles finished third. Frank Robinson joined the Orioles in 1966, and Baltimore went on to its first World Series.

Brooks hit .269 with 23 homers and 100 RBI that year. In 1968, Earl Weaver became the Orioles manager, and Brooks had the chance to star for a team that would finish first or second in eight of the next nine years.

Robinson's work in the 1970 World Series earned him MVP honors; he hit .583 in the ALCS, and .429 in the fall classic with two homers and a highlight reel full of defensive gems. The vanquished Reds nicknamed him "Hoover" after the affair, expounding on his tag of the "human vacuum cleaner."

Robinson was the Orioles regular third baseman for 19 years. In 23 big league seasons, he had over 20 homers six times, and had over 80 RBI eight times. He collected 2,848 hits, 268 home runs, and 1,357 RBI. Though he topped the .300 mark only twice, his career average was .267. He led American League third basemen in fielding average in 11 seasons, including five years and then four years consecutively. He also led circuit hot corner men in assists eight times, putouts and double plays three times, and total chances per game twice. After retiring in 1977, he became a baseball broadcaster in Baltimore. Personable and very popular among baseball fans everywhere, Robinson's induction into the Hall of Fame in 1983 drew one of the largest crowds ever.

Top: *Robinson scored his first run for the Baltimore Orioles in 1956 and his 1,232nd and last regular-season tally in 1977.* Above: *No player will ever again wear No. 5 for the Orioles and the probability is that no one ever again will play 23 seasons in a Baltimore uniform.*

Major League Totals

BA	G	AB	R	H	2B	3B	HR	RBI	SB
.267	2,896	10,654	1,232	2,848	482	68	268	1,357	28

LUIS ERNESTO APARICIO
CHICAGO A.L. 1956-1962, 1968-1970
BALTIMORE A.L. 1963-1967
BOSTON A.L. 1971-1973
REGULAR SHORTSTOP FOR ALL OF HIS 18 SEASONS.
SET MAJOR LEAGUE CAREER RECORDS FOR MOST
GAMES (2,581), ASSISTS (8,016), CHANCES ACCEPTED
(12,564) AND DOUBLE PLAYS (1,553) BY A SHORTSTOP;
AND HAS MOST A.L. PUTOUTS (4,548). LED A.L. IN
FIELDING 8 TIMES. TOPPED LEAGUE IN STEALS
HIS FIRST 9 SEASONS. BEGINNING STOLEN BASE
RENAISSANCE. A.L. ROOKIE OF THE YEAR IN 1956.

Shortstop
Chicago White Sox
 1956-1962; 1968-1970
Batimore Orioles
 1963-1967
Boston Red Sox 1971-1973

WHILE SHORTSTOP LUIS Aparicio was patrolling American League infields from the mid-1950s to the 1970s, he was widely regarded as one of the best fielders at that position that the game has ever seen. Along with White Sox teammate Nellie Fox Luis formed one of the best keystone combinations in baseball history.

Luis Ernesto Aparicio y Montiel was born in 1934 in Maracaibo, Venezuela, to one of the most highly regarded baseball players in that country's history. Luis Aparicio Sr. was the best shortstop in Venezuela for 25 years, and he passed on his skill to his son. Luis Jr. took over his father's position on the town team in 1953, and was signed by the Chicago White Sox in '54.

"Little Looie" so impressed the White Sox during his two years in the minors that the White Sox traded their starting shortstop, Chico Carrasquel (also a Venezuelan native), to make room for Aparicio in 1956. He made an immediate impact on the league, hitting .266 with a league-best 21 stolen bases and winning the Rookie of the Year Award.

Aparicio was also the catalyst of a "Go-Go Sox" team that challenged the Yankees dominance in the 1950s. After being a runner-up for several years, the Sox finally won the flag in 1959. They finished dead last in home runs but first in steals. All-Star Aparicio teamed with keystone partner Nellie Fox as each led the league at their positions in putouts, assists, and fielding percentage. Fox won the Most Valuable Player Award, and Luis was second in the voting.

Aparicio's 56 steals in 1959 (his previous best was 29) not only led the league, but represented a new level of performance for Luis, a level that left the rest of the league in the dust. He posted totals of 51, 53, 31, 40, and 57 over the next five seasons, but only one rival was able to swipe more than 30 during the same span. He won nine consecutive stolen base titles, a record that has never been broken. Along with Maury Wills of the Dodgers, Aparicio was a vanguard of an emerging generation that relied on speed.

Aparicio was unparalleled as a defensive player. He played more games at shortstop (2,581), was involved in more double plays (1,553), and threw out more men than any shortstop in history. He had more assists than any other shortstop and won nine Gold Gloves in three decades. He led AL shortstops in fielding average in eight seasons, assists seven times, and putouts four times. Luis was inducted into the Hall of Fame in 1984.

Top: Aparicio clearly was born to play shortstop, so much so that he never performed for a single inning at any other position in his 20-year professional career. Right: This is the union suit Aparicio wore in 1969 as a member of one of the franchise's poorest nines. Only the expansion Seattle Pilots prevented the Sox from finishing in the AL West basement.

Major League Totals

BA	G	AB	R	H	2B	3B	HR	RBI	SB
.262	2,599	10,230	1,335	2,677	394	92	83	791	506

FRANK ROBINSON

FRANK ROBINSON CINCINNATI N.L., BALTIMORE A.L., LOS ANGELES N.L., CALIFORNIA A.L., CLEVELAND A.L., 1956-1976 FIRST TO BE CHOSEN MOST VALUABLE PLAYER IN BOTH LEAGUES -- N.L. IN 1961 AND A.L. IN 1966. SET RECORDS BY HITTING HOMERS IN 32 DIFFERENT PARKS AND WITH PAIR OF GRAND-SLAMMERS IN SUCCESSIVE INNINGS IN 1970. FOURTH IN HOMERS (586), FIFTH IN EXTRA BASES ON LONG HITS (2,450), SIXTH IN TOTAL BASES (5,373). ON RETIRING LED N.L. IN SLUGGING PCT. IN 1960-61-62 AND A.L. IN BATTING, HOMERS, RUNS BATTED IN, TOTAL BASES AND SLUGGING PCT. IN 1966.

Outfielder
Cincinnati Reds 1956-1965
Batimore Orioles
  1966-1971
Los Angeles Dodgers 1972
California Angels
  1973-1974
Cleveland Indians
  1974-1976

Top: *In his rookie season, Robinson topped the senior loop in being hit by pitches.* Below: *Only once in his career, in '66, was he a homer champ, but he was so consistent that he hit 15 or more dingers for 19 straight years.*

FRANK ROBINSON HOLDS TWO distinctions; he was the first player to win Most Valuable Player awards in both leagues and was the first African-American manager in major league baseball.

Born in 1935, Frank Robinson signed with the Cincinnati Reds in 1953, after a career as a three-sport star at Oakland's McClymonds High School, where he played with Curt Flood and Vada Pinson (both of whom were signed by the Reds). That year with Ogden of the Pioneer League, Frank batted .348 with 17 homers and 83 RBI in 72 games. He led the '54 Sally League with 112 runs scored while batting .336 with 25 homers and 110 RBI.

By 1956, Robinson was with Cincinnati and won the Rookie of the Year Award by leading the league with 122 runs and hitting .290 with an NL-rookie-record-tying 38 homers. He was a fine defensive outfielder, winning a Gold Glove in 1958, and was very quick on the bases. He produced similar offensive stats from 1957 to 1960, solidifying his position as one of the top outfielders in the National League.

Frank led the Reds to a pennant in 1961, leading the league with a .611 slugging percentage. He also batted .323 with 37 homers, 117 runs scored, 124 RBI, and 22 stolen bases. He was named National League MVP. He led the NL with a .624 slugging percentage in 1962, the

third consecutive season he led the circuit in that category. He also led the league with 51 doubles and 134 runs scored. He had his worst season statistically as a Red in 1963, when he hit .259 with 21 homers and 91 RBI in 140 games.

In 1966, when Robinson was 30, the Reds traded him to the Orioles. Reds general manager Bill DeWitt said, "Robinson is not a young 30 years of age." All he did was win the Triple Crown, became the only man to win MVP awards in both leagues, and hit .286 with two homers as the O's beat the Dodgers in the 1966 World Series. In 1968, Earl Weaver took the helm in Baltimore and they won three straight pennants and another championship in 1970. Robinson displayed outstanding skills as a team leader as well as playing fine baseball. In 1972 he was traded to the Dodgers, and he hit 30 homers and drove in 97 runs for the Angels in 1973.

In 1974, Robinson went to the Cleveland Indians on waivers, and in '75 became the first African-American manager in baseball as player-manager of the Indians. He batted over .300 nine times, had over 30 homers 11 times, and had over 100 RBI in six seasons. Only Babe Ruth, Willie Mays, and Hank Aaron socked more homers. Robinson was inducted into the Hall of Fame in 1982.

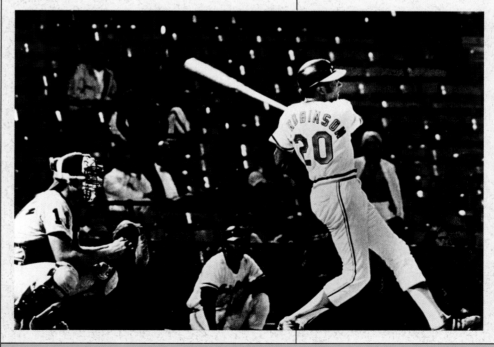

Major League Totals										
BA	G	AB	R	H	2B	3B	HR	RBI	SB
.294	2,808	10,006	1,829	2,943	528	72	586	1,812	204

WILLIE McCOVEY

WILLIE LEE McCOVEY
"STRETCH"
SAN FRANCISCO, N.L. 1959-1973, 1977-1980
SAN DIEGO, N.L. 1974-1976
OAKLAND, A.L. 1976
TOP LEFT-HANDED HOME RUN HITTER IN N.L.
HISTORY WITH 521. SECOND ONLY TO LOU GEHRIG
WITH 18 CAREER GRAND SLAMS LED N.L. IN HOMERS
THREE TIMES AND RBI'S TWICE. N.L. ROOKIE OF
YEAR IN 1959, MVP IN 1969 AND COMEBACK PLAYER
OF THE YEAR IN '77 TEAMED WITH WILLIE MAYS
FOR AWESOME 1-2 PUNCH IN GIANTS' LINEUP.

First baseman
San Francisco Giants
  1959-1973; 1977-1980
San Diego Padres
  1974-1976
Oakland Athletics 1976

Top: *When McCovey collected 137 free passes in 1970, he tied Roy Cullenbine's major league record for the most walks in a season by a first baseman.*
Right: *This is one of the last uniform jerseys worn by the most popular player ever to perform for the San Francisco Giants.*

T HE "OTHER" WILLIE ON THE 1960s San Francisco Giants, Willie McCovey was one of the great sluggers of the decade, averaging 30 homers each year and leading the league in round-trippers three times and homer percentage four times.

Willie Lee McCovey (born in 1938) was such an outstanding baseball player that as a youngster he played on men's teams in his Mobile, Alabama, hometown. He was signed by the Giants in 1955, and led the Georgia State League with 113 RBI, in 113 games. He made it to the Pacific Coast League by 1958, where the first baseman hit .319 with 89 RBI that year. While that performance should have earned him a spot in San Francisco out of spring training in 1959, he was assigned to the PCL again; the Giants had '58 NL Rookie of the Year Orlando Cepeda playing first base. After McCovey batted .372 with a league-best 29 homers and 92 RBI in 95 PCL games in 1959, he was called up to San Francisco. In the last 52 games of the '59 season, Stretch belted 13 homers with a .354 average and was named NL Rookie of the Year.

In 1960, however, McCovey's performance took such a dive he was returned to the minors. In 1961 and '62 he hit pretty well, socking a combined 38 home runs in about a season's worth of at bats. But in the same two years, Cepeda hit 81 homers with 256 RBI. They were both first basemen—and unsatisfactory outfielders—but they took their turns at first and in the field until Cepeda's knee injury in 1966 prompted his trade to St. Louis.

The Giants won the pennant in 1962. In the ninth inning of the seventh game, McCovey was at bat with the winning run on second. He hit a line drive—"the hardest ball I ever hit," he said—directly at Yankee second baseman Bobby Richardson. A hit to either side would have given the Giants a championship, and Stretch would have been the hero. Unfortunately, a World Series victory never came. In 1971, the Giants lost to the Pirates in the NLCS, though Willie hit .429 with two homers. McCovey won the National League MVP Award in 1969, the middle year in a three-year span of outstanding production. He led the circuit in slugging percentage from 1968 to '70.

Stretch, as popular as he was, was traded to the Padres in 1974, where he spent most of three seasons. In 1977, he returned to the Giants, and had one more good season, batting .280 with 28 homers and winning NL Comeback Player of the Year. He tied Ted Williams on the all-time home run list with 521. Willie was elected to the Hall of Fame in 1986.

						Major League Totals				
BA	G	AB	R	H	2B	3B	HR	RBI	SB
.270	2,588	8,197	1,229	2,211	353	46	521	1,550	26

JUAN MARICHAL WON MORE games than any pitcher during the 1960s, with 191. In addition, he was the greatest control pitcher of his time—he walked just 709 men in over 3,500 innings—with a delivery that defied logic. The timing oddities and whirl of motion that resulted from his high-kick windup baffled hitters for 16 seasons.

Juan Antonio Marichal y Sanchez (born in Laguna Verge, Dominican Republic in 1937) as a youngster learned to pitch using a homemade baseball. He gleaned enough to be signed by the Giants in 1958. He led the Midwest League in 1958 with 21 wins and a 1.87 ERA, and he led the Eastern League in '59 with 18 wins and a 2.39 ERA. In half a season at Tacoma of the Pacific Coast League, he was 11-5.

Called up to San Francisco in 1960, Marichal was immediately an effective pitcher. He was 6-2 with a 2.66 ERA that year, and had his worst ERA of the decade in 1961 when he was 13-10 with a 3.89 ERA. In 1963, Marichal led the league in wins, going 25-8. That year he lost to Sandy Koufax's no-hitter, but Marichal won his next start by no-hitting Houston. He also encountered Warren Spahn, each going all the way in a 16-inning Giants win. It was the first of six 20-win seasons in seven years for "Manito," each season posting ERAs under 3.00.

On August 22, 1965, with the Dodgers and the Giants in a tight pennant race, Marichal

was pitching against Koufax. That historic feud erupted in a brawl two days earlier. Juan had thrown a couple of purpose pitches, and when Dodger catcher John Roseboro asked Koufax to dust Marichal, Sandy refused. Marichal, apparently convinced that Roseboro's return throw to Koufax came too close to hitting him in the ear, took the bat and cracked the Dodger receiver in the head a couple of times. The benches emptied, erupting into one of the most vicious brawls in baseball history. Willie Mays played peacemaker, leading Roseboro from the fray, his uniform stained with Roseboro's blood. Marichal was suspended and fined, and since the Giants finished just two games back, his absence was costly.

The incident may have prevented Marichal from doing better in awards voting ("The Dominican Dandy" never won a Cy Young Award), as well as his Hall of Fame induction, for which Roseboro campaigned. Juan was inducted in 1983. He was one of the best righthanders of the 1960s, finishing in the top three in wins five times and ERA three times. He was particularly tough on the Dodgers, beating them in 37 of 55 lifetime decisions. He spent his last season, however, with the '75 Dodgers.

Pitcher
San Francisco Giants
1960-1973
Boston Red Sox 1974
Los Angeles Dodgers 1975

Left: Marichal's autograph graces this copy of the June 10, 1966, issue of Time. *He was also the most underappreciated righty. Though he notched 25 or more victories on three occasions, he never won a Cy Young Award.* **Top:** *Marichal kicked his lead leg higher than any other successful pitcher in modern times.*

			Major League Totals						
W	**L**	**ERA**	**G**	**CG**	**IP**	**H**	**ER**	**BB**	**SO**
243	142	2.89	471	244	3,509.1	3,153	1,126	709	2,303

Pitcher
St. Louis Cardinals
1959-1975

This is a ticket to the game in which Gibson fanned a World Series-record 17 Tigers on the way to a five-hit shutout.

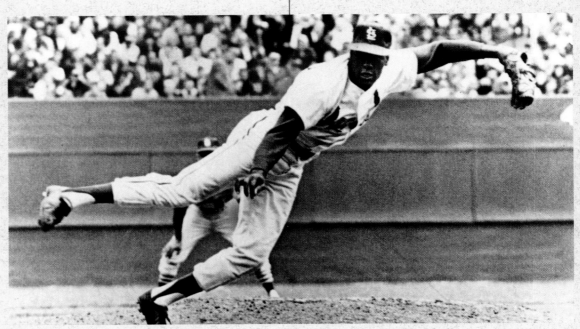

In 1968, Gibson had the most dazzling season of any pitcher since the dead-ball era.

IN THE 1960s, WHEN POWER pitchers ruled the game, there were few as as dominant as Bob Gibson. He was among the most exciting and successful of World Series performers, setting records and winning championships for the St. Louis Cardinals.

Robert Gibson (born in 1935) grew up in the slums of Omaha, Nebraska, and overcame a heart murmur and asthma as a child to become an outstanding athlete in both baseball and basketball. The Kansas City Monarchs offered him a contract after his high school graduation, but he turned it down to play both sports at Creighton University. The Cardinals signed him to a contract in 1957, and he played an unimpressive season in their farm system. After the season, he played basketball with the Harlem Globetrotters, which he did for only one year. From 1957 to 1960, he was generally unimpressive on the mound, and he didn't receive many starts. In 1961, Johnny Keane became the Cardinals manager, and he put Gibson in the starting rotation to stay.

Though Bob led the league in walks that year, he won 13 games. The following season he struck out 208 hitters, the first of nine seasons of 200-plus Ks—on his way to the record for strikeouts during the decade. In 1963, he went 18-9. In 1964, he was 19-12 and led the Cardinals to a World Series.

Gibson was intimidating in World Series play, winning a National League record seven games and losing only two as the Cards won two World Championships, in 1964 and 1967, and lost one in 1968. He won two games in the 1964 fall classic, and notched an ERA of 1.00 while winning three games in 1967.

In 1968, Gibson won both the MVP and Cy Young awards (as did Denny McLain in the AL), helping to prompt a lowering of the mound and a reduced strike zone. His record was 22-9, with a NL-record 1.12 ERA, and a league-best 268 strikeouts. He pitched 13 shutouts, and one-fifth of all his decisions were shutouts. In the World Series that year, he had a single-game record 17 strikeouts.

Pride played a role in Gibson's character and his success. He had to stay in a private home during his first spring training in 1958, and the struggle to overcome racial barriers stayed with him. He helped force the Cardinals' Florida hotels to accept black players in the early 1960s.

Gibson won another Cy Young in 1970 for his 23-7 showing. He had over 20 wins in five seasons, and had double figures in 14 consecutive years. He was a tremendous athlete, with 24 lifetime home runs and nine consecutive Gold Gloves. Gibson was inducted in 1981.

Major League Totals

W	L	ERA	G	CG	IP	H	ER	BB	SO
251	174	2.91	528	255	3,884.2	3,279	1,258	1,336	3,117

A signed Yaz shirt. Playing for 23 years helped him to notch 3,419 career hits but diminished his career batting average.

A GREAT HITTER FOR SEVERAL seasons and a very good hitter for many years, Carl Yastrzemski performed the impossible: replacing Ted Williams.

Carl Michael Yastrzemski (born in 1939) grew up in Southampton, New York, the son of an amateur baseball player. Carl played shortstop beside his third baseman father on the local team, and when Carl was age 18, he was pursued by several pro teams. He spurned them to attend Notre Dame in 1958, but after one year he decided that he wanted to turn professional. He visited a Yankee tryout camp and felt that he wasn't treated well, so he signed with the Red Sox. In 1959, he led the Carolina League with a .377 batting average, and in 1960 led the American Association with 193 base hits.

Williams retired after the 1960 season, and Yaz was moved into his left field spot. He batted .266 in his first season in '61, and improved to a .296 batting average and 94 RBI in his sophomore year. He won his first batting title in 1963 with a .321 average, and showed good power and a good eye. In 1965, he led the AL with a .536 slugging percentage and 45 doubles, and in '66 led the circuit with 39 doubles.

The Red Sox, a ninth-place team in 1966, won the pennant on the last day of the 1967 season, in the tightest race in American League history. Yaz won the Triple Crown that year, hitting .326 with a career-best 44 homers and 121 RBI, the last man to win a Triple Crown. He hit .522 with five home runs and 22 RBI in the final two weeks of the season. He was devastating in the final series against the Twins, going 7-for-8 and playing stellar defense. He was named the AL MVP. In the World Series, he hit .400 with three homers, but the Sox lost in seven.

In 1968, Carl won the batting title with the lowest average ever, at .301. In 1969 and 1970 he hit 40 homers. Aside from his Triple Crown season, he only hit as many as 28 one other time. He had an upright, distinctive stance, his bat almost straight up-and-down. Ted Williams said that Yaz "reminded me of myself at that age—I mean he positively quivered waiting for that next pitch." Yaz swung a potent bat for 23 seasons, patrolling left field expertly for the Red Sox as the master of the Green Monster.

Yastrzemski is the only AL player to get over 3,000 hits and 400 home runs, and when he retired, he had more at bats than any player other than Pete Rose. Carl was inducted into the Hall of Fame in 1989.

CARL MICHAEL YASTRZEMSKI
"YAZ"
BOSTON, A.L., 1961-1983
SUCCEEDED TED WILLIAMS IN FENWAY'S LEFT FIELD IN 1961 AND RETIRED 23 YEARS LATER AS ALL-TIME RED SOX LEADER IN 8 CATEGORIES. PLAYED WITH GRACEFUL INTENSITY IN RECORD 3,308 A.L. GAMES. ONLY A.L. PLAYER WITH 3,000 HITS AND 400 HOMERS. 3-TIME BATTING CHAMPION. WON MVP AND TRIPLE CROWN IN 1967 AS HE LED RED SOX TO "IMPOSSIBLE DREAM" PENNANT.

Outfielder; first baseman
Boston Red Sox 1961-1983

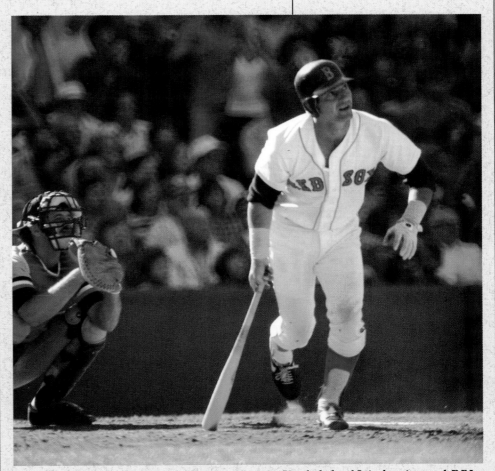

The last player to win a Triple Crown, in 1967, Yaz led the AL in batting and RBI and tied Harmon Killebrew for the home run title. His bat carried the Red Sox down the stretch for Boston's first flag since 1946.

Major League Totals

BA	G	AB	R	H	2B	3B	HR	RBI	SB
.285	3,308	11,988	1,816	3,419	646	59	452	1,844	168

CHAPTER SEVEN

New Frontier
Growth and Prosperity

I N THE FIRST YEAR OF DIVISIONAL PLAY, THE 1969 "Miracle Mets" won the World Championship seven years after having the worst record of any expansion club. The other three teams in the playoffs that year—Baltimore, Minnesota, and Atlanta—had shifted from their original locales.

The greatest shift in the way the game was played occurred in 1973, when the American League uni-laterally adopted the designated hitter. That year, the composite league batting average rose 20 points to .259. The following year, Hank Aaron became baseball's career home run king, Mike Marshall became the first relief pitcher to win the Cy Young, and Lou Brock broke Maury Wills's single-season stolen base record.

While records were falling on the field, players were reaping the benefits of a salary explosion fueled by arbitration and free agency. In 1976, an arbitrator's ruling regarding the option clause in the standard player's contract made free agency a reality. A new Basic Agreement between players and owners created a complex re-entry system granting free agency to veterans with more than six years of service. Bidding wars sparked by the advent of free agency sent baseball salaries on a steep upward spiral after 1976. The average major league salary had jumped from $34,000 in 1971 to $185,000 in 1980 and $597,537 in 1990. Mike Schmidt peaked at a perfect time. In the 1980s alone, Schmidt earned $17,076,738—more than the combined incomes of the five Presidents that held office during Mike's career.

Billy Williams's jersey as a member of the 1970s Oakland A's. He was the model of consistency. In his first 13 full seasons, he never collected fewer than 20 home runs or 84 RBI.

Opposite page: *Tom Seaver won three Cy Young awards and one-quarter of all Mets games from 1967 to 1977.* **Below:** *This is an autographed ball from Fergy Jenkins. With 284 career wins, he holds the record for the most victories by a pitcher born outside the United States.*

BILLY LEO WILLIAMS
CHICAGO, N.L. 1959 - 1974
OAKLAND, A.L. 1975 - 1976
SOFT-SPOKEN, CLUTCH PERFORMER WAS ONE OF MOST RESPECTED HITTERS OF HIS DAY. BATTED SOLID .290 OVER 18 SEASONS SOCKING 426 HOME RUNS. HIT 20 OR MORE HOMERS 13 STRAIGHT SEASONS. 1961 N.L. ROOKIE OF YEAR. 1972 N.L. BATTING CHAMPION WITH .333. HELD N.L. RECORD FOR CONSECUTIVE GAMES PLAYED WITH 1117.

Outfielder
Chicago Cubs 1959-1974
Oakland Athletics
1975-1976

Even though Williams stands no better than second in any of the Cubs' major career batting departments, many consider him the most valuable all-around offensive performer in the club's history.

BILLY WILLIAMS—WHO IS BEST remembered for his flawless swing—was a model of the quiet, consistent star. He established a National League record by playing in 1,117 consecutive games. He had more than 20 homers and more than 80 RBI in 13 consecutive seasons.

Billy Leo Williams was born in 1938 in Whistler, Alabama, which is near Mobile. His high school didn't have a baseball team, so when he was young he played with the semipro Mobile Black Bears, a farm team for the Negro Leagues that had prepared Hank Aaron in 1950. Williams was signed by the Cubs in 1956, and from 1957 to 1960 he rose steadily through the Cubs system, batting over .300 in four different minor leagues. In Houston of the American Association in 1960, Billy batted .323 with 26 home runs and 80 RBI. Rogers Hornsby, who was the batting instructor for the Chicago farm system, was so enamored of Billy's swing that he exhorted the Cubs to promote Williams.

The Cubs complied, installing Williams in the outfield in 1961 and his 25 homers and .278 average earned him NL Rookie of the Year

This button was handed out to Cubs fans who came out to Wrigley Field on "Billy Williams Day" in 1969.

honors. In his first seven seasons he struck out more than he walked, but over the final seven, the reverse was true. He never struck out more than 84 times in a season, and he drove in or scored more than 100 runs eight times. Advice and inspiration from Hornsby made Billy a more disciplined hitter. Willie Stargell called Williams's swing "poetry in motion," with its short arc and snapping wrists. From 1962 to 1969, he had from a .276 to .315 batting average, with 21 to 34 homers, 84 to 108 RBI, and 87 to 115 runs scored.

Although the Cubs had Ernie Banks, Ron Santo, and Ferguson Jenkins during much of Williams's career, the team never made it to postseason play. In 1970, Billy hit a career-high 42 homers and led the NL with 205 base hits and 137 runs scored. He also had 129 RBI, a .322 batting average, and a .586 slugging percentage. In 1972, he led the league with a .333 average and a .606 slugging average. He also had 37 homers, 95 runs scored, and 122 RBI. Both years he finished second to Johnny Bench in MVP voting, although Billy was named Player of the Year by *The Sporting News*

Williams batted over the .300 mark five times and topped 200 hits in a season three times. Traded to Oakland after the 1974 season, he was a designated hitter for the next two years. He popped 23 homers in 1975 to help the A's win their fifth straight divisional title. After the 1976 season, he retired to become a hitting instructor for the Cubs. Williams was elected to the Hall of Fame in 1987.

			Major League Totals							
BA	G	AB	R	H	2B	3B	HR	RBI	SB
.290	2,488	9,350	1,410	2,711	434	88	426	1,475	90

IN 1964, THE CHICAGO CUBS acquired Ernie Broglio, Bobby Shantz, and Doug Clemens from the Cards for Paul Toth, Jack Spring, and Lou Brock. Hitting .251 for the Cubs at the time of the trade, Brock went on to hit .348 the rest of the season, as the Cardinals overcame a six and one-half game deficit in two weeks to win the NL pennant. He hit .300 with a homer and five RBI in the 1964 World Series as the Cardinals won. Brock ruled left field in St. Louis for 15 more seasons.

Louis Clark Brock (born in 1939) was a lefthanded pitcher in high school, but he switched to the outfield when he went to Southern University in 1958. He played there for three seasons, then signed with the Cubs in 1961. He led the Northern League with a .361 batting average and 117 runs in 128 games that year, and was in Chicago to stay in 1962. He batted reasonably well in those two years, hitting .263 and .258 in 1962 and '63, with 73 and 79 runs scored, though he was an inferior outfielder.

In 1965, Lou scored 107 runs and stole 63 bases, while batting .288. He swiped an NL-high 74 bases in 1966, getting his first stolen base crown. Brock was an aggressive player, saying, "Base-running arrogance is just like pitching arrogance or hitting arrogance. You are a force, and you have to instill that you are a force to the opposition. You have to have utter confidence."

Lou led the Cards to two consecutive NL pennants in 1967 and '68. He led the NL with 113 runs in '67, and had a career-high 21 homers. In 1968, he led the circuit with 46 doubles and 14 triples. In each of those World Series, he hit over .400 and stole seven bases.

Brock stole 51 bases in 1970, but he didn't lead the league, losing out to Bobby Tolan. Lou led the NL from 1966 to 1969, and from 1971 to 1974. In 1970 and '71, he had more than 200 base hits and 100 runs scored a season, leading the NL with 126 in 1971. In 1974, a 35-year-old Brock stole 118 bases, breaking Maury Wills's 1962 single-season stolen base record of 104. Brock stole his 893rd base in 1977, breaking Ty Cobb's career record. When Lou turned in a .221 campaign in 1978, at age 39, he refused to retire on a down note. He returned for a final season in '79, batted .304 at age 40, earned his 3,000th hit, and stole 21 bases in 120 games. He ended his career with 938 stolen bases, and was

This is a jersey worn by Brock late in his career. He went out with a bang, hitting .304 in his major league finale.

present when Rickey Henderson broke both records. Brock earned eight stolen base titles, scored over 90 runs ten times, batted .300 in eight seasons, and had over 200 base hits four times. Lou was inducted in 1985.

LOUIS CLARK BROCK
CHICAGO N.L., 1961-1964
ST. LOUIS N.L., 1964-1979
BASEBALL'S ALL-TIME LEADER IN STOLEN BASES WITH 938. SET MAJOR LEAGUE RECORD BY STEALING OVER 50 BASES 12 TIMES AND N.L. RECORD WITH 118 STEALS IN 1974. LED N.L. IN STOLEN BASES 8 TIMES. COLLECTED 3,023 HITS DURING 19 YEAR CAREER AND HOLDS WORLD SERIES RECORD WITH .391 BATTING AVERAGE IN 21 POST-SEASON GAMES.

Outfielder
Chicago Cubs 1961-1964
St. Louis Cardinals
1964-1979

No player has ever exploded more unexpectedly into stardom after a trade than Brock. Sent to the Cards in mid-1964, he hit nearly 100 points higher in St. Louis (.348) than he had in Chicago (.251).

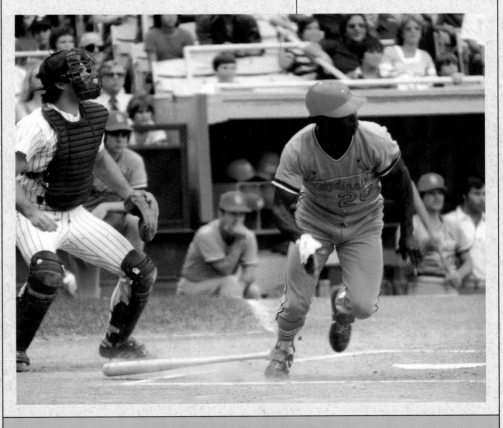

Major League Totals

BA	G	AB	R	H	2B	3B	HR	RBI	SB
.293	2,616	10,332	1,610	3,023	486	141	149	900	938

TOM YAWKEY

THOMAS AUSTIN YAWKEY

GAVE BASEBALL MORE THAN FOUR DECADES OF
DEDICATED SERVICE AS OWNER-PRESIDENT OF
BOSTON RED SOX FROM 1933 TO 1976. RATED
ONE OF SPORT'S FINEST BENEFACTORS. SET
PRECEDENT FOR A.L. IN 1936 AS FIRST TO
HAVE TEAM TRAVEL BY PLANE. HIS CLUB WON
PENNANTS IN 1946, 1967 AND 1975·· AND
NARROWLY MISSED IN 1948, 1949 AND 1972.
VICE-PRESIDENT OF A.L. FROM 1956 TO 1973.

THE DECLINE OF THE RED SOX that began with the sale of Babe Ruth to the Yankees in 1919 continued during the 1920s, and baseball interest in the Hub faded. In 1933, at age 30, Tom Yawkey bought the Red Sox for $1.5 million and spared nothing in his attempt to bring a World Championship to Boston. Although the Red Sox won pennants in 1946, 1967, and 1975, they lost each World Series in seven games.

Born Thomas Austin, Thomas Yawkey (1903-1976) was involved in baseball all his life. His grandfather, William Clyman Yawkey, was negotiating for the purchase of the Detroit Tigers when he died, in 1904. The sale was completed to Tom's uncle, William Yawkey. When Tom's father died, Uncle William adopted Tom; he eventually inherited the family lumber and mining business, which made him a millionaire.

After Yawkey bought the BoSox, he quickly hired Eddie Collins to oversee the baseball operations. Tom spent another $1.5 million to refurbish Fenway Park. Yawkey and Collins bought Lefty Grove, Joe Cronin, and Jimmie Foxx by 1936. Collins bought Bobby Doerr and Ted Williams on one scouting trip, and Boston finished second to the Yankees in 1938, 1939, 1941, and 1942. New manager Joe Cronin finally drove the team to a pennant in 1946.

Yawkey was very popular with his players and often worked out with them before games. He became so close to the Boston players and stars that he was often accused of "babying" them. Joe Cronin said Yawkey "was not only the team owner, he was the team's No. 1 fan." Though the team never triumphed, Yawkey revived the interest of the fans, who soon became (and remain) among the most devoted in the game. Yawkey reaped a full measure of enjoyment from his team, and from baseball.

The Red Sox' slow pace at signing black players cost them in the 1950s, and they were a fourth-place club most of the decade. In the 1960s, the bottom dropped out, and the Red Sox were generally lousy. In 1967, however, they went from ninth place to win the pennant. From that time, Boston was a solidly run franchise that never quite got over the top.

Yawkey was greatly respected by his peers in the baseball world, and from 1956 to 1973 he served as AL vice president. In 1980, four years after his death, the Veterans Committee elected him to the Hall of Fame. He was the sole owner of the Red Sox for 44 years, longer than anyone in baseball history. The Yawkey tradition lives on in the Red Sox organization, which was owned by Tom's widow Jean Yawkey until her death in 1992.

Right: *Yawkey and his wife Elise in 1936. Above: A Connie Mack and Yawkey autographed ball. One of Yawkey's first moves was to acquire Lefty Grove and Jimmie Foxx of Mack's A's. As a result, the Red Sox grew strong and remained so for the next two decades while the A's became a perennial doormat.*

WILLIE STARGELL WAS ONE OF the most potent power hitters of his time, performing as a mainstay of the Pittsburgh Pirates for 21 years, and retiring among the all-time leaders in home runs, slugging, and RBI.

Wilver Dornel Stargell (born in 1940) grew up in Alameda, California, and was a middle linebacker for his school's football team until he broke his pelvis in 1958. He signed with the Pirates in 1959, and he gradually increased his power through four stops in the Bucs' minor league chain. He hit .276 with 27 home runs and 82 RBI in 1962 with Columbus of the International League, and he was called up to Pittsburgh for good that year.

Stargell took over left field for the Bucs in '63 and had 11 homers and 47 RBI that year. Playing half his games in Forbes Field held down his power stats, but he still started a string of 13 straight 20-homer seasons in 1964, even though he played in only 117 games.

It was after the Pirates moved to Three Rivers Stadium in 1970 that the country took notice of Willie. After a good season in 1970—and a pennant for the Pirates—Stargell exploded in 1971. The Pirates won the pennant again, and Willie led the league with 48 homers and had 125 RBI, though he managed just a .208 average in the Series. The Pirates went back to the playoffs in 1972, 1974, and 1975. In 1973, he led the league with a .646 slugging percentage, 43 doubles, 44 homers, and 119 RBI. He is the only man to hit two balls out of Dodger Stadium, and his 269 homers were to be the most in the 1970s. But as his age started to catch up with him, his power began to wane. From 1974 through 1977, his home run totals fell steadily. In 1978, the 38-year-old "Pops" reached back, slugging .567 in 122 games with 28 homers and 97 RBI as the Pirates finished second.

In 1979, Stargell led the Bucs to the World Championship. Though he played in just 126 games, he hit 32 homers and .281, and then hit over .400 in the playoffs and Series with five homers. He tied with St. Louis first baseman Keith Hernandez in the voting for the NL MVP Award, and won both the NLCS and World Series MVPs. Willie was honored as much for his leadership as for his production. He was the leader of a team that was a family, as he encouraged the Pirates by example, drive, and handing out "Stargell Stars" to stick on their caps when they contributed to a victory. He suffered from a deteriorating arthritic condition and retired after the 1982 season. Willie was inducted in 1988.

Outfielder; first baseman
Pittsburgh Pirates
1962-1982

Above: *Stargell's No. 8 was retired by Pittsburgh in 1982.* Left: *Stargell seemed only to get better with age. Almost all of his most significant single-season achievements were achieved after he passed age 30. His most productive slugging season came in 1973 when he was 33 and six years later he became the oldest player ever to win an MVP Award.*

Major League Totals

BA	G	AB	R	H	2B	3B	HR	RBI	SB
.282	2,360	7,927	1,195	2,232	423	55	475	1,540	17

GAYLORD PERRY

GAYLORD JACKSON PERRY
SAN FRANCISCO, N.L. 1962-1971
CLEVELAND, A.L. 1972-1975
TEXAS, A.L. 1975-1977, 1980
SAN DIEGO, N.L. 1978-1979
NEW YORK, A.L. 1980
ATLANTA, N.L. 1981
SEATTLE, A.L. 1982-1983
KANSAS CITY, A.L. 1983
ACHIEVED PITCHERS' MAGIC NUMBERS WITH 314 WINS
AND 3,534 STRIKEOUTS. PLAYING MIND GAMES WITH
HITTERS THROUGH ARRAY OF RITUALS ON MOUND, WAS
PART OF HIS ARSENAL. 20-GAME WINNER 5 TIMES WITH
LIFETIME ERA OF 3.10. NO-HIT CARDS FOR GIANTS,
9/17/68. OUTSTANDING COMPETITOR. ONLY CY YOUNG WINNER
IN BOTH LEAGUES.

Pitcher
San Francisco Giants
   1962-1971
Cleveland Indians
   1972-1975
Texas Rangers 1975-1977;
   1980
San Diego Padres
   1978-1979
New York Yankees 1980
Atlanta Braves 1981
Seattle Mariners
   1982-1983
Kansas City Royals 1983

Above: Perry's travels took him to eight different major league teams in a dual quest for 300 wins and a World Series ring. Perry achieved the first goal but never the latter. In 1962, he pitched part of the season for the pennant-winning Giants but was not included on the team's World Series roster. Right: He reposes during a game in 1981.

GAYLORD PERRY—THE ONLY pitcher in history to have won the Cy Young Award in both leagues—fooled hitters and umpires for 22 years. He was an admitted proponent of the spitball, and entitled his autobiography *The Spitter and Me.* He contended that he rarely threw it, however, maintaining the idea that he might use a spitball was enough to put the hitter at a disadvantage. He heightened suspicion by his odd, herky-jerky delivery.

Gaylord Jackson Perry was born in 1938 in Williamston, North Carolina, the younger brother of Jim Perry by two years. Gaylord spent four years in the Giants' farm system, and he was first called to San Francisco in 1962 as a part-time starter. He was age 25 in 1964 when he became a regular starter, and he responded well, with a 2.75 ERA for the 1964 Giants. The next year his ERA ballooned to 4.19, but he rebounded with a 21-8 mark and a 2.99 ERA in 1966. He kept his ERA under 3.00 for four straight years, and he tossed a no-hitter in 1968 and led the league with 23 wins in 1970.

The Giants traded Perry to the Indians prior to the 1972 season (for Sam McDowell, on the way out by then). Perry responded by winning the Cy Young Award, at 24-16 with a 1.92

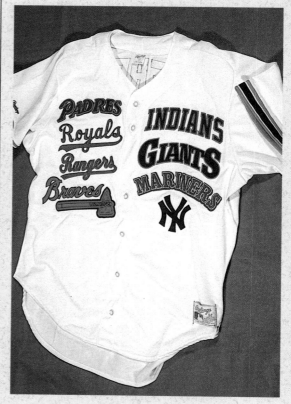

ERA. He was 19-19 in 1973, and in 1974 he was joined by his brother, Jim, on the Cleveland staff. Jim had pitched for the Tribe from 1959 to 1963, and in '74 he turned in a 17-12 record with a 2.96 ERA. Gaylord went 21-13 that year, and their 38 victories represented half of Cleveland's win total that year.

Although Gaylord won 70 games for Cleveland in just over three years, he was then traded to Texas. Three years later, he was traded back to the National League, and in 1978 he won the NL Cy Young Award with a 21-6 season for the Padres. Perry finally drew a suspension in 1979 for his foul play, then went calmly back to work. He kept moving, landing in Seattle in 1982, where he won his 300th game. He won his final four games for Kansas City in 1983 using a "puff ball" that had so much rosin on it that it billowed on its way to the plate.

Perry won 314 games with a remarkable 3.10 ERA, while playing on only one pennant-winning club. Jim had 215 career wins, and the brothers' 529 total was the highest until the Niekro brothers surpassed it in 1987. Gaylord's 3,534 strikeouts rank him No. 6 on the all-time list, and his 5,351 innings pitched are in history's top ten. Perry retired after the 1983 season and was elected to the Hall of Fame in 1991.

Major League Totals

W	L	ERA	G	CG	IP	H	ER	BB	SO
314	265	3.10	777	303	5,351	4,938	1,843	1,379	3,534

JOE MORGAN

LITTLE JOE MADE THE BIG RED Machine go. Joe Morgan is best remembered for being a catalyst for the World Champion Reds in 1975 and 1976. He also played more games at second base than anyone but Eddie Collins.

Joe Leonard Morgan was born in 1943 in Bonham, Texas, but his family moved to Oakland, California, when Joe was very young. His first hero was Jackie Robinson, but later Morgan emulated the play and the determination of Nellie Fox. After attending the same high school that produced Frank Robinson, Morgan signed with the Astros in 1963. In 1964, he was the Texas League MVP, batting .319 with 42 doubles, 12 homers, and 90 RBI.

In 1965, Morgan was the Houston second baseman. Houston coach Fox taught Joe a "chicken flap" of his left elbow while taking his batting stance, to remind him to keep his elbow high. The 5'7" second baseman hit .271 that year, with 14 home runs, 100 runs scored, and an NL-leading 97 bases on balls, and he finished second in Rookie of the Year voting to Los Angeles second baseman Jim Lefebvre. Joe notched 89 walks in 1966 despite missing time with a fractured knee cap. In 1968, he lost almost the whole season when he tore ligaments in his knee. He returned in 1969 to get 94 runs, had 102 runs in 1970, and 87 runs in 1971. The Astros and the Reds tied for fourth place in 1971, and each team was looking for a change. In one of the blockbuster trades of the decade, the Reds sent second baseman Tommy Helms and first baseman Lee May to Houston for outfielder Cesar Geronimo, pitcher Jack Billingham, and Morgan.

Second baseman
Houston Astros
  1963-1971; 1980
Cincinnati Reds
  1972-1979
San Francisco Giants
  1981-1982
Philadelphia Phillies 1983
Oakland Athletics 1984

When Joe got out of the Astrodome, his stats were enhanced. He hit 16 homers in 1972, 26 in '73, and 22 in 1974. His walk totals those three years were 115, 111, and 120, and he scored 122, 116, and 107 runs.

Morgan was the only second sacker in baseball history to be win back-to-back MVP awards, in 1975 and '76. In 1975, he batted .327 with 17 homers, 107 runs scored, 94 RBI, 67 stolen bases, and a league-best 132 bases on balls as the Reds won 108 games. Morgan batted .320 with 27 homers, 113 runs scored, 111 RBI, 60 swipes, and 114 walks in 1976.

Joe was a steady fielder and won five straight Gold Gloves from 1973 to '77. He led the Reds to another playoff berth in 1979. He then moved back to Houston in 1980, again appearing in the NLCS. In 1983, he joined the Phillies and appeared in his last World Series. Joe led the NL in walks four times and runs once. He never led the circuit in stolen bases, but he finished in the top three eight times. Joe was elected to the Hall of Fame in 1990.

Top: *Morgan was more than just the igniter of the 1970s Big Red Machine. In 1965, Morgan's first full season with Houston, he led the NL in walks as a rookie. Fifteen years later he returned to Houston for one season near the tag end of his career and again paced the NL in walks.* **Left:** *An Astros jersey worn by Joe Morgan.*

				Major League Totals					
BA	**G**	**AB**	**R**	**H**	**2B**	**3B**	**HR**	**RBI**	**SB**
.271	2,649	9,277	1,650	2,517	449	96	268	1,133	689

JAMES AUGUSTUS HUNTER
"CATFISH"
KANSAS CITY, A.L., 1965–1967
OAKLAND, A.L., 1968–1974
NEW YORK, A.L., 1975–1979
THE BIGGER THE GAME, THE BETTER HE PITCHED.
ONE OF BASEBALL'S MOST DOMINANT PITCHERS FROM
1970-76, WINNING OVER 20 FIVE STRAIGHT TIMES. COMPILED
224-166 MARK WITH 3.26 ERA BEFORE ARM TROUBLE
ENDED CAREER AT AGE 33. HURLED PERFECT GAME
VS. TWINS IN 1968. 1974 A.L. CY YOUNG AWARD WINNER.
5-3 IN 12 WORLD SERIES GAMES.

Pitcher
Kansas City Athletics
1965-1967
Oakland Athletics
1968-1974
New York Yankees
1975-1979

Top: For a five-year period in the early 1970s there was no better pitcher in the game than Hunter. Between 1971 and 1975, Catfish won 111 games, almost half of his 224 career total. Right: Hunter's uniform shirt in the early 1970s. The vest style was worn by the Oakland A's for several seasons over either green or gold undershirts.

JIM HUNTER SERVED HIS apprenticeship in the majors, never pitching in the minors. He rose from an 8-8 pitcher as a 19-year-old in Kansas City to Cy Young Award winner and the richest player in baseball. He was also part of two of the most successful and colorful teams of the 1970s.

James Augustus Hunter was born in 1946 in Hertford, North Carolina, and he earned celebrity as a schoolboy hurler, getting a 26-2 record with five no-hitters. A hunting accident cost him his right little toe as an 18-year-old, but Kansas City owner Charlie O. Finley signed Hunter for $75,000. Finley dubbed Jim "Catfish" in order to inject color into his image. On the injured list in '64, he didn't become a regular starter for Kansas City until 1965. He was named to the All-Star team for the first of eight times in 1966 and showed signs of things to come when he tossed a perfect game against the Twins in early 1968.

A lifetime 30-36 when the team moved to Oakland in 1968, Catfish won 18 games in 1970, and then 21 in 1971, the first of five straight seasons in which he passed the 20-win

mark. The A's grew to a powerhouse in the early 1970s, winning the World Series in 1972, 1973, and 1974. Catfish relied on a good fastball, guile, and pinpoint control. He won 21, 21, and 25 games those three years; he lost a combined total of 24. He was 4-0 in the three World Series. His 1974 season earned him Cy Young honors, as he posted a 25-12 record and a league-leading 2.49 ERA. When Finley failed to pay Hunter's insurance premium, as spelled out in his contract, Catfish also earned the right of free agency. Hunter was the first celebrated free agent of the era, commanding $3.75 million from George Steinbrenner for a five-year stint with the Yankees.

Catfish was 23-14 in his first year in pinstripes in 1975, and led the league with 30 complete games and 328 innings. The "Bronx Zoo" began to win, but Hunter began to develop arm trouble. The Yankees won pennants in 1976, 1977, and 1978, but Hunter was just 38-30. Although the Yankees won the Series in 1977, Catfish was rocked in just four and one-third innings of work. The Yanks repeated in 1978, and Hunter won the final game of the Series. After a 2-9 season in 1979, he retired at age 33. He continued to assist the Yankees in spring training but spent most of his time on his farm in North Carolina.

With a lifetime record of 224-166 and a 3.26 ERA, Catfish fanned at least 100 batters in 11 consecutive seasons—finishing with 2,012—but never walked more than 85. He ranks in the top ten in five World Series categories. Hunter was inducted in 1987.

Major League Totals

W	L	ERA	G	CG	IP	H	ER	BB	SO
224	166	3.26	500	181	3,448.1	2,958	1,249	954	2,012

JIM PALMER

THE IMAGE OF JIM PALMER AS a sex symbol, cultivated in his famous men's briefs advertisements, tends to diminish the ability the Baltimore righthander held as one of the game's top hurlers. Palmer won 20 games in eight seasons, won 15 games a dozen times, and gave up less than three earned runs a game for ten years.

James Alvin Palmer (born in 1945) received only one year of minor league seasoning before the Orioles promoted him in 1965. He was stationed in the bullpen most of that year. In 1966, he was inserted into the starting rotation (replacing Milt Pappas) and responded with a 15-10 record for the pennant-winning Birds. Jim gained his first bit of fame at age 20 by shutting out the Los Angeles Dodgers in game two of the World Series. The losing pitcher of that contest was Sandy Koufax, pitching in the final game of his career.

Palmer missed most of the 1967 and '68 seasons with an arm injury. After surgery corrected the problem, he came back in 1969 to win 16 games and lose only four, leading the AL with an .800 winning percentage. In 1970, he began a streak of four consecutive 20-win seasons. He led the league with a 2.40 ERA, going 22-9 for the 1973 Orioles to win his first Cy Young Award. Palmer had elbow problems in 1974, and went 7-12, with a 3.27 ERA. In 1975, for the second time in his career, he rebounded to become one of the top hurlers in baseball. He led the AL with a 2.09 ERA and 23 victories to win his second Cy Young. He led the league in victories in 1976 (earning another Cy Young) and 1977, and he had 21 wins in 1978.

Jim subscribed to the theory that most batters couldn't handle his high, tight fastballs, and he was right. He allowed his share of home runs, but in 3,948 innings, he never gave up a grand slam. Despite his various injuries, he led the league in innings pitched in four seasons. He started eight games over six World Series in his career. With Palmer on the staff, the Orioles won the AL West from 1969 to 1971, 1973 and '74, and 1979.

Jim and the Oriole manager for those AL East crowns, Earl Weaver, were both highly competitive and self-confident men. The two, thus, had many run-ins. Their relationship was not as rocky as believed by the fans of the day; the fact that Weaver and Palmer were quotable and were on the same team for 14 years added weight to that perception. Palmer retired in 1984, and he was named to the Hall of Fame in 1990. In spring training of 1991, he staged an ill-advised comeback attempt.

JAMES ALVIN PALMER
BALTIMORE, A.L., 1965-1984
HIGH-KICKING, SMOOTH-THROWING SYMBOL OF BALTIMORE'S SIX CHAMPIONSHIP TEAMS OF 1960's, 70's AND 80's. IMPRESSIVE NUMBERS INCLUDE 268 WINS WITH .638 PCT., EIGHT 20-WIN SEASONS, 2.86 ERA AND NO GRAND SLAMS ALLOWED OVER ENTIRE 19 YEAR CAREER. INTENSITY WAS TRADEMARK OF 3-TIME CY YOUNG WINNER, WHO COMBINED STRENGTH, INTELLIGENCE, COMPETITIVENESS AND CONSISTENCY TO BECOME ORIOLES' ALL-TIME WINNINGEST HURLER.

Pitcher
Baltimore Orioles
1965-1967; 1969-1984

Top: During his 20 seasons with the Orioles, Palmer was instrumental in bringing six pennants to Baltimore. In addition, he took wins in four ALCS. His record in postseason play is a banner 8-3. His last major league victory came, fittingly, in World Series action —game three of the 1983 fall classic. Left: An autographed 1984 ad disc of Palmer.

English's Salutes

Born - Oct. 15, 1945
Resides - Brooklandville, MD
Ht. 6'3", Wt. 194

Won-Lost 5-4
E.R.A. 4.23
S.O. 34

JIM PALMER
★ PITCHER ★
BALTIMORE ORIOLES
★ 1983 Champions ★

			Major League Totals						
W	L	ERA	G	CG	IP	H	ER	BB	SO
268	152	2.86	558	211	3,948.0	3,349	1,252	1,311	2,212

FERGUSON ARTHUR JENKINS, 1965-1966
PHILADELPHIA, N.L., 1965-1966
CHICAGO, N.L., 1966-1973, 1982-1983
TEXAS, A.L., 1974-1975, 1978-1981
BOSTON, A.L., 1976-1977
CANADA'S FIRST HALL-OF-FAMER. 284-226
LIFETIME WITH 3,192 STRIKEOUTS AND 3.34 ERA
DESPITE PLAYING 12 OF HIS 19 YEAR CAREER IN
HITTERS BALLPARKS-WRIGLEY FIELD AND FENWAY
PARK. WON 20 GAMES 6 SEASONS, INCLUDING 6
CONSECUTIVE, 1967 - 1972. CY YOUNG AWARD
WINNER, 1971. TRADEMARKS WERE PINPOINT CONTROL
AND CHANGING SPEEDS.

Pitcher
Philadelphia Phillies
    1965-1966
Chicago Cubs 1966-1973;
    1982-1983
Texas Rangers 1974-1975;
    1978-1981
Boston Red Sox
    1976-1977

A MASTER OF CONTROL, Ferguson Jenkins never walked more than 83 hitters in a season. He won 20 games a season for the Cubs from 1967 to 1972, and he is the only pitcher in baseball history to fan more than 3,000 batters while walking fewer than 1,000.

A 6'5" Canadian righthander out of Chatham, Ontario, Ferguson Arthur Jenkins (born in 1943) was discovered by the Phillies in 1962. He labored in the Philadelphia minor league organization for three and one-half years before being promoted in 1965. The Phillies used Fergy as a reliever, and after the Chicago Cubs obtained Ferguson from Philadelphia during the 1966 season, they put him in the bullpen. Cubs manager Leo Durocher decided to move Jenkins into the starting rotation at the end of the season, and he responded with two complete games. In 1967, he was 20-13 with a 2.80 ERA for the Cubs, the first of six consecutive 20-win seasons. He led the NL with 40 starts in 1968, and he went 20-15. He lost a record five decisions by the score of 1-0.

Jenkins's best season with the Cubs was 1971, when he led the league with 325 innings pitched and 24 wins, and posted a 2.77 ERA to earn the Cy Young Award. He was 20-12 in '72, but slipped to 14-16 in 1973. The Cubs, deciding that they needed a replacement for third baseman Ron Santo, sent Jenkins to Texas for Bill Madlock.

Fergie had one more outstanding season left in his arm. In 1974, he led the American League with a career-high 25 wins, lost 12, and fanned 225. Though he never won 20 games again, he continued to pitch effectively. In '75, he was 17-18 with a 3.93 ERA. Boston traded three players for him that winter, and although Jenkins hurt his foot, he was 12-11 with a 3.27 ERA. He had a run-in with Red Sox manager Don Zimmer in 1977, and Fergy was shipped back to Texas. He went 18-8 in 1978, won 16 and 12 games the next two years, and was back with the Cubs in 1982.

Jenkins led the league in strikeouts in 1969 and fanned more than 200 six times. Like other control pitchers, he gave up many homers; his 484 home runs allowed are the second most in history. Curiously, his highest total allowed in a season, 40, occurred in 1979 when he was with Texas. His career made him a fine Hall of Fame candidate, but an arrest for drug possession in Toronto in 1980 made his election problematic. In 1991, Jenkins was elected to the Hall of Fame by one of the closest margins in Cooperstown history.

Top: Jenkins had perhaps the best control of any pitcher in the modern era. His career strikeouts to walks ratio was better than 3-to-1 and he averaged only about 52.5 free passes per season in his 19-year career. In 1971, the year he won his lone Cy Young Award, Jenkins gave up a mere 37 walks in 325 innings. Right: A Jenkins jersey.

Major League Totals

W	L	ERA	G	CG	IP	H	ER	BB	SO
284	226	3.34	664	267	4,499.2	4,142	1,670	997	3,192

JOHNNY BENCH

In 1989, Bench became one of the youngest players ever voted into the Hall of Fame.

JOHNNY BENCH WAS THE BEST offensive and defensive catcher in baseball for more than a decade. The first player from the draft to be inducted into the Hall of Fame (in 1989), he had the greatest career of any catcher in National League history.

Born in Oklahoma City, Oklahoma, in 1947, Johnny Lee Bench grew up admiring the play of another Okie, Mickey Mantle. Bench's father was a semipro catcher, and he imparted the love of the game to John. Bench was an outstanding high school athlete, and Cincinnati drafted him on the second round of the 1965 draft. He was named the 1966 Carolina League Player of the Year, hitting 22 homers in 98 games. He had 23 homers at Buffalo in '67.

The Reds promoted Johnny in 1968. He was the National League Rookie of the Year with a .275 average, 15 homers, and 82 RBI, second on the club. He hit 26 homers in 1969. He also laid the foundations for a defensive reputation that was to become legendary. He led the '68 NL in putouts and assists, and popularized a one-handed catching method that gave him greater mobility and allowed him to better utilize his cannonlike right arm. He was so overpowering that baserunners simply didn't challenge him throughout much of his prime.

Bench won Most Valuable Player awards in 1970 and '72, leading the Reds to the playoffs both years. In 1970, at age 22, he was the youngest man to ever win the Award. He led the league with 45 homers and 148 RBI. It capped a meteoric rise to stardom that took even Bench

by surprise. His second MVP Award came two years later in 1972, after batting .270 with 40 home runs and 125 RBI.

Bench and the Reds won consecutive World Series in 1975 and '76, and the Big Red Machine won 210 games during those two seasons. John hit in the middle of a lineup that included Pete Rose, Joe Morgan, George Foster, Tony Perez, and Dave Concepcion. In the fourth and final game of the 1976 World Series, Bench had two homers and five RBI. He hit .533 for the Series, and won the World Series MVP Award.

Bench's 327 homers as a catcher were a record when he retired after the 1983 season, and he rates near the top in many defensive categories. He had 20 or more home runs in 11 seasons, drove in more than 100 runs six times, and won Gold Gloves from 1968 to 1977. During his last three seasons he played more games at first and third to extend his career. Bench drove in more runs in the 1970s than any other player, 1,013, and played in 11 All-Star games.

**Catcher
Cincinnati Reds 1967-1983**

The Reds waited about three years too long to convert Bench to a less taxing position. He caught 1,393 games for Cincinnati before he was age 30 and only 345 thereafter.

Major League Totals

BA	G	AB	R	H	2B	3B	HR	RBI	SB
.267	2,158	7,658	1,091	2,048	381	24	389	1,376	68

RODNEY CLINE CAREW
MINNESOTA, A.L., 1967-1978
CALIFORNIA, A.L., 1979-1985
BATTING WIZARD WHO LINED, CHOPPED AND
BUNTED HIS WAY TO 3,053 HITS. 7 BATTING TITLES
SURPASSED ONLY BY COBB AND WAGNER. USED
VARIETY OF RELAXED, CROUCHED BATTING STANCES
TO HIT OVER .300 15 CONSECUTIVE SEASONS,
ACHIEVING .328 LIFETIME. A.L. ROOKIE OF YEAR
IN 1967 AND A.L. MVP 10 YEARS LATER WHEN HE
BATTED .388 WITH 239 HITS. NAMED TO 18 STRAIGHT
ALL-STAR TEAMS. NATIONAL HERO IN PANAMA.

**Second baseman;
first baseman**
Minnesota Twins
1967-1978
California Angels
1979-1985

I N 1977, ROD CAREW MADE A valiant run at the .400 mark last topped by Ted Williams in 1941, though Rod fell just short at .388. He topped the .300 plateau 15 times and the .330 mark ten times, winning seven batting titles along the way. Carew was a master of the base hit, as he posted 200-plus hits in four seasons.

Born in the Panama Canal Zone in 1945, Rodney Scott Carew moved to New York when he was age 17. After high school he joined the Twins' organization in 1964. Promoted to Minnesota in 1967, Carew won the Rookie of the Year Award when he hit .292. He established his bat wizardry early, winning a batting title in 1969. Minnesota won the AL West in 1969 and '70; Carew and Co. ran into the Baltimore buzzsaw both years.

Carew won four straight AL batting titles from 1972 to 1975. As a second baseman, he was weak on the double play and had a below

Above: *A baseball autographed by Carew.*

average arm but compensated with good range. Unfortunately, the slightly built Carew took a pounding at second. Twins manager Gene Mauch moved Rod to first base to extend his career. In 1977, he responded with a serious run at a .400 season, hitting .388 and a league-leading 16 triples, 239 hits, and 128 runs. It was his sixth batting title, and the next closest hitter to Carew's .388 mark was NL batting champ Dave Parker at .338, making it the largest margin in baseball history. Carew was a runaway choice for the league's Most Valuable Player.

Rod was a master bunter—when he won the title in 1972 he had 15 bunt-hits, but not a single home run—and would astonish teammates by putting a handkerchief at various spots up and down the foul lines and dropping bunts onto it. In 1969, he stole home seven times, tying Pete Reiser's record. Carew had seasons of 35 swipes in 44 attempts and 27 in 35, and stole at least 23 in six out of seven seasons. He won his final batting title with a .333 mark in 1978.

After that season, Carew forced his own trade and ended up with the California Angels, where owner Gene Autry was trying to build a winner. The 1979 Angels went to the ALCS, and though Rod hit .412, they lost to the Orioles in four games. He failed to hit .300 in 1984 for the first time in 15 years. He returned in 1985 and hit .285, and became only the 16th man to collect 3,000 hits. He retired after the 1985 season with 3,053 hits. In 1991, Carew became the 22nd man to be elected to Cooperstown in his first year of eligibility.

When Rod Carew retired he had the highest career batting average of any player who had played in at least 1,000 games since Ted Williams retired in 1960.

Major League Totals

BA	G	AB	R	H	2B	3B	HR	RBI	SB
.328	2,469	9,315	1,424	3,053	445	112	92	1,015	353

WHEN TOM SEAVER WON 25 games to spirit the New York Mets to a stunning pennant in 1969, he earned the nickname "Tom Terrific." His 25 wins also set a Mets record that still stands. The previous mark had been 16, established by Seaver in his 1966 rookie season. Over the ensuing 17 seasons, Seaver would set a multitude of team and National League pitching records.

Unlike most pitching greats, George Thomas Seaver (born in 1944) was a virtual nonentity in high school. Not until he had served a Marine hitch and enrolled at the University of Southern California did he first begin to attract the notice of major league scouts. The Braves thought so highly of his collegiate mound work that they offered him a $40,000 bonus in 1966 to sign. His contract with the Braves was voided, however, by commissioner William Eckert, who ruled that the rights to Seaver would go in a specially arranged lottery to any team that agreed to match or top the Braves' bonus offer. By the luck of the draw, the Mets won the privilege of signing Seaver for a $50,000 bonus.

Seaver was the Mets staff ace for ten seasons. On three occasions (1969, 1973, and 1975) he won the Cy Young Award, and he twice hurled the Mets to a pennant. The team's second flag came in 1973 when Seaver earned his second Cy Young honor despite winning just 19 games, five fewer than Giants ace Ron Bryant. Seaver's stats in 1973 were bolstered, however, by both the NL ERA and strikeout crowns. In all, Seaver paced the senior circuit five times in whiffs. The last occasion, in 1976, marked the ninth consecutive season in which Tom had fanned at least 200 hitters to set a major league record.

During the 1977 season, Seaver was traded to Cincinnati to the shock of Mets fans. Although he twice led the NL in winning percentage,

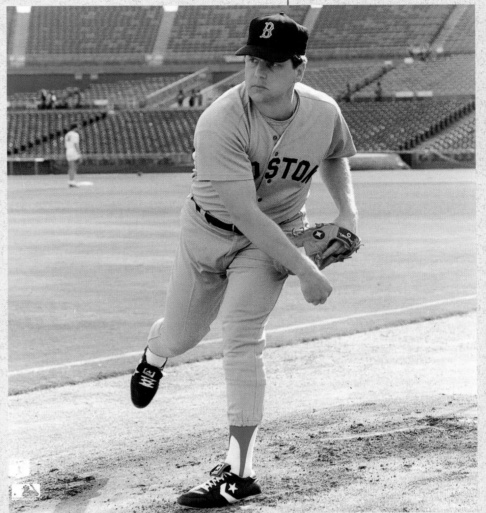

Tom Seaver made his last stop in the majors in Boston, near his Greenwich, Connecticut, hometown.

Seaver failed to bring the Reds a pennant. After six years in Cincinnati, he was reacquired by the Mets before the 1983 season. At age 39, Tom seemed destined to finish his career as a Met. Instead, after one last season in New York, he was drafted by the White Sox when the Mets, thinking him too old to be at risk, did not put his name on their list of protected players.

Seaver won 31 games in his first two seasons in the AL. When he started poorly in 1986, he was dealt to Boston. He retired with a .603 career winning percentage, the highest of any 300-game winner in the past half-century. Seaver set another record in 1992 when he was named on 98.8 percent of the ballots for enshrinement.

Pitcher
New York Mets
  1967-1977; 1983
Cincinnati Reds 1977-1982
Chicago White Sox
  1984-1986
Boston Red Sox 1986

Left: *When he hung up his spikes, in 1986, his 3,640 career strikeouts ranked him third on the all-time list.*

W	L	ERA	G	CG	IP	H	ER	BB	SO
\multicolumn{10}{c}{**Major League Totals**}
311	205	2.86	656	231	4,782.2	3,971	1,521	1,390	3,640

ROLLIE FINGERS

Pitcher
Oakland Athletics
    1968-1976
San Diego Padres
    1977-1980
Milwaukee Brewers
    1981-1985

Above: A clean-shaven Fingers started his career with the Athletics as a starter. Dick Williams finally decided that Rollie was best suited to come out of the bullpen. Top right: Fingers's memorabilia as a member of one of the most colorful World Championship teams in the century, the 1970s Oakland A's.

AFTER BRINGING ROLLIE Fingers up from the minors in 1969, the Oakland A's were uncertain what to do with him. For three seasons the A's shuttled him between the bullpen and periodic starting roles. Finally in 1971, after he was able to finish only four of his 35 career starts to date, Oakland manager Dick Williams decided Fingers was best suited for relief work. He responded with a team-leading 17 saves that year and 21 saves in 1972. In 1973, Williams again briefly tried Fingers as a starter before recognizing once and for all that Rollie's proper job was as a fireman. In the 11 remaining years of his career, Fingers never made another starting appearance.

Clean shaven when he first appeared on the major league scene, Roland Glen Fingers (born

in 1946) soon became known for having the longest mustache from tip to tip in major league history. His career high-point came in the 1974 World Series for the A's against the Dodgers. With the A's shooting for their third successive World Championship, Fingers won the first game of the Series with a four and one-third inning relief stint and then came through with two saves in the final two games. For his efforts, Fingers earned the Series MVP trophy.

After two more seasons with the A's, Rollie became a free agent at the end of the 1976 campaign. He signed a five-year pact at an estimated $1.5 million with the Padres. In each of his first two seasons in San Diego, he topped the senior loop in saves. His personal high of 37 saves came in 1978. In 1980, Fingers was swapped to the St. Louis Cardinals and then immediately shipped to the Milwaukee Brewers in the year's biggest deal.

Fingers had his finest season in the strike-abbreviated 1981 campaign. In 47 appearances, he collected a major league-leading 28 saves and etched a 1.04 ERA. His banner year garnered him both the MVP and the Cy Young awards but narrowly missed bringing Milwaukee a division crown. When the Brewers broke through the next year to win their first pennant, an ailing elbow forced Fingers to watch their World Series loss to the Cardinals from the sidelines.

Elbow problems shelved Fingers for all of the 1983 season, but he rebounded strongly in 1984 to post 23 saves and a 1.96 ERA. The 1985 campaign proved to be his last, however, when he sagged to a career-worst 1-6 record and 5.04 ERA, with 17 saves. He compiled a major-league record 341 saves. Fingers was voted to the Hall of Fame in 1992.

Major League Totals

W	L	ERA	G	SV	IP	H	ER	BB	SO
114	118	2.90	944	341	1,701.0	1,474	548	492	1,299